Informatik-Fachberichte 176

Subreihe Künstliche Intelligenz

Herausgegeben von W. Brauer in Zusammenarbeit mit dem
Fachausschuß 1.2 „Künstliche Intelligenz und
Mustererkennung" der Gesellschaft für Informatik (GI)

H. Trost (Hrsg.)

4. Österreichische Artificial-Intelligence-Tagung

Wiener Workshop
Wissensbasierte Sprachverarbeitung

Wien, 29.-31. August 1988

Proceedings

Springer-Verlag
Berlin Heidelberg New York
London Paris Tokyo

Herausgeber

Harald Trost
Universität Wien
Institut für Medizinische Kybernetik und Artificial Intelligence
Freyung 6/2, A–1010 Wien, Österreich

Programmkomitee

Georg Dorffner	Universität Wien
Walter von Hahn	Universität Hamburg
Hans Haugeneder	Siemens AG München
Wolfgang Heinz	Universität Wien
Gerard Kempen	University of Nijmegen
Markus Kommenda	TU Wien
Dieter Metzing	Universität Bielefeld
Hans Uszkoreit	IBM Stuttgart
Wolfgang Wahlster	Universität Saarbrücken

CR Subject Classifications (1987): F.4.1-2, H.3.1, I.2.3-4, I.2.7, I.5.4, J.5

ISBN-13:978-3-540-50180-0   e-ISBN-13:978-3-642-73998-9
DOI: 10.1007/978-3-642-73998-9

CIP-Titelaufnahme der Deutschen Bibliothek.
Workshop Wissensbasierte Sprachverarbeitung «1988, Wien»: Proceedings /
4. Österreichische Artificial-Intelligence-Tagung : Wien, 29.-31. August 1988 /
H. Trost (Hrsg.). – Berlin; Heidelberg; New York; London; Paris; Tokyo: Springer, 1988
    (Informatik-Fachberichte; 176: Subreihe künstliche Intelligenz)
    Auf d. Haupttitels. auch: Wiener Workshop Wissensbasierte Sprachverarbeitung
    ISBN-13:978-3-540-50180-0

NE: Trost, Harald [Hrsg.]; GT

2145/3140 – 543210 – Gedruckt auf säurefreiem Papier

Vorwort

Die vierte Österreichische Artificial-Intelligence-Tagung fand vom
29.-31.August 1988 an der Universität Wien statt. Im Gegensatz zu den
früheren Tagungen, die den Gesamtbereich der Artificial Intelligence
abdeckten, befaßte sie sich mit einem speziellen Teilgebiet, der
wissensbasierten Verarbeitung natürlicher Sprache. Diese Tatsache
fand auch im Haupttitel der Tagung, "Wiener Workshop für
Wissensbasierte Sprachverarbeitung 1988", ihren Ausdruck.

Zwei Gründe waren ausschlaggebend für diese Themenwahl: Einmal ist die
Verarbeitung natürlicher Sprache eines der aktivsten Teilgebiete der
Artificial Intelligence, das auch über eine breite Palette von
Anwendungen verfügt. Zum anderen wollten die Veranstalter diese Tagung
zum Anlaß nehmen, speziell auf die Verarbeitung deutscher Sprache
einzugehen. Da die Mehrzahl der Formalismen und Algorithmen im
Hinblick auf das Englische mit seinem wesentlich anderen Aufbau
entwickelt wurde, ergeben sich bei ihrer Anwendung auf das Deutsche
praktische und theoretische Probleme. Diese aufzuarbeiten sowie die
Zusammenarbeit zwischen AI-Forschern und Linguisten im deutsch-
sprachigen Raum zu verbessern, waren die Ziele dieser Tagung.

Die Tagung gliederte sich in einen allgemeinen Teil sowie zwei
Workshops zu den Themen 'Generierung' und 'Unifikationsgrammatiken'.
Ich möchte an dieser Stelle den Organisatoren dieser Workshops, Herrn
Dr.Dietmar Rösner und Frau DI Karin Harbusch, herzlich für Ihre Mühe
und Ihren großen Einsatz danken.

Die 24 Beiträge dieses Bandes - von etwa 40 eingereichten - geben
einen Eindruck von der Breite des Gebiets, von gesprochener Sprache
über Morphologie, Syntax und Semantik bis hin zur Darstellung von
Weltwissen, und geben gleichzeitig Einblick in den aktuellen Stand der
Forschung.

Nicht zuletzt möchte ich allen danken, die zum Gelingen dieser Tagung
beigetragen haben: den Mitgliedern des Programmkomitees, die die
wissenschaftliche Qualität der Tagung gewährleisteten, und den
Mitgliedern des Organisationskomitees, ohne deren freiwillige
Mitarbeit bei der Organisation diese Tagung nicht hätte stattfinden
können.

Wien, im August 1988   Harald Trost

Inhaltsverzeichnis

Knowledge Representation Problems
For Natural Language Understanding

Graeme Hirst
Department of Computer Science
University of Toronto
Toronto, CANADA M5S 1A4

Abstract

In artificial intelligence these days, just about anything that's any good is knowledge-based'. Consequently, knowledge representation formalisms are big business, and are available in a wide range of styles and colors to suit the various demands of consumers in the marketplace. In this paper, I want to argue that consumers in the natural language understanding research community are not as well served as they might be, and many of their needs have been overlooked.

For a rule-based expert system, it is often perfectly adequate to represent knowledge in a set of condition-action rules of greater or lesser complexity. In natural language understanding, however, knowledge representation plays two separate roles, both of which place stronger demands on it than a simple production-rule system. The first is for a knowledge base of facts about the world that the system can use when it has to decide which readings of an ambiguous sentence don't make sense, which ones do, and of the ones that do which is the most likely to have been intended by the speaker. The second is to represent the meaning of the input itself---to serve, in other words, as a semantics.

These two roles are fairly distinct, and might well be served by a different KR formalism for each. However, there are good a priori reasons for wanting to use the same formalism for both. First, the sentences the system reads will often be facts about the world that are to be added to the knowledge base or questions whose answer is to be sought therein. Second, the process of interpreting the input will often involve asking questions of the knowledge base about fragments of the semantics (or proposed semantics) of the sentence; this would be easier if one formalism were used throughout. (In Hirst 1987 I describe an NLU system that uses Frail, a frame-based formalism, for both tasks.)

In this paper, I will investigate exactly what is required of a KR in these roles in NLU, where some of the problems lie, and where we might look for some of the solutions. I take as a starting point the idea that we need a structured representation with a denotational semantics. I assume that, other things being equal, a compositional representation is to be preferred -- that is, a representation in which the meaning of the whole is a systematic function of the meaning of the parts from which it is constructed. For example, if we have representations of "on Tuesday" and "Ross kissed Nadia" we could combine them in some fairly obvious way to get the representation of "Ross kissed Nadia on Tuesday".

I will give little time to issues of tractability (cf. Levesque and Brachman), but rather emphasize questions that are prior to such issues. Also, I won't address problems in representations that just try to describe the world or the laws of physics or commonsense (Hayes, Lenat, Hobbs, etc).

References:

Brachman R.J., Levesque H.J.(1984). The Tractability of Subsumption in Frame-Based Description Languages, in Proc. of the 4th National Conference on AI (AAAI-84), Morgan Kaufmann, Los Altos, CA.

Hayes P.J.(1985). The Second Naive Physics Manifesto, in Brachman R.J., Levesque H.J.(eds.), Readings in Knowledge Representation, Morgan Kaufmann, Los Altos, CA.

Hirst, Graeme (1987). Semantic interpretation and the resolution of ambiguity, Cambridge University Press.

Generation and Recognition
of
Inflectional Morphology

John Bear
Artificial Intelligence Center
SRI International
333 Ravenswood Ave
Menlo Park, California 94025

Abstract

Koskenniemi's two-level morphological analysis system can be improved upon by using a PATR-like unification grammar for handling the morphosyntax instead of continuation classes, and by incorporating the notion of negative rule feature into the phonological rule interpreter. The resulting system can be made to do generation and recognition using the same grammars.

1 Introduction

Since Koskenniemi published his 1980 dissertation on two-level morphology it has met with mixed reviews. Many scholars have pointed to the declarativeness of the system as very desirable feature. The two-level formalism for expressing phonological generalizations has the obvious advantage that any description of phonological facts can be used as well for generation as recognition. Furthermore, working recognition systems have been built for several languages using this paradigm, and it seems to have the potential to be used in many more.

Detractors have pointed out that there are many unsolved problems with the two-level paradigm. In particular, using a system of continuation classes to describe the morphosyntactic regularities of a language is cumbersome at best. Furthermore, while it has been demonstrated how to do recognition using continuation classes, it is not nearly so clear how to use them in doing generation. With regard to the model's handling of phonology, the use of arbitrary diacritics within words for encoding information, such as exceptionality, is considered by many to be unwieldy and highly undesirable. Even more undesirable is the need to manipulate transition tables for finite-state transducers rather than some form of phonological rule.

The intent of this paper is to describe work that has been done to remedy these problems. The main point being argued here is that this general paradigm of two-level morphology is both theoretically and practially useful. The text that follows presents my system for dealing with English inflectional morphology. This system has been implemented in Quintus Prolog, and in Common Lisp. It can be used for doing both recognition and generation of words. This work is based on the ideas of Koskenniemi [10,11,12], Karttunen and Wittenburg [7], and Shieber [15].

2   Basic Paradigm

There is a lexicon of morphemes. Each morpheme has two parts: a spelling and a collection of features and values. I use a unification grammar, so the collections of features are just directed acyclic graphs (dags). The spelling of a morpheme is what would be found in a dictionary. For instance, the English noun stem "spy" might have the following entry in the lexicon:

```
spelling: spy
features: [cat: noun_stem
           lex: spy
           type: regular]
```

There are two sets of rules describing linguistic phenomena. There are phonological rules (actually orthographic), which describe mappings between the spellings of morphemes, as they appear in the lexicon, and the spellings that occur in text. And there are morphosyntactic rules, which constitute a unification-based grammar specifying which morphemes may combine with which, and what the resulting dag (or feature set) should be.

The challenge is to arrive at two sets of declarative, reversible rules that may be used conjointly for both generation and recognition of word forms. The recognition task is clear. Given a word, e.g., "spies," one would like the recognizer to produce, for instance, the dag

```
[cat: noun
 number: plural
 type: regular
 stem: spy].
```

Given that, the generation task becomes clear. Given a dag like the one immediately above, a generator should produce the word "spies," and not, for instance, "spys," or "spis," or "spyes."

Two types of mappings are involved here. One is the mapping of dictionary spellings to spellings of words as they appear in text. For example:

```
''spy+s'' <-> ''spies.''
```

The other is the mapping between a dag representing a word as it appears in text and a sequence of morphemes that would combine to form it, e.g.

```
[cat: noun                        [cat: noun_stem
 number: plural        <->         lex: spy            +        [lex: s]
 type: regular                     type: regular]
 stem: spy].
```

When the program is set to generate, it is given a dag as input and then it applies rules of the grammar to arrive at a sequence of dags, each representing a morpheme. It extracts a morpheme's spelling from each of the dags to produce a sequence of morphemes. In the foregoing example, it would find the list [spy, s]. A morpheme boundary character is inserted between each pair of morphemes to give: spy+s. This last string serves as input to the phonological component. The phonological component decides which surface spellings might correspond to that string. In this case, there is only one alternative: spies.

The rest of this paper describes in more detail how the two grammars are used.

3   Morphosyntax

The morphosyntactic grammar is based on PATR (Shieber 1986), with an augmentation for doing disjunction based on an algorithm described by Karttunen (1984). The rules are all necessarily binary. They state how two dags can be combined to form a third. They can also be interpreted as specifying how a given dag can be decomposed into two others. Appendix 1 contains several of the verb formation rules used by this system.

In doing recognition, the parser is primed with a dag whose only feature is [category: empty]. The parser then proceeds through the word until it finds a string of characters that can constitute a morpheme. When it finds such a string, it retrieves the dag associated with it and then looks for a rule in the grammar telling how to unify the dag just found with the "empty" dag. If there is such a rule, it will describe how to build a new dag. This new dag is carried along as the parser looks farther down the word until another morpheme is found. The comparison process is then repeated with the new morpheme's dag, and the dag that was being carried along.

Of course, the first morpheme that is found might be one that is not destined to lead anywhere. To handle such cases, the parser also continues down the word as if the morpheme just found were not really a morpheme. In short, every time a morpheme is found, two paths must be pursued. One path assumes that the morpheme will indeed be part of the final analysis, while the other assumes that it will not.

In doing generation, the process is reversed. The engine starts with a dag and tries to find a rule telling how to decompose it. There might be more than one, of course. In that case, all the possible paths are followed. When a rule is found that tells how to decompose the dag at hand, two new dags are built and the generation engine is told to try to decompose one of them while simply remembering the other. This process continues until the generator is trying to decompose the dag [category: empty]. At that point it ceases doing decompositions and assembles a list of morphemes from the list of dags. This list of morphemes is passed as input to the phonology component whose task is to produce the appropriate spelling of the word.

4   Phonology and Orthography

The philosophy behind the phonological component is that there are two types of strings we are concerned with: morphemes in the lexicon and words in the text. When morphemes in the lexicon combine to form words, sometimes spelling changes happen. For instance (to use the "spy" example again), at the lexical level we could have the verb stem "spy" and the ending "s". At the text or surface level, we have "spies." We may talk of the following mapping:

```
(lexical level)     s   p   y   +   s

                    |   |   |   |   |

(surface level)     s   p   i   e   s.
```

We use two devices to describe the possible mappings between surface and lexical (underlying) strings of characters. One device is the list of feasible pairs of characters. It tells us which characters may ever correspond to which other characters. The default in this system is that any lexical alphabetic character (a-z) may correspond to itself on the surface, while lexical diacritics may correspond to the empty string (written as 0). In the example with "spy+s" above, the list of feasible pairs would need to indicate that, for instance, a lexical /s/ may correspond to a surface /s/; a lexical /p/ may correspond to a surface /p/; a lexical /y/ may correspond to a surface /i/, and so on. The converse is also true. If we know that a lexical /y/ may correspond to a surface /i/, then we also know that a surface /i/ may correspond to a lexical /y/.

The other device we use to describe possible mappings between surface and underlying strings is that of two-level constraints. The two-level constraints employed in this system are an outgrowth of those of Koskenniemi [10], of Karttunen and Wittenburg [7], and of Karttunen, Koskenniemi and Kaplan [5].

The basic idea is to stipulate constraints on when a certain lexical character is allowed to correspond to a certain surface character (and vice versa). Two different kinds of constraints are used: those which specify that certain string pairs are never allowable, and those that specify a certain character pair is only allowable in a certain context. There is third type of constraint that combines the other two. This last type looks very similar in form to a generative phonological rule, but it has additional power in that the context may refer to characters at both levels.

For instance the constraint:

```
+ --> e  /  {x | z | y/i | s ( h ) | c h }  _  s,
```

abbreviates a combination of two simpler constraints:

```
+/e  allowed in context  {x | z | y/i | s ( h ) | c h }  _  s
```

and

```
+/0  disallowed in context  {x | z | y/i | s ( h ) | c h }  _  s.
```

The rules have several abbreviatory conventions, – for example, any character appearing by itself in the context really means a pairing of a lexical occurrence of that character with a surface occurrence. When a rule mentions a lexical character that is different from the surface character it is paired with, the pair is written with a slash, as is the pair y/i in the rule above. The symbol 0 is used to represent the empty string.

Sometimes it is necessary or desirable to be able to write a general constraint and then mark certain morphemes as exceptions to it. This can be done with negative rule features. For instance, if some morpheme were an exception to the rule given above, (and the rule had the name epenthesis1), then the morpheme's entry in the lexicon would contain the notation "-epenthesis1", meaning that the epenthesis1 constraint need not hold of that morpheme. The use of negative rule features is described in more detail in another paper [3].

5 Conclusion

Many of the original objections that linguists have had to Koskenniemi's two-level model for doing computational morphology are no longer valid. Solutions to them have been found. There are elegant ways of dealing with the morphosyntax. There are also nice ways of dealing with exceptions to phonological rules. Moreover, it is possible to use the same grammars for both generation and recognition.

Acknowledgments

I have benefited greatly from conversations with Lauri Karttunen and Kimmo Koskenniemi on the general problem of two-level phonology. I would also like to thank Stuart Shieber for discussions on the topic of unification grammars. This research was funded by the Defense Advanced Research Projects Agency under Office of Naval Research Contract N00014-85-C-0013.

References

[1] Bear, John (1985) "Interpreting Two-level Rules Directly," presented at a Stanford workshop on finite-state morphology.

[2] Bear, John (1986) "A Morphological Recognizer with Syntactic and Phonological Rules," *COLING 86*.

[3] Bear, John (1988) "Two-level Rules and Negative Rule Features," to appear in the proceedings of COLING 88.

[4] Karttunen, Lauri (1983) "Kimmo: A General Morphological Processor," in *Texas Linguistic Forum #22*, Dalrymple et al., eds., Linguistics Department, University of Texas, Austin, Texas.

[5] Karttunen, Lauri, Kimmo Koskenniemi and Ronald Kaplan (1987) "TWOL: A Compiler for Two-level Phonological Rules," distributed at the 1987 Summer Linguistic Institute at Stanford University, Stanford, California.

[6] Karttunen, Lauri (1984) "Features and Values," in *COLING 84*.

[7] Karttunen, Lauri and Kent Wittenburg (1983) "A Two-level Morphological Analysis Of English," in *Texas Linguistic Forum #22*, Dalrymple et al., eds., Linguistics Department, University of Texas, Austin, Texas.

[8] Kay, Martin (1983) "When Meta-rules are not Meta-rules," in K. Sparck-Jones, and Y. Wilks, eds. *Automatic Natural Language Processing*, John Wiley and Sons, New York, New York.

[9] Kay, Martin (1987) "Nonconcatenative Finite-State Morphology," paper presented at a workshop on Arabic Morphology, Stanford University, Stanford, California.

[10] Koskenniemi, Kimmo (1983) *Two-level Morphology: A General Computational Model for Word-form Recognition and Production.* Publication No. 11 of the University of Helsinki Department of General Linguistics, Helsinki, Finland.

[11] Koskenniemi, Kimmo (1983) "Two-level Model for Morphological Analysis," *IJCAI 83*, pp. 683-685.

[12] Koskenniemi, Kimmo (1984) "A General Computational Model for Word-form Recognition and Production," *COLING 84*, pp. 178-181.

[13] Schane, Sanford (1973) *Generative Phonology*, Prentice Hall, Englewood Cliffs, New Jersey.

[14] Selkirk, Elizabeth (1982) *The Syntax of Words*, MIT Press, Cambridge, Massachussetts.

[15] Shieber, Stuart (1986) *An Introduction to Unification-Based Approaches to Grammar*, CSLI Lecture Notes Series, Stanford University, Stanford, California.

```
Appendix 1 (Morphosyntax)
% Some of the verb rules from this system's English grammar.
%   verb --> empty + verb_stem
%     1       2        3
 <2 cat> = empty
 <3 cat> = verb_stem
 <3 type> = regular
 <1 type> = <3 type>
 <1 cat> = verb
 <1 word> = <3 lex>
 <1 form> = {inf
     [tense: pres
       pers:  {1 2}
       nbr: {pl sg}] } .
%   verb --> empty + verb_stem
%     1       2        3
 <2 cat> = empty
 <3 cat> = verb_stem

 <3 type> = irregular
 <1 type> = <3 type>
 <1 cat> = verb
 <1 word> = <3 word>
 <1 form> = <3 form> .
%  verb --> verb + ing
%   1       2     3
 <2 cat> = verb
 <3 lex> = ing
 <2 form> = inf
 <1 cat> = verb
 <1 word> = <2 word>
 <1 form> = [tense: pres_part] .
%  verb --> verb + ed
%   1       2    3
 <3 lex> = ed
 <2 cat> = verb
 <2 form> = inf
 <2 type> = regular   % to prevent "sleeped"
 <1 cat> = verb
 <1 word> = <2 word>
 <1 form> = [tense: {past_part past}] .
%  verb --> verb + s
%   1       2    3
 <3 lex> = s
 <2 cat> = verb
 <2 form> = inf
 <1 cat> = verb
 <1 word> = <2 word>
 <1 form> = [tense: pres
     pers: 3
     nbr: sg] .
```

```
% verb --> empty  +  verb_past
%  1         2           3
 <2 cat> = empty
 <3 cat> = verb_past
 <1 cat> = verb
 <1 word> = <3 word>
 <1 form> = [tense: past] .
```


Appendix 2 (Lexicon)
```
ed
[]
.

ing
[]
.

s
[]
.

try
[cat: verb_stem
 type: regular]
.

spy
[cat: verb_stem
 type: regular]
.

banjo
- epenthesis2
[cat: noun_stem
 type: regular]
.

piano
- [epenthesis2 epenthesis3]
[cat: noun_stem
 type: regular]
.

box
- gemination
[cat: verb_stem
 type: regular]
.
```

Appendix 3 (Phonology)
```
%%%  -*- Mode: PROLOG -*-
epenthesis1:
'+' --> e  /  {x | z | y/i | s ( h ) | c h }  _  s.
epenthesis2:
'+' --> e / o _ s.
epenthesis3:
'+'/e allowed in context  o  _  s.      % Allow words like 'banjoes'.
epenthesis4:
0/e allowed in context  z  '+'/z _ s.
gemination:
'+' --> c1 / {cC | q u} vV c1 _ {0/vV | vV} where c1 is in cC.
y_spelling:
y  --> i  /  cC  _  '+'/'='  cC.
y_spelling:
y  --> i  /  cC  _  '+'/'='  e  cC.    % For spied, tried,
elision:
e  --> 0  /  cC  _  '+'/0  { e | i }.
elision:
e  --> 0  /  vV  _  '+'/0  e.

elision:
e  --> 0  /  i/y  _  '+'/0  vV.
elision:
e/0  allowed in context  c_CG  _  '+'/0  a.
ie_spelling:
i  --> y  /  _  e/0  '+'/0  i.
ie_spelling:
1  --> 0  /  _  e/0  '+'/0  1 y.
ie_spelling:
e  --> 0  /  1/0  _  '+'/0  1 y.
```

Appendix 4
List of feasible pairs in addition to the pairs (x,x), where x is
any alphabetic character:
(',0), (1,0), (e,0), (i,y), (y,i), (+,b), (+,d), (+,f), (+,g), (+,1),
(+,m), (+,n), (+,p), (+,r), (+,s), (+,t), (+,z), (+,e), (+,0)

MORPHIX
A Fast Realization of a Classification–Based Approach to Morphology

Wolfgang Finkler and Günter Neumann
University of Saarbrücken
D–6600 Saarbrücken 11
Federal Republic of Germany
fine@fb10vax.informatik.uni-saarland.dbp.de

Abstract

This paper presents an alternative approach to the use of the Finite State Automata for morphology in inflectional languages. The essential feature is the use of the morphological regularities of these languages to define a fine–grained word–class–specific subclassification. Morphological analysis and generation can be performed at the level of this classification by means of simple operations on n–ary trees. This approach has been implemented in the package MORPHIX which handles all inflectional phenomena of the German language. In spite of the complexity of the German inflection, the average time required to analyse a word is between 0.01 and 0.02 cpu–seconds.

1 Introduction

In order to develop a package for the morphological analysis and generation, it is necessary to consider requirements of linguistics and computer science. Important properties for the integration of a package into natural language systems are: portability, the possibility of extension, and efficiency. As a precondition for a useful integration as a package a wide range of morphological phenomena has to be dealt with. During analysis and generation, linguistical methods should be used in the same manner to structure and to process the morphological characteristics.

Based on the generative phonology there have been several approaches to the treatment of morphological phenomena in inflectional languages by means of Finite State Automata (FSA). FSA describe the morphological regularities of transformations from stems to surface forms and vice versa. The transitions of the automata are directed by testing characters [Kos83] or character strings[Kay82] of the surface form and the underlying lexical representation. Koskenniemi demonstrated that this approach is capable of both morphological analysis and production of word forms for a wide class of inflectional languages [Kos84]. Kay showed how a two–level account might even be given for nonconcatenative morphological phenomena [Kay87].

The starting point of our classification–based approach[1] is to consider morphological regularities as the basis for the definition of a fine–grained word–class–specific classification. Besides morphosyntactic features, phonological phenomena e.g. gemination of a consonant are also used

---

[1]The work presented here is being supported by the German Science Foundation (DFG) in its Special Collaborative Program on AI and Knowledge–Based Systems (SFB 314), project N1 (XTRA).

in refining the classification. This approach is applicable to all languages where such regularities can be identified. Classification–based systems for German morphology already exist but with the restriction that they either handle only morphological analysis e.g. [Ber83], [Son80] or generation e.g. [Bus83], or that they consider only single categories [Sch72]. An approach which is able to handle both morphological analysis and generation is described in [TD85]. In contrast to the classification used there our hierarchical classification serves to structure two central knowledge sources of our model: the stem lexicon and the inflectional allomorph lexicon (IAL). The stem lexicon contains information about the classification of each stem. The IAL relates each inflectional morph to all its possible combinations of morphosyntactic information (the IAL contains 131 entries). In order to be able to disambiguate the morphosyntactic information of an inflectional morph, the various possibilities are differentiated with the help of the classification. Each entry in the IAL is an n–ary tree, the nodes of which describe the classes and the leaves of which contain the appropriate inflectional information (examples of such trees: see figure 1). During the morphological analysis of word forms, the classes which are found in the lexicon direct the traversal of the n–ary tree associated to the candidate inflectional morph which was segmented out of the word form. The fundamental data structures used in our approach to verify or to reject previous segmentations of a word form are the n–ary trees in the IAL. In computer science, there is an abundance of simple and efficient algorithms to operate on trees, thus allowing our model to be implemented efficiently.

The basis of both the Finite State Automata approach and the classification–based approach are the morphological regularities of inflectional languages.

In the Finite State Automata approach, rules are set up and compiled into automata. During morphological analysis the transitions of the Finite State Automata are directed by the actual word form. The determination of which morphological phenomena are present is made in the course of the transitions.

In our classification–based approach, the regularities are used to define classes. Words with the same morphological phenomena are grouped together in classes. Since the classes are contained in the lexicon entries of stems, the morphological analysis entails only simple operations:
– lexicon access to extract classification information
– traversal of an n–ary tree which is found under the segmented inflectional allomorph.

The storage of classes in the lexicon entries reduces the processing–time of the morphological analysis compared to the Finite State Automata approach, where the membership to the class has to be tested directly on each word. Therefore it is appropriate to use a classification–based approach in a package for morphology.

2 The Package MORPHIX

Our classification–based approach of morphological computation has been realized in MORPHIX, a morphological package for natural language systems (NLS's) with German as the input language. A wide range of word classes has been covered so that MORPHIX can be integrated into NLS's.

In designing our package, we opted for a word–level analysis, meaning that MORPHIX has to compute all readings of a given word form. The disambiguation of the results can be achieved by components of the NLS which have syntactic and semantic knowledge at their disposal.

2.1 Inflecting vs. Non–inflecting Word Classes

In inflectional languages, a division of word classes is possible into those which are not capable of inflection – e.g. prepositions, conjunctions, adverbs – and those which are – e.g. nouns, verbs and adjectives.

These linguistic facts are modelled in MORPHIX. Word forms belonging to non–inflecting word classes are stored in a word form lexicon. For such forms only the lexical access is necessary without trying to decompose the word form into candidate stem and inflectional morph pairs. For example, without regarding these facts, one might try to split off the possible inflectional suffix *er* from the German adverb *immer* ('always'), although it is a non–inflecting word. As the non–inflecting word classes are closed and domain independent, the word form lexicon belongs to the fixed lexical knowledge of the package regardless of the specific NLS.

2.2 Segmentation of Inflecting Word Classes

The first step in analyzing forms which are not found in the word form lexicon or which are marked as homographs is to decompose them into candidate stems and corresponding prefixes and suffixes. This process is highly language–specific since at least the inflectional morpheme inventory varies from one language to another. With the information stored in the IAL, MOR-PHIX first separates the longest possible inflectional suffix from the input word. Because all possible stems for a word form have to be found, it is necessary to split a complex suffix into its parts and to concatenate the stem with these parts step by step. The information about the parts of complex suffixes is contained in the IAL beside the n–ary trees for each inflectional allomorph.

In analogy, a corresponding process is done to split off all possible prefixes to handle prefix/suffix combinations.

For example, for the input word *rasten*, the process of segmentation yields as result no possible prefix and the following possibilities for stems and suffixes:

ra – sten, ras – ten, rast – en, raste – n, rasten – ∅

Further analysis will show that the three stems *ras* ('to race'), *rast* ('to rest', 'rest') and *raste* ('notch') will lead to correct results.

2.3 Morphophonological Alternation in the Stem

In languages where irregular or even suppletive stems occur in addition to inflectional morphs to form surface word forms, it is possible that the segmentation process may not yield the canonical stems. In such cases either the corresponding canonical stems can be obtained algorithmically or the irregular stems can be stored in the stem lexicon and related to the canonical ones.

In the German language, for instance, there are nouns which form their plural with an inflectional suffix plus umlaut in the stem. Nouns having this feature can be grouped together [Sch72]. An example of such a noun is the German word *haus* ('house'). As previously described, the segmentation process of *häusern* (dative plural of 'house') leads to the following combinations of stems and suffixes:

häus – ern, häuser – n, häusern – ∅

The canonical stem *haus* is not contained in any of these candidate stems, so the morphological analysis would fail. Because umlaut often occurs in German and since its reduction is efficient to implement, umlaut will be reduced for all candidate stems in the segmentation process. Therefore, it is sufficient to store only the canonical stems of such nouns in the stem lexicon. In the example, the augmented segmentation process thus obtains the following additional combinations:

haus – ern, hauser – n, hausern – ∅

Changes in the stems of irregular verbs are more difficult to handle than the umlaut phenomenon in nouns. Particular verbs can form their irregular stems by umlaut or ablaut alternations. For example, the German verb *fahren* ('to drive') takes four different stems: the canonical stem *fahr* and the irregular stems *fähr*, *fuhr* and *führ*. In MORPHIX, the irregular stems are stored in the stem lexicon with a pointer to their canonical stem. This method is more efficient than the reduction of irregular stems to their canonical stems algorithmically during segmentation, especially since the number of irregular verbs is limited in German (about 200).

2.4 The Use of the Classification

In the further analysis of the word form thus segmented, MORPHIX determines which of the proposed combinations of stem and affixes describe correct segmentations of the word form. A segmentation is correct if the stem can be found in the lexicon and if the inflectional morpheme in conjunction with the stem represents a grammatical well–formed word form. The algorithm that accepts or rejects each previously derived segmentation is as follows:

- Try to access the stem in the stem lexicon.
- If an entry exists, extract the classification information and construct search–paths containing the classes, otherwise reject this segmentation.
- Extract the n–ary tree from the IAL and match the search–paths within the n–ary tree.
- For each search–path test: If both, the matching succeeds and the next subtree in the n–ary tree is a leaf, then the segmentation was correct. If no leaf could be reached, the combination of stem and inflectional morph was not correct.
- For successful search–paths, collect the stem of this segmentation and the morphosyntactic information that is found in the leaf as a part–result of the algorithm.

Before giving a detailed example, we explain how the German verbs are classified in MOR-PHIX. First, we consider **morphosyntactical** features. In section 2.3, we mentioned that several irregular stems may be needed to produce all forms of a verb. The irregular stems are grouped into four different classes according to [Bus83]. These classes express the use of a stem within its paradigm, for example that a particular non–canonical stem is used to form the past tense. Disjoint verb types are defined by the combination of these classes. MORPHIX makes use of 11 verb types which express different degrees of irregularity. To illustrate this, we explain the classification of the German verb *fahren* ('to drive'). *fahren* uses four different stems to build all its inflectional forms:

verb–stem	used to build forms of	coded in the lexicon as
führ	subjunctive	VGFD
fuhr	past indicative	VGFC
fähr	2nd/3rd singular present indicative	VGFB
fahr	else	VGFA

Verbs which use four stems in this manner for their inflectional forms belong to verb type 6 in our classification. Most verbs inflect using only the canonical stem, the so–called weak verbs classified as verb type 1.

So far the classification has only considered morphosyntactic features. However, it is possible to use **morphophonological** features to refine the existing classification. In inflectional languages, phonological requirements often lead to morphophonological alternation in the stem coda or inflectional suffix. In German, these alternations consist in the insertion or elision of segments at the juncture between stem and suffix. It can be determined from the nature of the stem coda whether and which alternations occur. In MORPHIX therefore, the irregular stem classes are partitioned into disjoint subclasses.

The subclass A2 of canonical stems (coded as VGFA) may serve here as example:

- It contains all elements that use the canonical stem to form the present 2nd sg and whose stem coda is either "d" or "t". To build the present 2nd sg forms of verbs of this subclass an "e" is inserted between the stem and the regular suffix *st* – e.g. *du arbeit-e-st* ('you work').

A consequence of this refined classificaton is the requirement of the IAL that in the n–ary tree for the suffix *st* no path containing the class A2 as a node is allowed to reach a leaf containing the morphosyntactic information *present 2 sg*. If such a path existed then wrong forms such as *arbeitst* would be analysed.

Example

- input word: *rasten*
- successful lexicon access for the stems (cf. 2.2):

ra	:	((WORTART nomen) (GENUS mas) (SG 0))
ras	:	((WORTART verb) (VTYP 1) (VGFA A4))
rast	:	((WORTART verb) (VTYP 1) (VGFA A2))
rast	:	((WORTART nomen) (GENUS fem) (SG 0) (PL 4))
raste	:	((WORTART nomen) (GENUS fem) (SG 0) (PL 3))

- build the search–paths:

$$verb--vtype--1--VGFA--A4 \quad\Big\} \quad for \quad ras$$

$$\left.\begin{array}{l} verb--vtype--1--VGFA--A2 \\ nomen--sg--0 \\ nomen--pl--4 \end{array}\right\} \quad for \quad rast$$

$$\left.\begin{array}{l} nomen--sg--0 \\ nomen--pl--3 \end{array}\right\} \quad for \quad raste$$

- extract the n–ary trees for the suffixes *ten*, *en* and *n* from the IAL:

  e.g.

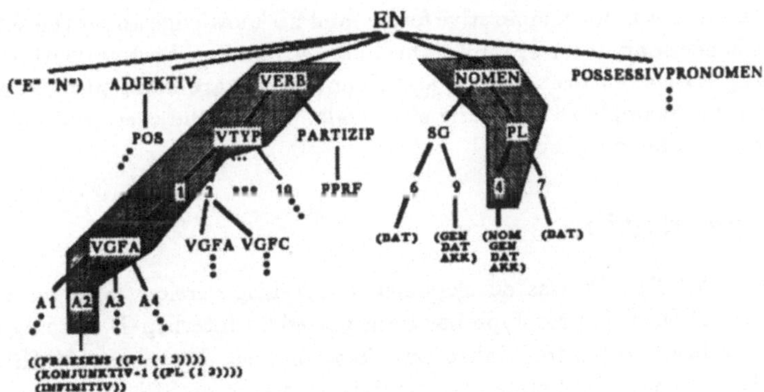

Figure 1: the n–ary tree for the suffix *en*

- result for the morphological analysis of *rasten*:

  (*ras*   (WORTART verb) (FLEXION ((imperfekt ((pl (1 3))))) (konjunktiv-2 ((pl (1 3))

  (*rast*   (WORTART nomen) (FLEXION ((fem ((pl (nom gen dat akk)))))))

  (*rast*   (WORTART verb)
         (FLEXION ((infinitiv) (praesens ((pl (1 3))))) (konjunktiv-1 ((pl (1 3)))))))

  (*raste*   (WORTART nomen) (FLEXION ((fem ((pl (nom gen dat akk)))))))

2.5   Generation of Word Forms

It is possible to use our approach in the opposite direction, i.e. to produce word forms (see [FN88] for the use of MORPHIX in the how-to-say component of a natural language generation system). This requires that the canonical stems in the stem lexicon have additional pointers to their irregular stems. The input structures for the generation process are a canonical stem and the morphosyntactic information for the desired surface form. The algorithm for this task is as follows:

- Try to access the canonical stem in the stem lexicon.
- If an entry exists, extract the classification information, otherwise the stem lexicon is insufficient and a clarification dialog can be started to augment the lexicon.
- Compute the correct stem for the desired inflection with the help of the lexicon entry and construct a search–path for the IAL. The morphosyntactic description from the input constitutes the last element of the search–path.
- This search–path is matched against all n–ary trees of the IAL which are relevant for the desired category.
- The root of the unambiguous entry of the IAL which matches the search–path is the correct inflectional morph and appended to the computed stem.

2.6   The Clarification Dialog

The user is able to augment the MORPHIX lexicon interactively by means of a clarification dialog. Because it is easy to compile a domain–specific lexicon, the integration of the package into natural language systems with different domains is thus facilitated.

The clarification dialog guarantees that only syntactically well–formed lexicon entries are constructed, thus requiring no user knowledge about the internal structure of the lexicon. Only linguistic knowledge is required of the user in the clarification dialog – for example, whether an adjective gets an umlaut in its comparative form – and no knowledge about the subclassification of word classes is necessary – for example which classes handle adjectives with this feature. In addition, existing lexicon entries are used and computations are made to relate stems to their subclassification, for example to check the stem coda. Hence, the user need not carry out the entire classification of an entry by hand.

3   Implementation

The prototype of MORPHIX was developed in Franz–Lisp version 38.79 on a VAX–11/780 under UNIX 4.2. BSD. This prototype has been ported to Interlisp–D running on a XEROX 1108, and has also been ported to Zetalisp and Common Lisp. It runs on SYMBOLICS and TI EXPLORER lisp–machines and on several workstations such as SUN 3, MicroVax II and HP 9000/350.

Run time evaluation was carried out for these environments with a stem lexicon of about 6000 entries. The average cpu–time required for the analysis of one input word is listed below:

Computer	Lisp–Dialect	CPU–Seconds/Word
XEROX 1108	Interlisp–D	0.040
SUN 3	Common Lisp	0.024
TI EXPLORER I	Zetalisp	0.019
VAX – 8700	Franz Lisp	0.016
SYMBOLICS 3640	Zetalisp	0.014
HP 9000/350	Common Lisp	0.009
VAX – 8700	Kyoto Common Lisp	0.005

These run–time evaluations were performed for the prototype of MORPHIX [FN86] that didn't handle all aspects of the classification–based approach. Now we have implemented the approach described in this paper in a new version of MORPHIX. Although, this version has increased the linguistic power of the prototype its average run–time per word is 0.02 cpu–seconds on a SYMBOLICS 3640.

4   Example of an Application

MORPHIX has been integrated into the syntactic component SB–PATR which is part of XTRA (eXpert TRAnslator), a natural language access system for expert systems [XTR87]. SB–PATR is a reimplementation of the D–PATR system, a development environment for unification–based grammars [Kar86]. With the PATR formalism, there has been developed XTRAGRAM a unification grammar for German sentences [Har86]. To integrate MORPHIX into SB–PATR, only the word classes and their inflectional information from the MORPHIX output had to be mapped onto the categories of XTRAGRAM (see figure 2 for the context–free part of a parsed sentence).

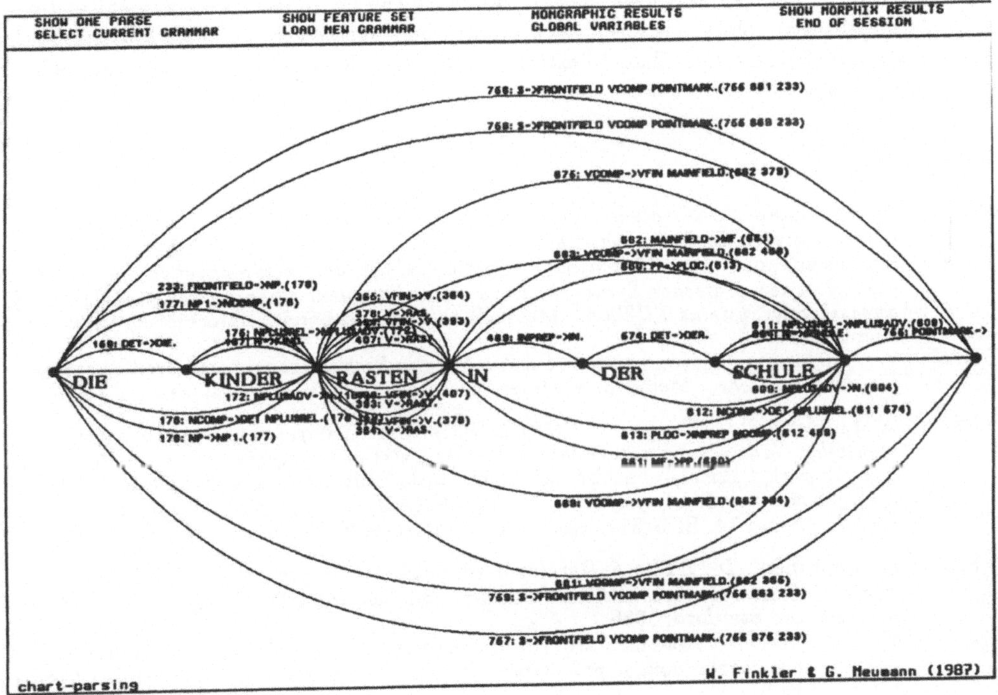

Figure 2: context–free part of the sentence: *Die Kinder rasten in der Schule.*

The integration of the package MORPHIX into SB–PATR resulted in the following overall improvements:

- During the parse of an input sentence, it is possible to insert entries for unknown words into the stem lexicon with the help of the clarification dialog. The parsing algorithm is just interrupted and then resumed after the clarification dialog is finished. Without MORPHIX, SB–PATR was not able to obtain a result for input sentences containing unknown words.

- The installation of MORPHIX with its stem lexicon of about 6000 entries enables XTRA-GRAM to use approximately 60000 surface forms instead of storing all these forms in a word form lexicon, which would have been necessary without the integration of MOR-PHIX.

These facts and the excellent run time behavior of MORPHIX illustrate the power that is made available to a natural language system by such a package.

5 Conclusion

Due to the very abstract level of description for morphological phenomena used in our approach, the course of morphological analysis is easy to understand. The use of a hierarchical classification can be represented directly by means of n–ary trees. For this reason the testing of performed segmentations can be done with simple algorithms in order to traverse these trees. The realization of MORPHIX shows that our approach can be implemented very efficiently as well. Although morphology has often been studied and handled in computer programs, the demand for MORPHIX - more than 10 external institutes - demonstrates the necessity of such a portable package.

References

[Ber83] H. Bergmann. *Lemmatisierung in HAM-ANS*. Memo ANS-10, Fachbereich Informatik, Universität Hamburg, 1983.

[Bus83] S. Busemann. *Oberflächentransformationen bei der automatischen Generierung geschriebener deutscher Sprache - Entwurf und Implementierung des modularen und anpassbaren Systems SUTRA*. Master's thesis, Fachbereich Informatik, Universität Hamburg, 1983.

[FN86] W. Finkler and G. Neumann. *MORPHIX - Ein hochportabler Lemmatisierungsmodul für das Deutsche*. Memo 8, Fachbereich Informatik, Universität des Saarlandes, 7 1986.

[FN88] W. Finkler and G. Neumann. *POPEL-HOW: Eine Komponente zur parallelen, inkrementellen Generierung natürlichsprachlicher Sätze aus konzeptuellen Einheiten*. Technical Report, SFB 314, Fachbereich Informatik, Universität des Saarlandes, 1988.

[Har86] K. Harbusch. *A First Snapshot of XTRAGRAM, a Unification Grammar Based on PATR*. Memo 14, SFB 314, Fachbereich Informatik, Universität des Saarlandes, 12 1986.

[Kar86] L. Karttunen. *D-PATR. A Development Environment for Unification-Based Grammars*. Technical Report, SRI International and Center for the Study of Language and Information, Stanford, 1986.

[Kay82] M. Kay. When meta-rules are not meta-rules. In Sparck-Jones & Wilks, editor, *Automatic natural language processing*, University of Essex, Cognitive Studies Centre, 1982. CSM-10.

[Kay87] M. Kay. Nonconcatenative finite-state morphology. In *3rd Conference of the European Chapter of the ACL*, pages 2–10, University of Copenhagen, Copenhagen, Denmark, 1987.

[Kos83] K. Koskenniemi. Two-level model for morphological analysis. In *IJCAI 1983*, pages 683–685, Karlsruhe, 1983.

[Kos84] K. Koskenniemi. A general computational model for word-form recognition and production. In *COLING 1984*, pages 178–181, Stanford University, California, 1984.

[Sch72] G. Schott. Automatic analysis of inflectional morphems in german nouns. *Acta Informatica*, 1:360–374, 1972.

[Son80] Sonderforschungsbereich 100, editor. *SALEM: Ein Verfahren zur automatischen Lemmatisierung deutscher Texte*. Niemeyer, Tübingen, 1980.

[TD85]   H. Trost and G. Dorffner. A system for morphological analysis and synthesis of german texts. In D. Hainline, editor, *Foreign Language CAI*, Croom Helm, London, 1985.

[XTR87]   *Künstliche Intelligenz - Wissensbasierte Systeme*. Frühjahr 1987. SFB - 314 Arbeits- und Ergebnisbericht für die Jahre 1985 - 1986 - 3/1987.

Determinatoren und Quantoren
in einer kategorialen Unifikationsgrammatik des Deutschen

Petra Maier
Universität Tübingen
Uhlandstr. 18
D-7400 Tübingen

Petra Steffens
IBM Deutschland GmbH
UP WT LILOG
Postfach 800880
D-7000 Stuttgart 80

1. Problemstellung

Gegenstand der vorliegenden Untersuchung ist die Beschreibung von Nominalphrasen im Rahmen einer kategorialen Unifikationsgrammatik, wobei der Schwerpunkt der Analyse auf Kongruenz- und Abfolgephänomenen im pränominalen Bereich liegt.

Die Beschreibung der <u>Kongruenzphänomene</u> ist als eher technisches Problem anzusehen, da die Datenlage bekannt ist. Hervorzuheben ist in diesem Zusammenhang allerdings, daß innerhalb der Nominalphrase nicht nur Übereinstimmung hinsichtlich Kasus, Genus und Numerus herrschen muß, sondern auch die Deklination eine Rolle spielt. Dabei unterscheidet man beim Adjektiv drei Deklinationsformen: schwach, stark und gemischt. Ob ein Adjektiv stark, schwach oder gemischt zu deklinieren ist, richtet sich nach dem vorausgehenden Determinator bzw. Quantor[1] , wie die nachfolgenden Beispiele veranschaulichen.

(1) der rote Wein / dem roten Wein   - schwache Deklination
(2) roter Wein / rotem Wein   - starke Deklination
(3) sein roter Wein / seinem roten Wein   - gemischte Deklination

Die Beschreibung der <u>Abfolgeregularitäten</u> im pränominalen Bereich erweist sich vor allem im Hinblick auf die Quantoren als problematisch, da deren Kombinations- und Stellungsmöglichkeiten nur teilweise semantisch motivierbar sind. So läßt sich zwar die Unakzeptabilität von (4) semantisch erklären, nicht aber das unterschiedliche syntaktische Verhalten der Quantoren "all_" oder "sämtlich_" in (5) oder die unterschiedlichen Kombinationsmöglichkeiten der Kardinalzahlen "10" und "hundert" in (6).

(4) * viele wenige Rosen
(5a) die sämtlichen Rosen
(5b) * die alle Rosen
(6a) * viele 10 Studenten
(6b) viele hundert Studenten

Daß die Quantoren hinsichtlich ihres syntaktischen Verhaltens eine sehr heterogene Gruppe darstellen wird auch an den Beispielen (7) bis (11) deutlich. So gibt es Quantoren, die sowohl vor als auch nach einem Adjektiv stehen können und die sich zugleich hinsichtlich anderer Kriterien wie z.B. Koordination, Deklinationsverhalten und

---

[1]   Als "Determinatoren" bezeichnen wir den definiten Artikel, die Possessiva sowie die Demonstrativa. Als "Quantor" bezeichnen wir (in einem vorerst nicht-technischen Sinne) Ausdrücke, die in irgendeiner Weise quantifizierend auf der Denotatsmenge ihrer Bezugsnomen operieren. Beispiele für Quantoren sind "viel_", "kein_", "all_" oder die Kardinalzahlen.

Modifizierbarkeit wie Adjektive verhalten:

(7a) die schönen vielen/?wenigen/5 gelben Häuser
(7b) die schönen hohen/?höchsten gelben Häuser
(8a) die zahlreichen und schönen Blumen
(8b) die teuren und schönen Blumen
(9a) die zu wenigen Rosen
(9b) die zu teuren Rosen

Andere Quantoren hingegen verhalten sich syntaktisch eher wie Determinatoren. So stellen sie an ein nachfolgendes Adjektiv eine Deklinationsforderung und können nicht nach einem Determinator auftreten:

(10a) keine roten Rosen
(10b) * die keinen roten Rosen
(11a) viele rote Rosen
(11b) die vielen roten Rosen

Analysen der beschriebenen Phänomene wurden bisher hauptsächlich im Bereich der X'-Syntax durchgeführt (Jackendoff 1977, Vater 1986a und 1986b, Haider 1986). Zwar streben diese Ansätze eine Formalisierung der postulierten theoretischen Konzepte an, doch mangelt es ihnen oft an observationeller Adäquatheit; das heißt: viele der beobachtbaren Phänomene, vor allem spezielle Abfolgephänomene im Deutschen wie (12), (13) oder (14), bleiben weitgehend unberücksichtigt.

(12) einige wenige Rosen
(13) all die vielen Rosen
(14) diese meine Schwestern

Den Ansätzen im Rahmen der X'-Theorie stehen verschiedene Beschreibungen der Nominalphrase in Grammatiken des Deutschen gegenüber (z.B. "Duden" 1984 und "Grundzüge" 1980). Während diese Grammatiken zwar darum bemüht sind, die Fülle der sprachlichen Phänomene möglichst umfassend zu beschreiben, sehen sie es nicht als ihre Aufgabe an, die postulierten Regularitäten zu formalisieren. Wir halten es daher für erforderlich, die Analyse der Determinatoren und Quantoren neu aufzurollen, mit dem Ziel, die heterogene Klasse der Quantoren unter spezieller Berücksichtigung ihrer morphologischen und syntaktischen Eigenheiten neu zu strukturieren.

Untersucht man nun die Quantoren, insbesondere im Hinblick auf ihre Ähnlichkeit mit den Adjektiven (beispielsweise hinsichtlich ihrer Komparierbarkeit, der Möglichkeit zur prädikativen Verwendung, des Deklinationsverhaltens oder der Koordination, etc.), so ergibt sich die in Abbildung 1 dargestellte Skala, deren beide Pole durch ein mehr oder weniger "Adjektiv-haftes" Verhalten gegeben sind. [2]

Wie Abbildung 1 zeigt, unterscheiden wir insgesamt drei Gruppen von Quantoren:

■ Quantoren, die -ähnlich wie Determinatoren- von einem nachfolgenden Adjektiv eine bestimmte Deklinationsform fordern und die nicht nach einem Determinator auftreten können; wir bezeichnen diese Gruppe mit "Q1".

■ Quantoren, die -ähnlich den Adjektiven- keine Deklinationsforderung haben und die zugleich einem Determinator folgen können; wir bezeichnen diese Gruppe mit "Q3".

■ Quantoren, die sich sowohl wie Adjektive als auch wie Determinatoren verhalten, wie die Konstruktionen (15) und (16) illustrieren.

(15a) beide roten Rosen
(15b) * rote beide Rosen
(16a) die beiden schönen Rosen
(16b) die schönen beiden Rosen

Wir bezeichnen diese Quantoren mit "Q2".

---

[2] In der Skala sind durch die vertikale Schraffur diejenigen Quantoren gekennzeichnet, die eine eigene Deklinationsforderung haben und durch die horizontale Schraffur diejenigen Quantoren, die sich wie Adjektive verhalten.

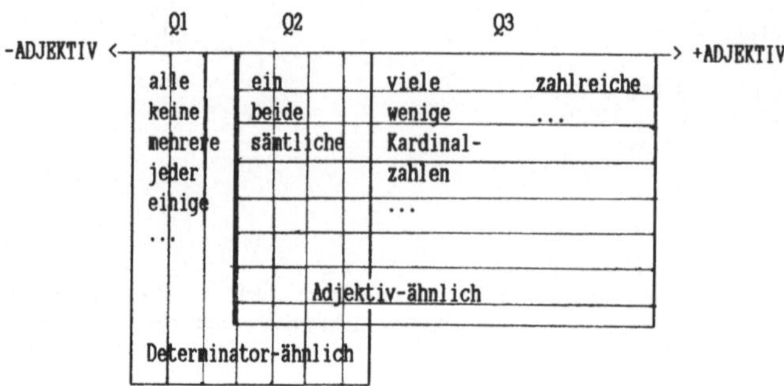

Abbildung 1. Quantoren und Adjektive

Im folgenden wollen wir den syntaktischen Eigenschaften dieser drei Gruppen im Rahmen einer kategorialen Unifikationsgrammatik Rechnung tragen. Dabei werden wir Q3-Quantoren als Untergruppe der Adjektive und Q1-Quantoren ähnlich den Determinatoren behandeln. Der Doppelfunktion der Q2-Quantoren wird durch eine spezielle Behandlung Rechnung getragen.

2. Kategoriale Unifikationsgrammatik

Kategoriale Unifikationsgrammatiken (KUG) vereinen die universale Ausdruckskraft Unifikations-basierter Formalismen mit der konzeptuellen Einfachheit kategorialer Grammatiken. Wir wollen in diesem Abschnitt auf einige wesentlichen Eigenschaften des von uns verwendeten Unifikationsformalismus eingehen und die Codierung kategorialgrammatischer Information an einem Beispiel veranschaulichen.

Der von uns verwendete Unifikationsformalismus heißt STUF (Stuttgart Type Unification Formalism). STUF, in vielerlei Hinsicht eine Erweiterung von PATR-II (Shieber et al. 1983) und Ait-Kaci's Typenrepräsentationsformalismus (Ait-Kaci 1984), wurde im Rahmen des Projekts LILOG der IBM Deutschland GmbH entwickelt und in verschiedenen Versionen implementiert (s. Bouma et al. 1988 und Uszkoreit 1987). STUF erlaubt es, lexikalisches und syntaktisches Wissen weitgehend uniform darzustellen, nämlich in der Form gerichteter Graphen. Betrachten wir hierzu ein Beispiel:

(17)

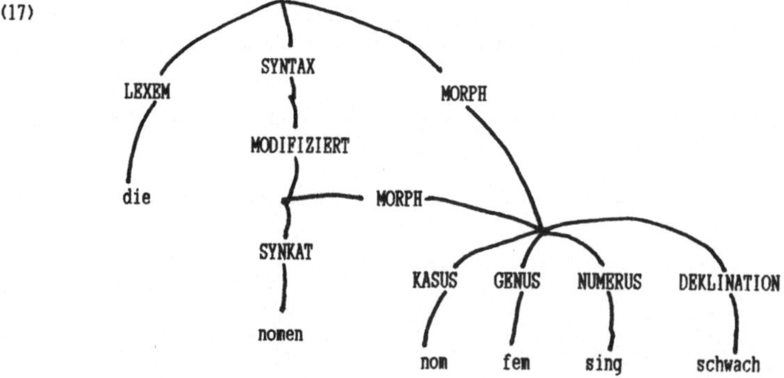

Neben den morphologischen Eigenschaften des LEXEMs "die" beschreibt dieser Graph das syntaktische Verhalten des bestimmten Artikels: "die" MODIFIZIERT "nomen", für die MORPHologische Kongruenz gefordert wird. Die Bedingung der morphologischen Kongruenz kommt dadurch zum Ausdruck, daß sowohl der Pfad, der aus der Kante "MORPH" besteht, als auch der Pfad, der sich aus den Kanten "SYNTAX", "MODIFIZIERT" und

"MORPH" zusammensetzt, auf den gleichen Teilgraphen zeigen. Wir sprechen in diesem Fall von einer "reentranten" Struktur.

Graphen können "atomar" und "komplex" sein. Atomare Graphen sind entweder leer oder bestehen aus einer alphanumerischen Zeichenkette, wie beispielsweise "sing". Atome schreiben wir im folgenden immer klein. Komplexe Graphen bestehen aus einer oder mehreren Kanten, die ihrerseits auf Graphen zeigen. Kantennamen schreiben wir im folgenden immer groß. Statt von "Kanten", die "auf Graphen zeigen", sprechen wir auch von "Attributen" und ihren "Werten", wobei wir im Falle atomarer Graphen auch den Begriff "Merkmal" und im Falle komplexer Graphen den Begriff "Merkmalsstruktur" verwenden.

Im folgenden wollen wir Graphen allerdings nicht zeichnerisch, sondern in STUF-Notation darstellen. Der in (17) dargestellte Graph wird in STUF folgendermaßen notiert:

```
(18)  <LEXEM> = die
      <MORPH GENUS> = fem
      <MORPH NUMERUS> = sing
      <MORPH KASUS> = nom
      <MORPH DEKLINATION> = schwach
      <SYNTAX MODIFIZIERT SYNKAT> = nomen
      <SYNTAX MODIFIZIERT MORPH> = <MORPH>.
```

Pfade werden in STUF also in spitze Klammern eingeschlossen, wobei ein Pfad der Wurzel des Graphs umso näher ist, je weiter links in der Klammer er steht. Reentranz wird in STUF durch die Gleichsetzung zweier Pfade ausgedrückt. Neben der Gleichheit und der Unifikation ist auf Graphen die Operation der Disjunktion, notiert durch ";", definiert. Wollte man beispielsweise neben der Nominativform des Artikels "die" auch seine Akkusativform berücksichtigen, so ließe sich die vierte Zeile in (18) durch (19) ersetzen.

```
(19)  <MORPH KASUS> = [nom;akk].
```

STUF bietet die Möglichkeit, Graphen zu benennen. Auf diese Weise kann auf "Pakete" syntaktischen bzw. lexikalischen Wissens mit einem frei gewählten Namen referiert werden. Ähnlich wie Shieber (1984) wollen wir solche Teilgraphen "Templates" nennen. Templates können beliebig in anderen Teilgraphen und natürlich auch in anderen Templates angesprochen werden. Im Fall lexikalischer Einträge ist der Template-Name das zu beschreibende Lexem selbst. (20) zeigt an zwei Beispielen, wie Templates definiert und zur Strukturierung lexikalischer Information verwendet werden.

```
(20)  die := FEM [NOM;AKK] SING.
      der := [[MASK NOM];[FEM [DAT;GEN]] SING.

      FEM  := <MORPH GENUS> = fem.
      MASK := <MORPH GENUS> = mask.
      NOM  := <MORPH KASUS> = nom.
      AKK  := <MORPH KASUS> = akk.
      GEN  := <MORPH KASUS> = gen.
      DAT  := <MORPH KASUS> = dat.
      SING := <MORPH NUMERUS> = sing.
```

Wir wollen die Beschreibung des von uns verwendeten Unifikations-Formalismus nun abschließen und noch kurz darauf eingehen, wie sich kategorialgrammatische Konzepte in Unifikations-basierten Formalismen darstellen lassen. Detaillierte Ausführungen hierzu finden sich in Uszkoreit (1986) und in Zeevat et al. (1986).

Zur Darstellung von Kategorien führen wir ein Attribut SYNKAT (für "SYNtaktische KATegorie") ein, dessen Werte Merkmalsstrukturen für atomare oder komplexe Kategorien sind. Atomare Kategorien wie N (für Nomen) oder S (für Satz) wollen wir als atomare Graphen darstellen. Um komplexe Kategorien wie N\S (für intransitive Verben) zu repräsentieren, führen wir drei weitere Attribute ein: WERT, ARGUMENT und RICHTUNG. Die kategoriale Information für Eigennamen wie "Hans" und intransitive Verben wie "singt" ließe sich dann folgendermaßen in Graphenschreibweise übersetzen:

(21)   Hans: singt:

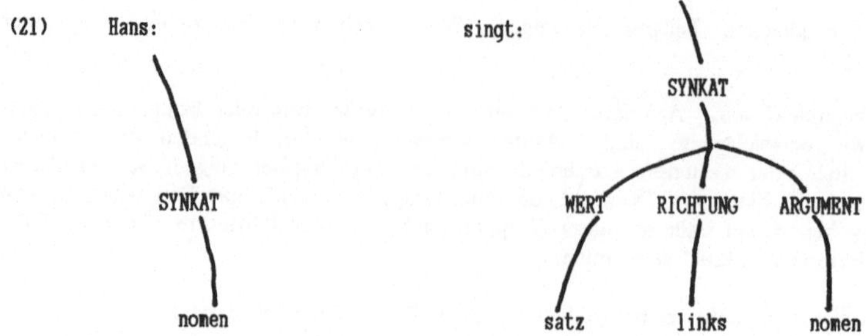

Für unsere Analyse der Determinatoren und Quantoren verwenden wir ausschließlich die Operationen der Rechtsapplikation (A --> A/B B) und der Linksapplikation (B --> A A\B). Sie werden in STUF durch die Graphenapplikation realisiert (s. König 1987). Wird beispielsweise die Regel der Linksapplikation (LA) angewendet, so wird die Merkmalsstruktur (22) mit den jeweiligen Funktor- und Argumentgraphen unifiziert und als Ergebnis der Teilgraph übergeben, auf den der Pfad < FA_WERT > zeigt.

(22) LA:

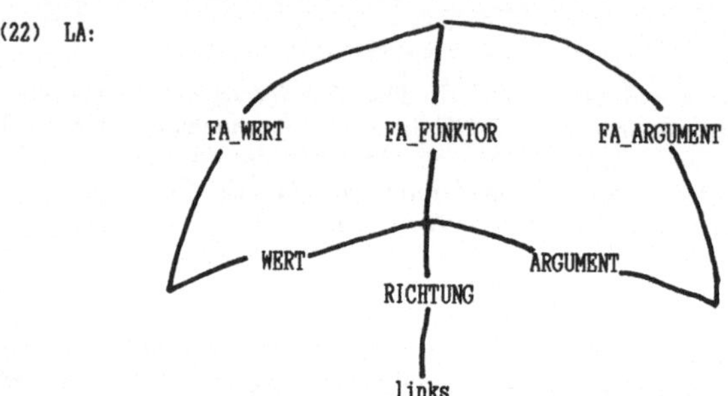

Die Ableitung für den Satz "Hans singt." läßt sich dann wie in Abbildung 2 gezeigt, darstellen.

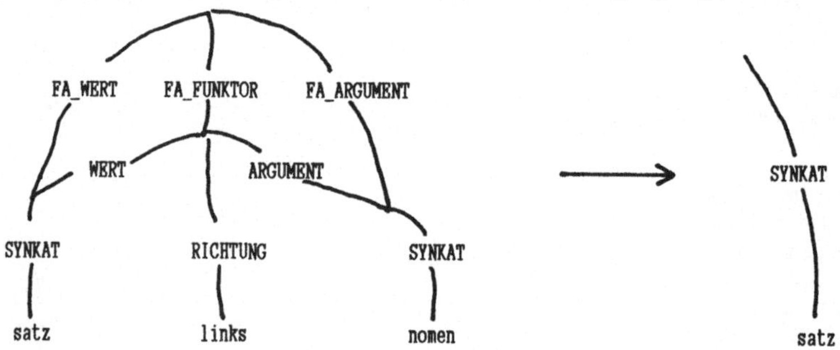

LA ⊔ Hans ⊔ singt[3]

Abbildung 2. Ableitung eines Satzes in einer KUG

Im folgenden werden wir syntaktische Kategorien allerdings nicht in STUF-Schreibweise, sondern in ihrer gewohnten Form (z.B. "N/N") notieren, wobei wir die mit der Wert-, Argument- bzw. Funktorkategorie assoziierten Merkmalsstrukturen in eckigen Klammern rechts neben die jeweiligen Kategoriensymbole (z.B. "N/N[SCHWACH] [SING FEM]") schreiben und Reentranz durch Koindizierung markieren.

---

[3]   Das Symbol "⊔" bezeichnet die Unifikationsoperation.

3. Lexikalische Markierung von Determinatoren und Quantoren

Wie die in Abschnitt 1 angeführten Beispiele verdeutlichen, muß eine Grammatik für Determinatoren und Quantoren auf verschiedenen Beschreibungsdimensionen operieren. Wir wollen im folgenden drei Beschreibungsdimensionen unterscheiden:

- **Die morphologische Dimension.** Durch geeignete morphologische Kennzeichnungen ist zum einen dafür zu sorgen, daß die Determinatoren und Quantoren mit ihren Bezugsnomen in Kasus, Genus und Numerus übereinstimmen und zum anderen, daß die Deklination der Bezugsnomen, d.h. der in den Bezugsnomen auftretenden Adjektive, mit den Deklinationsforderungen des Determinators oder Quantors übereinstimmt.

- **Die kategoriale Dimension.** Durch die Zuweisung zu einer geeigneten syntaktischen Kategorie wird die syntaktische Umgebung eines Determinators bzw. Quantors grob charakterisiert; das heißt, es wird explizit (durch die zugewiesene Argument-Kategorie) und implizit (durch die Prozesse, die auf der zugewiesenen Wert-Kategorie operieren) festgelegt, welches seine kategoriale Umgebung ist; es wird ferner bestimmt, welche Position er relativ zu seinem Bezugsnomen hat und es wird gesagt, welche Funktor-Argument-Beziehungen zwischen ihm und seiner Umgebung vorliegen.

  Bei unserer Analyse der Determinatoren und Quantoren gehen wir von einer Kategorialgrammatik aus, deren atomare Kategorien S (für Satz) und N (für alle Nominalkonstruktionen) sind. Determinatoren und Quantoren sind demnach komplexen Kategorien zuzuweisen. Da wir Determinatoren und Quantoren gleichermaßen als Funktoren auffassen, die Nominalkonstruktionen auf andere Nominalkonstruktionen abbilden, weisen wir sie der Kategorie N/N zu.

- **Die subkategoriale Dimension.** Da die durch die syntaktischen Kategorien gegebenen Möglichkeiten zur Beschreibung der Umgebung eines Determinators bzw. Quantors im allgemeinen noch keine korrekte und erschöpfende Beschreibung seiner Distribution zulassen, ist es notwendig, neben einer Charakterisierung auf der kategorialen Ebene eine Beschreibung auf einer feiner granulierten Ebene vorzunehmen, die wir im folgenden "subkategoriale Dimension" nennen wollen. Während auf der kategorialen Dimension beispielsweise festgelegt wird, daß sich der bestimmte Artikel "die" mit einem Nomen, beispielsweise zu "die Rosen", verbindet, erlauben es die auf der subkategorialen Dimension vorgenommenen Spezifikationen, Verbindungen wie "die vielen Rosen" zu generieren und Verbindungen wie "die keinen Rosen" auszuschließen.

Wir wollen uns nun zuerst den Quantoren der Gruppen Q1 und Q3 zuwenden (als typische Vertreter dieser Gruppen werden wir die Quantoren "kein_" bzw. "viel_" betrachten) und geeignete morphologische und subkategoriale Attribute für ihre Beschreibung festlegen; die spezielle Problematik der Q2-Quantoren soll im Anschluß daran, in Abschnitt 4, diskutiert werden. Auf die kategoriale Beschreibungsebene wollen wir im folgenden nicht mehr eingehen, da in Abschnitt 2 bereits erläutert wurde, wie sich atomare und komplexe Kategorien als STUF-Graphen repräsentieren lassen.

3.1 Morphologische Attribute

Um die Interaktion zwischen Determinatoren und Quantoren und ihren Bezugsnomen hinsichtlich Genus, Kasus, Numerus und Deklinationsverhalten zu steuern, führen wir für die morphologische Analysebene die folgenden Attribute und Werte ein:

GENUS: mask, fem, neut

NUMERUS: plu, sing

KASUS: nom, gen, dat, akk

DEKLINATION: schwach, stark, gemischt

Dabei werden bei Anwendung der funktionalen Applikation die morphologischen Merkmale der Funktorkategorie mit den morphologischen Merkmalen der Argumentkategorie unifiziert und an die Wertkategorie vererbt. Nehmen wir nun an, daß die genannten Attribut-Wert-Paare ihrerseits die Werte eines Attributs MORPH darstellen und daß für jedes der genannten morphologischen Merkmale ein gleichnamiges Template, wie beispielsweise

```
MASK:= < MORPH GENUS > = mask.
```

definiert wurde, so lassen sich die folgenden (partiellen) lexikalischen Einträge für den Q1-Quantor "keine" und die Q3-Quantoren "viele" und "5" angeben.

```
keine:=    [[PLU [NOM;AKK] GEMISCHT] ;
            [SING ....            ]].

viele:=    [[PLU [NOM;AKK] STARK] ;
            [SING ...          ]].

5:=        [PLU].
```

Hierzu ist folgendes zu sagen. Während die Merkmale für Genus, Kasus und Numerus konstant eine Eigenschaft des Lexems selbst beschreiben, verhält sich das Attribut DEKLINATION gewissermaßen "janusköpfig". Sofern es einen Q3-Quantor charakterisiert, macht es eine Aussage über diesen Quantor selbst: so hat "viele" im Plural das Merkmal "stark", weil seine eigene Flexion die des starken Deklinationsparadigmas ist. Sofern DEKLINATION einen Q1-Quantor charakterisiert, macht es eine Aussage über die morphologische Form, die ein nachfolgendes Adjektiv haben muß: so hat "keine" das Merkmal "gemischt", weil dies die Form ist, die von einem nachfolgendem Adjektiv gefordert wird.

3.2 Subkategoriale Attribute

Mit einer Zuweisung der Determinatoren und Quantoren zur Kategorie N/N lassen sich nun zwar Verbindungen wie (23), (24a) und (25a) bilden; ungrammatische Abfolgebeziehungen der Art "* Adjektiv Q1", "* Adjektiv Determinator" oder "* Determinator Q1", wie sie beispielsweise in (24b) und (25b) vorliegen, wird durch eine solche Kategorisierung jedoch nicht Rechnung getragen.

(23)   rote Rosen
(24a) die roten Rosen
(24b) * roten die Rosen
(25a) keine Rosen
(25b) * die keinen Rosen

Um Konstruktionen wie (24b) und (25b) auszuschließen, in denen ein Determinator bzw. ein Q1-Quantor einem anderen pränominalen Element folgt, ist eine Charakterisierung der Determinatoren und Quantoren auf der subkategorialen Ebene erforderlich. Dabei wollen wir folgendermaßen vorgehen: jeder Determinator und jeder Quantor weist der Konstruktion, zu der er sich mit einem Nomen verbindet, gewisse Merkmale zu, die seine Anwesenheit signalisieren, und fordert seinerseits von seinem "Argument-Nomen" gewisse Merkmale, die die An- oder Abwesenheit anderer Determinatoren und Quantoren signalisieren. Da mit Hilfe dieser Merkmale die Distribution der Determinatoren und Quantoren gesteuert wird, wollen wir -parallel zum Attribut MORPH- ein Attribut DISTRIBUTION einführen, das seinerseits Attribute als Werte annimmt. Zu den Werten des Attributs DISTRIBUTION zählt ein Attribut MODIFIKATION, das die Werte "nil", "q1" und "det" annehmen kann. Dabei signalisiert

■ "nil", daß die vorliegende Nominalkonstruktion weder einen Q1-Quantor noch einen Determinator enthält;

■ "q1", daß die vorliegende Nominalkonstruktion einen Q1-Quantor enthält;

■ "det", daß die vorliegende Nominalkonstruktion einen Determinator enthält.

Nehmen wir an, daß für jeden Wert des Attributs MODIFIKATION ein mit dem Merkmal namensgleiches Template definiert ist, so läßt sich die subkategoriale Charakterisierung von Nomen, Adjektiven, Quantoren der Gruppen Q1, Q2 und Q3 und für Determinatoren folgendermaßen angeben:

```
Nomen:                      N[NIL]

Adjektive und Q3-Quantoren:  N[NIL]/N[NIL]

Q1-Quantoren:               N[Q1]/N[NIL]
```

```
Q2-Quantoren:          N[NIL]/N[NIL]

Determinatoren:        N[DET]/N[NIL]
```

Q1-Quantoren zeichnen sich dadurch aus, daß sie keinem anderen Quantor oder Determinator folgen. Dem wird in den vorausgehenden subkategorialen Charakterisierungen dadurch Rechnung getragen, daß das Merkmal, das die Anwesenheit eines Q1-Quantors signalisiert, für keine der angeführten Argumentkategorien spezifiziert ist. Die Argumentkategorie von Determinatoren ist mit dem MODIFIKATIONS-Merkmal "nil" gekennzeichnet, da sich Determinatoren gleichermaßen mit Nominalkonstruktionen verbinden, in denen ein Adjektiv bzw. ein Q2- oder Q3-Quantor auftritt. Da sich Verbindungen mit einem Determinator jedoch weder wie Nomen ohne Determinator noch wie Verbindungen mit einem Quantor der Gruppe Q1 verhalten, ist die Wertkategorie von Determinatoren mit einem von "nil" und "q1" verschiedenen Merkmal zu kennzeichnen. Wir wählten hierfür "det". Die bisher eingeführten subkategorialen Kennzeichnungen erlauben es nun, Verbindungen wie (26a), (27) oder (28a) zu generieren und blockieren gleichzeitig Konstruktionen wie (26b) oder (28b).

(26a) keine roten Rosen
(26b) * die keinen Rosen
(27)   viele Rosen
(28a) die vielen Rosen
(28b) * vielen die Rosen

Durch das Attribut MODIFIKATION wird also gewährleistet, daß Determinatoren und Q1-Quantoren in der Nominalphrase an erster Stelle stehen (Konstruktionen der Art "all_ Determinator" sind dabei gesondert zu behandeln). Allerdings wird durch dieses Attribut den mehr oder weniger idiosynkratischen Kombinationsmöglichkeiten der Quantoren untereinander noch nicht Rechnung getragen. Würden wir nämlich die Anwesenheit von Quantoren der Gruppen Q2 und Q3 durch kein weiteres Merkmal signalisieren, könnten sie sich ohne Unterschied mit Quantoren der Gruppe Q1, beispielsweise zu (29) oder (30), verbinden.

(29) ? keine beiden Mädchen
(30) * alle wenigen Mädchen

Um nun eine weitere Beschränkung der Abfolgemöglichkeiten unter den Quantoren zu realisieren erweitern wir den Wertebereich des Attributs DISTRIBUTION um ein weiteres, binäres Attribut, das wir QFILTER nennen wollen. Ähnlich wie das Attribut DEKLINATION erfüllt auch dieses Attribut eine Doppelfuntion: charakterisiert es einen Q1-Quantor, besagt es, ob sich der Quantor mit einem Q2- oder Q3-Quantor verbinden kann - falls ja, hat QFILTER den Wert "plus", falls nein, den Wert "minus"; charakterisiert es einen Q2- oder Q3-Quantor signalisiert es dessen Anwesenheit durch den Wert "plus". Die subkategoriale Information für die Quantoren "keine" und "viele" ist dann folgendermaßen zu ergänzen[4] :

```
keine:= N[Q1]/N[NIL, QFILTER=minus].

viele:= N[NIL, QFILTER=plus]/N[NIL].
```

Allerdings kann von Q1-Quantoren nicht generell gesagt werden, daß sie sich nie mit Q2- oder Q3-Quantoren verbinden. So existieren beispielsweise die folgenden, mehr oder weniger idiosynkratischen, Verbindungen:

(31) manch eine Rose
(32) einige wenige Rosen
(33) keine 4 Leute
(34) jede 5 Stunden
(35) alle 20 Rosen
(36) alle beiden Mädchen

Um solchen Verbindungen gerecht zu werden, sehen wir vor, daß eine Nominalkonstruktion Information über die lexikalische Gestalt desjenigen Modifikators enthält, der sich zuletzt mit ihr verbunden hat. Nehmen wir an, daß diese Information mit einem Attribut MODLEX assoziiert ist, das seinerseits zur Wertemenge des Attributs

---

[4] Wir wollen bei der Spezifikation lexikalischer Information auf Pfade jeweils nur durch Nennung der untersten Kante des Pfades Bezug nehmen, falls dies eindeutig ist. Anstatt "<DISTRIBUTION QFILTER> = nil" schreiben wir also "QFILTER = nil".

DISTRIBUTION gehört. Verbindungen wie (31), (32) oder (33) kann dann folgendermaßen Rechnung getragen werden.

```
manch:= N[Q1]/N[NIL, QFILTER=plus, MODLEX=ein].

einige:= N[Q1]/N[[NIL, QFILTER=minus] ;
                [NIL, QFILTER=plus, MODLEX=wenig]].

keine:= N[Q1]/N[[NIL, QFILTER=minus] ;
               [NIL, QFILTER=plus, MODLEX=card]].
```

Nachdem wir nun mit Hilfe kategorialer und subkategorialer Attribute den Kookkurenzbeschränkungen von Determinatoren und Quantoren Rechnung getragen haben, stellt sich die Frage, wann eine nach unseren Regeln aufgebaute Nominalkonstruktion als Nominalphrase fungiert. Dieser Frage wollen wir im nächsten Abschnitt nachgehen.

4. Ein Merkmal für "NP-Status"

Bisher verwendeten wir zur kategorialen Charakterisierung von Nomen und pränominalen Elementen eine einzige atomare Kategorie, nämlich N. Diese Kategorie sahen wir sowohl für Nominalkonstruktionen vor, die bereits den Status einer Nominalphrase haben, wie z.B. "Bare Plurals" oder Verbindungen wie "Determinator Nomen", als auch für Nominalkonstruktionen, die keine Nominalphrasen sind, wie z.B. unmodifizierte "Count Nouns" im Singular. Es stellt sich nun die Frage, auf welche Weise dem unterschiedlichen "Nominalphrasen-Status" dieser Nominalkonstruktionen Rechnung getragen werden kann. Prinzipiell lassen sich hierbei zwei Vorgehensweisen unterscheiden:

1. Man erweitert die Menge der atomaren Kategorien um eine Kategorie NP und weist beispielsweise Determinatoren der Kategorie NP/N zu. Nominalkonstruktionen, die sich syntaktisch sowohl wie Nomen als auch wie Nominalphrasen verhalten, wie z.B. "Bare Plurals" oder "Mass Nouns", wären dann entweder doppelt zu kategorisieren oder durch entsprechende unäre Regeln von N nach NP zu überführen.

2. Der NP-Status jeder Nominalkonstruktion wird durch ein binäres Merkmal explizit signalisiert. "Bare Plurals" oder "Mass Nouns" wären beispielsweise hinsichtlich eines solchen Merkmals positiv, unmodifizierte "Count Nouns" im Singular negativ zu kennzeichnen.

Da wir sowohl Mehrfachkategorisierungen vermeiden, als auch die Anzahl der verwendeten Regeltypen so klein wie möglich halten wollen, werden wir die zweite der genannten Alternativen aufgreifen. Wir führen daher ein weiteres, binäres Distributionsattribut, NP, ein, das folgendermaßen verwendet wird:

unmodifizierte Count-Nomen im Singular:
N[NP = minus]

unmodifizierte Nomen im Plural, Eigennamen und unmodifizierte Mass-Nomen:
N[NP = plus]

Determinatoren und Q1-Quantoren:
N[NIL, NP = plus]/N[NIL]

Adjektive und Q3-Quantoren mit schwacher oder gemischter Deklination im Plural:
N[NIL, NP = minus]/N[NIL]

Adjektive und Q3-Quantoren mit starker Deklination im Plural:
N[NIL, NP = < 1 >]/N[NIL, NP = < 1 >]

Adjektive mit schwacher oder gemischter Deklination im Singular:
N[NIL, NP = minus]/N[NIL]

Adjektive mit starker Deklination im Singular:
    [N[NIL, NP= < 1 >]/N[NIL, NP= < 1 >, MASS] ;
    [NIL, NP = minus]/N[NIL, COUNT]][5]

Da für die Deklinationsform von Determinatoren nicht zwischen starker, schwacher und gemischter Form unterschieden zu werden braucht, markieren sie ihre Wertkategorie grundsätzlich als NP. Das gleiche gilt -bis auf wenige Ausnahmen- für Q1-Quantoren[6] .

Wir haben bisher noch nicht gesagt in welcher Weise wir der Doppelfunktion von Q2-Quantoren Rechnung tragen. Dabei läßt sich gerade an den Q2-Quantoren die linguistische Relevanz des Attributs NP verdeutlichen. Würden wir nämlich ohne Rückgriff auf ein solches "NP-Status-Attribut" festzulegen versuchen, welche Nominalkonstruktionen als Nominalphrasen fungieren können, ergäbe sich das folgende Problem. Da eine Verbindung "Adjektiv Nomen" im Plural nur dann eine Nominalphrase ist, wenn das Adjektiv stark dekliniert ist, wäre solchen Verbindungen nur dann Nominalphrasen-Status zuzugestehen, wenn sie mit der Merkmalsstruktur STARK unifizieren. Demnach wäre aber eine Nominalkonstruktion wie (38) keine Nominalphrase, da "beide_" von einem nachfolgenden Adjektiv schwache Deklination fordert und daher morphologisch als schwach gekennzeichnet ist.

(38) beide roten Rosen

Nun könnte man allerdings das Deklinationsverhalten von "beide" einmal hinsichtlich seiner Argumentkategorie und zum anderen hinsichtlich seiner Wertkategorie spezifizieren; also beispielsweise:

    beiden: [N[NIL, GEMISCHT]/N[NIL, SCHWACH]] PLU DAT

    beiden: [N[NIL, SCHWACH]/N[NIL, SCHWACH]] PLU DAT

    beiden: [N[NIL, STARK]/N[NIL, SCHWACH]] PLU DAT

Dies allerdings würde bedeuten, daß man für eine Konstruktion wie (39) annimmt, daß "beiden älteren Schwestern" anders dekliniert ist als die Teilkonstituente "älteren Schwestern"; denn Genitivattribute fordern starke Deklination, wohingegen der Quantor "beide_" schwache Deklination fordert.   .

```
(39) Karls   beiden   älteren   Schwestern
                     ─────────────────────────
                            schwach
     ────>   ─────────────────────────
     stark           stark
```

Allerdings erscheint uns diese Annahme linguistisch nicht adäquat. Der Doppelfunktion von Q2-Quantoren kann jedoch dann auf einfache und intuitiv plausible Weise Rechnung getragen werden, wenn man annimmt, daß Quantoren ihre Wertkategorie hinsichtlich NP-Status markieren. Q2-Quantoren sind dann nämlich sowohl als Q1- als auch als Q3-Quantoren zu kategorisieren, wobei sie ihre Wertkategorie im ersten Falle immer, im zweiten Falle nur dann als Nominalphrase markieren, wenn sie selbst stark dekliniert sind. Für die Quantorenformen "beide" und "beiden" ergeben sich dann die folgenden lexikalischen Einträge.

    beide: [N[Q1, NP=plus]/N[NIL]] [NOM;AKK] PLU SCHWACH.

    beiden: [N[Q1, NP=plus]/N[NIL]] DAT PLU SCHWACH.

    beiden: [N[NIL, NP=minus]/N[NIL]] PLU [SCHWACH;GEMISCHT].

---

[5] Mit "MASS" und "COUNT" seien Merkmalsstrukturen bezeichnet, die angeben, ob es sich bei einem Nomen um ein Mass- oder Count-Nomen handelt.

[6] Die Ausnahmen bilden die Sonderfälle "jede_", "jedwede_" und "jegliche_", die in Verbindung mit dem unbestimmten Artikel "ein_" dessen Deklinationsforderung erfüllen, wie an Beispiel (37a) und (37b) ersichtlich wird.

    (37a) einer jeden Frau
    (37b) * einer jeder Frau

Wir haben in diesem Abschnitt gezeigt, wie durch die Einführung eines "NP-Status-Attributs" einerseits Mehrfachkategorisierungen bzw. unäre Regeln (z.B. für "Bare Plurals") vermieden werden können und wie zum anderen den speziellen morphologischen Eigenschaften der Q2-Quantoren auf elegante Weise Rechnung getragen werden kann. Wird der NP-Charakter einer Nominalkonstruktion nun allerdings nicht durch ihre Kategorie, sondern durch ein Attribut reflektiert, heißt dies, daß Konstruktionen, die ihrerseits auf Nominalphrasen operieren, den Wert dieses Attributs explizit "testen". Funktoren der Kategorie X/NP bzw. NP\X (wobei "X" eine beliebige atomare oder komplexe Kategorie bezeichnet) sind demnach der Kategorie X/N bzw. N\X zuzuweisen und zusätzlich subkategorial folgendermaßen zu charakterisieren: X/N[NP = plus] bzw. N[NP = plus]\X.

5. Zusammenfassung

Den Ausgangspunkt der vorliegenden Arbeit bildeten Kongruenz- und Abfolgephänomene im pränominalen Bereich. Für eine formale Beschreibung dieser Phänomene im Deutschen erwiesen sich bisherige Ansätze, die vor allem im Bereich der X'-Syntax angesiedelt sind, als deskriptiv inadäquat. Wir unterzogen Determinatoren und Quantoren daher einer eigenen Analyse, bei der die Abgrenzung der Quantoren von den Adjektiven im Vordergrund stand. Dabei ergab sich eine Unterteilung der Quantoren in drei Gruppen. Eine Behandlung dieser drei Gruppen im Rahmen einer KUG erforderte die Einführung verschiedener Attribute, die es uns erlaubten vielen der zumeist semantisch nicht motivierbaren Kookkurrenzbeschränkungen Rechnung zu tragen (einen Überblick über die von uns verwendeten Attribute und ihre jeweiligen Wertemengen bietet der "Merkmalsbaum" in Appendix I).

Die von uns dargestellte Behandlung pränominaler Elemente wurde in verschiedenen Testversionen fragmentarisch implementiert, wobei uns die Entwicklungsumgebung des LILOG-Prototyp I zur Verfügung stand. Für die Zukunft ist geplant, die hier vorgestellten Arbeiten zur Syntax deutscher Nominalphrasen mit den Ansätzen auf dem Gebiet der kompositionellen und lexikalischen Semantik zusammenzuführen, die derzeit im Projekt LILOG im Rahmen des Prototyp I getestet und weiterentwickelt werden. Des weiteren soll untersucht werden, inwiefern die hier beschriebenen syntaktischen Eigenschaften von Determinatoren und Quantoren mit semantischen Eigenschaften korrelieren, wie sie beispielsweise im Rahmen des auf Barwise/Cooper (1981) zurückgehenden Ansatzes der "Generalized Quantifiers" (eine neuere Darstellung findet sich etwa in Hamm (1986)) beobachtet wurden.

Appendix I: Merkmalsbaum

Abbildung 3 stellt die in den vorausgehenden Abschnitten beschriebenen Attribute zur Morphologie und Distribution pränominaler Elemente sowie ihre jeweiligen Wertemenge als Baumstruktur dar. Dabei sind die mit "&" bezeichneten Knoten des Baumes konjunktiv, die mit "V" bezeichneten Knoten disjunktiv zu interpretieren; das heißt: im Falle einer konjunktiven Verzweigung kann ein Lexem mit allen sich an die Verzweigung anschließenden Attributen bzw. Merkmalen charakterisiert werden; im Falle einer disjunktiven Verzweigung nur mit einem.

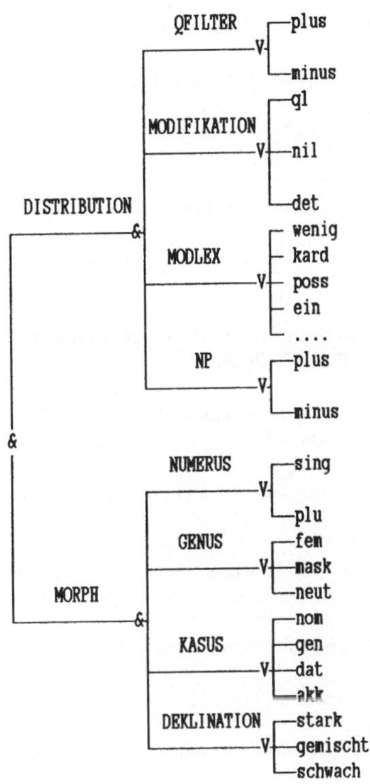

Abbildung 3. Merkmalsbaum

Literatur

Ait-Kaci H. (1984): A Lattice Theoretic Approach to Computation Based on a Calculus of Partially Ordered Type Structures. Ph.D. Thesis. University of Pennsylvania.

Barwise J., Cooper R. (1981): Generalized Quantifiers and Natural Language. In: Linguistics and Philosophy 4. 159-219.

Bouma G., E. König, H. Uszkoreit (1988): A Lexical Unification-Based Approach to Syntactic and Semantic Processing. In: IBM Journal of Research and Development. (erscheint demnächst)

"Duden" (1984): DUDEN - Grammatik, Bd.4. Mannheim: Bibliographisches Institut.

"Grundzüge" (1980): Heidolph et al.: Grundzüge einer deutschen Grammatik. Berlin: Akademie-Verlag.

Haider H. (1986): Die Struktur der deutschen NP. Ms. Universität Stuttgart.

Hamm F. (1986): Generalisierte Quantoren und semantische Prinzipiensysteme. In: Linguistische Berichte 103. 201-223.

Jackendoff, R. (1977): X'-Syntax: A Study of Phrase Structure. Cambridge (Ma.): The M.I.T. Press.

König E. (1987): Methoden der Semantikkonstruktion in Unifikationsgrammatiken. Diplomarbeit. Universität Stuttgart.

Shieber S. et al. (1983): The Formalism and Implementation of PATR-II. In: Research on Interactive Acquisition and Use of Knowledge. SRI International, Menlo Park, California.

Shieber S. (1984): The Design of a Computer Language for Linguistic Information. In: Shieber S., L. Karttunen, F. Pereira (1984): A Compilation of Papers on Unification-Based Formalisms. SRI Technical Note 327. 4-16

Uszkoreit H. (1988): The Stuttgart Type Unification Formalism. LILOG Report 16. IBM Deutschland, UP Wissenschaft, LILOG Stuttgart.

Uszkoreit H. (1986): Categorial Unification Grammars. In: Proceedings of the 11th International Conference on Computational Linguistics, Bonn. 86-100.

Vater H. (1986a): Zur Abgrenzung der Determinantien und Quantoren. In: Vater (1986c). 13-31.

Vater H. (1986b): Zur NP-Struktur im Deutschen. In: Vater (1986c). 123-145.

Vater H. (ed.) (1986c): Zur Syntax der Determinantien. Studien zur deutschen Grammatik, 31. Tübingen: Gunter Narr.

Zevat H., E. Klein, J. Calder (1986): Unification Categorial Grammar. ms. Centre for Cognitive Science, University of Edinburgh.

THE PROBLEM OF OVERGENERATION IN PARSING PROCESSES AND THE AID OF LINGUISTIC GENERALIZATIONS

Stefanie Schachtl

Siemens AG, Muenchen

ZTI INF 23

Otto-Hahn-Ring 6

8 Muenchen 83

Federal Republic of Germany

The aim of this paper is to show by means of a simple example from German noun-phrase syntax how the appropriate linguistic generalizations succeed in overcoming the problem of overgeneration in parsing processes. The phenomenon which is discussed here is rarely mentioned in the linguistic literature and is clarified and formalized for the first time in this paper .

1. When working on applied natural language processing, the linguist is often faced with surprising defects in his knowledge of grammar. In this paper I would like to describe such a phenomenon and the results it triggered: an encounter with a problem posed in German noun-phrase syntax. Writing an NP-grammar in the LFG-format (see BRESNAN 1982) which is compatible with the parser described in (BLOCK/HUNZE 1986) and which applied the traditional descriptive devices of NP-syntax revealed a specific problem. It is necessary first to give a short account of the relevant syntactic phenomena in order to elucidate the situation:

German grammar allows for a genitive attribute to occur in front of or after the head noun:

(1) *Peters (NPgen) Haus (NPnom) wurde verkauft.*
    Peter's house was sold.
(2) *Das Haus (NPnom) Peters(NPgen) wurde verkauft.*
    Peter's house was sold.

A noun like *Peter* may be interpreted as a proper noun and equally as a count noun. Each interpretation coincides with a specific syntactic behaviour. The morphological form of the proper noun in the genitive singular is phonetically identical (syncrete) with that of the count noun in the plural in all cases, cf. (3):

(3) *Peters (NP acc pl) habe ich nicht getroffen.*
   I didn't meet any Peters.

Of course an NP-grammar of German has to allow for all these constructions to be parsed in an adequate way.
And now for the surprise: While only one interpretation exists for the native speaker for an NP, e. g. , *Marias Frauen* , the parser will find four of them. At a first glance there is nothing to hinder the parser from generating any of the four forms :
Marias is either singular or plural, *Frauen* must be plural. *Marias* is genitive singular and is syncrete in all cases in the plural, *Frauen* is also syncrete in all cases. If these two nouns, which may both occur without an article, are to be analysed as an NP, one of them must be marked with the genitive case. Everything else will be okay, according to traditional NP grammars for German. This gives the following results: *Marias* is an attribute and *Frauen* is the head, *Marias* is either singular or plural, two readings are accepted by the parser (case variations of *Frauen* not counted). But *Marias* can also be the head and *Frauen* the genitive attribute in the postnominal position, and again *Marias* can be genitive singular or plural (in all cases): two more readings are accepted (excluding case variations in the plural). Now take the following sentence as an example:

(4) *Die Frage ist, ob Frauen Marias Schwestern Maedchen malen.*
   (see below).

Six readings of this sentence are accepted by the native speakers (due to insufficient morphological case marking, and, depending on focus and scrambling, marked in different degrees):

i) [NPnom NPgen sg] NPdat NPacc:
    The question is whether Mary's women will paint (any) girls for (their) sisters.
ii) NPnom [NPgen sg NPdat] NPacc:
    The question is whether (any) women will paint (any) girls for Mary's sisters .
iii) [NPnom NPgen sg] NPacc NPdat:
    The question is whether Mary's women will paint (their) sisters for (any) girls.
iv) NPnom [NPgen sg NPacc] NPdat
    The question is whether (any) women will paint Mary's sisters for girls.
v) [NPdat NPgen sg] NPnom   NPacc
    The question is whether for Mary's women (their) sisters will paint (any) girls.

vi) NPdat [NPgen sg NPnom] NPacc
   The question is whether for (any) women Mary's sisters will paint (any) girls.
But now the attributive NPs become involved, and the parser will find the following readings:
ia) *[NPgen NPnom pl] NPdat NPacc
   The question is whether women's Marys will paint (any) girls for (their) sisters.
ib) *NPnom [NPdat pl NPgen]   NPacc
   The question is whether (any) women will paint (any) girls for their sisters' Marys.
ic) *NPnom [NPgen pl NPdat]   NPacc
   The question is whether (any) women will paint (any) girls for Marys' sisters.
id) *NPnom NPdat pl [NPgen   NPacc]
   The question is whether (any) women will paint (their) sisters' girls for Marys.
ie) *NPnom NPdat pl [NPacc   NPgen]
   The question is whether (any) women will paint any girls' sisters for Marys.

...

To emphasize once more: these readings are predicted to be grammatical - neither the NP-grammar nor any other part of the grammar will reduce them, but on the contrary the grammatical readings which are parsed by the other parts of the grammar will be multiplied by the ones parsed here.
Take for example the faculty of German *malen* which allows the NPdat and the NPacc to be omitted as well, in this way some new derivations emerge that involve attribution:

vii) *NPnom [NPakk pl [NPgen   NPgen]]
   The question is whether any women will paint their sisters' girls' Marys.
viii)*NPnom [[NPgen pl NPgen] NPakk]
   The question is whether Mary's sisters' women will paint any girls.
xi) *[NPnom [[NPgen sg [NPgen NPgen]]
   The question is whether Marys' sisters' girls' women will paint.

 A grammar which allows for such an output is not to be called a German grammar. This fact remains, even if diverse strategies like heuristic weights etc., are applied afterwards to filter out the bad readings.
In the following sections I will propose a syntactic analysis for this phenomenon. I will also present an LFG treatment of German noun-phrases which respects this analysis, and is consequently not overgenerating.

2. As explained in the chapter before, the traditional approach to German np syntax fails in capturing the right generalization for this phenomenon. Why is this so?
Morphological case-marking is traditionally handled with declension paradigms. e.g. the German declension paradigm for *Frauen* in the plural is:
die Frauen(nom) *der Frauen*(gen) *den Frauen*(dat) *die Frauen*(acc).

The indefinite plural in German is marked by the absence of the determiner. Taken together this means that wherever the morphological form *Frauen* appears, it will appear in the correct grammatical case for which the position demands (henceforth genitive position, dative position, etc.) but this prediction is obviously incorrect. In (5) there should be two acceptable readings, due to the occurrence of the case marked NP without lexical governor: one with *Frauen* marked [case = dat] as a free complement of the matrix verb ("free" meaning the verb is not subcategorized for it) and one with an attributive reading for *Frauen* marked [case = gen]. But in fact the sentence has but one single acceptable reading, the one with Frauen in the dative case.

(5) *Er hat das Haus Frauen gekauft.*
   He bought the house for (some) women.

This behaviour is not restricted to genitive NPs in the attributive reading. A couple of German verbs are subcategorized for a genitive NP, cf. *sich bedienen* in (6).

(6) *Er bedient sich der Frauen, um Karriere zu machen.*
   He uses the women, in order to further his own career.

Again the occurence of Frauen without determiner (the indefinite plural) leads to ungrammaticality, like in (7).

(7) **Er bedient sich Frauen, um Karriere zu machen.*
   He uses (some) women, in order to further his own career.

And the same holds equally for the genitive complements of other lexical heads.
This clearly shows: Morphological case marking is not sufficient to allow for an NP in genitive positions. That there is morphological case in these NPs is unquestionable. There is case just as well as there is case via agreement in the uninflected adjective *lila* in (8):

(8) *Grosse quergetreifte lila Kravatten mag er besonders.*
   He especially likes huge striped violet ties.

The difference between inflected and uninflected adjectives and the difference between invariable and distinctive declension paradigms of nouns is the same with regard to case theory: there simply is no difference. Case theory has to generalize over sufficiently and insufficiently marked lexical items and it overgeneralizes with respect to the genitive. That is why traditional grammar fails here.

3. There are however simple nouns which are perfect in genitive positions without determiner or modifier : the proper names.

(9) *Er kauft das Haus Marias.*
   He bought Mary's house .
(10) *Er bediente sich Marias, um Karriere zu machen.*
   He used Mary, in order to further his own career

Interesting enough, though, the genitive *s* in these forms does not appear in the declension paradigm for these nouns. It is ungrammatical when they do not have the proper noun reading, and therefore must have a lexically realized determiner position, e.g. in (11):

(11) *Er kauft das Haus des schoenen Peter.*
   He bought the beautiful Peter's house.
(12)**Er kauft das Haus des schoenen Peters.*

Not being a consequence of a morpho-lexical process then, it is not astonishing when the *s*-suffixation of the genitive of proper nouns takes part in the occurence restriction for genitive NPs.
Another problematic case from this point of view is the behaviour of nominalized adjectives. These too may occur without a determiner in the genitive position (see Plank (1979)):

(13) *Den Forderungen Glaeubiger kommt der Papst ungern nach.*
   The pope ceases to fulfill the demands of the faithful .

The restriction is suppressed only in the case of a non-lexicalized interpretation. The genitive form of the nominalized adjective *Glaeubiger* (of the faithful) is phonetically identical with the genitive plural form of the noun *Glaeubiger* (of the creditors) for which the restriction holds. The sentence becomes ambiguous if the genitive case is sufficiently marked like in (13).

(14) *Den Forderungen vieler Glaeubiger kommt der Papst ungern nach.*
   The pope ceases to fulfill the demands of many of the faithful / the creditors.

There are lexicalized adjective nominalizations which continue to display the declension paradigm for adjectives, but their occurrence is blocked in the relevant positions:

(15)**Den Forderungen Beamter kommt der Papst ungern nach.*
   The demands of (the) officials, the pope ceases to fulfill.

In this respect , much depends on how non-lexicalised adjective nominalizations are dealt with. The above fact might serve in defending the hypothesis that there is a position of the head noun which is empty in non-lexicalized adjective nominalizations (cf. Haider (1987), Olsen (1987)). But regardless which analysis for adjective nominalization may prove to be correct, the above fact indicates that we are dealing again with a syntactic phenomenon, not with a lexical one.

4. Now that these two apparent counterexamples (proper nouns which are genitive marked and adjective nominalizations) are overcome, it seems justified to provide the following restriction for the occurrence of genitive NPs :

NPs in a genitive position must include a grammatical formative independent of the morphological form of the head noun.

Apart from the head noun itself (as in the case of proper names) this grammatical formative may be carried by a variety of adjacent categories: adjectives, inflected numerals, determiners, the possessive pronoun, and, at least for most speakers, even by another genitive marked NP if it is fronted:

(16) *Er bedient sich schoener Frauen um Karriere zu machen.*
   He uses pretty women in order to further his own career.
(17) *Er bediente sich zweier (two) Frauen um Karriere zu machen.*
(18) *Er bediente sich einiger (some) Frauen um Karriere zu machen.*
(19) *Er bediente sich seiner (his) Frau um Karriere zu machen.*
(20) *Er bediente sich Peters (Peter's) Frau um Karriere zu machen.*

This is exactly the generalization we wanted, which predicts, why *Marias Frauen* has only one reading: only the morphological form of *Marias* in the genitive singular carries the necessary grammatical formative for the genitive position. Neither *Frauen* nor *Marias* in the plural interpretation are able to carry the desired grammatical formative, they would need an adjacent category to carry it.
It is relatively easy to represent this restriction in a sufficiently structured grammar and thereby achieve the correct results in the parsing processes - a working proposal for this will be given in the next section - but it is hard to foresee what the existence of such an restriction implies for syntactic case theory, especially for the until now least controversial part of it: the morphological case.

5. I will give now a characterization of how the generalization discussed in the previous chapters could be represented by an np-grammar in an LFG-format. The comments in this chapter refer only to what is necessary for the description of the generalization, but they are founded in the description of the whole np-grammar which was developed for the LFG-parser mentioned in the first chapter. The grammar works as follows:
In the position of the head noun, a feature structure is created subsuming all syntactic information about the NP, which is to be gathered from the lexical entry of the noun.

This feature structure is called "gkopf" (signifying "grammatischer Kopf"), cf.:($\uparrow$ gkopf kas) = (# kas).

Attribution by adjectives is uniformly represented as adjunction to the maximal projection of the head noun (nmax). This projection is maximal in the sense that all complement positions of the head noun must be filled before this step in the derivation is chosen. Adjunction is represented in a recursive PSR :

nmax --> { [:a1 adj] / [:a2 adj] / [:a3 adj] } [:nmax] .
/*a1, a2, a3, nmax serve as labels for attaching the f-equations, see below*/

F-structure reflects the derivation via adjunction in that it includes a new feature structure called "skopf" (signifying "semantischer Kopf") with each new instance of adjective attribution. This new feature structure "skopf" indicates the scope of the adjoined adjective, and subsumes all feature structures of the previous derivations. This is the effect of the following f-equation associated with the position of nmax:

nmax: ($\uparrow$ skopf) = $\downarrow$.

Note that the simple gathering of the adjectival f-structures into a set will not do for the semantic purposes.

The rules of the semantic component consequently are able to resolve these recursively embedded structures, but the syntactic rules are not. Therefore the feature structure which contains the features which are relevant for the syntactic behaviour of the NP, the "gkopf" , must be raised by each step in the derivation:

nmax: ($\uparrow$ gkopf) = ($\downarrow$ gkopf).

That means that the feature structures in "gkopf" remain constant in their embedding during every step of derivation, whereas in contrast to this one may have different values of the same feature structures in different "skopf"s, due to the different depth of embedding, as shown before.

This is exactly what is needed for the determination of the value of the feature structure that is to indicate the capability of an NP to occur in a genitive position. The strategy for achieving the correct results is now obvious: the value for this feature, called "kt" (signifying "Kasustraeger") is set to 'minus' in the position of the head noun. If a nominal modifier is adjoined, this feature structure is embedded in "skopf" and the value of a new feature "kt" is determined. This determination depends on whether the adjective is inflected or not (in case of an uninflected numeral, see section three), which information may either be brought about by a lexical feature structure of the modifier itself or drawn from the morphological component.

In case another instance of adjunction takes place, this last "kt" is embedded again in "skopf" , a new one is determined, and so forth until the last instance of adjunction has taken place. This is done by the following f-equations (uninflected adjectives excluded), associated with the respective positions in the PSR, mentioned above.

a1: ($\downarrow$ spec) = kard,
  ($\downarrow$ ktm) = plus, /* inflected numerals*/
  ($\uparrow$ kt) = plus;

a2: ($\downarrow$ spec) = kard,
  ($\downarrow$ ktm) = minus, /* uninflected numerals*/
  ($\uparrow$ kt) = ($\uparrow$ skopf kt);

a3: ($\downarrow$ spec) = adj, /*adjectives*/
  ($\uparrow$ kt) = plus;

nmax: ($\uparrow$ skopf) = $\downarrow$,
  ($\uparrow$ gkopf) = ($\downarrow$ gkopf);

n: ($\uparrow$ kt) = minus.

In the next step of the derivation, the information that is encoded in the determiner position is added. This step is obligatory even if the determiner position is not lexically realized, for this information is also necessary, for, e.g. the determination of the definiteness of an NP or the agreement of the adjective. A noun with the value 'plural' for the feature "agreement", occurring without determiner, must be indefinite, this is the information which is added by the f-equations that are associated with this "empty" determiner position.

d1 --> { [: det] / [:j1 jump] / [:j2 jump] / [:j3 jump] / [:j4 jump] } [:nmax].

There are five relevant differentiations between the information bundles which are associated with the determiner position:
First: the determiner position is realized by a lexical category. Apart from the information about the declension paradigm for adjectives and definiteness, the information is given that all NPs which are derived in this way may appear in genitive positions: the feature "kt" is set to the value 'plus', regardless what value the "kt" of "skopf" has. This feature is now subsumed under "gkopf", being syntactically relevant and henceforth remaining constant :

det: ($\uparrow$ gkopf kt) = plus.

Second: the determiner position is not lexically realized, and the value of the feature "agreement" is 'singular'. This derivation gives correct results only if the head noun belongs to the lexical class of minus count nouns . In this case the value of "kt" depends on whether the noun was attributed by an inflected adjective or not, i.e. the value of "kt" in "gkopf" is the same as the value of "kt" in the last "skopf". This fact is reflected in the following f-equation:

j1: ($\uparrow$ gkopf count) = minus , ($\uparrow$ gkopf agr) = sg3,
   ($\uparrow$ gkopf kt) = ($\uparrow$ skopf kt) .

Third: the same holds for nouns in the indefinite plural:

j2: ($\uparrow$ gkopf agr) = pl3, ($\uparrow$ gkopf def) = indef,
   ($\uparrow$ gkopf kt) = ($\uparrow$ skopf kt) .

Fourth: the syntactic properties of proper nouns are determined in the fourth bundle of f-equations including the semantic characterization as proper nouns. For "kt" the value can be easily determined in this case, it is invariably 'plus' (see section four):

j3: ($\uparrow$ gkopf count)   {proper loc},   /*proper and local names lexical classes*/
   ($\uparrow$ gkopf agr)   = sg3,   /* plural is indefinite*/

   ˜($\uparrow$ gkopf ngea),   /* may not be attributed*/
   ˜($\uparrow$ gkopf aat),

   ($\uparrow$ gkopf def) = proper.   /* semantic characterization*/

   ($\uparrow$ gkopf kt) = plus,

Fifth: The c-structure position of prenominal genitive attributes and the possessive pronoun differs from the determiner position in this proposal. This is due to the controversy over the phrase structure of NPs, and the adopting of the hypothesis roughly outlined in Abney (1986), see Haider (1987) for German, which states that the syntactic structure of arguments in the phrasal categories should be described as a maximal projection of the determiner position. F-equations follow this c-structure mechanism with the binary feature "praeNP" which is set to 'plus' in the case of prenominal attributes and set to 'minus' in the case of all other choices of realizing the determiner positon, in order to prevent either the co-occurence of prenominal attributes and an article or two interpretations of other nouns without a determiner. As clarified in the previous sections, not only the possessive pronoun, which is morphologically marked, but also the genitive NP which may occur in this position allow for the entire NP to appear in a genitive position. Due to this observation, the value of "kt" must be set to 'plus' in this case:

j4: (↑ praeNP)   = plus,
     (↑ gkopf kt) = plus,
     (↑ gkopf def) = def.

What remains now is to add to each f-equation that requires the genitive marking of an NP in the syntactic component another f-equation that requires the value of "kt" to be 'plus'.

NOTE:

This work is part of the WISBER joint project of the University of Hamburg, Nixdorf Computer Company, SCS and Siemens AG. This project is sponsored by a grant of the Federal Ministery of Research and Technology.

ACKNOWLEDGEMENTS:

Many thanks go to my colleagues, Hans-Ulrich Block, Robert Frederking, Manfred Gehrke, Hans Haugeneder and Rudolf Hunze, who always held me in check in time when I was lead astray by the facts, and to Joachim Jacobs who also gave me precious hints.

References:

Abney, Steven (1986): *Functional elements and licensing*. Abstract to a talk given at the GLOW-Colloquium (1986), Gerona, Spain.

Block, Hans-Ulrich/Hunze, Rudolf(1986): *Incremental Construction of c- and f-structure in an LFG-Parser (Siemens)* in: Proceedings of the 11th International Conference on Computational Linguisitics, COLING '86, Bonn. pp. 490-493.

Bresnan, Joan (1982) (ed.): *The Mental Representation of Grammatical Relations.* (Cambridge 1982).

Haider, Hubert (1987): *Die Struktur der deutschen NP.* To aappear in: Zeitschrift fuer Sprachwissenschaft, Goettingen.

Olsen, Susan (1987): *Das substantivierte Adjektiv im Deutschen und Englischen: Attribuierung vs. syntaktische Substantivierung.* (to appear) in: Folia Linguistica.

Plank, Frans (1979): *Encoding grammatical relations: acceptable and unacceptable non-distinctness.* in: Fisiak, Josef: Historical Morphology. (Tuebingen 1979), pp 289 - 324.

Wo trifft 'treffen' 'Treffen'?
Zur semantischen Repräsentation nominalisierter Verben*

Carola Reddig, Universität des Saarlandes

Zusammenfassung

Der folgende Beitrag befaßt sich mit der Verarbeitung von Nominalisierungen von Verben, einem im Deutschen sehr häufig auftretenden Phänomen. Zugrundegelegt wird eine auf KL-ONE basierende Repräsentation, die (für Nominalisierungen von Verbkonzepten) den semantischen Zusammenhang - in Form gemeinsamer Attributdeskriptionen - sowie den funktionalen Unterschied - ausgedrückt durch differierende Positionen in der Konzepthierarchie - zwischen einemVerb und seiner Nominalisierung expliziert. Der an dieser Wissensrepräsentation orientierte Prozeß der semantischen Analyse nominalisierter Ausdrücke wird vorgestellt. Für Rollennominale (Substantivierungen von Verbaspekten) werden Repräsentationsmöglichkeiten diskutiert.

I Einleitung

(1) "Die Regierungschefs *trafen* sich zu einem Arbeitsfrühstück."

(1') "Anschließend wurde das *Treffen* von allen als 'ergiebig' bezeichnet."

(2) "In der 83. Minute *traf* Völler zum wiederholten Male nur die Querlatte."

(2') "Ein *Treffer* wollte ihm an diesem Tage nicht gelingen." (Frankfurter Rundschau vom 16.11.87)

Keine Frage: Die Nomina "Treffen" und "Treffer" aus den Sätzen (1') und (2') haben einiges mit dem Verb "treffen" des jeweilig vorangehenden Satzes zu tun. Nicht nur, daß sie, morphologisch gesehen, *Substantivableitungen* dieses Verbstammes sind; auch ihre *Bedeutung* läßt sich regelhaft aus der des Verbs ableiten: "Treffen" ist ein Abstraktum mit dem Prädikatsinhalt von "treffen" als Bedeutung, und der "Treffer" ist - als Konkretum - das Resultat des "treffen"-Konzeptes[1]. Zudem bezieht sich das "Treffen" aus (1') anaphorisch auf den Sachverhalt des "treffen"-Satzes (1); Nominalisierungen haben also auch, was ihren *referentiellen Gehalt* anbelangt, enge Bezüge zu ihrem Wortstamm.

Wenn natürlichsprachliche KI-Systeme als Zugangssysteme zu wissenschaftlichen Daten- oder Wissensbeständen (Datenbank- oder Expertensystemen) fungieren, werden sie mit Verb-Nominalisierungen stark konfrontiert: "In der neueren Geschichte der deutschen Sprache kann [...] die stärkere Ausnutzung der komprimierten Satzbauweise durch Nominalisierungen [...], vor allem in der Literatur-, Wissenschafts- und Öffentlichkeitssprache als Entwicklungstendenz nachgewiesen werden." (v. Polenz 85, S.40). Die Verarbeitungsprobleme bestehen nun darin, daß

- auf Seiten der *Syntax* das Verb von seiner Nominalisierung durch die Zuordnung zu ganz verschiedenen syntaktischen Kategorien getrennt ist;

- auf der Ebene der *Semantik*, wenn der Informationsgehalt der Äußerung Unterscheidungsmerkmal ist, die Abbildung auf ein und dieselbe semantische Repräsentation wünschenswert erscheint ;

- dasselbe für die inferentielle Verarbeitung gilt: Aus beiden Formulierungen: a) "Gestern kam es in KL zu panikartigen Reaktionen in der Bevölkerung, weil MacDonald's *geschlossen* wurde." und b) "Aufgrund der *Schließung* von MacDonald's kam es gestern in KL zu panikartigen Reaktionen in der Bevölkerung." sollten dieselben Informationen ableitbar sein;

---

* Dieser Bericht entstand mit Unterstützung der Deutschen Forschungsgemeinschaft (DFG) im Sonderforschungsbereich KI - Wissensbasierte Systeme (SFB 314), Teilprojekt N1 (XTRA: eXpert TRAnslator)

[1]wenn auch, im Beispiel (2,2') und zu Völlers Leidwesen, kein Resultat der beschriebenen Situation.

- auf der Ebene des Dialoggedächtnisses jedoch die Unterscheidung wieder relevant wird, insbesondere für Prozesse der Anaphoraauflösung und -generierung, der Referentenidentifikation und -spezifikation allgemein.

Nominalisierungen sind zwar syntaktisch gesehen Nominalphrasen, semantisch gesehen aber (zumindest sehr ähnlich den) Verben. Darum ist das Ziel der Bedeutungsanalyse von nominalisierten Verben, einerseits möglichst wenige zusätzliche Verarbeitungs*prozeduren* (neben den ohnehin vorhandenen NP- und Verbkonzeptbehandlungen) zu benötigen, und andererseits die Redundanz in der Wissens*repräsentation* zu minimieren.

II Nominalisierungen im Deutschen

Verbnominalisierungen machen den größten Teil der Substantivableitung im Deutschen aus (DUDEN 84); sie lassen sich in zwei Gruppen einteilen:

1) Abstrakta, die *Prädikatsinhalte* beschreiben, und

2) Konkreta, die verschiedene *Satzgliedinhalte* thematisieren.

Im einzelnen erfüllen sie die in Abb.1 dargestellen Bezeichnungsaufgaben.

	Substantivableitungen für	Beispiel	bezeichnen vor allem
Abstrakta	Prädikatsinhalte	Treffen Prüf-ung	Vorgänge. Handlungen (action), Eigen-schaften, Zustände, Verhalten und Verhältnisse (quality)
Konkreta	Subjektinhalte	Prüf-ender Leucht-er	Lebewesen, insbesondere Personen, vereinzelt auch Sachen (agent)
	Objektinhalte	Gekochtes Prüf-ling Erzeug-nis	vereinzelt Personen (patiens), sonst Ge-genstände (product) und Stoffe (material)
	instrumentale Adverbialinhalte	Bohr-er Ge-hör	Gegenstände, Organe (instrument)
	lokale Adverbialinhalte	Näh-erei Sultan-at	Arbeitsstätten (location), Zuständigkeits-bereiche

Abb.1: Bezeichnungsaufgaben nominalisierter Verben
(nach DUDEN: Die Grammatik, mit ergänzenden Beispielen)

Prädikatsinhalte werden (neben formverändernden Ableitungen) in erster Linie durch substantivierte Infinitive verbalisiert und bezeichnen damit eine **ACTION**[2], einen **PROCESS** oder einen **STATE**. *Subjektinhalte* sind häufig (wiederum neben "echten" Substantivierungen) in Nominalisierungen des Partizip Präsens dargestellt und bezeichnen den *Urheber* (**agent**) einer Handlung. Objektinhalte können häufig durch Partizip Perfekt-Nominalisierungen im Neutrum realisiert werden, die das Ergebnis (**result**) der im Verb genannten Tätigkeit bezeichnen; **patiens, counterpart** oder **benefactive** lassen sich durch personenbezeichnende substantivierte Maskulina/Feminina derselben Form realisieren.

---

[2]In diesem Kapitel erwähnte Begriffe, die in der Funktional-semantischen Struktur (vgl. Kap. IV) als Bezeichnungen für Konzepte der Repräsentationssprache SB-ONE (s. Kap. III) auftreten, sind in fettgedruckten Großbuchstaben hervorgehoben, solche, die sich als FSS-Rollen-Namen wiederfinden, entsprechend in Kleinbuchstaben.

Kap. IV und V der vorliegende Arbeit beschäftigen sich mit der Nominalisierung von Prädikatsinhalten, also vollständigen Konzepten. Konkreta bezeichnen, wie die obigen Hervorhebungen bereits andeuten, einzelne Attributdeskriptionen des Ausgangsverbkonzepts; damit entsprechen sie - in der KL-ONE Terminologie (Brachman, Schmolze 85) - den 'roles', genauer gesagt: den Füllern einer bestimmten Rolle. Mit solchen - nach der Terminologie von (Finin 80a,b) - als *role nominals*, Rollennominale bezeichneten Nominalisierungen setzt sich Kap. VI auseinander.

III Das System XTRA und seine Wissensrepräsentationssprache - ein Überblick

Ziel des XTRA-Projekts ist die Entwicklung eines natürlichsprachlichen Zugangssystems zu verschiedenen Expertensystemen. Das System ist stark modularisiert, um die domänenunabhängigen Teile, die für jedes Hintergrund-Expertensystem identisch bleiben, von den domänenspezifischen, an die neue Anwendung jeweils anzupassenden Moduln separieren zu können. Gleichzeitig sind die Wissensbasen des Systems so konzipiert, daß sie von den verschiedenen Prozessen - z.B. der Analyse und der Generierung - gemeinsam genutzt werden können. Zentral im XTRA-System ist die Wissensrepräsentationssprache SB-ONE (Kobsa 88), ein Mitglied der KL-ONE Familie. Diesen Formalismen gemeinsam ist die Unterteilung des Wissens in eine generelle Ebene des definitorischen Wissens und eine individuelle Ebene zur Formulierung von Sachverhalten über einzelne Entitäten. Strukturierte konzeptuelle Objekte, die *Konzepte*, sind die 'building blocks' beider Ebenen. Sie sind in einer definitorischen Taxonomie, einem Vererbungsnetz, angeordnet, und mittels *Rollen* strukturiert, die potentielle Relationen zwischen Objektklassen (auf der generellen Ebene) oder tatsächlich bestehende Relationen zwischen Elementen dieser Klassen (auf individualisierter Ebene) formulieren. Rollen und ihre Füller, ergänzt um Angaben über Quantität und Modalität dieser Rolle, machen die Attributdeskriptionen aus.

Wie alle KL-ONE-artigen Repräsentationsformalismen unterstützt SB-ONE zum einen die Reasoningprozesse in KI-Programmen, und eignet sich zum anderen sehr gut dazu, Modelle der zu repräsentierenden Domäne auf Papier zu strukturieren (Cercone, McCalla 87). Diese Eigenschaften machen SB-ONE interessant nicht nur für die "klassische" Modellierung des *Weltwissens*, sondern auch für die Darstellung und Verarbeitung des *sprachbezogenen semantischen Wissens* des Systems, d.h. zur Definition einer "Semantik-Grammatik". Und in diesem zweifachen Sinne wird SB-ONE in XTRA auch eingesetzt: Die *Funktional-semantische Struktur* (FSS) enthält in ihrem generellen Teil ($FSS_{general}$) Wissen über die semantische Wohlgeformtheit sprachlicher Ausdrücke. Sie klassifiziert sie nach semantischen Kriterien (Kasusrahmen, Sorten) und definiert, wie sie zu semantisch korrekten (und vom System interpretierbaren) komplexen Ausdrücken kombiniert werden können. Die individualisierte Ebene dieser Wissensbasis ($FSS_{individual}$) stellt dann die Satzsemantik einzelner Benutzereingaben dar. Die *Satzsemantische Analyse* nutzt dabei die SB-ONE Funktionen zur korrekten Individualisierung als Entscheidungskriterium für die Wohlgeformtheit eines Ausdrucks. Die *Referenz-semantische Interpretation* überträgt Strukturen aus $FSS_{individual}$ in die Weltwissensbasis, die *Conceptual Knowledge Base* (CKB), die zweite in SB-ONE formulierte Wissensbasis des XTRA-Systems. Über die Referentiellen Objekte des Dialoggedächtnisses sind die korrelierenden Strukturen aus FSS (auch die aus früheren Erwähnungen) und CKB gleichzeitig zugreifbar.

IV Semantische Repräsentation von Verbkonzepten und ihren nominalisierten Formen

In XTRA, wie auch in anderen wissensbasierten sprachverarbeitenden Systemen (z.B. in SNePS, vgl. (Shapiro, Rapaport 87)), ist also das sprachliche Wissen deklarativ in einem Wissensnetz abgelegt, in einem Formalismus, der zuläßt, dieses Wissen in zweifacher Hinsicht zu nutzen:
- als "Grammatik" zur semantischen Analyse von Benutzereingaben ($FSS_{general}$)
- und als "Daten", auf denen verschiedene Reasoningprozesse - z.B. des Dialoggedächtnisses - arbeiten können ($FSS_{individual}$)

Die Definition eines generellen FSS-Konzepts besteht zum einen aus der Definition seiner Superkonzepte und damit in der Einordnung in semantische Kategorien allgemeineren Typs, zum anderen aus seiner lokalen internen Struktur, ausgedrückt durch Rollen, die seine (obligatorischen oder fakultativen) funktionalen Dependenten beschreiben, also die potentiellen Relationen zwischen Individualisierungen dieses Konzepts und denen anderer Konzepte. Argumentstrukturen von Prädikaten, Valenzen und freie Angaben, können so unterschieden, strukturelle Teile einer Phrase und mögliche Modifikatoren formuliert werden. Die explizite Repräsentation von Rollen mit Namen für jedes Argument des Prädikats bzw. seiner Nominalisierung macht es möglich, die Anzahl der Argumente eines Prädikats variabel zu halten. Damit können verschiedene Anwendungen desselben Verbs (z.B. auch in nominalisierter Form) mit demselben Konzept repräsentiert werden, zunächst unabhängig von möglichen Differenzen in der Valenz.

Zwar sind die Bedeutungen einer Satz- und der entsprechenden Nominalformulierung aus Sicht ihres Informationsgehalts identisch, und es spricht aus diesem Blickwinkel viel dafür, identische FSS-Strukturen für beide aufzubauen. Die Funktional-semantische Struktur erfüllt aber mehrere Funktionen im System, neben der Repräsentation der Satzsemantik auch die, die Basisstruktur für Dialogprozesse (Anaphoraauflösung, Referentenidentifikation und -spezifikation allgemein) bereitzustellen. Darum werden Nominalisierungen von Verben in der FSS so repräsentiert, daß
- die Definitionen und damit die Positionen von Prädikats- und Nominalkonzepten in der $FSS_{general}$ unterschiedlich sind,
- sie aber weitestgehend identische Attributbeschreibungen besitzen, die das Nominalkonzept vom Prädikat via 'superc link' erbt, so daß
- sie wieder auf die gleichen Strukturen der Weltwissensbasis überführt werden können,
- für die Prozesse des Dialoggedächtnisses der sprachliche Unterschied aber erhalten bleibt.

Wie in Kap. II erläutert, stehen in dieser Arbeit die Nominalisierungen von Prädikats*inhalten* im Vordergrund. Somit befinden wir uns in der Funktional-semantischen Struktur (vgl. Abb. 2) in der Subhierarchie ausgehend von **ABSTRACT THING**. DUDEN (84) unterscheidet die Abstrakta in sogenannte Verbalabstrakta, worunter Handlungs-, Vorgangs- und Ereignisbezeichnungen fallen, und Zustandsbezeichnungen aus Verben, die einen erreichten Zustand bezeichnen. Häufig ist jedoch diese Zustandsbedeutung das Ergebnis einer Bezeichnungsverschiebung[3] von Vorgangsabstrakta; daher wird in der FSS diese etwas künstliche Unterscheidung nicht explizit durch die Einführung entsprechender Subkonzepte von **ABSTRACT THING** nachvollzogen, sondern direkt die Kategorisierung abge-

---

[3] unter 'Bezeichnungsverschiebung' versteht der DUDEN den Bedeutungswandel einer regelhaft gebildeten Form von der Standardinterpretation hin zu einer speziellen Semantikbelegung, die regelhaft nur anderen Formen vorbehalten ist.

bildet, die wir auch in der **PREDICATE**-Hierarchie finden: **ACTION CONTENT, PROCESS CONTENT, EVENT CONTENT**, und **PROPERTY CONTENT**. Sie haben Superkonzepte sowohl in der **THING**- als auch in der **PREDICATE**-Hierarchie, erben also Attributdeskriptionen wie **det** (Determiner) *und* die case frames (**agent...**).

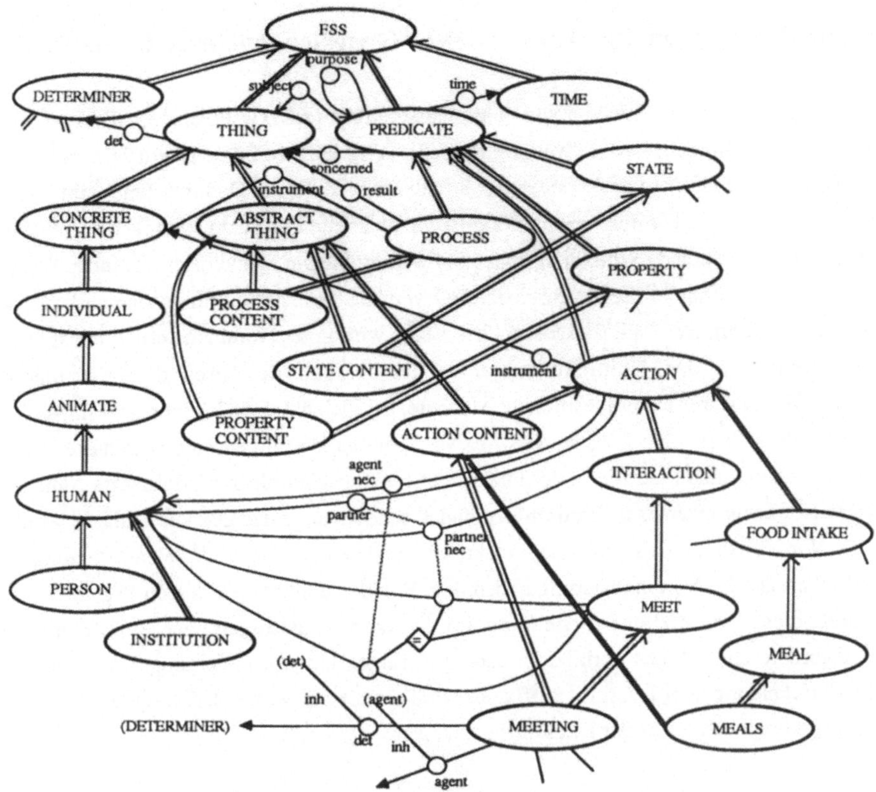

Abb. 2: Ausschnitt aus der Funktional-Semantischen Struktur
(mit Auslassungen an einigen Stellen)

Diese Repräsentation von Nominalisierungen von Verb*konzepten* bedient sich ausschließlich des vorhandenen Inventars von SB-ONE-Elementen. (Brachman 78), der die Bedeutungsrepräsentation von Nominalisierungen (als Teil von Nominalkomposita) als Testdomäne für die Mächtigkeit seines '*SI-net formalism*' wählt, definiert hierfür eine ganze Reihe zusätzlicher struktureller Sprachelemente, z.B.

DFACTIVE: ein Vererbungslink (auf individualisierter Ebene!), der einem EVENT die PROPOSITION dieses EVENTs unterordnet; hierdurch entsteht eine Verdopplung der entsprechenden Konzepte auch auf individualisierter Ebene;

DACTIVITY/PROCESS: ein genereller 'inheritance link', der aus einer Klasse von Aktionen, als Prozess betrachtet, einen 'abstract nominal node' ableitet;

DACTIVITY/COMPL-ACTION: entsprechend für Nominalisierungen mit der Bedeutung der Menge der abgeschlossenen Aktionen;

DGEN: definiert - wiederum als Subkonzeptrelation, aber vom abstract nominal des Ausgangs-verbkonzepts - die *Struktur* eines einzelnen EVENTs (noch nicht das Individuum selbst!), was zu einer Vermischung von Sprachstruktur, referentieller Interpretation und Wissensrepräsentation führt.

Diese Repräsentation ließe das Problem sehr elegant handhaben. Da sie allerdings den Gesamtformalismus erheblich aufbläht, da insbesondere die Semantik der speziellen inheritance-Typen im Verhältnis zum "normalen" DSUPERC link nur angedacht wurde, ist diese Lösung im KL-ONE-Formalismus (Brachman, Schmolze 85) nicht operationalisiert worden.

V Nominalisierungen im Analyse- und Generierungsprozeß von XTRA

Untersuchungen über den Gebrauch von Nominalisierungen (z.B. (v. Polenz 85, Teubert 79)) stellen fest, daß dabei der Sprecher zwar "weniger Sprache", d.h. kürzere Sätze produziert, der Hörer dafür aber größere Anstrengungen des Verstehens auf sich nehmen muß. Dadurch liegt - im System - die Haupt"last" der Analyse auf der semantischen Ebene, während die Syntax weniger Anhaltspunkte für eindeutig zu interpretierende Strukturen findet und weitergibt. Der syntaktisch scheinbar übersichtliche Ausdruck ist nicht ohne weiteres durchsichtig, weil die Sprachökonomie teuer erkauft wird mit semantischer Vagheit. Das Akkusativobjekt des Verbs wird unter Nominalisierung meist ebenso zum Genitivattribut wie das Nominativsubjekt ("der Besuch des Freundes" ist mehrdeutig), Präpositionalphrasen werden präpositionale Attribute, bei gleichbleibender Präposition. Nach (Teubert 79) jedoch läßt sich für den größten Teil der Verbnominalisierungen eine regelhafte Übertragung feststellen, wodurch nicht nur die in der Funktional-semantischen Struktur definierte Nähe des Verb- und seines Nominalkonzeptes theoretisch begründet, sondern auch das Lexikon entlastet werden kann, indem die Nominalisierung als generelle syntaktische Regel eingeführt wird[4]. Wenn allerdings, wie dies häufig der Fall ist, die Nominalisierung neben dem Prädikatsinhalt auch dessen Ergebnis bezeichnen kann, muß diese zusätzliche Bedeutung im Lexikon eingetragen werden. Zahlreiche nicht systematisierbare Ausnahmen verhindern zudem uneingeschränkte Ableitungsregeln über die Form (d.h. die Entscheidung über Infinitiv, Suffix oder Präfix etc.) der Nominalisierung, ein Problem für die Generierungskomponente, das der Lexikonentlastung entgegensteht.

Für Nominalisierungen (wie für andere syntaktische Konstrukte auch) verfügt die Satzsemantische Analyse über eine Menge von Regeln zur Überführung aus der Ergebnisstruktur der Syntaxanalyse in die entsprechende FSS-Struktur. Das entscheidende Problem bei Nominalisierungen, sowohl bzgl. der Repräsentation als auch der Analyse, ist jedoch die *Modalität* der Rollen der Attributdeskription, die vom **PREDICATE** geerbt wird: Sie ist *syntaktisch* gesehen immer optional, *semantisch* bei indefiniten Deskriptionen als *generic default* zu ergänzen, und bei *anaphorischen* Ausdrücken durch Referentenidentifikation zu ermitteln. SB-ONE schreibt jedoch vor, daß Rollen eines Konzepts (z.B. **MEET**) bei der Attributdeskription eines Subkonzepts (wie **MEETING**) nur spezialisiert, die Modalität also nur verschärft werden darf. Die in XTRA gewählte Lösung orientiert sich teilweise an (Dahl et al. 87). Die syntaktische Korrektheit der Eingabe kann auf der Ebene der Semantikanalyse vorausgesetzt werden. Wenn in der FSS eine Rolle also als 'necessary' bezeichnet ist, so ist sie *semantisch* notwendig und muß entweder - falls mit default versehen - mit einer generisch zu interpretierenden Individualisierung des Rollenrestriktionskonzepts versehen werden, oder anderenfalls über die Referentenidentifikation - den nächsten Schritt der Bedeutungsanalyse - aus dem Faktenwissen des Systems ergänzt werden. Für die Generierungskomponente ist die vorgestellte FSS-Repräsentation

---

[4]Es bleibt zu untersuchen, ob entsprechend auch die Definition der **PREDICATE-CONTENT** Konzepte in der FSS automatisiert werden kann; derzeit werden sie - wie alle übrigen - über den SB-ONE Editor definiert.

Voraussetzung für ein inkrementelles Aufbauen von FSS-Strukturen: Sie macht die Entscheidung, ob auf der natürlichsprachlichen Oberfläche ein Satz oder eine Nominalisierung das gewählte Konzept wiedergeben soll, nach Aufbau der Attributstruktur noch möglich.

Um *anaphorische Referenz auf Ereignisse*, die über ganze Sätze eingeführt wurden, auflösen zu können, verzeichnen das Dialog Sequence Memory und der Set of Referential Objects (beides Bestandteile des Linguistic Dialog Model) Referenzobjekte hierfür, die also nicht zu einer NP auf der Oberfläche korrespondieren. Auf einen Sachverhalt, über eine Assertion eingeführt, kann später referiert werden, indem eine NP mit der Nominalisierung des ursprünglichen Verbs gebildet wird. In den Beispielen des Kap. I

    (1) "Die Regierungschefs *trafen* sich zu einem Arbeitsfrühstück."

    (1') "Anschließend wurde das *Treffen* von allen als 'ergiebig' bezeichnet."

kann der referentielle Gehalt der NP "das Treffen" berechnet werden, indem die Funktional-semantische Struktur aus Abb. 3 gegen das Dialoggedächtnis gematcht wird, in dem sich - im aktuellen context space[5] - auch die Struktur aus Abb. 4 befindet; der match, der nicht auf Identität, sondern auf Verträglichkeit[6] überprüft, gelingt, so daß die entsprechende Individualisierung der Conceptual Knowledge Base von XTRA für die Referentenidentifikation in Frage kommt[7]. Da die Rollen **agent** und **partner** des **MEETING**-Konzeptes in Abb. 3 obligatorisch sind, werden sie *default*mäßig[8] mit einer Individualisierung des value restriction-Konzepts belegt, mit definitem Determiner, da auch das

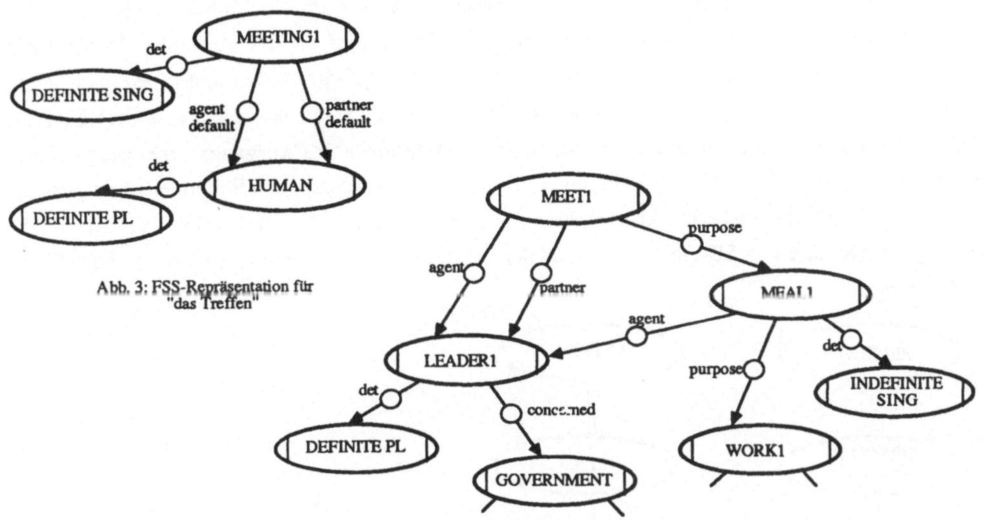

Abb. 3: FSS-Repräsentation für "das Treffen"

Abb. 4: (vereinfachte) FSS-Repräsentation für "Die Regierungschefs trafen sich zu einem Arbeitsfrühstück"

[5] ein 'context space' ist ein Element des Dialog Context Models (einer weiteren, von N. Reithinger entwickelten Komponente des Dialoggedächtnisses) und beschreibt die aktuelle Dialogsituation bzgl. rhetorischer Prädikate, Focus und verfügbaren Referenzobjekten.

[6] Der SB-ONE Matcher, der hierfür verwendet wird, wird derzeit in einem Fortgeschrittenenpraktikum unter der Leitung von R.-M. Jansen-Winkeln entwickelt.

[7] als ein Kandidat unter möglicherweise mehreren, für die der Match gelingt oder die durch inferentielle Prozesse über der aktuellen Wissensbasis berechnet werden.

[8] Der Default-Mechanismus in SB-ONE individualisiert die Füller-Konzepte entsprechend gekennzeichneter notwendiger Rollen, falls in der Input-Struktur kein korrespondierender Ausdruck gefunden wurde; die default-Markierung bleibt erhalten, um das Überschreiben durch den Match-Prozeß zuzulassen.

MEETING1 definit - und damit im Diskurs bekannt - ist. Die Repräsentation für "Arbeitsfrühstück", **MEAL1**, - wiederum ein durch Nominalisierung gewonnenes Abstraktum - und "Regierungschef", **LEADER1** - ein Konkretum, das den Subjektinhalt des Prädikats **LEAD** nominalisiert, vgl. Kap. VI - sind vereinfacht dargestellt.

Auch die Generierungskomponente nutzt zur Erzeugung solcher anaphorisch gebrauchten Nominalphrasen die explizite Verbindung zwischen einem Prädikatskonzept und seinem Abstraktum, die sie - ausgehend von der individualisierten FSS, die ihr das Dialoggedächtnis über einen Pointer vom entsprechenden Referenzobjekt liefert - über die $FSS_{general}$ erreichen kann. Der Behandlung von Satzanaphern kommt hier zugute, daß in SB-ONE **THING**s und **PREDICATE**s strukturell gleichbehandelt werden, eine Eigenschaft des Repräsentationsformalismus, die auch (Allen 87, S. 353f) als wichtig für die Eignung als Basis für natürlichsprachliche Systeme betont.

VI Rollennominale: Nominalisierungen von Konkreta

Die Linguistik bezeichnet Ableitungen wie "Sendung" aus "senden", "Fahrer" aus "fahren" als Konkreta-Nominalisierungen, in der KI (nach der von (Finin 80a,b) eingeführten Terminologie[9]) spricht man von *role nominals*, Rollennominalen, was sowohl nach Kasusrahmen- als auch nach KL-ONE-Terminologie zu interpretieren ist. Viele Nominalisierungen von Verben (insbesondere solche, die auf -ung enden) bezeichnen nicht nur den Geschehensablauf, den Prädikatsinhalt, sondern auch den Abschluß oder das Ergebnis (**result**) eines Geschehens; oder aber sie sind zu *Sach-* ("Kleidung"), *Raum-* ("Wohnung") oder *Personen*bezeichnungen ("Bedienung") geworden und fallen damit nicht mehr unter das FSS-Konzept **ABSTRACT THING**, sondern sind Subkonzepte von **CONCRETE THING**. Konkreta bezeichnen also einzelne Attributdeskriptionen des Ausgangsverbkonzepts; damit entsprechen sie - in der SB-ONE Terminologie - Rollen, genauer gesagt: den Füllern einer bestimmten Rolle. Für die "Regierungschefs" (Abb. 4) wäre eine Repräsentation wünschenswert wie in Abb. 5, die aber nicht der Syntax von SB-ONE genügt, da der inheritance link nur zwischen Konzepten definiert werden kann.

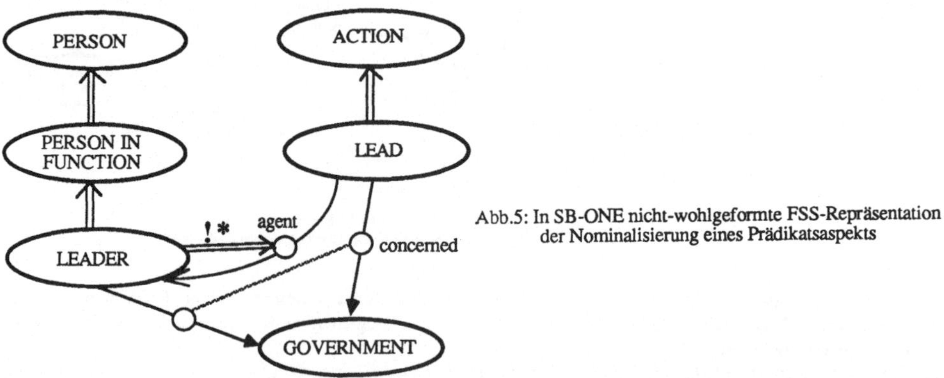

Abb.5: In SB-ONE nicht-wohlgeformte FSS-Repräsentation der Nominalisierung eines Prädikatsaspekts

---

[9]Finin benutzt die Bezeichnung 'role nominals' allerdings auch für die "echten" Nomina, die keine abgeleiteten Formen sind, deren Bedeutung sich jedoch als agent, als instrument etc. eines Verbkonzepts definieren läßt (z.B. "Pilot"); ich benutze den Begriff hier i.e.S. für die Nominalisierungen von Verbaspekten. Selbstverständlich sollten "echte" Nomina und bedeutungsgleiche Rollennominale auf die gleichen FSS-Strukturen abgebildet werden.

Brachman schlägt in (Brachman 78) eine ähnliche Repräsentation von Rollennominalen vor, für die er wiederum einen neuen 'nominalization link type' einführt: den DROLE link. Abb. 6 zeigt die Ableitung eines 'agentive nominal concept'; es erbt seine Attributdeskriptionen, dem DROLE link folgend, als

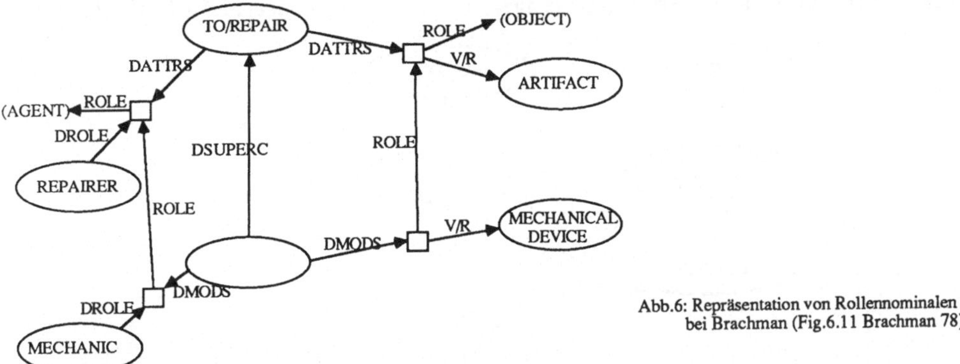

Abb.6: Repräsentation von Rollennominalen bei Brachman (Fig.6.11 Brachman 78)

Inverse zu den erreichbaren DATTRS von TO/REPAIR. Während in Abb.5 die Nicht-Wohlgeformtheit bzgl. SB-ONE darin besteht, daß Attributvererbung von einer Rolle aus nicht definiert ist, präsentiert Abb.6 einen speziellen inheritance link, der in KL-ONE nicht operationalisiert ist. Mit den bisher zur Verfügung stehenden Methoden KL-ONE-artiger Sprachen können solche Beziehungen nur in der einen Richtung - der Rolle vom Prädikat zum Subkonzept von **THING** - definiert werden.[10]

(Finin 80a,b) führt - für die Analyse von Komposita mit Rollennominalen - strukturelle Regeln ein:

a) RULE: Concept + RoleNominal ; Bsp: "cat food"

b) RULE: RoleNominal + Concept ; Bsp: "pilot school" ,

die Interpretationen erzeugen, in denen

a) der Modifier ('CAT') das Konzept modifiziert, auf das sich das Rollennominal bezieht ('FEED')

b) die Modifikation nicht durch das erste Kompositionsglied ('PILOT') selbst erfolgt, sondern durch dasjenige Konzept, von dem sich das Rollennominal herleitet ('FLY').

Unklar bleibt bei diesem Ansatz die Repräsentationen von Rollennominalen *in* der frame-basierten Repräsentationssprache, d.h. *außerhalb* der Interpretationsregeln, wo 'food' als 'an object of (a to-eat)' beschrieben ist. Allerdings weist Finin darauf hin, daß sich Rollennominale ganz ähnlich verhalten wie *Relativsätze* (mit leichter Focusverschiebung), und aus dieser Beobachtung läßt sich eine mögliche Repräsentation ableiten: Relativsätze konstituieren in der Funktional-semantischen Struktur eine bestimmte, für alle **THING**s definierte Attributdeskription in Form der Rolle **rel-mod** zu **PREDICATE**, die als Inverse zu einer beliebigen case-role des **PREDICATE** definiert ist. Die konzeptuelle Repräsentation von "die Person, die die Regierung führt" würde aufgrund der value restriction der **agent**-Rolle von **LEAD** vom eigentlichen head-Konzept **PERSON** spezialisiert werden zur Struktur aus Abb. 7. Der gewünschten Definition für "Regierungschef" (aus Abb.5) kommt diese Repräsentation schon sehr nahe: Statt des nicht-wohlgeformten 'superconcept link' von **LEADER** zur

---

[10](Freeman 81) schlug allerdings als KL-ONE-Erweiterung ein QUA concept vor, das als Repräsentation für einen generellen Rollenfüller intendiert war; da der Classifier jedoch bei der Behandlung der dadurch entstehenden verschiedenen Ebenen "explodieren" würde, wurde der QUA-link in KL-ONE nicht operationalisiert. Die KL-ONE-Sprache QUIRK (Bergmann , Gerlach 87) kennt ein Macro-artiges QUA, das sich mittels inverser Rollen (vgl. auch Abb.7) in die Basis-Sprachkonstrukte übersetzen läßt. Inwieweit sich dieser Ansatz zur Repräsentation von Rollennominalen eignet, ist noch zu prüfen; ich danke Jürgen Allgayer für den Hinweis.

agent-Rolle führen wir eine - ebenso definitorische - Rolle **predicative aspect** (als Verallgemeinerung der **rel-mod** Rolle) ein; die **concerned**-Information zu erschließen bzw. zu repräsentieren, ist dann ein zweistufiger Prozeß, analog der Finin'schen Interpretationsregeln:

LEADER = predicative aspect <u>inverse</u> **agent** of **LEAD** with **concerned = GOVERNMENT**

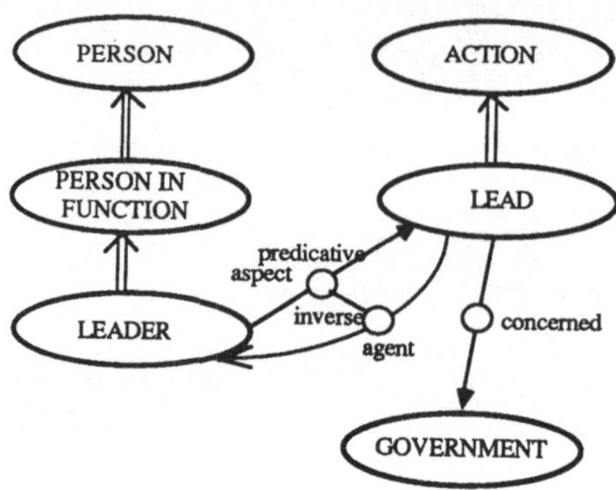

Abb.7: Repräsentationsmöglichkeit für
Konzeptaspekte und für Relativsätze

Im Gegensatz zu Nominalisierungen von Verbkonzept*inhalten* kommt die Repräsentation von Konzept*aspekten* damit zwar nicht ohne Erweiterung des Formalismus aus; allerdings scheint die hier vorgeschlagene zum einen weniger gravierend als die Definition neuer 'inheritance links' (Relationen zwischen Rollen läßt SB-ONE auch an anderen Stellen zu, z.B. als role value maps), zum anderen ist sie - wie das Beispiel des Relativsatzes zeigt - weniger eng auf das spezielle Problem der Nominalisierungen zugeschnitten und beschreibt damit einen generelleren Typ von (Sprach-) Wissensstrukturen.

VII Erweiterungen

Neben der Nominalisierung von Verben tritt im Deutschen auch die "umgekehrte" Wortbildung auf, wenn auch nicht ebenso häufig: die "Verbalisierung" von Nomina, das Ableiten eines Verbs aus einem gegebenem Nomen, wie in 'stationieren' oder 'positionieren'. Wünschenswert und mit den diskutierten Methoden möglich erscheint es auch hier, den Zusammenhang zwischen Nomen und abgeleitetem Verb zu repräsentieren (das Nomen bezeichnet wiederum ein Rollennominal)[11].

Einige KI-Arbeiten zur Repräsentation von Nominalisierungen haben als Hauptziel die Behandlung von Nominalkomposita, z. B. neben den schon erwähnten (Brachman78, Finin 80a.b) auch (Isabelle 84, McDonald 81, Sparck Jones 83). Mit den hier vorgestellten Lösungen - und unter der Voraussetzung, daß sich Prädikatsaspekte in SB-ONE adäquat repräsentieren lassen - lassen sich (teilweise) auch solche Wortbildungen analysieren, denn viele Nominalkomposita setzen sich aus nominalisierten Verben plus einem case frame-Argument zusammen. Bei der Überführung des Prädikatsinhalts in ein Abstraktum kann das Subjekt als ein (das erste) Kompositionsglied mitgenannt werden ("Siegersprung"). "Prüfergebnis" ist ein Beispiel für einen Prädikatsaspekt mit vorangestelltem Prädikat. Die Schwierigkeit, solche Nominalkomposita zu analysieren, liegt allerdings bereits in der morphologischen

---

[11]Allerdings sind mir bisher keine linguistischen Untersuchungen bekannt, die ein Regelwerk zur *semantischen* Ableitung von Verben aus Nomina aufstellen, auf das ein KI-System aufbauen könnte.

Komponente eines NLS; ist die Fuge gefunden, reichen die bisherigen (in den vorangegangenen Kap. vorgestellten) Prozesse und Strukturen aus, um die (evtl. alternativen) Relation(en) zwischen den Komponenten zu finden, falls eines der Kompositionsglieder eine Verbnominalisierung ist[12].

Ein weiteres Problem ist das der Frequenz: Manche Nominalisierungen aus Verben enthalten eine (im DUDEN) sogenante *frequentative Komponente* des *wiederholten oder andauernden* Tuns (oft verbunden mit der Bewertung "das dauert länger als erwünscht/erwartet"); Beispiele hierfür sind "Bummel-ei", "Ge-Keife". Mit -er Suffix dagegen lassen sich (maskuline) Bezeichnungen für eine *einmalige* Verhaltensäußerung oder Bewegung (bzw. deren Ergebnis) bilden ("Hopser", "Seufzer", "Ausrutscher"). (Dahl et al. 87) weisen darauf hin, daß der für die Verarbeitung wesentlichste Unterschied zwischen einem Verb und seiner Nominalisierung darin liegt, daß bei der letzteren eine Tempusangabe fehlt oder nur implizit vorhanden ist: "The fact that nominalizations are untensed while clauses normally are tensed means that an alternative treatment of time is required for nominalizations." Es ist bisher ungeklärt, wie diese Bedeutungskomponenten in der FSS widergespiegelt werden können, da sie anscheinend starke pragmatische Züge tragen.

VIII Literatur

Allen, James (1987): Natural Language Understanding. Menlo Park: The Benjamin/Cummings Publ. Comp.

Bergmann, Henning; Gerlach, Michael (1987): QUIRK - Implementation einer TBox zur Repräsentation begrifflichen Wissens. Hamburg: WISBER Memo Nr.11 (2. erw. Aufl.)

Brachman, Ronald J. (1978): A Structural Paradigm for Representing Knowledge. BBN Report No. 3605, Cambridge. MA: Bolt Beranek & Newman Inc.

Brachman, R.; Bobrow, R.; Cohen, P.; Klovstad, J.; Webber, B.; Woods, W. (1979): Research in Natural Language Understanding. Annual Report. BBN Report No. 4274, Cambridge. MA: Bolt Beranek & Newman Inc.

Brachman, R.J. and Schmolze, J.G. (1985): "An Overview of the KL-ONE Knowledge Representation System." Cognitive Science 9, 172-216.

Cercone, Nick and McCalla, Gordon (eds.): The Knowledge Frontier - Essays in the Representation of Knowledge. New York: Springer 1987.

Dahl, D.A., Palmer, M.S., Passonneau, R.J. (1987): "Nominalizations in PUNDIT". Proc. 25th ACL, Stanford.

DUDEN (1984): Grammatik der deutschen Gegenwartssprache. Mannheim: Bibliographisches Institut.

Fillmore, Charles (1971): "Types of Lexical Information". in: D. Steinberg, L. Jakobovits (eds.): Semantics. Cambridge University Press.

Finin, Tim (1980a): The Semantic Interpretation of Compound Nominals. PhD Thesis, Univ. of Illinois.

Finin, Tim (1980b): "The Semantic Interpretation of Nominal Compounds." Proc. 1st AAAI'80.

Freeman, Michael (1981): "The QUA link." Proc. 1981 KL-ONE Workshop, Fairchild Rep. No. 618.

Hobbs, Gerald (1983): "An Improper Treatment of Quantification in Ordinary English". Proc. 21st ACL.

Isabelle, Pierre (1984): "Another Look at Nominal Compounds." Proc. of COLING'84

Kobsa, Alfred (1988): The SB-ONE Knowledge Representation Workbench. SFB 314, FB Informatik, Universität des Saarlandes (in preparation).

McDonald, David B. (1981): "COMPOUND: A Program that Understands Noun Compounds." Proc. 7th IJCAI'81.

v. Polenz, Peter (1985): Deutsche Satzsemantik. Sammlung Göschen 2226, Berlin: W. de Gruyter.

Shapiro, Stuart and Rapaport, (1987): "SNePS Considered as a Fully Intensional Propositional Semantic Network." in: Nick Cercone and Gordon McCalla (eds.)

Sparck Jones, Karen (1983): "So what about parsing compound nouns?" in: Sparck Jones, K.; Wilks, Y. (eds.): Automatic Natural Language Parsing. Chichester: Ellis Horwood ltd. 1983

Teubert, Wolfgang (1979): Valenz des Substantivs. Düsseldorf: Schwann.

---

[12] (Sparck Jones 83) betont allerdings, daß die Problemfälle unter den Nominalkomposita gerade nicht unter diesen zu finden sind; denn im allgemeinen besteht ja das Analyseproblem im Auffinden der Relation zwischen den Kompositionsgliedern.

Automatische Messung der Dauer von Lauten in lautsprachlichen Äusserungen *

Dieter Gilg   Remo Leber   Karl Huber

Institut für Elektronik

Fachgruppe Sprachverarbeitung

ETH Zürich

Zusammenfassung

Automatische Messung der Dauer von Lauten in lautsprachlichen Äusserungen ist gleichbedeutend mit der Segmentierung eines Sprachsignals aufgrund der zugehörigen phonetischen Umschrift. Die Kenntnis der exakten phonetischen Umschrift kann dabei darüber entscheiden, ob eine Segmentierung erfolgreich ist oder nicht. Aus diesem Grund wurde der folgende Ansatz gemacht: Ausgehend von einer wortweisen Transkription wird in einem ersten Schritt versucht, alle möglichen durch Regeln gegebenen Varianten von phonetischen Sequenzen eines Satzes zu bestimmen. In einem zweiten Schritt wird die beste dieser Varianten ermittelt und gleichzeitig auf das Sprachsignal abgebildet.

1   Einleitung

Messungen der zeitlichen Länge einzelner Segmente in natürlicher Lautsprache sind beispielsweise notwendig, um Modelle für die Dauersteuerung in der Sprachsynthese aufzustellen. Üblicherweise wurden solche Messungen anhand von Spektrogrammen vorgenommen [1] [2]. Dieses Vorgehen ist zeitraubend, und es fragt sich deshalb, ob die Messung der Dauer von Lauten nicht automatisiert werden kann. Ein automatisches Verfahren ist allerdings nur dann vorteilhaft, wenn es zuverlässig arbeitet und die resultierenden Daten präzise sind, so dass nicht wiederum viel Zeit für die Kontrolle benötigt wird. Die Messung von Lautlängen ist an sich mit viel Unsicherheit verbunden, denn die Grenze zwischen zwei benachbarten Lauten ist in den meisten Fällen nicht eindeutig auszumachen und kann nur mit einem gewissen Mass an Willkür festgesetzt werden.

Für Zwecke der Sprachsynthese ist es erforderlich, die Lautdauermessungen in Bezug zu setzen zur Synthese, d. h. die Messungen einzelner Segmente auf dieselben Konventionen zu basieren, worauf dann auch die Steuerung der Länge der Grundelemente basiert. Die Messungen sind erfolgreich, falls der darauf basierende Steueralgorithmus natürlich klingende synthetische Lautsprache erzeugt (wenigstens was die zeitliche Struktur betrifft). Die Erzeugung synthetischer Sprache bietet somit ein Mittel, die Konventionen für die Lautdauermessungen festzulegen oder zu verändern.

Die automatische Messung von Lautlängen ist gleichbedeutend mit der Segmentierung (labeling, time alignment) eines Sprachsignals aufgrund der zugehörigen phonetischen Transkription. In bestehenden Verfahren wird dies häufig in zwei Schritten vollzogen: In einem ersten Schritt wird aufgrund von Stationaritäts- und Instationaritätsbedingungen eine erste Struktur bestimmt,

---

*Die Arbeiten zu diesem Thema wurden im Rahmen einer Diplomarbeit ausgeführt

auf die dann im zweiten Schritt die phonetische Sequenz abgebildet wird [3] [4]. Solche Segmentierungsverfahren arbeiten zuverlässig und werden für die Analyse von Lautsprache eingesetzt [5].

Für eine erfolgreiche Segmentierung ist allerdings die exakte phonetische Umschrift Voraussetzung. Wird kontinuierliche Sprache segmentiert und nicht nur einzelne isolierte Wörter, so ist die phonetische Umschrift ohne Kenntnis der lautsprachlichen Realisierung nicht immer vollständig vorauszusagen, denn es gibt grosse Variationsmöglichkeiten abhängig vom Sprechstil und vom Sprechtempo. Diese möglichen Variationen verhalten sich jedoch zu einem grossen Teil regelhaft [6], und sie können berücksichtigt werden, indem nicht nur eine einzige phonetische Sequenz, sondern eine aufgrund von Regeln gebildete Menge von Sequenzen als Ausgangsbasis für die Segmentierung verwendet wird.

Das hier beschriebene Verfahren umfasst deshalb eine Komponente, die die anhand des Aussprachewörterbuches transkribierten Wörter aufgrund von Regeln zur Koartikulation und Lautvariation in ein Transitionsnetz überführt, das die Menge aller möglichen phonetischen Sequenzen beschreibt. In einem zweiten Schritt wird aus den möglichen Sequenzen mittels Optimierung die am besten angepasste ausgewählt, wobei sie gleichzeitig auch auf das Signal abgebildet wird.

2 Beschreibung des Verfahrens

2.1 Beispiel einer Segmentierung

Verfolgen wir den Ablauf der Segmentierung anhand des flektierten unbestimmten Artikels "einen" innerhalb des Teilsatzes "... verriet einen riesigen ...". Die Information, die dem Prozess zur Verfügung gestellt werden muss, ist die wortweise phonetische Transkription laut Aussprachewörterbuch mit zusätzlichen Informationen über Akzentuierung, Wortklasse und Phrasen- bzw. Satzgrenzen.

$$\ldots f\varepsilon r - [2]ri : t \; [F]ai - n\partial n \; [2]ri : -zI - g\partial n \; \ldots$$

"[2]" bezeichnet den Sekundärakzent, "[F]" bezeichnet ein Formwort. Auf diese Zeichensequenz werden Regeln zur Assimilation und Elision und Regeln zur Bildung von schwachen Formen angewandt. Erzeugt wird damit ein Transitionsnetz, das die meisten möglichen phonetischen Sequenzen beschreibt. Das zugehörige Netz zu "einen" im obigen Kontext ist in Figur 1 dargestellt.

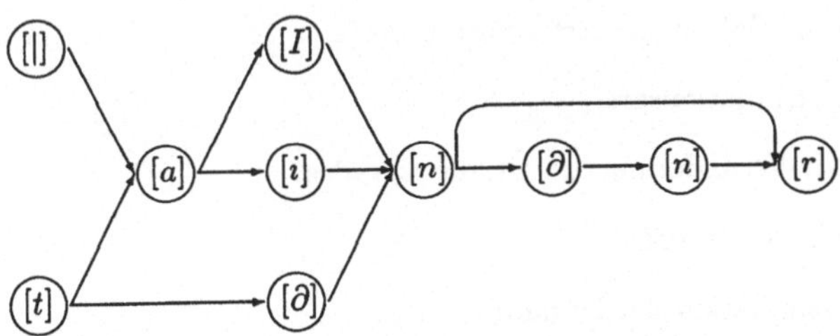

Figur 1: Dieses Transitionsnetz beschreibt die möglichen phonetischen Sequenzen von "einen" in der Umgebung "... verriet einen riesigen ...".

In einem zweiten Schritt wird dieses Transitionsnetz auf das Sprachsignal abgebildet. Gleichzeitig wird der beste Weg durch obiges Netz durch Minimierung einer Kostenfunktion bestimmt. Das Resultat davon ist die Segmentierung in Figur 2.

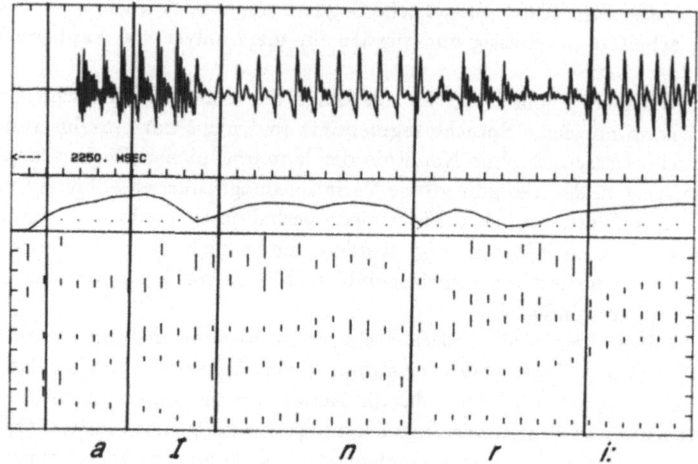

Figur 2: Das Resultat der Segmentierung anhand des Transitionsnetzes von Figur 1. Es ist der Signalverlauf (oben), der Leistungsverlauf (Mitte) und der Verlauf der Maxima im Spektrum dargestellt. Der Abstand einzelner Rastermarkierungen beträgt 10 ms. Die Segmentierung ist mittels vertikaler Linien markiert. Als vokalische Variante wurde [I] anstelle von [i] gewählt. Der Schwa-Laut [∂] wurde als elidiert betrachtet.

Wir erhalten die am besten angepasste phonetische Sequenz und zugleich die Dauer der einzelnen Laute. In diesem Fall wurde für den Diphtong /ai/, der biphonematisch gewertet ist, die vokalische Variante [I] anstelle von [i] gewählt. Weiter wurde der Schwa-Laut [∂] als elidiert betrachtet.

2.2 Generierung phonetisch-allophonischer Varianten

Hier soll näher auf die Generierung der phonetisch-allophonischen Varianten eingegangen werden. Die Transformation der Eingangssequenz in das Transitionsnetz berücksichtigt die folgenden Möglichkeiten zur Assimilation, Elision und Variantenbildung [6]:

- Elision von [r], [∂] und [t],

- regressive und progressive Assimilation des Artikulationsortes,

- regressive Assimilation der Artikulationsart,

- Einsparung von Bewegung zur Veränderung des Öffnungsgrades,

- progressive Assimilation der Stimmlosigkeit,

- regressive und progressive Assimilation der Nasalität,

- Geminatenreduktion,

- Sonorisierung,

- vokalische Varianten,

- Sprosskonsonanten,

- schwache Formen.

Die Transformationsregeln können in Form von kontextabhängigen Ersetzungsregeln formuliert werden:

$$A \longrightarrow B \;/\; C\_D$$

Der Laut A kann in den Laut B übergehen, falls er im Kontext C und D steht, wobei B im Falle einer Elision auch ein Leerelement sein kann. Transformationen dieser Art wurden für einen in Prolog geschriebenen Regelinterpreter formuliert [7]. Diese Transformationen benötigen in manchen Fällen jedoch ausser der Information über die benachbarten Laute noch zusätzliche Informationen über die Akzentuierung, die morphologische Struktur, die Wortart und die Satz- und Phrasengrenzen. Diese können als zusätzliche Bedingungen neben den Kontextbedingungen für jede einzelne Regel aufgestellt werden. Eine der Schwierigkeiten ist dabei, eine geeignete Reihenfolge für die Abarbeitung der Transformationsregeln zu finden. Um alle möglichen Varianten zu erhalten, müssten im Grunde auf jede aus einer Transformation hervorgegangene Sequenz wieder alle anderen Regeln angewandt werden. Dies würde aber zu weit führen. Es ist deshalb sinnvoll, eine Abfolge von Transformationen festzulegen, die die wahrscheinlichsten phonetischen Sequenzen erzeugt. Die Abfolge der Transformationen wurde in dieser Arbeit durch Versuche bestimmt [8].

2.3 Segmentierung anhand eines Transitionsnetzes

Die eigentliche Segmentierung und Bestimmung der Lautlängen wird anhand des im ersten Schritt erzeugten Transitionsnetzes vorgenommen. Das Transitionsnetz beschreibt die möglichen Zustände, die während des Optimierungsprozesses beim sequentiellen Durchlaufen des Signals angenommen werden können.

Der Optimierungsprozess arbeitet auf einer parametrisierten Signaldarstellung. Die einzelnen Parameter, die abschnittweise in einem zeitlichen Abstand von 5 bis 10 ms berechnet vorliegen, sind die spektrale Enveloppe (oder LPC-Spektrum), die momentane Leistung im Signal und die Grundfrequenz, falls der Signalabschnitt periodisch ist. Bei der Abbildung der einzelnen abstrakten Zustände auf den kontinuierlichen Signalverlauf muss eine Zuordnung von Merkmalen im Signalparameterbereich zu einzelnen phonetischen Elementen gemacht werden. Für jedes phonetische Element (ob Pause oder Lautvariante) wird eine Beschreibung des möglichen Verhaltens der Signalparameter in einer Datenbasis abgelegt. Dabei wird berücksichtigt, dass einzelne phonetische Ereignisse abhängig von ihrer Position unterschiedlich realisiert sein können. Beispielsweise können Vibranten sowohl periodisch als auch aperiodisch realisiert sein.[1] Zusätzlich zu den signalparametrischen Merkmalen Spektrum, Leistung und Periodizität wird für jedes einzelne phonetische Element auch die minimale und maximale Länge in der Datenbasis eingetragen. Für einen Zustand im Transitionsnetz wird aufgrund der zugehörigen Eintragungen in der Datenbasis für verschiedene Längenvarianten, die im Bereiche der minimalen und maximalen Länge liegen, eine Kostenfunktion berechnet. Verschiedenartige Anteile steuern dabei zur Kostenfunktion bei. Je nach Charakter des jeweiligen Segmentes wird aufgrund der vorhandenen Energie im Signal, aufgrund der vorhandenen oder fehlenden Periodizität oder der Abweichung von einem Referenzspektrum ein Kostenanteil hinzugefügt. Es ist dabei wichtig sicherzustellen, dass die aufgrund verschiedenartiger Merkmale berechneten Kostenanteile vergleichbar bleiben, d. h. das durchnittliche aufgrund der Energie oder der Periodizität berechnete Kostenniveau soll

---

[1]Man beachte, dass das phonologische Merkmal Stimmhaftigkeit nicht unbedingt der Periodizität im Signalparameterbereich entsprechen muss.

ungefähr gleich gross sein wie das aufgrund der spektralen Abweichung berechnete. Die Minimierung der Kostenfunktion und die Optimierung des Pfades und der Längenvarianten erfolgt nach dem Prinzip der dynamischen Programmierung [9].

Die Wahl der besten lautlichen Varianten, die Bestimmung der Lautlängen und die Abbildung auf den Signalverlauf geschieht also in einem einzigen Durchgang. Entscheidungen an einem bestimmten Punkt werden aufgrund aller möglichen verfügbaren Informationen getroffen und nicht nur aufgrund einer einzelnen Grösse. Dieses Prinzip verhilft dem Verfahren zu seiner Mächtigkeit.

Das Verfahren ist teilweise in Modula-2 und teilweise in Prolog implementiert. Teile, die numerische Berechnungen durchführen (und sich deshalb für eine Formulierung in Prolog nicht eignen) sind in Modula-2, Teile, die auf die phonetische Datenbasis zugreifen und Entscheide treffen, sind in Prolog formuliert. Diese Aufteilung ist möglich dank eines Prolog-Interpreters, der eine Schnittstelle für Modula-2-Prozeduren besitzt [10].

Der Kern der Optimierung sieht vereinfacht in Prolog formuliert folgendermassen aus:

```
finde_besten_weg(ende).
finde_besten_weg(Aktuelle_Stufe) :-
    bearbeite_stufe(Aktuelle_Stufe),
    weitere_stufe(Aktuelle_Stufe, Naechste_Stufe),
    finde_besten_weg(Naechste_Stufe).

bearbeite_stufe(Stufe) :-
    transition(Vorherige_Stufe, Vorheriges_Ele, Stufe, Ele, Art),
    laut_eigenschaft(Ele, Art, Voi, Ene, Zen),
    bester_weg(Vorherige_Stufe, Vorheriges_Ele, Vorherige_Kosten),
    laut_laenge(Ele, Art, Laenge),
    prozess(Voi, Ene, Zen, Laenge, Stufe, Ele, Lokale_Kosten),
    Akkum_Kosten is Vorherige_Kosten + Lokale_Kosten,
    mimimum(Stufe, Ele, Vorherige_Stufe, Vorheriges_Ele, Akkum_Kosten).
bearbeite_stufe(_).
```

Das Prolog-Prädikat 'finde_besten_weg' geht sequentiell alle Stufen durch, bis das Ende erreicht ist. Eine einzelne Stufe wird abgearbeitet, indem ein Übergang zur vorherigen Stufe hergestellt wird ('transition'), die Eigenschaften des aktuellen Lautelementes geprüft werden ('laut_eigenschaft'), der Pfad, der bis zum vorherigen Element führt, aktiviert wird ('bester_weg'), eine gültige Lautlänge gewählt wird ('laut_laenge'), die lokalen Kosten für das aktuelle Element mit der gewählten Länge bestimmt werden ('prozess'), die akkumulierten Kosten berechnet werden ('Akkum_Kosten') und in einem letzten Schritt die akkumulierten Kosten verglichen werden mit den akkumulierten Kosten, die für alternative Varianten berechnet wurden ('minimum'). Das letzte Subgoal 'minimum' initiiert ein Backtracking. Es wird solange Backtracking gemacht, bis alle alternativen Übergänge, Lauteigenschaften und Lautlängen auf einer einzelnen Stufe abgearbeitet sind.

3 Ergebnisse

Das Verfahren wurde bis jetzt an ungefähr 70 Sätzen eines Sprechers ausgetestet. Für die Beurteilung des Verfahrens muss eine Unterscheidung zwischen globalem Verhalten und lokalem Verhalten gemacht werden. Das globale Verhalten meint die grobe zeitliche Zuweisung phonetischer Elemente zum Signalverlauf. Das globale Verhalten hat beispielsweise versagt, wenn das

Ende der phonetischen Sequenz nicht mit dem Ende des Signalverlaufes zusammenfällt, das Verfahren also völlig ausser Tritt fällt. Das lokale Verhalten meint die Präzision der Zuordnung einzelner phonetischer Elemente. Das beschriebene Verfahren hat in allen analysierten Sätzen eine richtige globale Zuordnung geliefert, falls sich in der Menge der phonetischen Sequenzen eine richtige, d. h. zuweisbare Sequenz befand. Selbst in Fällen mit starken Störungen im Signal (Störgeräuschen, die von der Aufnahme herrührten) fiel das Verfahren nie ausser Tritt.

Das lokale Verhalten ist sehr stark von den einzelnen Lauten abhängig. Einige Laute wie der Aspirant, aber auch der Lateral passen sich stärker an ihre Umgebung an und sind deshalb schlechter von den Nachbarlauten abzugrenzen als andere. Folgen zwei Nasale aufeinander, so sind sie ebenfalls schlecht voneinander abzugrenzen. Eine Durchsicht der analysierten Sätze ergibt, dass ungefähr 1–2% der Segmente schlecht von ihren Nachbarsegmenten abgegrenzt werden.

Die Präzision der Zuordnung ist auch abhängig von der Rasterung der möglichen Längen, diese Rasterung bestimmt jedoch sehr stark die Rechenzeit der Analyse.

Die Figuren 3 und 4 zeigen zwei Signalausschnitte als Resultat der automatischen Segmentierung. Figur 3 zeigt einen Ausschnitt aus "... riesigen Flieder ...", Figur 4 einen Ausschnitt aus "... riesigen Tisch ...". In Figur 3 wird der Schwa-Laut [∂] als elidiert angesehen, während er in Figur 4 als vorhanden betrachtet wird. Offensichtlich handelt es sich in Figur 3 um einen Fall regressiver Fernassimilation, ausgelöst durch den Laut [ʃ] des nachfolgenden Wortes "Flieder".

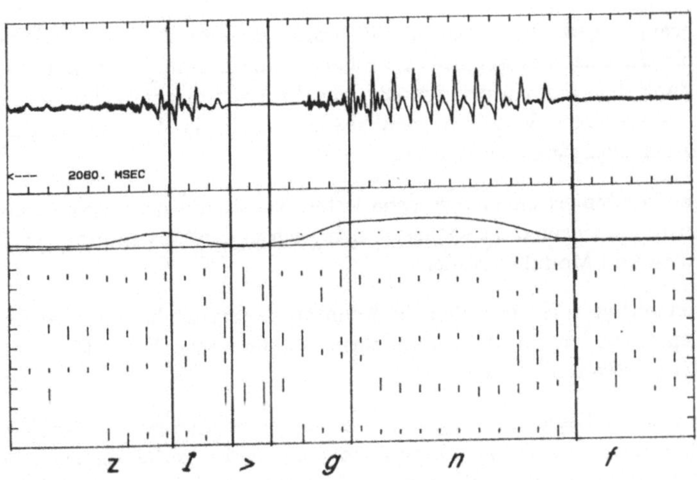

Figur 3: Ein Ausschnitt aus der Umgebung "... riesigen Flieder ...". Der Schwa-Laut [∂] wird in diesem Fall als elidiert betrachtet.

4   Schlussfolgerungen

Das beschriebene Verfahren arbeitet sehr zuverlässig in dem Sinne, dass in den untersuchten Testsätzen keine globalen Fehler auftreten. Es sind die folgenden Eigenheiten des Verfahrens, die sich günstig auf die Robustheit auswirken:

- Die Abbildung geschieht in einem einzigen Schritt. Dabei wird an einer bestimmten Stelle das gesamte vorhandene Wissen über ein Segment bezüglich signalphonetischer Eigenschaften (spektrale Eigenschaften, Intensitätsverlauf, Periodizität) gleichzeitig für einen

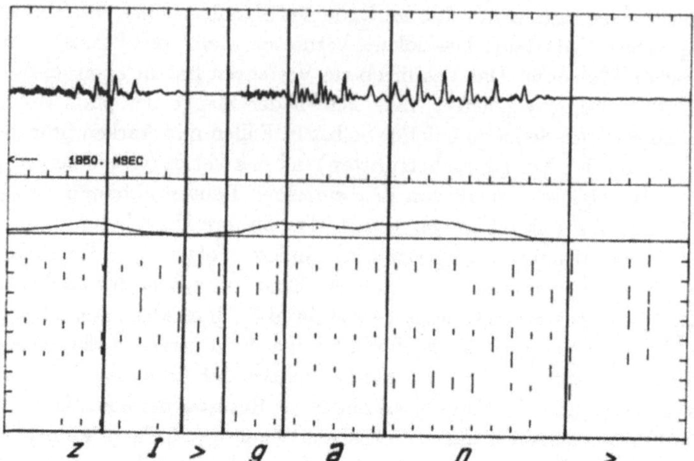

Figur 4: Ein Ausschnitt aus der Umgebung "... riesigen Tisch ...". In diesem Fall wird der Schwa-Laut [∂] als nicht elidiert betrachtet.

Entscheid herangezogen. Dies macht den Entscheid sicherer. Zusätzlich wird ein Entscheid nicht lokal für ein einzelnes Segment getroffen, sondern umfasst mehrere Segmente (dies ist möglich dank dem Prinzip der dynamischen Programmierung). Im Gegensatz dazu ist es in einem zwei-stufigen Verfahren nicht mehr möglich, Fehler, die auf der ersten Stufe gemacht wurden, rückgängig zu machen.

- Das Verfahren kombiniert einen wissensbasierten Ansatz mit dem algorithmischen der dynamischen Programmierung. Dies spiegelt sich auch in der Verwendung der Programmiersprachen Prolog und Modula-2 wider.

- Das Verfahren verfügt nicht nur über die Kenntnis der signalphonetischen Realisation einzelner Segmente, sondern auch über mögliche allophonische Varianten, die an einer bestimmten Stelle auftreten können.

Der Übergang von der Segmentierung aufgrund der phonetischen Umschrift zur Spracherkennung ist ein fliessender. In diesem Sinne kann man dieses Verfahren auch betrachten als Erkennung von Sprache aufgrund unvollständiger Erwartungen.

Literaturverzeichnis

[1] D.H. Klatt. Synthesis by rule of segmental durations in English sentences. In Lindblom B. and Öhman S., editors, *Frontiers of Speech Communication Research*, pages 287–301, Academic Press, 1979.

[2] K. Bartkova and Ch. Sorin. A model of segmental duration for speech synthesis in french. *Speech Communication*, (6):245–260, 1987.

[3] J.P. van Hemert. Automatic segmentation of speech into diphones. *Philips Technical Review*, 43(9):233–242, sept 1987.

[4] H.C. Leung and V.W. Zue. A procedure for automatic alignment of phonetic transcriptions with continuous speech. In *Proceedings ICASSP V1*, pages 2.7.1–2.7.4, IEEE, 1984.

[5] V.W. Zue. The use of speech knowledge in automatic speech recognition. *Proceedings of IEEE*, 73(11):1602–1615, nov 1985.

[6] K.J. Kohler. *Einführung in die Phonetik des Deutschen.* Volume 20 of *Grundlagen der Germanistik*, Erich Schmidt Verlag, Berlin, 1977.

[7] Ch. Traber. Documentation to the rule interpreter. 1986. Institut für Elektronik ETH Zürich.

[8] D. Gilg and R. Leber. Erkennung der lautlichen Einheiten in der gesprochenen Sprache. Febr. 1988. Diplomarbeit am Institut für Elektronik der ETH Zürich.

[9] E.V. Denardo. *Dynamic Programming Models and Applications.* Prentice Hall, Englewood Cliffs, N.J., 1982.

[10] Ch. Traber. Prolog V2.0 User Manual. 1988. Institut für Elektronik ETH Zürich.

Prosodiesteuerung in der Sprachsynthese

Sigismund Frenkenberger, Markus Kommenda
Institut für Nachrichtentechnik und Hochfrequenztechnik
Technische Universität Wien

0. Zusammenfassung

Dieser Aufsatz behandelt die Probleme einer natürlich klingenden Prosodiesteuerung im Rahmen der Sprachsynthese. Zunächst wird das am Institut für Nachrichtentechnik und Hochfrequenztechnik in Wien entwickelte Sprachausgabesystem "Graphon" (1) beschrieben, im speziellen die Vorgangsweise bei der Bestimmung von Phrasengrenzen und Akzenten. Die aus der Literatur bekannten Effekte bezüglich Prosodie werden im Hinblick auf ihre Verwendbarkeit in "Graphon" behandelt.

Es wird ein Modell zur Beschreibung der Sprachgrundfrequenz mit Hilfe von Gipfelmustern vorgestellt, welches an gehobene Wiener Umgangssprache angepaßt wurde. Zur Überprüfung des Modells wurde der Sprachgrundfrequenzverlauf natürlicher Sprache gelöscht und durch den künstlich generierten ersetzt.

1. Das Sprachausgabesystem "Graphon"

Wie bei jedem Text-to-Speech-System erfolgt auch in Graphon die Umsetzung von orthographisch eingegebenem Text in Sprache in mehreren Teilschritten (1).

Im ersten Schritt, der sog. Textvorverarbeitung, wird die Eingabe in eine einheitliche Form gebracht, d.h. es werden alle Abkürzungen ausgeschrieben, Großbuchstaben unter Berücksichtigung ihres Informationsgehalts in Kleinbuchstaben umgesetzt, Datumsangaben behandelt usw.

Im nächsten Schritt erfolgt die Graphem-Phonem-Umsetzung. Diese stützt sich auf eine morphologische Analyse der eingegebenen Wörter mit Hilfe eines Lexikons von etwa 2500 häufigen Morphen (Stämmen, Präfixen, Derivationssuffixen, Flexionsendungen und Fugen). Zugleich wird jedes Wort einer von 6 verschiedenen Wortklassen zugeordnet (Nomen, Verb, Adjektiv, Konjunktion, Personalpronomen, Rest).

Aufbauend auf dieser Information ist es möglich, Abfolgen von Wörtern bestimmter Klassen zu Phrasen zusammenzufassen und für diese Akzent und Intonationsmotiv zu bestimmen. Die grundlegenden Ideen dazu wurden von H. Zinglé (2) übernommen: Phrasen sind dadurch gekennzeichnet, daß jeweils ein Wort gegenüber allen anderen akzentuiert ist und daß am Ende ein charakteristischer Tonhöhenverlauf auftritt, welcher ansteigt, sofern es sich nicht um die letzte Phrase eines Aussagesatzes handelt.

Für die Zerlegung von Sätzen in Phrasen wurde eine Liste von etwa 300 Mustern angelegt, wobei jedes aus Wortklassensymbolen und Symbolen für Interpunktionszeichen besteht. Diese Liste wird im wesentlichen sequentiell durchsucht, bis ein Muster paßt. Dieses enthält Marker für Hauptakzent und Phrasengrenze und erlaubt so die Bestimmung eines Betonungsverlaufs und gegebenenfalls das Einfügen von Sprechpausen. Weiters wird für jede Phrase durch Auswertung der Interpunktion ein Intonationsmotiv (terminal, progredient oder interrogativ) festgelegt.

Im nächsten Schritt muß die Transkription mit Hilfe phonetischer Regeln verfeinert werden, um Reduktion und allophonischer Variation Rechnung zu tragen. Weiters muß die klassifikatorische Information über Akzent, Rhythmus und Intonationsmotiv in quantifizierte Verläufe für Sprachgrundfrequenz, Lautdauern und Intensität umgesetzt werden, damit schließlich die für den jeweils verwendeten Sprachsynthetisator notwendigen Parameter berechnet und diesem für die eigentliche Synthese übergeben werden können.

2. Die Prosodischen Parameter

2.1 Sprachgrundfrequenz (F0)

Es gibt zahlreiche Aufsätze über Intonation und über Sprachgrundfrequenzverlauf, die alle von syntaktischen, semantischen oder pragmatischen Überlegungen ausgehen und großteils deskriptiver Natur sind. In Graphon wurde nun nicht der Versuch unternommen, die hierarchische Struktur von Sätzen vollständig zu analysieren, und semantische und pragmatische Kriterien waren von vornherein ausgeklammert. Darum seien hier nur jene aus der Literatur bekannten Phänomene angeführt, die lediglich auf die syntaktische Oberfläche, so wie sie in Graphon analysiert wird, Bezug nehmen.

Selbstverständlich geht dadurch ein Teil dessen, was durch die Sprache ausgedrückt werden kann, verloren. Beispielsweise können wir nicht zwischen den beiden Realisierungen des Satzes: *"Die Sekretärinnen schreiben."*, einmal als Antwort auf die Frage: *"Was tun die Sekretärinnen?"* und einmal auf die Frage: *"Wer schreibt?"*, unterscheiden. Wenn also ein Computer den Inhalt dessen, was er sagt, "nicht versteht", so ist der einzig gangbare Weg der, nach einer möglichst neutralen Intonation zu suchen. So schreibt Janet Pierrehumbert (3, S.985):

"Insofar as possible, the system should mimic natural speech but because this is not always possible, the system should also minimize the abrasiveness of deviations."

Bei Untersuchungen am F0-Verlauf ist es zunächst notwendig, eine geeignete Beschreibungsform desselben zu wählen. Je nachdem, was man untersuchen will, werden sich verschiedene Beschreibungsformen verschieden gut eignen. Für automatische Intonationsgenerierung bieten sich folgende Möglichkeiten an:

** Man selektiert bestimmte ausgezeichnete Punkte der F0-Kontur und bildet die Kontur durch Interpolation der einzelnen Punkte (3).

** Man klassifiziert die Kontur nach Tonübergängen, d.h. man bestimmt eine Folge von Anweisungen, die jeweils die Tonbewegung festlegen (3) (4).

** Man beschreibt die Kontur durch Überlagerung vordefinierter Gipfelmuster (5).

Für die hier beschriebene Anwendung erscheint die Gliederung nach Gipfelmustern am geeignetsten, da dadurch einerseits hinreichend Abstraktion durchgeführt wird, und andererseits dennoch jene Phänomene, die zu modellieren beabsichtigt ist (Akzentsetzung, Intonationsmotive) , gut wiedergegeben werden können.

2.1.1. Die Gipfelmuster

Zunächst wird über die gesamte Phrase eine Basislinie gelegt. Darauf werden nun sogenannte Gipfel aufgesetzt. Ein Gipfel ist ein F0-Verlauf, der aus einem Anstieg und einem Abfall besteht. Ein jeder Gipfel ist durch 3 Punkte charakterisiert, deren zeitliche Lage relativ zu bestimmten Punkten um die betonte Silbe (Silbenbeginn, Vokalbeginn, Vokalende und Ende der letzten unbetonten Silbe) fixiert wird:

** Anfangspunkt (A), welcher auf der Basislinie liegt und den Beginnzeitpunkt festlegt,

** Gipfelpunkt (G), welcher eine bestimmte Anzahl von Halbtönen oberhalb der Basislinie liegt,

** Endpunkt (E), welcher wiederum auf der Basislinie (oder auch etwas unterhalb derselben) liegt.

Kohler (7) hat in seinen Arbeiten vor allem terminale Äußerungen untersucht. Zu ihrer Beschreibung unterscheidet er drei verschiedene Gipfelmuster: den frühen, den mittleren und den späten Gipfel. Schließlich definiert man noch ein terminales (Basislinie gegen Ende verstärkt abfallend) bzw. progredientes (Basislinie am Ende ansteigend) Phrasenende, und berücksichtigt die Deklination, indem man bei mehreren an sich gleich hohen Gipfeln den späteren Gipfel etwas tiefer ansetzt. Auch in Bereichen wo kein Gipfelmuster wirksam ist, sollte ein leichter F0-Abfall vorhanden sein. Damit hat man eine Beschreibungsform für F0-Konturen in Händen, die bereits recht brauchbare Resultate liefert.

2.1.2. IF0 und CF0

Darauf aufbauend gibt es noch zahlreiche Erscheinungen der Mikroprosodie, die zu einer wesentlich komplizierteren Struktur der F0-Konturen natürlicher Sprache führen als die, die mit dem relativ einfachen Modell erstellt werden können, aber sie sind von eher untergeordneter Bedeutung. Zwei davon seien hier kurz angeführt:

** IF0: Jeder Vokal hat eine ihm eigene inhärente Sprachgrundfrequenz. Bereits in den fünfziger Jahren wurde diese Tatsache von House und Fairbanks beschrieben (8). Aber auch in neuester Zeit gibt es einige Arbeiten, die sich mit diesem Thema auseinandersetzen (9) (10). Auffallend bei den zwei letztgenannten Arbeiten ist, daß die Größe des Effekts, den sie konstatieren, nicht dieselbe ist. Während Gartenberg die Variation in einer Größenordnung von etwa 5 Hertz ansetzt, spricht Möbius von einem Unterschied von etwa 25 Hertz.

** CF0: Beide Arbeiten beschäftigen sich auch mit dem Effekt des artikulatorischen Einflusses auf die F0-Kontur, wobei sie jene Fälle untersuchen, in denen in einer betonten Position ein Vokal auf einen stimmlosen Plosiv oder Frikativ folgt. Es stellt sich heraus, daß der Vokal in diesem Kontext mit einem höheren F0-Wert einsetzt als zu erwarten wäre.

2.2 Dauer

Für das Deutsche gilt, daß prinzipiell die Tendenz dahin geht, alle Phrasen mit derselben Länge zu realisieren. Da nun die Silbenanzahl für jede Phrase verschieden ist, führt dies dazu, daß die Silbendauer negativ proportional zur Silbenanzahl ist. Natürlich bleiben solche Dauervariationen in einem gewissen Rahmen. Weitere Variationsmöglichkeiten bieten die Sprechpausen.

Hoequist und Kohler (11, S. 8) sprechen in diesem Zusammenhang vom "foot compression effect".

"The syllable durations are negatively related to the number of syllables in a foot, that is, the more syllables in the foot, the less is the average syllable duration."

Einige Zeilen weiter erwähnt Kohler dann daß:

"FO increases with increasing speech rate"

Des weiteren hängt die tatsächlich realisierte Länge noch von dem vorausgehenden Phonem ab. Gewisse Phoneme wirken sich längend, gewisse kürzend auf das nachfolgende Phonem aus.

Schließlich hat noch jedes Phonem eine ihm eigene intrinsische Dauer.

2.3. Vokalreduktion und Intensität

Zwei weitere aus der Literatur bekannte Effekte seien hier nur in aller Kürze angeführt.

** Vokalreduktion:
Es hat sich gezeigt, daß Vokale in jener Qualität (ausgedrückt z.B. durch Formantwerte), in der sie auftreten, wenn sie isoliert gesprochen werden, im Satzzusammenhang selten vorkommen. Man stellt sich vor, daß durch die Bewegung der Artikulatoren (Zunge, Lippen, Velum, usw.) bei den Übergängen zwischen den Phonemen die für die einzelnen Phoneme typischen Einstellungen nur sehr kurz, wenn überhaupt, erreicht werden. Je schneller also gesprochen wird, desto geringer wird die Wahrscheinlichkeit, daß eine bestimmte Zielposition von den Artikulatoren eingenommen wird. Dies äußert sich im Vokaldreieck dadurch, daß in Abhängigkeit von der Vokaldauer die Position der einzelnen Vokale mehr oder weniger weit in das Zentrum des Vokaldreiecks (Schwa-Laut) rückt (12).

** Intensität:
Ein sehr schwer zu beschreibendes, aber dennoch nicht zu leugnendes Phänomen ist die Variation der Intensität mit dem Grad der Betonung. Schwer zu beschreiben ist dies deshalb, weil jedes Phonem eine ihm eigene Intensität besitzt, weil sich der Wahrnehmungseindruck der Lautstärke bei gleichbleibendem Energiegehalt ändert, wenn die Energie in einem anderem Frequenzbereich zu liegen kommt, weil bei transienten Vorgängen (Plosive) es überhaupt fraglich ist, ob die Bildung der Momentanenergie sinnvoll ist. Dennoch erkennt man bei Betrachtung des Zeitsignals, daß die Amplitude in betonten Silben meist größer ist als in unbetonten.

3. Meßanordnung

Wie in Punkt 1 bereits beschrieben, werden in Graphon die Akzente einer Äußerung dadurch bestimmt, daß die gesamte Äußerung in sogenannte Akzentphrasen gegliedert wird, wobei die Phrasenmuster in einer Tabelle gespeichert sind. Von dieser Tabelle wurde eine kleine Anzahl von Mustern ausgewählt (etwa 25). Bei der Auswahl der Phrasen wurde darauf geachtet, daß sowohl lange als auch kurze Phrasen, sowohl endbetonte als auch nicht endbetonte und sowohl Phrasen in terminaler als auch in progredienter Stellung vorkommen. Diese wurden in einen kurzen Text gekleidet:

Mein Großonkel, der ein großer Bastler war, hat ein schönes Auto gebaut. Weil er viel gearbeitet hat, starb er noch in jungen Jahren. Alle seine Verwandten erbten etwas, und wir bekamen sein schönes Auto. Und wir fanden sehr großes Wohlgefallen an der Erbschaft. Ich durfte, und ich sollte als erster mit dem Auto fahren. "Wo wollen wir hinfahren?", fragte mein Vater. "Schön ist, was blau ist, darum fahren wir ins Gebirge!", gab ich zur Antwort. Opa meckerte:"Schön ist, was grün ist, warum fahren wir ins Gebirge!". Ich schlichtete den Streit:"Schön ist, was mir gefällt, darum fahren wir ins Gebirge!".

Dieser Text wurde von 7 Sprechern auf Band gesprochen. Alle Sprecher, es waren 4 Frauen und 3 Männer aller Altersgruppen, waren gebürtige Wiener und haben auch immer in Wien gelebt. Da sie zudem alle studiert hatten oder noch studierten, schien die Annahme berechtigt, daß die Ergebnisse der einzelnen Sprachproben insofern vergleichbar sein würden, als daß es sich jedesmal um dieselbe dialektale Variante des Österreichischen (gehobene Wiener Umgangssprache) handelt. Bei den Aufnahmen wurde folgendermaßen vorgegangen:

Der Text wurde dem Sprecher zunächst in unbehandelter Form vorgelegt, d.h. als gewöhnlicher, maschingeschriebener Text. Nachdem der Sprecher den Text vorgelesen hatte, bekam er denselben Text noch einmal, nur daß jetzt die Phrasengrenzen und die Phrasenakzente markiert waren. Nachdem er sich den Text durchgelesen hatte (um sich an die vorgeschriebene Akzentuierung zu gewöhnen), mußte er auch diesen Text vorlesen.

Die erste Aufnahme diente vor allem dazu, Schwächen des Systems im bezug auf richtiges Setzen der Phrasenakzente oder der Phrasierung allgemein aufzudecken. Die eigentlichen Messungen wurden dann anhand der bewußt akzentuierten Aufnahmen gemacht. Alle Messungen wurden am Institut für Phonetik und digitale Sprachverarbeitung in Kiel durchgeführt.

4. Die Messungen und deren Interpretation

Zunächst wurden für den gesamten Text über Kopfhörer die Akzente bestimmt, um sie dann mit den Soll-Werten für die Akzentpositionen (Ausgabe Graphon) zu vergleichen. So wurden 2 Textversionen (1 männl. und 1 weibl. Sprecher) ermittelt, bei denen alle Akzente "richtig" realisiert waren (richtig hier im Sinne der Vorgabe).

4.1. Ergebnisse

Bei dem Versuch, die analysierten F0-Konturen mittels Gipfelmustern zu beschreiben, gab es schon bald Probleme. Kohler untersuchte nur terminale Äußerungen (6), sodaß er mit drei Gipfelmustern das Auslangen finden konnte, wohingegen hier ein zusammenhängender Text gegeben war.

Ein weiteres Problem bestand darin, daß Kohler vor allem Sprache aus dem norddeutschen Sprachraum untersucht hat, während es sich hier um eine österreichische Dialektvariante handelt. Es zeigte sich, daß sehr oft betonte Silben vorhanden sind, die eine niedrigere Sprachgrundfrequenz haben als ihre Umgebung, und daß sehr oft Betonung einfach durch einen F0-Abfall (F0-Bewegung) auf dem Vokal realisiert wird.

Um die gefundenen F0-Konturen adäquat zu beschreiben, wurde ein viertes Muster - das sogenante Anstiegsmuster - hinzugenommen. Beim Anstiegsmuster steigt nach einem kur- zen F0-Abfall die Grundfrequenz kontinuierlich bis ans Ende des Musters an, um schließ- lich sehr steil zur Basislinie abzufallen.

Für die automatische Generierung eines Sprachgrungfrequenzverlaufes ergibt sich nun folgende Vorgangsweise:

Als Ausgangspunkt dient eine gedachte Grundlinie mit der Bezugsfrequenz 1. Darauf wird dann ein linearer Deklinationsverlauf multipliziert, d.h. der Anfangspunkt jeder Phrase wird auf einen bestimmten Frequenzwert (160 Hz) gesetzt und ebenso der Endpunkt jeder Phrase (80 Hz).

Die Zeitpunkte für die einzelnen Vokalanfänge, Gipfelpunkte, Vokalenden liegen bereits fest, d.h., es wurden die Berechnungen der einzelnen Vokaldauern bereits durchgeführt, sodaß für jeden Vokal die Grundlinie an den entsprechenden Zeitpunkten mit einem be- stimmten Faktor (<>1), der die inhärente Sprachgrundfrequenz beschreibt, multipliziert werden kann.

Im nächsten Schritt werden die Gipfelmuster auf die Grundlinie übertragen, wobei jedes Gipfelmuster durch die bereits gekennzeichneten Zeitpunkte A G E festgelegt wird. Da die Gipfelmuster auf 1 normiert definiert sind, können sie einfach multiplikativ auf die bereits errechnete F0-Kontur übertragen werden.

Im letzten Schritt werden dann alle Teile, die rauschförmige Anregung besitzen, als solche markiert, und die CF0-Effekte durch Anhebung von F0 unmittelbar nach stimmlosen Plosiven und Frikativen um etwa 15 Hz berücksichtigt.

Zur Überprüfung des Modells wurde am Institut für Phonetik und digitale Sprachverarbeitung folgendes Experiment gemacht: Mit Hilfe des Programmpakets SSP (7) wurde der bereits erwähnte Text analysiert.

Durch Abhören des Tonbandes waren bereits die Akzentpositionen in eine phonetische Repräsentation des Textes eingetragen worden. Wiederum auditiv wurde nun für jeden Akzent eines der 4 Gipfelmuster gesetzt, wobei vor allem auf den Tonhöhenverlauf geachtet wurde. So kam es mitunter auch vor, daß auf Grund der wahrgenommenen Sprachgrundfrequenzbewegung ein entsprechendes Gipfelmuster gesetzt wurde, obwohl ursprünglich kein Akzent an dieser Stelle perzipiert worden war.

Zusätzlich war es noch erlaubt, die Gipfel entweder mit voller oder mit halber Ausprägung zu setzen. Für jede progrediente Phrase wurde ein weiteres Intonationsmuster gesetzt, welches dafür sorgt, daß die Sprachgrundfrequenz von der Position des letzten Akzentes bis zum Ende der Phrase linear bis etwa 200 Hz ansteigt. Terminale Phrasen wurden nicht extra behandelt, da, wie bereits oben erwähnt, jede Phrase zunächst eine Grundlinie erhält, die am Phrasenanfang bei 160 Hz und am Phrasenende bei 80 Hz liegt.

Somit wurde der gesamte Text auf phonetischer Ebene beschrieben, wobei für die Beschreibung des F0—Verlaufes insgesamt nur 9 Symbole notwendig waren. Diese Beschreibung legte aber bereits einen konkreten F0—Verlauf fest, sodaß dieser für eine Resynthese des Textes verwendet werden konnte. So wurde also der gesamte Text einmal mit dem natürlichen, vom SSP Programm ermittelten F0—Verlauf und einmal mit dem durch die Gipfelmuster erzeugten F0—Verlauf resynthetisiert.

Beide Ergebnisse wurden schließlich mehreren Personen vorgespielt. Eines der überraschenden Ergebnisse war die Tatsache, daß bei einer bestimmten Phrase die Version mit dem künstlichen F0—Verlauf bevorzugt, d.h. für die natürliche Kontur gehalten wurde. Abbildung 1 zeigt sowohl die natürliche als auch die künstliche F0-Kontur für eben diese Phrase (*"weil er viel gearbeitet hat"*). Bemerkenswert dabei ist, daß die Abweichungen der beiden Konturen bei *"gearbeitet hat"* vom Hörer praktisch nicht wahrgenommen werden. Die unterschiedliche Höhe des mittleren Gipfels bei *"viel"* ist zwar deutlich zu hören, hier wird aber der künstliche F0—Verlauf bevorzugt.

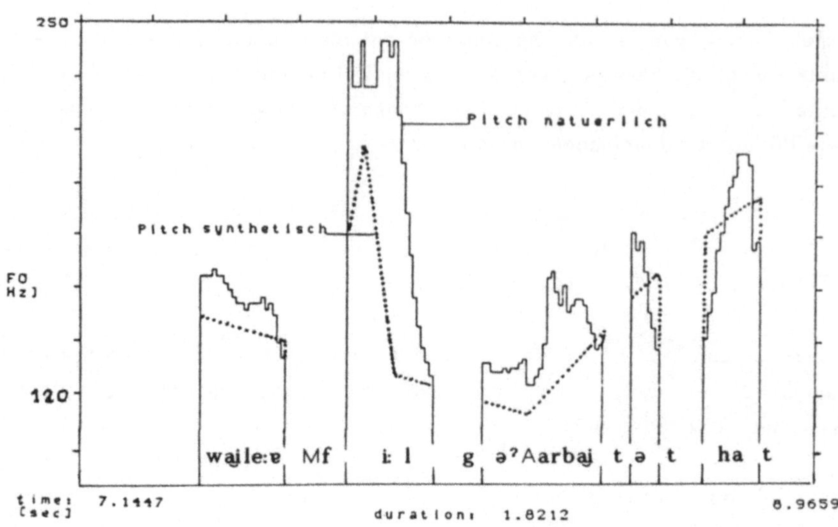

Abb.1: Natürlicher und synthetischer Sprachgrundfrequenzverlauf für die Äußerung:
"*...weil er viel gearbeitet hat*".   (M...mittlerer Gipfel A...Anstiegsmuster)

4.2 Ausblick

Ausgehend von natürlicher Sprache mit gelöschtem Sprachgrundfrequenzverlauf konnte mit dem beschriebenen Verfahren wiederum Sprache mit natürlich klingender Prosodie erzeugt werden. In einem nächsten Schritt soll der künstliche FO-Verlauf synthetischer Sprache aufgeprägt werden. Dabei ist zu erwarten, daß der Einfluß der mangelhaften Dauer- und Intensitätssteuerung und der noch nicht erfaßten Vokalreduktion augenfällig werden wird. Verbesserungen durch eine Einbeziehung der unter 2.2 und 2.3 beschriebenen Effekte sind geplant.

Danksagung

Alle Messungen wurden am Institut für Phonetik und digitale Sprachverarbeitung in Kiel durchgeführt. Für das Entgegenkommen von Prof. K. Kohler und seiner Mitarbeiter und für ihrer Hilfestellung bei der Interpretation der Meßergebnisse sei ihnen an dieser Stelle herzlicher Dank ausgesprochen.

Das Projekt wird vom Fonds zur Förderung der wissenschaftlichen Forschung unterstützt.

Literaturliste:

1. Bauer S., M.Kommenda, A.Pounder: Graphem-Phonem-Umsetzung: Lexikon versus Regelkatalog. Proc. der Jahrestagung der Gesellschaft für Linguistische Datenverarbeitung e.V. Bonn, März 1987. S.18-25.

2. Zinglé, H.: Traitement de la prosodie allemande dans un systèm de synthèse de la parole. Thèse pour le Doctorat d'État, Université de Strasbourg II, 1982.

3. Pierrehumbert J.: Synthesizing Intonation.
J. Acoust. Soc. Am. 70(4), Okt. 1981. S.985 - 995.

4. House J., M. Johnson: Enlivening the Intonation in Text-To-Speech Synthesis, an "Accent-Unit" Model. Proc. of the 11th ICPHS, Se.6.5, Tallin, 1987.

5. Kohler K.J.: Einführung in die Phonetik des Deutschen. Grundlagen der Germanistik, 20. Erich Schmidt Verlag, Berlin 1977.

6. Kohler K.J.: Funktionen von F0-Gipfeln im Deutschen. Proc. Jahrestagung der Gesellschaft für Linguistische Datenverarbeitung e.V., Bonn, März 1987, S.133-140.

7. Kohler K.J., W.J.Barry: Phonetic Data Processing at Kiel University, Developments and Applications. Arbeitsberichte des Instituts für Phonetik und digitale Sprachverarbeitung in Kiel (AIPUK), Nr.22, April 1982.

8. House A.S., G.Fairbanks: The Influenoo of Consonantal Enviroment upon the Secondary Acoustical Characteritics of Vowels. JASA 25, 1953. S.105ff.

9. Gartenberg R.D.: Artikulatorische Fakten in der Ausprägung von Intonationsmustern. Schriftliche Hausarbeit zur Erlangung des Grades eines Magisters Artium der Philosophischen Fakultät der Christian-Albrechts-Universität zu Kiel. 1987.

10.Möbius B., A. Zimmermann, W. Hess: Microprosodic Fundamental Frequency Variation in German. Proc. of the 11th ICPHS in Tallin, 1987. Se. 7.3.

11. Hoequist C.E., K.J.Kohler: Summary of Speech Rate Perception at Kiel.
AIPUK Nr.22, April 1986. S. 7-27.

12.Rietveld A.C.M., F.J. Koopmans van Beinum: Vowel Reduction and Stress. Speech Communication 6, North-Holland, 1987. S.217-229.

Flexible Generierung von natürlichsprachigen Abstracts aus Textrepräsentationsstrukturen[1]

Gabi Sonnenberger
Universität Konstanz
Informationswissenschaft
Projekt TWRM-TOPOGRAPHIC
Postfach 5560
7750 Konstanz

Abstract

Es wird die Generierungskomponente des Volltextinformationssystems TWRM-TOPO-GRAPHIC vorgestellt, die im Retrievaldialog unter Berücksichtigung textueller Wohlge-formtheitsbedingungen benutzerspezifische natürlichsprachige Abstracts erzeugt. Aus-gangsbasis der Generierung sind die vom Textkondensierungssystem TOPIC erstellten Textrepräsentationsstrukturen. Die Generierung wird in zwei Phasen, in eine konzeptuelle und in eine morphosyntaktische Phase, aufgeteilt. Schwerpunkt der Generierung wie auch der Darstellung ist die konzeptuelle Phase mit den Schritten: Identifizierung der relevanten Konzepte aus den Textrepräsentationsstrukturen, Abgleich mit den Benutzerinteressen und Auswahl und Anordnung der relevanten Konzepte im Text mittels Diskursstrategien.

1. Einführung

Vielfach wird gefordert,[2] daß Länge, Komplexität und Abstraktionsniveau eines Abstracts sowie der angebotene Inhalt die jeweiligen Benutzerinteressen reflektieren sollen. Allerdings konnte diese Forderung bisher nicht befriedigend erfüllt werden, da Abstracts in der Regel *einmalig* für *einen* bestimmten Zweck und *einen* angenommenen Benutzertyp angefertigt wurden. Mit der nachfolgend vorgestellten Gene-rierungskomponente des kooperativen Volltextinformationssytems TWRM-TOPOGRAPHIC *(Hammwöh-ner/Thiel 1987)* wird jedoch ein Schritt hin zur Erfüllung dieser Forderung gemacht, indem ausgehend vom selben Text (bzw. dessen Repräsentation) *benutzerangepaßte* Abstracts mit unterschiedlichem The-menschwerpunkt und unterschiedlicher Ausführlichkeit produziert werden. Derart situationsspezifische Abstracts erfordern, im Gegensatz z.B. zum Abstracting-System SUSY *(Fum/Guida/Tasso 1982)*, in dem der Benutzer Schemata angeben muß, die die Textanalyse und die Erstellung des Abstracts steuern, kein Eingreifen des Benutzers, sondern werden durch Auswertung der Vorgaben, die die kooperative Dialogführung des TWRM-TOPOGRAPHIC-Systems[3] aus dem bisherigen Dialogverlauf abgeleitet hat, produziert.

In den ersten, auf statistischen Verfahren beruhenden Ansätzen des automatischen Abstracting, die von *(Luhn 1958)* ausgingen und trotz aller Verbesserungen letztlich unbefriedigend blieben, da sie aus dem Text extrahierte Sätze ohne textuelle Organisation unverbunden nebeneinander stellten, wurde ein Abstract direkt über den Text gewonnen. Die gegenwärtige Beschäftigung mit der Präsentation von

---

[1]   Dieser Beitrag entstand im Rahmen des TWRM-TOPOGRAPHIC-Projekts, das vom Bundesministerium für Forschung und Tech-nologie (Projektträger Gesellschaft für Mathematik und Datenverarbeitung) unter dem Kennzeichen 102 0018 1 gefördert wird.

[2]   z.B. *(DIN 1426 1973)*, *(Fum/Guida/Tasso 1982)* und *(Kuhlen 1984)*

[3]   Auf die kooperative Dialogführung des TWRM-TOPOGRAPHIC-Systems und seine flexible, situationsspezifische Wissenspräsentation (Textwissen wird auf unterschiedlichem Abstraktionsniveau und in der jeweils adäquaten Präsentationsform entweder graphisch, natürlich-sprachig oder tabellarisch aufbereitet dargestellt) wollen wir hier nicht weiter eingehen, s. hierzu *(Hammwöhner/Kuhlen/Thiel 1987)*.

Textwissen[4] läßt, wie *(Kuhlen 1988)* ausführt, einen entscheidenden Paradigmenwechsel erkennen, indem versucht wird, nicht mehr aus den Texten selbst, sondern aus semantischen Repräsentationen der Texte Darstellungen der Textinhalte zu erstellen[5]. Diesen Weg beschreitet auch TWRM-TOPOGRAPHIC, dessen Basis für die Präsentation von Textwissen *semantische Repräsentationsstrukturen* (Textkondensate) sind, die vom Textkondensierungssystem TOPIC erstellt wurden.

Ausgehend von den TOPIC-Textkondensaten wird unter Berücksichtigung *textueller Wohlgeformt-heitsbedingungen* organisierter Text erzeugt, der die speziellen Erwartungen, die an ein Abstract gestellt werden und die in zahlreichen Arbeiten (z.B. *(DIN 1426 1973)*, *(Borko/Chatman 1963)*, *(Pfeiffer-Jäger 1980)*) dokumentiert sind, erfüllt. Diese Arbeiten unterscheiden verschiedene Abstract-Formen; als Haupt-formen werden üblicherweise das indikative und das informative sowie ihre Mischform, das indikativ-informative textuelle Abstract, genannt. Da die TOPIC-Textkondensate, wie nachfolgend erläutert wird, die thematischen Schwerpunkte eines Textes vorwiegend auf indikativem Niveau beschreiben, jedoch auch signifikante Fakteninformation beinhalten können, ist somit die Möglichkeit zur Erzeugung in-dikativer als auch indikativ-informativer Abstracts gegeben. Die Hauptforderung, die an diese beiden Abstracttypen gestellt wird, ist die, den wesentlichen Textinhalt kurz und prägnant anzuzeigen bzw., im Fall des indikativ-informativen Abstracts, auch teilweise wiederzugeben.

2. Repräsentationsstrukturen der TOPIC-Textkondensate

TOPIC *(Hahn/Reimer 1986)* analysiert deutschsprachige Texte, vollständige Zeitschriftenartikel aus dem Gebiet der Informations- und Kommunikationstechnologie, und überführt thematisch zusammen-hängende Textabschnitte in eine Themenbeschreibung,[6] im weiteren auch **Textkonstituente** genannt. Ausgehend von diesen Textkonstituenten wird durch Ableitung weiterer Konstituenten, die in verall-gemeinerter Form die Gemeinsamkeiten der beteiligten Textkonstituenten beschreiben, ein sogenannter **Textgraph** (das Textkondensat) gebildet, dessen Knoten die Textkonstituenten zugeordnet sind. Die Kanten des Textgraphen zeigen die Abstraktionsbeziehungen an, die zwischen den Textkonstituenten existieren. Eine **Themenbeschreibung**, die eine Textkonstituente ausmacht, ist als hierarchisches Netz aufgebaut, dessen Knoten Frames und, je nach Spezifität, auch Slots und Sloteinträge zugeordnet sind, die die thematisch relevanten Konzepte des Textabschnitts repräsentieren. Eine Vernetzung thematisch relevanter Konzepte durch die Ober-/Unterbegriffs- und Prototyp/Instanz-Relation ist ebenfalls möglich. Zur weiteren Erläuterung soll Graphik-1 dienen, die einen Textgraphen-Ausschnitt zeigt, bestehend aus zwei Textkonstituenten, die jeweils einen thematisch zusammenhängenden Textabschnitt beschreiben, und einer abgeleiteten Textkonstituente, die deren Gemeinsamkeit in verallgemeinerter Form beschreibt.

---

[4]   Hier ist bewußt ein allgemeinerer, umfassenderer Ausdruck gewählt worden, weil mit dem Paradigmenwechsel auch andere alternative Formen der Darstellung von Textwissen möglich geworden sind.

[5]   wie z.B. im FRUMP-System (DeJong 1982), das aber von Repräsentationen kürzerer Texte (die meist nur einen Abschnitt umfassen) ausgeht und außerdem keine Abstracts, sondern kurze Zusammenfassungen der Ausgangstexte, in denen Handlungsabläufe im Vordergrund stehen, erstellt.

[6]   Eine ausführlichere Beschreibung der Textkondensierungsergebnisse enthält *(Reimer/Hahn 1988)*.

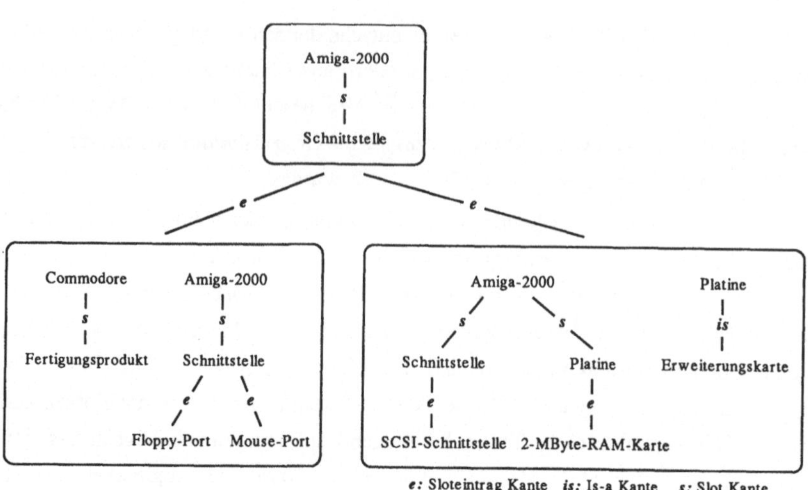

Graphik 1: Textgraphen-Fragment

Die beschriebenen TOPIC-Textkondensate sind zusammen mit dem Volltext in einer Textwissensbasis abgelegt. Aus dieser Wissensbasis werden im TWRM-TOPOGRAPHIC Retrievaldialog aufgrund der Ähnlichkeit zwischen der Suchfrage des Benutzers und der Textrepräsentation diejenigen Repräsentationen ausgewählt, deren Textinhalte geeignet scheinen, die Suchfrage zu beantworten. Zur Beurteilung der Relevanz werden dem Benutzer Abstracts angeboten, die aus den ausgewählten Textgraphen generiert werden.

3. Generierung natürlichsprachiger Abstracts aus den TOPIC-Textkondensaten im TWRM-TOPOGRAPHIC Retrievaldialog

Zwar liegt mit dem TOPIC-Textgraphen bereits eine kondensierte Textrepräsentation vor, da aber TOPIC die Relevanz eines Konzeptes bezüglich eines Textabschnitts beurteilt, können im Textgraphen auch Themenbeschreibungen enthalten sein, die zwar für einen Textabschnitt, aber nicht für den gesamten Text von zentraler Bedeutung sind. Da es Ziel eines Abstracts ist, den wesentlichen Textinhalt (mit gegebenenfalls signifikanter Fakteninformation) bereitzustellen, müssen deshalb zunächst die zentralen Textthemen und die zu ihnen gehörigen Konzepte identifiziert werden. Diese bezüglich des Textes relevanten Textthemen sind je nach Interessensschwerpunkt und gewünschter Ausführlichkeit jedoch nicht für jeden Benutzer gleichermaßen relevant, so daß eine weitere Bewertung durch Analyse der Vorgaben der Dialogführung (z.B. der Suchfrage des Benutzers) zur Bestimmung der aktuell relevanten Konzepte stattfinden muß.

Nachdem entschieden ist, welche Konzepte im Abstract ausgedrückt werden sollen, muß ein **Textplan** erstellt werden, der festlegt[7]

- welche Konzepte zusammengehören und in einem Satz ausgedrückt werden sollen,

---

[7]   Vgl. zur skizzierten Problematik auch *(Clippinger/McDonald 1983)*, *(Cook/Lehnert/McDonald 1984)*, *(Danlos 1984)*, *(Mann/Moore 1981)* und *(McKeown 1986)*.

- welche lexikalischen und syntaktischen Realisierungen am besten geeignet sind, die Beziehung zwischen den Konzepten auszudrücken,
- in welcher Reihenfolge die Sätze angeordnet werden sollen, wie sie zusammenhängen und wie dies verdeutlicht werden kann.

Es muß also die Generierung von zusammenhängendem Text gewährleistet werden, der sowohl die Expansion der einzelnen Textthemen und ihre Abgrenzung gegenüber anderen Themen (**Textkohäsion**), als auch die textuelle Relationierung der Themen (**Textkohärenz**) erkennen läßt,[8] und darüberhinaus die speziellen Anforderungen, die an ein Abstract gestellt werden, erfüllt.

3.1 Textgenerierungs-Modell

Die Textgenerierung wird in dem nachfolgend detaillierter dargestellten Modell in zwei Phasen, in eine konzeptuelle und in eine morphosyntaktische Phase, aufgeteilt.[9] In der **konzeptuellen Phase** wird entschieden, welche Konzepte aus dem Textgraphen im Abstract ausgedrückt, wie sie gruppiert und angeordnet werden sollen, und welche lexikalischen und syntaktischen Realisierungen geeignet sind, diesen Inhalt auszudrücken. Aufgabe der **morphosyntaktischen Phase** ist die Transformation der erarbeiteten Struktur in natürliche Sprache.

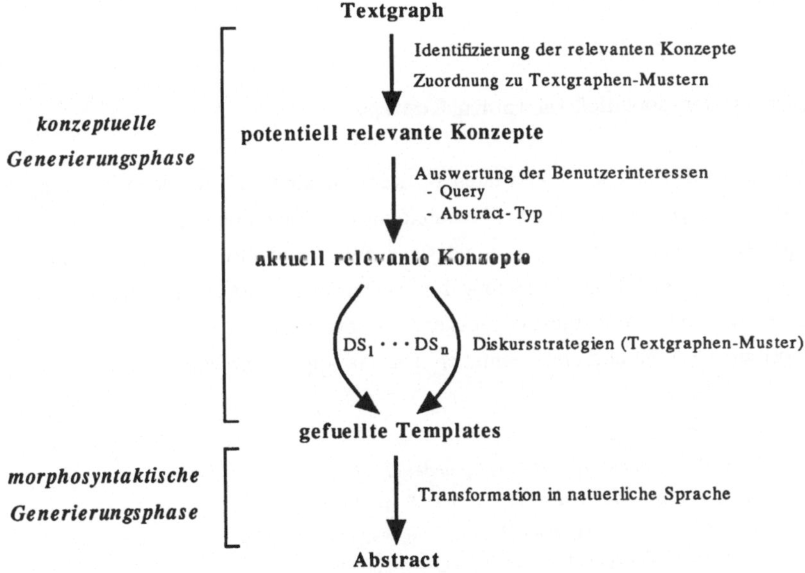

Graphik 2: Textgenerierungs-Modell

---

[8] Zur Unterscheidung von Textkohäsion und Textkohärenz s. a. (Hobbs 1983).

[9] Die Aufgabenteilung folgt im wesentlichen der in *(McKeown 1986)*.

Die angestrebte Funktionalität erfordert keine vollständig natürlichsprachige Generierung, so daß hier bei der Generierung vorgefertigte Satzmuster (**Templates**) verwendet werden, die Lücken enthalten, in welche die ausgewählten Konzepte eingesetzt werden.

Das hier kurz skizzierte Textgenerierungs-Modell legt den Schwerpunkt auf die Erstellung des Textplans, dementsprechend konzentriert sich die weitere Darstellung ganz auf die konzeptuelle Generierungsphase.

3.2 Konzeptuelle Generierungsphase

Da im Abstract der wesentliche Textinhalt kurz und prägnant angezeigt bzw. wiedergegeben werden soll, werden in einem ersten Schritt der konzeptuellen Phase die zentralen Textthemen und die zu ihnen gehörigen Konzepte identifiziert, also diejenigen Konzepte bestimmt, die aufgrund ihrer Bedeutung im Text **potentiell relevant** sind. Danach werden aus ihnen durch Auswertung der Vorgaben der Dialogführung, die die Benutzerinteressen reflektieren, diejenigen bestimmt, die für die gegebene Dialogsituation **aktuell relevant** sind.

Die ausgewählten relevanten Konzepte werden aufgrund ihrer thematischen Relationierung typischen Mustern zugeordnet. Speziell auf die verschiedenen Muster abgestimmte **Diskursstrategien**[10] steuern sowohl die Auswahl und Anordnung der Konzepte im Text als auch das Einsetzen der Konzepte in adäquate Templates.

3.2.1 Bestimmung der potentiell relevanten Konzepte

Die Bestimmung der potentiell relevanten Konzepte beginnt mit der Identifizierung der zentralen Textthemen. Ein Konzept aus einer Themenbeschreibung des Textgraphen soll als ein zentrales Textthema (**Hauptthema**) gelten, wenn es im Text in mindestens zwei Abschnitten als thematisch relevant bewertet wurde (also nicht nur von lokaler Bedeutung ist), selbst durch andere thematisch relevante Konzepte näher spezifiziert wird und darüberhinaus genügend spezifisch ist, um Aussagekraft zu besitzen. Formal lautet die Regel zur Bestimmung eines zentralen Themas folgendermaßen:

$$main\_topic\,(Main\_Topic) :\Longleftrightarrow$$
$$\exists tg\_node,\ tg\_node',\ tg\_node'' \in tg\_nodes\,(TG) :$$
$$\exists graph \in graphs\,(tg\_node) : \exists graph' \in graphs\,(tg\_node') :$$
$$\exists graph'' \in graphs\,(tg\_node'') : \exists i,\ i' \in tbg\_nodes\,(graph) :$$
$$\exists j \in tbg\_nodes\,(graph') : \exists k \in tbg\_nodes\,(graph'') :$$
$$\neg\,(tg\_node = tg\_node') \wedge \neg\,(tg\_node = tg\_node'') \wedge \neg\,(tg\_node' = tg\_node'') \wedge$$
$$Main\_Topic = j = i' \wedge is\_slot\_link\,(i,\ i') \wedge$$
$$(is\_a\,(j,\ k) \vee inst\,(j,\ k))$$

---

[10] Bei der Textgenerierung werden vielfach Diskursstrategien zur Auswahl der Informationen aus dem relevanten Ausschnitt der Wissensbasis und zu ihrer Anordnung im Text verwendet (vgl. z.B. *(Mann 1984)* und *(McKeown 1986)*).

Anschließend werden die zu einem Hauptthema gehörigen Konzepte bestimmt und gemäß ihrer Relation zum Hauptthema unterteilt in:[11]

- **Generische Klasse** (Prototyp oder Oberbegriff des Hauptthemas)
- **Hauptthema**
- **Merkmal** (ein Slot des Hauptthemas)
- **konkrete Angabe zu einem Merkmal** (Sloteintrag zu einem Merkmal)

Sind die potentiell relevanten Konzepte des Textgraphen derart bestimmt und thematischen Blöcken zugeordnet, werden aufgrund der Relationierung dieser Blöcke verschiedene, typische Textgraphen-Muster unterschieden:[12]

- **Einzelnes Hauptthema:**
  Bei der Klassifizierung des Textgraphen wird ein einziges Hauptthema bestimmt, das durch Merkmale und konkrete Angaben zu den Merkmalen näher spezifiziert wird.

- **Vergleichende Gegenüberstellung mehrerer verwandter Hauptthemen:**
  Bei diesem Muster werden mehrere Hauptthemen bestimmt, die alle derselben generischen Klasse angehören. Da sie darüberhinaus auch gemeinsame Merkmale besitzen, kann daraus geschlossen werden, daß die Hauptthemen vergleichend gegenübergestellt werden.

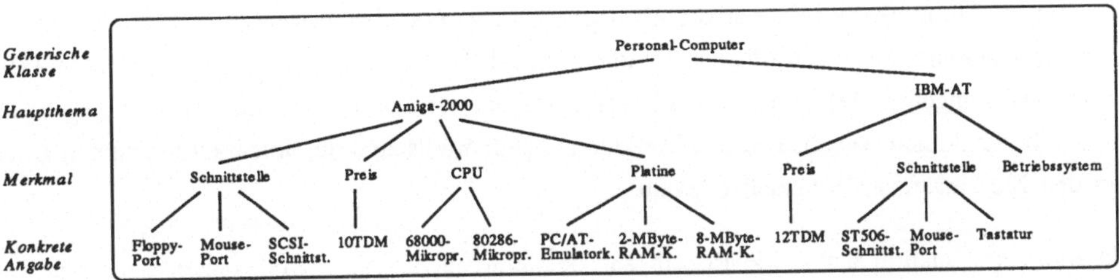

Graphik 3: Beispiel für die Relationierung der potentiell relevanten Konzepte im Textgraphen-Muster "Vergleichende Gegenüberstellung mehrerer verwandter Hauptthemen"

- **Mehrere, einfach linear relationierte Hauptthemen:**
  Auch hier werden bei der Klassifizierung des Textgraphen mehrere Hauptthemen bestimmt. Dabei ist eines der näher spezifizierenden Konzepte des einen Hauptthemas ein anderes Hauptthema des Textgraphen, das wiederum näher spezifiziert wird. Gibt es mehr als zwei Hauptthemen, sind sie fortlaufend auf diese Weise relationiert.

---

[11] Die Regeln zur Bestimmung dieser Kategorien von potentiell relevanten Konzepten sind ebenfalls formal beschrieben, s. hierzu *(Sonnenberger 1988)*

[12] Diese Muster stellen Grundmuster dar, aus denen sich durch Kombination weitere, komplexere Muster ableiten lassen.

3.2.2 Auswahl der aktuell relevanten Konzepte

Nachdem die für die Generierung eines Abstracts potentiell relevanten Konzepte bestimmt sind, werden die Vorgaben der Dialogführung ausgewertet, um aus ihnen diejenigen auszuwählen, die für die gegebene Dialogsituation aktuell relevant sind. Derzeit vorgesehen sind optionale Angaben über den gewünschten Abstract-Typ sowie die Query (Suchfrage) des Benutzers in Form semantisch relationierter Konzepte.

- **Abgleich mit der Query:**
  Durch den Abgleich mit der Query werden aus den potentiell relevanten Konzepten diejenigen ausgewählt, die geeignet sind die Suchfrage des Benutzers zu beantworten, die anderen aber eliminiert. Damit es nicht zu einer Überbewertung der Relevanz des nachgewiesenen Textes kommt, muß jedoch auch der Teil des Textinhaltes angezeigt werden, der keinen direkten Bezug zur Suchfrage hat; d.h. es werden unter Beibehaltung der thematischen Relationierung die gesuchten Textthemen so detailliert wie möglich, die anderen nur so detailliert wie nötig beschrieben.

- **Abstract-Typ:**
  Der Parameter 'Abstract-Typ', für den die Werte 'indikativ' oder 'indikativ-informativ' angegeben werden können, beeinflußt die Ausführlichkeit des zu generierenden Abstracts. Von einem indikativen Abstract wird erwartet, den wesentlichen Textinhalt anzuzeigen, ohne jedoch konkrete Informationen zu nennen. Ein indikativ-informatives Abstracts soll ebenfalls den wesentlichen Textinhalt anzeigen, aber darüberhinaus zu den wichtigsten Textthemen auch (im Ausgangstext enthaltene) konkrete Detailinformation angeben. Dementsprechend wird auch hier verfahren: Wird 'indikativ' angegeben, entfallen die konkreten Angaben zu den Merkmalen, andernfalls sind die potentiell relevanten Angaben zu den Merkmalen auch aktuell relevant.

In formaler Notation lauten die Regeln zur Bestimmung der aktuell relevanten Konzepte folgendermaßen:[13]

$$
\begin{aligned}
&akt\_rel\_feature\,(Feature,\ Main\_Topic,\ TG\_Pattern,\ Query) :\Longleftrightarrow \\
&\qquad main\_topic\,(Main\_Topic) \wedge pot\_rel\_feature\,(Feature,\ Main\_Topic) \wedge \\
&\qquad (\ TG\_Pattern = comparison \wedge \forall M' : main\_topic\,(M') \wedge \\
&\qquad\ pot\_rel\_feature\,(Feature,\ M') \vee \\
&\qquad\ main\_topic\_in\_focus\,(Main\_Topic,\ Query) \vee \\
&\qquad\ \neg\exists M'' : main\_topic\,(M'') \wedge main\_topic\_in\_focus\,(M'',Query))
\end{aligned}
$$

---

[13] Die bestimmten Hauptthemen des Textes und deren generische Klassen sind, wie oben erläutert wurde, unabhängig von den Vorgaben der Dialogführung in jedem Fall aktuell relevant, so daß sich die Beschreibung zur Bestimmung der aktuell relevanten Konzepte auf die Kategorien 'Merkmal' und 'konkrete Angabe' beschränkt.

$$akt\_rel\_value\,(Value,\ Feature,\ Main\_Topic,\ TG\_Pattern,\ Query,\ Abstract\_Typ) :\Longleftrightarrow$$
$$(TG\_Pattern = comparison \lor TG\_Pattern = single) \land$$
$$Abstract\_Typ = ind. - inform. \land main\_topic\,(Main\_Topic) \land$$
$$akt\_rel\_feature\,(Feature,\ Main\_Topic,\ TG\_Pattern,\ Query) \land$$
$$pot\_rel\_value\,(Value,\ Feature,\ Main\_Topic) \land$$
$$(\ main\_topic\_in\_focus\,(Main\_Topic,\ Query) \lor$$
$$\neg\exists M' : main\_topic\,(M') \land main\_topic\_in\_focus\,(M',\ Query)\,) \land$$
$$(\ feature\_in\_focus\,(Feature,\ Main\_Topic,\ Query) \lor$$
$$\neg\exists F' : pot\_rel\_feature\,(F',\ Main\_Topic) \land$$
$$feature\_in\_focus\,(F',\ Main\_Topic,\ Query)\,)$$

Werden diese Regeln auf die in Graphik-3 dargestellten potentiell relevanten Konzepte angewendet, ergeben sich für die angegebene Query folgende aktuell relevante Konzepte:

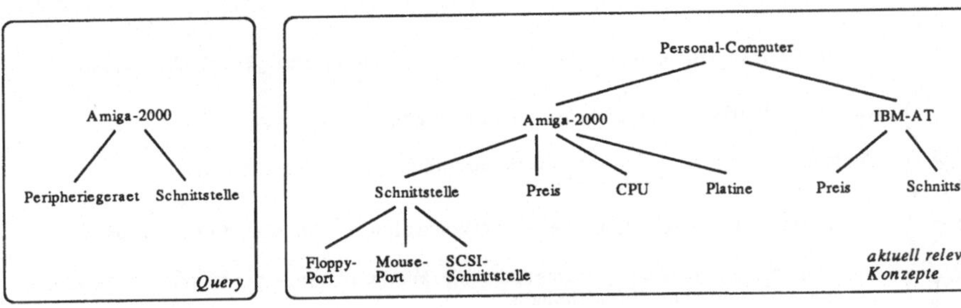

Graphik 4: Beispiel zur Bestimmung der aktuell relevanten Konzepte

3.2.3 Diskursstrategien

Dem beschriebenen Auswahlmechanismus zur Bestimmung der relevanten Konzepte ist eine Ordnung der Konzepte inhärent, da die ausgewählten Konzepte verschiedenen Themenblöcken zugeordnet werden, und die Themenblöcke aufgrund ihrer thematischen Relationierung typische Muster bilden. Mit der dadurch erarbeiteten Struktur ist die Basis für die Generierung von kohäsivem und kohärentem Text gegeben, da sowohl die Expansion der einzelnen Themen als auch ihre Relationierung erkennbar ist. Daneš *(Daneš 1974)* hat die Anordnung und Relationierung von Themen in Texten untersucht und dabei drei Haupttypen der thematischen Progression erarbeitet, die ebenfalls kombiniert werden können. Diese drei Haupttypen der thematischen Progression korrespondieren mit den zuvor vorgestellten Textgraphen-Mustern:

Thematisches Progressionsmuster:	Textgraphen-Muster:
konstantes Thema	einzelnes Hauptthema
einfache lineare Progression	mehrere, einfach linear relationierte Hauptthemen
abgeleitetes Thema	vergleichende Gegenueberstellung mehrerer verwandter Hauptthemen

Ursprünglich wurden die thematischen Progressionsmuster bei der Analyse bzw. Beschreibung von Texten verwendet; hier dienten sie dazu, Kriterien abzuleiten für eine sinnvolle lineare Anordnung der Themenblöcke im Text. Aus der Zuordnung der typischen Muster zu den thematischen Progressionsmustern von Daneš und der Operationalisierung der Konventionen[14] zur Erstellung eines Abstracts wurden Regeln in Form von Diskursstrategien abgeleitet, die die lineare Anordnung sowohl der Themenblöcke als auch der einzelnen Konzepte im Text steuern. Durch speziell auf die verschiedenen typischen Muster abgestimmte Diskursstrategien wird im letzten Schritt der konzeptuellen Phase die Generierung von zusammenhängendem Text realisiert. Mit jedem Schritt einer Diskursstrategie werden zusammengehörige Konzepte und ein dazu passendes Template ausgewählt, in dessen Lücken die Konzepte eingesetzt werden. Für das Textgraphen-Muster "Vergleichende Gegenüberstellung mehrerer verwandter Hauptthemen" lautet z.B. die Diskursstrategie, als vereinfachtes Übergangsnetzwerk dargestellt, folgendermaßen:[15]

Graphik 5: Diskursstrategie zur Behandlung des Textgraphen-Musters "Vergleichende Gegenüberstellung mehrerer verwandter Hauptthemen"

Die in den einzelnen Schritten der Diskursstrategie ausgewählten und gefüllten Templates bilden zusammen ein Text-Template, das von der morphosyntaktischen Phase in natürliche Sprache transformiert wird. Die Arbeitsweise der Diskursstrategien soll an nachfolgendem Beispiel verdeutlicht werden, das einen Schritt der oben genannten Strategie detaillierter beschreibt.

Beispiel

Durch Anwendung der Diskursstrategie auf die aktuell relevanten Konzepte in Graphik-4 wird im ersten Schritt das Template[16]

"Der Artikel handelt über ((?ART_DET) (GENERIC_CLASS)) (MAIN_TOPICS)."

---

[14] wie z.B. der, daß in indikativ-informativen Abstracts der indikative Teil vor dem informativen stehen soll.

[15] Den Übergängen auf der rechten Seite des Netzwerks ist die Ausführung des angegebenen Schrittes der Diskursstrategie zugeordnet, wohingegen denen der linken Seite keine Aktionen zugeordnet sind.

[16] Die Darstellung der Templates ist leicht vereinfacht; zur Notation der Templates, wie auch der morphosyntaktischen Phase s. *(Sonnenberger 1988)*.

ausgewählt. Die Platzhalter des Templates, "MAIN_TOPICS" und "GENERIC_CLASS", (die anzeigen an welcher Stelle, mit welcher Kategorie von relevanten Konzepten und mit wievielen Konzepten die Lücken gefüllt werden können) werden durch die in diesem Schritt ausgewählten Konzepte "Personal-Computer" (gemeinsame generische Klasse der Hauptthemen) sowie "Amiga-2000" und "IBM-AT" (Hauptthemen) ersetzt, so daß das Template anschließend lautet:

"Der Artikel handelt über ((?ART_DET) (Personal-Computer)) (Amiga-2000, IBM-AT)."

Nach Ausführung der weiteren Schritte dieser Diskursstrategie und Transformation in der morphosyntaktischen Phase ergibt sich folgendes Abstract (die aus dem Textgraphen ausgewählten Konzepte sind kursiv gesetzt):[17]

Der Artikel handelt über die *Personal-Computer Amiga-2000* und *IBM-AT*. Die *Schnittstellen* und die *Preise* der *Personal-Computer* werden vergleichend gegenübergestellt. Für den *Amiga-2000* gibt es die *Schnittstellen Mouse-Port*, *Floppy-Port* und *SCSI-Schnittstelle*. Ausserdem wird auf die *Platinen* und auf die *CPUs* des *Amiga-2000* eingegangen.

4. Zusammenfassung

Es ist eine Textgenerierungskomponente vorgestellt worden,[18] die aus semantischen Textrepräsentationsstrukturen unter Berücksichtigung textueller Wohlgeformtheitsbedingungen benutzerspezifische Abstracts erzeugt, indem

- aus der Textrepräsentation die zentralen Textthemen und die ihnen zugehörigen Konzepte bestimmt werden,
- ein Abgleich der textrelevanten Konzepte mit den Benutzerinteressen stattfindet,
- aufgrund der thematischen Relationierung der Konzepte verschiedene typische Muster unterschieden werden und
- speziell auf die verschiedenen Muster abgestimmte Diskursstrategien unter Verwendung von Templates die Produktion von kohäsivem und kohärentem Text steuern.

---

[17] Zum Vergleich, wären in der Diskursstrategie die *potentiell* relevanten und nicht die *aktuell* relevanten Konzepte berücksichtigt worden, würde das Abstract lauten:
"Der Artikel handelt über die *Personal-Computer Amiga-2000* und *IBM-AT*. Die *Schnittstellen* und die *Preise* der *Personal-Computer* werden vergleichend gegenübergestellt. Für den *Amiga-2000* gibt es die *Schnittstellen Floppy-Port*, *Mouse-Port* und *SCSI-Schnittstelle*. Der *IBM-AT* hat die *Schnittstellen Tastatur*, *Mouse-Port* und *ST506-Schnittstelle*. Als *Preis* wird für den *Amiga-2000 10.000DM* und für den *IBM-AT 12.000DM* genannt. Ausserdem wird auf das *Betriebssystem* des *IBM-AT* sowie auf die *Platinen* und auf die *CPUs* des *Amiga-2000* eingegangen. Es gibt die *Platinen PC/AT-Emulatorkarte*, *2-MByte-RAM-Karte* und *8-MByte-RAM-Karte* für den *Amiga-2000*. Der *68000-Mikroprozessor* und der *80286-Mikroprozessor* sind die *CPUs* dieses *Personal-Computers*."

[18] Zur Realisierung des Modells wurde in beiden Phasen ein einheitlicher Grammatikformalismus (Augmented Transition Networks) verwendet; die Implementierung erfolgte auf einem CADMUS-Rechner 9200 in PROLOG.

Literaturverzeichnis

Borko, H. / Chatman, S. (1963): Criteria for Acceptable Abstracts: A Survey of Abstracters' Instructions.
In: American Documentation. April 1963, pp.149-160

Clippinger, J.H.Jr. / McDonald, D.D. (1983): Why Good Writing is Easier to Understand.
In: Proceedings of the 8th International Joint Conference on Artifical Intelligence. Karlsruhe, 1983, pp.730-732

Cook, M.E. / Lehnert, W.G. / McDonald, D.D. (1984): Conveying Implicit Content in Narrative Summaries.
In: COLING-84: Proceedings of the 10th International Conference on Computational Linguistics. Stanford, 1984, pp.5-7

Daneš, F. (1974): Functional Sentence Perspective and the Organization of the Text.
In: F. Daneš (ed): Papers on Functional Sentence Perspective. Prague: Academia, 1974, pp.106-128

Danlos, L. (1984): Conceptual and Linguistic Decisions in Generation.
In: COLING-84: Proceedings of the 10th International Conference on Computational Linguistics. Stanford, 1984, pp.501-504

DeJong, G. (1982): An Overview of the FRUMP System.
In: W. Lehnert; M. Ringle (eds.): Strategies for Natural Language Processing. Hillsdale/NJ, London: Erlbaum, 1982, pp.149–176

DIN 1426 (1973): Inhaltsangaben in Information und Dokumentation. Berlin: Beuth, 1973

Fum, D. / Guida, G. / Tasso, C. (1982): Forward and Backward Reasoning in Automatic Abstracting.
In: J. Horecky (ed.): COLING-82: Proceedings of the 9th International Conference on Computational Linguistics. Prague, 1982, pp.83–88

Hahn, U. / Reimer, U. (1986): TOPIC Essentials.
In: COLING-86: Proceedings of the 11th International Conference on Computational Linguistics. Bonn, August 1986, pp.497-503

Hammwöhner, R. / Kuhlen, R. / Thiel U. (1987): TWRM-TOPGRAPHIC: Automatische Textkondensierung mit flexiblem graphikgestütztem Retrieval und Wissenspräsentation.
Universität Konstanz, Informationswissenschaft (Bericht TOPOGRAPHIC-8/87), 1987

Hammwöhner, R. / Thiel, U. (1987): Content Oriented Relations between Text Units — a Structural Model for Hypertexts.
In: Hypertexts '87 Papers, Chapel Hill/North Carolina. 1987, pp.155–174

Hobbs, J. R. (1983): Why is Discourse Coherent?
In: Neubauer (ed.): Coherence in Natural Language Texts. Hamburg: Buske, 1983, pp.29–70

Kuhlen, R. (1984): Some Similarities and Differences between Intellectual and Machine Text Understanding for the Purpose of Abstracting.
In: Proc. IRFIS 5, Heidelberg 1983. Amsterdam: North-Holland, 1984, pp.87-109

Kuhlen, R. (1988) Information Retrieval: Verfahren des Abstracting.
Erscheint in: W. Lenders (ed.): Computational Linguistics, Handbücher zur Sprach- und Kommunikationswissenschaft, Berlin etc.: de Gruyter, 1988

Luhn, H. P. (1958): The Automatic Creation of Literature Abstracts.
In: IBM Journal of Research and Development 2. 1958, pp.159–165

Mann, W.C. / Moore, J.A. (1981): Computer Generation of Multiparagraph English Text.
In: American Journal of Computational Linguistics 7, Nr.1. 1981, pp.17-29.

Mann, W.C. (1984): Discourse Structures for Text Generation.
In: COLING-84: Proceedings of the 10th International Conference on Computational Linguistics. Stanford, 1984, pp.367-375

McKeown, K.R. (1986): Language Generation: Applications, Issues, and Approaches.
In: Proceedings of the IEEE, Vol. 74, No. 7. 1986, pp.961-968

Pfeiffer-Jäger, G. (1980): Referat und Referieren.
In: Germanistische Linguistik 1-2. 1980, pp.1-180

Reimer, U. / Hahn, U. (1988): Text Condensation as Knowledge Base Abstraction.
In: Proc. of the CAIA-88: 4th Conference on Artificial Intelligence Applications. San Diego/California, March 14–18, 1988

Sonnenberger, G. (1988): Generierung von natürlichsprachigen Abstracts mittels Templates aus Frame-Repräsentationsstrukturen einer Textwissensbasis.
Universität Konstanz, Informationswissenschaft (Bericht TOPOGRAPHIC-10/88, in Bearb.), 1988

Anwendung einer logischen Grammatik zur Generierung deutscher Texte

Konrad Jablonski, Armin Rau, Johannes Ritzke
Nixdorf Computer AG, Paderborn
Abt. Expertensysteme/Man-Machine-Interface

1. Einleitung

Im Beitrag wird anhand des Systems NUGGET (Natural language User friendly Generator of GErman Text) gezeigt, in welchem Maß und in welcher Form eine logische Grammatik als Basis für die Generierung natürlichsprachlicher Texte des Deutschen eingesetzt werden kann. NUGGET umfaßt Module zur Herstellung einer semantisch-pragmatischen Standardrepräsentation, zur Textorganisation, zur Erzeugung syntaktischer Strukturbeschreibungen aus der Standardrepräsentation, zur Vereinfachung der Strukturbeschreibungen durch Pronominalisierung und zur Erzeugung morphologisch korrekter Lexemketten. Das Modul zur syntaktischen Strukturbeschreibung basiert auf einer Definite Clause Grammar (DCG). Das Gesamtsystem NUGGET fungiert als Textgenerierungskomponente im Beratungssystem WISBER (*), das im Rahmen eines BMFT-Projekts als Prototyp entwickelt wurde. Die Komponente selbst ist vollimplementiert in Prolog und wurde über den Anwendungsrahmen in WISBER hinaus als eigenständige Komponente zur Produktreife gebracht und für entsprechende Anwendungen zur Verfügung gestellt wie z.B. als natürlichsprachliche Erklärungskomponente der Expertensystemshell TWAICE (**) im aktuellen Release (vgl. näher in JABLONSKI/RAU/RITZKE 1987, 1988). NUGGET bestimmt, WIE ein Text generiert werden soll. Dies betrifft die Komponente der Generierung, die im Rahmen einer Klassifizierung wie bei McKeown (MCKEOWN 1985:7) taktische Generierung genannt wird. Die taktische Generierung baut auf einer strategischen Komponente auf, die das WAS der Äußerung bestimmt, d.h. die semantisch-pragmatischen Informationen (Inhalte und Funktionen) liefert, nach denen in der taktischen Komponente die Form des Textes bestimmt wird.

NUGGET besitzt zur strategischen Komponente einer jeweiligen Applikation eine nach dem Blackboardprinzip konzipierte und genau definierte Schnittstelle, über die semantisch-pragmatische Repräsentationen übertragen werden. Die Repräsentation ist in der propositionalen Sprache ARPS (Anwendungsorientierte Repräsentation für Pragmatik und Semantik) geschrieben bzw. wird in diese übersetzt. ARPS ist eine eigens entwickelte Repräsentationssprache mit Operator-Operanden-Strukturen, die Inhalte von Texten, pragmatische und textuelle Funktionen von Textteilen und situative Informationen repräsentieren (s. 3.4).

Bisher realisierte natürlichsprachliche Systeme verfügen meist nicht über Textgenerierungsmodule mit umfangreichen syntaktischen Subkomponenten. Da es sich hier in der Regel um prototypische Realisierungen handelt, an denen das Funktionieren des Systems im Prinzip gezeigt werden soll, ergibt sich keine zwingende Notwendigkeit, Texte größeren Umfangs zu generieren, also in der im erwähnten Sinn taktischen Komponente einen umfangreichen Sprachausschnitt zu bearbeiten. Soll allerdings ein System in der Lage sein, einen großen Sprachausschnitt abzudecken, wie es von einem produktreifen System erwartet wird, ist es notwendig, auch die Komponente, die das WIE der Textgenerierung betrifft, in größerem Umfang zu realisieren. Wichtige Konstruktionskriterien sind dabei die Dimension und Form einer hier eigenständigen syntaktischen Komponente sowie ihr Zusammenwirken mit Semantik und Pragmatik bzw. Morphologie.

2. Einsatz einer logischen Grammatik zur Textgenerierung

Logische Grammatiken gehen zurück auf die "Metamorphosis Grammars" von Colmerauer (COLMERAUER 1978), aus denen heraus sich ein Paradigma unterschiedlicher logischer Grammatiken entwickelte, unter denen die Definite Clause Grammar (DCG, PEREIRA/WARREN 1980, PEREIRA/SHIEBER 1987) und ihre Derivate (z.B. EXtraposition Grammar (XP) PEREIRA 1981) die bekanntesten und erprobtesten sind (vgl. dazu GAZDAR 1987:1172, SHIEBER 1985:33). Eine DCG zeichnet sich durch drei Eigenschaften aus, die sie als Mittel zur Beschreibung natürlicher Sprache und als Grundlage auch für die Generierung relevant machen:

- Nonterminale Symbole können Argumente besitzen, wodurch es möglich wird, bei der Abarbeitung der Grammatik einen Strukturbaum zu verwalten,
- über Argumente können ebenfalls Agreements definiert werden, so daß Grammatikregeln kontextabhängig werden,
- den Grammatikregeln können zusätzliche Bedingungen assoziiert werden, die in arbiträrem Prologcode formuliert sind (vgl. dazu auch BLOCK/GEHRKE/HAUGENEDER/HUNZE 1985).

Neben der Tatsache, daß die DCG als Sprachbeschreibungsmittel beim Parsing (vgl. STERLING/SHAPIRO 1986) und -wenn auch nur als Teilkomponente eines Generierungssystems und in kleinerem Rahmen- auch für die Generierung (vgl. DERR/MCKEOWN 1984) benutzt wurde, gaben diese Eigenschaften den Ausschlag, in NUGGET als Kern zur syntaktischen Generierung die DCG als unifikationsbasierte Grammatik zu wählen. Darüberhinaus begünstigte der in vielen Prolog-Dialekten vorhandene Präcompiler, der deklarativ formulierte Grammatikregeln in Prolog-Klauseln umsetzt, diese Entscheidung. Darüberhinaus legt die Prolog-Umgebung die Wahl einer logischen Grammatik nahe, da hier der Inferenzmechnismus von Prolog als Parser bzw. Algorithmus zur Generierung effizient nutzbar ist:

> *A beautiful characteristic of logic programming is that grammars*
> *for natural (and artifical) languages can be expressed easily as*
> *logic programs...Thus analysis and synthesis are forms of infe-*
> *rence, and grammars, being simply axiom systems, are declarative*
> *in nature ... Furthermore, analysis and synthesis can be quite*
> *efficient when the logic programming language is Prolog and the*
> *grammar is expressed directly as a Prolog program. (WALKER (ed.)*
> *et al. 1987:316)*

Die in NUGGET realisierte DCG deckt den durch die derzeitigen Aufgaben - (Generierung umfangreicher Erklärungstexte in einem Expertensystem mit einer mittleren
Länge von ca. einem Bildschirm und Generierung von flexiblen Systemäußerungen in
einem Beratungssystem) - abgesteckten Sprachausschnitt des Deutschen mit ca. 250
Regeln ab. Daraus ergibt sich eine generative Mächtigkeit von ca. 300 000 Strukturbeschreibungen, wenn man Regelrekursionen nicht mitzählt, und folgender Leistungsumfang:

Aussagesaetze, Entscheidungs- und Ergänzungsfragesaetze, kausale Nebensaetze und
Korrelatsaetze mit Vollverben; Aussagesaetze, Entscheidungs- und Ergänzungsfragesaetze, kausale und konditionale Nebensaetze, Korrelatsaetze, Objekt- und Rela-
tivsaetze mit Kopula; beliebige Koordination aller Haupt- und Nebensaetze; je
Teilsatz bis zu sieben Nominalkomplexe, die selbst aus beliebig vielen koordi-
nierten Nominalkonstruktionen bestehen können; bis zu fünf Nominalkomplexe können
dabei Präpositionalphrasen sein; Nominalkonstruktionen können komplex (NP +
Genitiv-NP), einfach und quantifiziert sein, sowie definit, indefinit bzw. ohne
Artikel stehen; Relativsatzanschluß an jede NP ist möglich; Modalisierung der
Vollverben (auch zweifach)

Das für diesen Leistungsumfang erforderliche Vokabular wird je nach Anwendungsdo-
mäne aus einem 6000 Einträge umfassenden Grundwortschatz extrahiert und um dort
nicht verzeichnete Lexeme durch ein graphisch unterstütztes Lexikonentwicklungsmo-
dul semiautomatisch ergänzt. Das domänenspezifische Laufzeitlexikon umfaßt jeweils
einige hundert Einträge.

3. Beschreibung sprachlicher Phänomene durch eine Definite Clause Grammar

Bei der hier angestrebten Evaluierung der Definite Clause Grammar bezüglich eines
umfangreichen Ausschnitts der deutschen Sprache sind zwei Betrachtungsebenen zu
unterscheiden. Zum einen ist eine logische Grammatik auf der Grundlage von Horn-
Klauseln (Definite Clauses) ein Formalismus zur Beschreibung einer (natürlichen)
Sprache und ihrer Regelhaftigkeiten. Dies betrifft die deklarative Interpretier-
barkeit der DCG, wodurch sie sich z.B. von ATN's unterscheidet:

However, unlike an ATN, a DCG can also be understood as a description of a language. (...) As Woods put it (referring to CFG's), 'by looking at a rule, the consequences of that rule for the types of construction that are permitted are immediately apparent'. (PEREIRA/WARREN 1980; S.259)

Zum anderen liegt bei der DCG zusätzlich eine prozedurale Interpretation nahe, bei der die Verwendung der Grammatik-Regeln im Rahmen eines Parsing- oder Generierungs-Programms betrachtet wird. Diese Interpretation ergibt sich v.a. aus der Tatsache, daß eine im DCG-Formalismus niedergeschriebene Grammatik je nach Codierungsart entweder direkt als logisches Programm anzusehen ist oder durch einen Compile-Vorgang in ein logisches Programm überführt wird, das dann von einem Prolog-Interpreter ausgeführt werden kann.

Diese problemlose Überführung einer deklarativen Beschreibung einer natürlichen Sprache in ein ausführbares Programm zur Analyse oder Generierung von Sätzen der entsprechenden Sprache ist einerseits die große Stärke der DCG, andererseits führt sie leicht zur Vermischung der beiden beschriebenen Betrachtungsweisen, was PEREIRA/SHIEBER (1987:73) dazu veranlaßt, die Unterscheidung der formalen Sprache DCG und der ausführbaren Prolog-DCG-Regeln zu betonen. Bei der folgenden Beurteilung der Eignung der Definite Clause Grammar anhand ausgewählter sprachlicher Phänomene werden beide Betrachtungsebenen stets getrennt berücksichtigt, was auch dadurch seinen Ausdruck findet, daß auf der deklarativen Ebene eine logische Notation der Regeln, auf der prozeduralen Ebene die Prolog-Grammar-Rule-Notation verwendet wird.

3.1 Kongruenz morpho-syntaktischer Merkmale

Eine reine Phrasenstruktur-Grammatik (PSG), die lediglich die zulässigen Expansionen der Kategorien beschreibt, läßt sich als DCG formalisieren, wie folgendes Beispiel zeigt:

$$NP(P0,P1) \wedge VP(P1,P2) \Rightarrow S(P0,P2)$$

Nun ist offensichtlich, daß eine aus solchen Regeln bestehende kontextfreie Grammatik die Regularitäten einer natürlichen Sprache nicht korrekt beschreibt, weil es Kontextabhängigkeiten gibt, z.B. notwendige Kongruenzen morpho-syntaktischer Merkmale einzelner Konstituenten und satzpositionsbezogene Kasusrestristriktionen. Solche notwendigen Kongruenzen können problemlos in einer DCG ausgedrückt werden, indem die Wahrheitsbedingungen durch Einführung entsprechender Argumente verschärft werden:

$$NP(P0,P1,NUMBER,PERSON) \wedge VP(P1,P2,NUMBER,PERSON) \Rightarrow S(P0,P2)$$

Die leichte Umsetzbarkeit einer solchen Horn-Klausel in eine natürlichsprachliche Form zeigt, wie sehr der Aussage "Furthermore, DCG's seem eminently suitable as a formalism for theoretical work- ..." (PEREIRA/WARREN 1980:269) zuzustimmen ist.

Auf der prozeduralen Betrachtungsebene der top-down, depth-first, left-to-right Verarbeitung der Grammatik-Regeln kommt dem Backtracking zentrale Bedeutung zu. Auf der Grundlage der deklarativ formulierten Abhängigkeiten morpho-syntaktischer Merkmale wird solange nach Lösungen gesucht, bis in einem lokalen Teilbaum alle notwendigen Kongruenzen durch Unifizierung der entsprechenden Argumente hergestellt sind. Der Backtracking-Resolutions-Mechanismus ermöglicht dabei sowohl die Weitergabe von Argument-Instanziierungen von einem Tochter-Knoten zum Mutter-Knoten als auch vom Mutter-Knoten zu einem Tochter-Knoten, sowie von einem Tochter-Knoten zu einem anderen (von rechts nach links und links nach rechts). Folgendes Beispiel von NUGGET-Grammatikregeln (ohne strukturbildende Argumente) soll dies verdeutlichen:

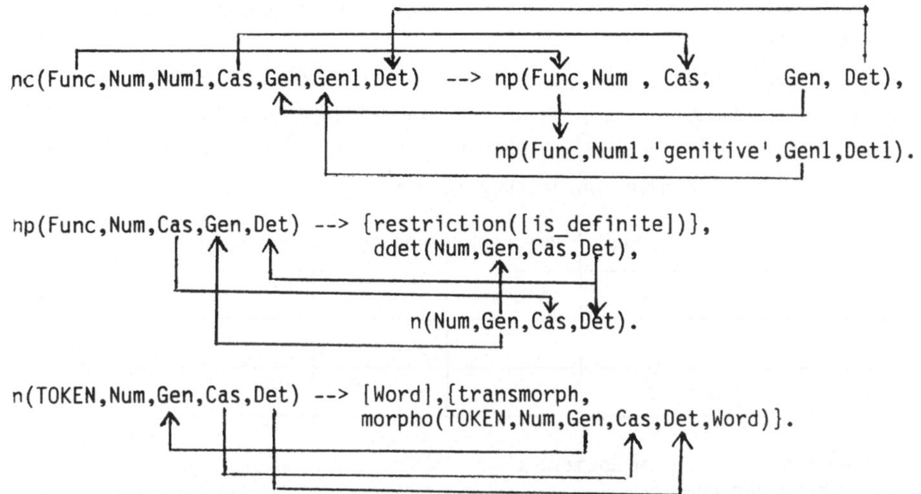

Die Pfeilrichtung gibt die Instanziierungsreihenfolge der Argumente an, wobei ein rückwärts gerichteter Pfeil auf die Ausnutzung des Backtrackingmechnismus hinweist. Das Prädikat 'morpho' in Schweifklammern ruft die morphologische Komponente auf, wobei auch der Lexikonzugriff erfolgt.

3.2 Wortstellung und Fokussierung

Zur Behandlung aller zulässigen Wortstellungen im Satz incl. Fokussierung, Fragesatz- und Relativsatzstellung könnte man jeweils spezielle DCG-Regeln formulieren. In NUGGET wurde jedoch eine Erweiterung der Ausdrucksfähigkeit des DCG-Standardformalismus unter Ausnutzung der vorhandenen Mittel 'Argument-Übergabe' und 'Hinzufügung restringierender logischer Terme' vorgenommen. Diese Erweiterung bedeutet, daß als zusätzliche Verschärfung der Wahrheitsbedingungen einer Regel Angaben über die Funktion zu nominalen Kategorien hinzutreten und eine zusätzliche Bedingung über die korrekte Verteilung der Funktionen formuliert wird. Als wesentliche Funktionen wurden angesetzt:

1.) ACTOR: für das grammatische Subjekt; 2.) OBJECT: für das grammatische Akkusativ-Objekt bzw. eine präpositional angeschlossene obligatorische Ergänzung; 3.) RECEIVER: für das grammatische Akkusativ-Objekt; 4.) GOAL: für das grammatische

Dativ-Objekt; 5.) TIME,LOC,MODE: für freie Ergänzungen der Zeitangabe, Ortsangabe
oder Umstandsangabe (Funktionen angelehnt an HALLIDAY 1985:31; 101-157)

Folgendes verkürztes Beispiel soll die Verwendung der Funktionen auf der deklarativen Ebene demonstrieren (die bereits besprochenen Argumente morpho-syntaktischer
Art werden zur Vereinfachung ausgelassen):

$$FOCUS\text{-}NP(P0,P1,FOCUS\text{-}FUNC) \land V(P1,P2) \land NP(P2,P3,NP1\text{-}FUNC) \land$$
$$NP(P3,P4,NP2\text{-}FUNC) \land PREPNP(P4,P5,PNP\text{-}FUNC) \land$$
$$PREDICATION(P1,P2,FOCUS\text{-}FUNC,NP1\text{-}FUNC,NP2\text{-}FUNC,PNP\text{-}FUNC)$$
$$=> S(P0,P5)$$

Es wird somit zunächst nur festgelegt, welche Konstituenten aufeinander folgen dürfen. Die einschränkende Bedingung, welche Verteilungen der Funktionen zulässig
sind, erfolgt durch den logischen Term PREDICATION, der bei folgenden Beispiel-
Verteilungen die entsprechenden Wahrheitswerte hat:

Satz	Wahrheitswert	FOCUS-FUNC	NP1-FUNC	NP2-FUNC	PNP-FUNC
1)	true	actor	object	—	time
2)	true	—	actor	goal	—
3)	false	object	—	—	loc

1.) Der Mann sah den Hund im Sommer.
2.) Sah der Mann den Hund ?
3.) * Den Hund sah gestern im Wald.

Die zulässigen Verteilungen sind abhängig vom jeweiligen Verb und seinen obligatorischen oder fakultativen funktionalen Komplementen. Aus diesem Grund heißt der
logische Term PREDICATION und führt als zusätzliche Argumente die Begrenzungspunkte
von V (also P1 und P2). In der beschriebenen Weise kann nicht nur das Problem der
verschiedenen Wortstellungen in Aussage-, Frage- bzw. Relativsätzen deklarativ
gelöst werden, sondern auch das Problem unterschiedlicher Anzahl von Elementen im
Satz (die leere Funktion korrespondiert mit einer nicht realisierten Konstituente).
In gleicher Weise ist die genaue Berücksichtigung der vom Verb zugelassenen Subka-
tegorisierungen möglich. Erwähnenswert ist, daß den genannten Phänomenen rein
deklarativ Genüge getan werden kann, ohne prozedural Movement-Operationen auf einer
Basis-Struktur zu benötigen. Auch werden die Probleme der "Filler-Gap-
Dependencies" (PEREIRA/SHIEBER 1987:117) bzw. Long-Distance-Dependencies deklarativ gelöst. Die Tatsache, daß ein "Gap is licensed by the previous occurence of the
filler" (ebda.), wird auf der Ebene der zulässigen Verteilungen der Funktionen
berücksichtigt. Trägt z.B. die Fokus-Konstituente die leere Funktion ('--'), so
muß eine der Konstituenten, die nach dem Verb stehen, die ACTOR-Funktion tragen
(Inversion von Subjekt und grammatischem Prädikat). Andererseits kann eine Funkti-
onszuweisung OBJEKT an die Fokus-Konstituente (Filler) nur mit einer leeren Funktion (Gap) bei einer Konstituente nach dem Verb korrespondieren. Zu diesem Zweck

wurde auf eine separate Kategorie VP verzichtet und statt dessen theoretisch zugrundegelegt, daß in der syntaktischen Struktur neben der Verb-Kategorie alle nominalen Konstruktionen auf der gleichen Ebene liegen. Probleme des PP-Attachment (Desambiguierung syntaktischer Ambiguitäten) werden durch o.g. Ansatz nur insofern bearbeitet, als die den verschiedenen Lesarten entsprechenden syntaktischen Strukturen durch die Grammatik beschrieben werden.

Bei unserem Ansatz der funktional erweiterten DCG genügen die im letzten Kapitel (3.1) beschriebenen Ausdrucksmöglichkeiten zur Herstellung der korrekten Kongruenzen und Werte morpho-syntaktischer Argumente nicht mehr, da damit von vornherein festgelegt wird, welche Konstituenten wie kongruieren. Stattdessen müssen logische Bedingungen formuliert werden, die in Abhängigkeit der Verteilung der funktionalen Argumente die entsprechenden Oberflächen-Kasus zulassen bzw. zurückweisen und die eine Kongruenz-Bedingung bezüglich des flektierten Verbs und jeweils der Konstituente, die die Funktion ACTOR trägt, formulieren. Dies soll unmittelbar auf der prozeduralen Betrachtungsebene an einem Beispiel aus NUGGET (ohne strukturgenerierende Argumente) für nicht-modalisierte Aussagesätze gezeigt werden:

```
rep_s --> {predication_test(FOCUS_FUNC, NC1_FUNC, NC2_FUNC,
                     PNC1_FUNC, PNC2_FUNC, PNC3_FUNC, PNC4_FUNC)},
          {restriction(no_modality)},

          focus(FOCUS_FUNC,NUM1,CAS1,PRP1,PER1),
          v(VPART1, [FOCUS_FUNC,   CAS1,NUM1,PER1,PRP1],
                    [NC1_FUNC,     CAS2,NUM2,PER2,_   ],
                    [NC2_FUNC,     CAS3,NUM3,PER3,_   ],
                    [PNC4_FUNC,    CAS7,_   ,_   ,PRP7],
            Num,Per,Tense,Mood),
          coord_gnc(NUM2,Gen1,CAS2,NC1_FUNC,PER2),
          coord_gnc(NUM3,Gen2,CAS3,NC2_FUNC,PER3),
          prepnc(PNC1_FUNC,CAS4,PRP4),
          prepnc(PNC2_FUNC,CAS5,PRP5),
          prepnc(PNC3_FUNC,CAS6,PRP6),
          prepnc(PNC4_FUNC,CAS7,PRP7),
          vpart(VPART1).
```

Ein Repräsentativsatz (rep_s) expandiert (d.h.'ist genau dann wahr, wenn') zu einem fokustragenden Nominalkomplex (focus), einem flektierten Verb (v), sechs Komplementen (coord_gnc, prepnc = coordinated grouped nominal complex ohne und mit Präposition) und einem Verbpartikel (vpart). Die Argumente stehen für Funktionen, Numerus, Kasus, Genus und Person, sowie die Präpositionen, die fakultativ vor Nominalkomplexe treten. Die Konstituenten 'focus', 'coord_gnc' und die letzte 'prepnc' können die obligatorischen Funktionen realisieren, wohingegen die drei ersten 'prepnc' die freien Angaben der Zeit, des Orts und des Umstands realisieren können. Die zusätzliche Aufnahme der Argumente der obligatorischen Komplemente beim Verb ermöglicht die flexible Instanziierung und Unifizierung in Abhängigkeit vom Verb und den jeweiligen Komplementen. Die in Schweifklammern notierten zusätzlichen Goals 'predication_test' und 'restriction' machen die Expansion des Repräsentativsatzes von der Verteilung der Funktionen der Komplemente (vgl. oben logischer Term

'PREDICATION') und von den Informationen der semantisch-pragmatischen Repräsentation abhängig (s. 3.4). Bei der in unserer Implementation zentralen Abarbeitung
der Grammatik zur Generierung wird als erstes durch 'predication_test' die vom aus-
zuwählenden Verb zugelassene und der zu realisierenden Semantik entsprechende Verteilung der Funktionen vorgenommen, so daß bei der Expansion der einzelnen Konstituenten deren Funktions-Argumente bereits instanziiert sind. Bei der Expansion des
flektierten Verbs werden nun unter Berücksichtigung der Funktionen der obligatorischen Konstituenten deren Kasus und evtl. präpositionale Anschlüsse bestimmt. Ebenfalls wird eine Unifikation der Numerus- und Person-Argumente des flektierten Verbs
mit der jeweils ACTOR-realisierenden Konstituente vorgenommen, so daß jede obligatorische Konstituente das Satzsubjekt realisieren kann. Auf Grund ihrer deklarativen Mächtigkeit kann nur eine einzige Regel sämtliche aufgeführten Varianten
beschreiben.

3.3 Abriß der Beschreibung weiterer Phänomene

Die ausführliche Erläuterung der o.g. Phänomene erlaubt es, im folgenden nur abriß-
haft auf einige weitere Aspekte der Sprachbeschreibung mittels DCG und ihrer Verwendung in NUGGET einzugehen. Aus Gründen der ökonomischen Gestaltung der Grammatik
(mit möglichst wenigen Regeln soll ein möglichst großer Sprachumfang beschrieben
werden) wird in einer DCG die Optionalität fakultativer Satz-Konstituenten angewendet. Diese Optionalität besagt, daß eine zur Ableitung einer Ober-Kategorie (z.B.
Satz) notwendig abzuleitende Unter-Kategorie (z.B. nominale Kategorie) auch dann
wahr ist, wenn das leere Symbol ('EPSILON') vorliegt. (vgl. PEREIRA/WARREN
1980:245 + PEREIRA 1981:245)
      TRUE => NP(p0,p0)   (bzw. CONNECTS('EPSILON',p0,p0))
Prozedural betrachtet wird eine solche Beschreibung in NUGGET intensiv benutzt, da
so alle Konstituenten, die nicht semantisch fundiert sind (also zur Realisierung
der jeweiligen Semantik nicht erforderlich sind) durch das leere Symbol expandiert
werden und somit in der Satzoberfläche entfallen. Bei beispielsweise fünf optiona-
len Konstituenten kann eine Regel 32 Kombinationsvarianten beschreiben.

Ein Spezialfall dieser Optionalität von Konstituenten ist die Behandlung von infinitivischen Verben, die vom flektierten Modalverb abhängen. ('Er möchte das Auto
kaufen können.' vs. 'Er möchte das Auto kaufen.') Auch in solchen Fällen bietet
sich an, das satzabschließende infinitivische Modalverb als optional zu beschreiben. Auf der prozeduralen Ebene wird dies in NUGGET mit der Semantik entsprechend
verknüpft, d.h. wenn entsprechende Positionstypen vorliegen, die modale Abfärbung
erfordern, wird das optionale Modalverb realisiert. Andernfalls schließt der Satz
mit dem infinitivischen Vollverb.
Leicht nachvollziehbar und deutlich deklarativ ist die Verknüpfung syntaktischer
Regeln mit morphologischen Regeln im Formalismus der DCG. Eine anspruchsvolle

Beschreibung der Sprache verwendet kein in die Grammatik integriertes (Vollformen-) Lexikon. Vielmehr wird die logische Ableitung korrekt flektierter Lexeme über morphologische Relationen sichergestellt, die Grundformen und ihre morphologischen Merkmale (Numerus etc.) zu flektierten Lexemen in Beziehung setzen. Die morphologischen Relationen setzen an den terminalen Regeln der Grammatik als verschärfende Bedingungen an: Eine Kategorie ist genau dann wahr, wenn sie auf ein terminales Symbol abbildbar ist, das sich unter Berücksichtigung der Merkmale und der kategorie-bezogenen Relation als morphologisch korrekt erweist. Auf der prozeduralen Ebene der generierenden Anwendung der Grammatik sieht das in NUGGET so aus, daß ein String generiert wird, der die korrekt flektierte Form des ausgewählten Lexems darstellt.

3.4 Abbildung Semantik/Pragmatik auf Syntax

Die formulierte DCG beschreibt komplett den durch ihren Umfang definierten Sprachausschnitt, d.h. alle möglichen korrekten Sätze und ihre syntaktischen Strukturen über strukturbildende Argumente. Zwischen der syntaktischen Beschreibung und den zugrundeliegenden semantisch-pragmatischen Repräsentationen in ARPS besteht eine grundsätzliche Abbildungsrelation. Jeder mögliche Satz besitzt eine semantisch-pragmatische Entsprechung. Dies impliziert, daß für eine bestimmte semantisch-pragmatische Repräsentation nur ein bestimmter Teil der Grammatik und der Expansionen zu terminalen Symbolen wahr ist.

Bei der Formulierung von ARPS wurde auf Systematisierungen der Sprechaktheorie zurueckgegriffen. Beispiele:

EBENE	ARPS-Notation / * Beispiel
illokut. Rollen	is_spa(SPA_COUNTER,TYPE_OF_SPEECHACT) * is_spa(1,'EROTETICAL')
Positionstypen	is_position(POS_COUNTER,VIEWPOINT,RANGE_LIST,PREDICATION) * is_position(pos1(1),'SYSTEM',['WANTED_FACT'],state(1))
Propositionen: a)Praedikationen	is_state(STATE_COUNTER,PREDICATION_TYPE,ROLES_LIST) * is_state(state(1),'POSSESS',[possessor *= 'USER', possessed *= topic1(1)])
b)Referenzen	is_const(TOPIC,QUALIFIED,QUALIFIER) * is_const(topic(1),'Anlage_1', 'Laufzeit_1')

(Terminologie nach SEARLE 1971, WUNDERLICH 1976).

In ARPS werden semantische und pragmatische Informationen als Prolog-Facts notiert, wobei die Prädikatnamen semantisch-pragmatische Beschreibungsebenen wiedergeben und die Argumente deren Ausprägung. Um die Kohärenz einer Repräsentation herzustellen, werden Pointer in Form von Strukturen und Integers (state(1) oder 1) benutzt. So wird der im Beispiel für 'is_state' verwendete Pointer 'topic1(1)', der der Rolle 'possessed' zugeordnet ist, in 'is_const' aufgegliedert in eine Entität ('Anlage') und deren Eigenschaft ('Laufzeit').

Die Abbildungsrelation zwischen einer bestimmten Repräsentation und dem zugehörigen Ausschnitt der Grammatik wird zur Formulierung verschärfender logischer Wahrheitsbedingungen genutzt, die als logische Terme die semantisch-pragmatische Repräsentation evaluieren und den zutreffenden Ausschnitt der Abbildung von Semantik und Pragmatik auf Syntax beschreiben. In prozeduraler Sicht handelt es sich um 'Restriction'-Prädikate, die als zusätzliche Bedingungen in den unterschiedlichen Grammatikregeln definiert sind und bestimmen, ob die Regel zutrifft oder nicht. Im Prozeß der Textgenerierung werden die in der ARPS-Notation erwarteten semantischen und pragmatischen Informationen in der beschriebenen Art ausgewertet und somit die Form des jeweils angezielten Texts flexibel gesteuert. So führt die Evaluierung der ARPS-Basis bezüglich der RANGE-LIST des Positionstyps beispielsweise zur Restringierung der anwendbaren Grammatikregeln auf Regeln mit oder ohne Modalverb-Konstituente. Entsprechend ist die im Kapitel 3.2 beispielhaft angeführte 'rep_s'-Expansion ohne Modalverb genau dann wahr, wenn 'restriction(no_modality)' wahr ist, d.h. wenn die RANGE-LIST den Eintrag 'FACT' (für faktisch) und nicht etwa 'WANTED_FACT' (für gewünscht; vgl. obiges Beispiel) besitzt.

4. Abschließende Beurteilung

Fazit der beschriebenen Anwendung der DCG auf die Generierung deutscher Texte ist, daß eine DCG selbst im beschriebenen Umfang eine leicht zu handhabende und komfortabel zu erweiternde Beschreibung der Regularitäten der Zielsprache erlaubt und darüberhinaus eine deklarative Abbildung von Bedeutung und Funktion auf deren textuelle Realisierung möglich macht. Die von uns vorgenommenen funktionalen Erweiterungen sowie die durchgängige Ausnutzung von bestehenden Konzepten (wie Konstituenten-Optionalität) sind zudem die Grundlage für eine stark komprimierte Grammatik mit gleichwohl erheblicher generativer Kapazität.

Aus der prozeduralen Sicht der generierenden Verwendung der DCG kann zudem ein äußerst günstiges Laufzeitverhalten festgestellt werden, das sogar ohne Meta-Interpreter allein unter Ausnutzung des Prolog-Resolutionsmechanismus zustande gekommen ist. Für einen Text in Bildschirmlänge, der sich aus mehreren Sätzen zusammensetzt, werden auf einer TARGON/35 mit UNIX und IF-Prolog 12 CPU-Sekunden verbraucht. Diese Aussage kann jedoch nicht ohne genauere Überprüfung auf eine Parsing-Verwendung der DCG übertragen werden, da in einem solchen Kontext ein ungünstigeres Backtracking-Verhalten erwartbar ist.

(*) WISBER ist ein vom BMFT gefördertes Verbundprojekt; Partner sind: Nixdorf
Computer AG, SCS Organisationsberatung und Informationstechnik GmbH, Siemens AG,
Universität Hamburg, Universität Saarbrücken
(**) TWAICE ist eingetragenes Warenzeichen der Nixdorf Computer AG

4. Literaturverzeichnis

BLOCK,   Hans-Ulrich/Manfred Gehrke/Hans Haugeneder/Rudolf Hunze: "Neuere
                Grammatiktheorien und Grammatikformalismen" WISBER-Bericht 1; Mün-
                chen 1985 (= BLOCK/GEHRKE/HAUGENEDER/HUNZE 1985)

COLMERAUER, A.: "Metamorphosis Grammars"; in: L.Bolc (Hrsg.): Natural Language
                Communication with Computers; Lecture Notes in Computer Science; New
                York (Springer) 1978; S.133 - 189 (= COLMERAUER 1978)

DERR,   Marcia A./Kathleen McKeown: "Using Focus to Generate Complex and
                Simple Sentences"; in: Proceedings of 10th COLING 84; Stanford 1984;
                S. 319 - 326 (= DERR/MCKEOWN 1984)

GAZDAR,   Gerald: "The New Grammar Formalisms - A Tutorial Survey"; in: Pro-
                ceedings IJCAI 1987 (= GAZDAR 1987); S. 1172

HALLIDAY,   M.A.K.: "An Introduction to Functional Grammar"; London (Edward
                Arnold) 1985 (= HALLIDAY 1985)

JABLONSKI,   Konrad; Armin Rau; Johannes Ritzke: "Konzeption und Architektur des
                taktischen Textgenerierungssystems NUGGET"; WISBER-Memo 12; Pader-
                born 1987 (= JABLONSKI/RAU/RITZKE 1987)

JABLONSKI,   Konrad; Armin Rau; Johannes Ritzke: "NUGGET - Ein DCG-basiertes
                Textgenerierungssystem"; WISBER-Bericht; erscheint im Sommer 1988
                (=JABLONSKI/RAU/RITZKE 1988)

MCKEOWN,   Kathleen R.: "Text generation"; Cambridge (University Press) 1985
                (=MCKEOWN 1985)

PEREIRA,   F.C.N.: "Extraposition Grammar"; in: American Journal of Computatio-
                nal Linguistics (7) 1981; S. 243 - 256 (= PEREIRA 1981)

PEREIRA,   F.C.N./Stuart M. Shieber: "Prolog and Natural-Language Analysis";
                Stanford (CSLI Lecture Notes) 1987 (= PEREIRA/SHIEBER 1987)

PEREIRA,   F.C.N./D.H.D WARREN : "Definite Clause Grammars for Language Analy-
                sis - A Survey of the Formalism and a Comparison with Augmented
                Transition Networks". In: Artificial Intelligence 13, S. 231-278
                (=PEREIRA/WARREN 1980)

SEARLE,   John: "Sprechakte"; Frankfurt (Suhrkamp) 1971 (= SEARLE 1971)

SHIEBER,   Stuart M.: "An Introduction to Unification-Based Approaches to Gram-
                mar"; Chicago (University of Chicago) 1985 (= SHIEBER 1985)

STERLING,   L./ E. SHAPIRO : "The Art of Prolog"; Cambridge/Mass. (MIT-Press)
                1986 (= STERLING/SHAPIRO 1986)

WALKER,   Adrian (Hrsg.): "Knowledge Systems and Prolog"; Reading Mass. etc.
                (Addison Wesley) 1987 (= WALKER 1987)

WUNDERLICH, Dieter: "Studien zur Sprechakttheorie"; Frankfurt a.M. (Suhrkamp)
                1976 (= WUNDERLICH 1976)

Resolving Anaphoric References
in a
DRT-based Dialogue System

Robert E. Frederking
Manfred Gehrke

Siemens AG, München
ZTI INF 23

Abstract

The identification of the referents of pronouns and definite descriptions in natural language processing (NLP) is a formidable task. We present our approach to pronominal and definite references in a German language dialogue system that is currently being implemented. This approach combines immediate focus and a special purpose reasoner that uses a KL-ONE like taxonomy within a modified form of discourse representation theory (DRT) structure (KAMP 81, HUNZE 88).

Referencing discourse objects

In a discourse, new objects that the discourse deals with can be introduced in various ways. Consider for example the following text:

(1) **Ein Mann** hat *40000 DM* geerbt.

 A man has inherited *40000 DM*.

Here we have the indefinite introduction of 'ein Mann' and '40000 DM'.

(2) **Er will** {*die 40000 DM, das Geld, den Betrag*} anlegen.

 He wants to invest {*the 40000 DM, the money, the amount*}.

In addition to the pronominal reference of 'er' to 'ein Mann', there is a reference to '40000 DM' that can be established by repeating the phrase or by using a definite description (dB) that is in some sense equivalent to the reference object (RefO).

(3) **Deshalb geht er *zur Bank*,** um eine günstige Art der Geldanlage zu erfragen.

 Therefore he goes to *the bank* to ask for a profitable kind of investment.

Though it is a definite description, 'zur Bank' is not licensed by a previously mentioned RefO, but rather by the discourse establishing a context allowing for the definite introduction of 'Bank'.

(4) *Der Angestellte* rät ihm zu Pfandbriefen.

   The clerk advises him to an investment in bonds.

'Der Angestellte', which stands in a part-of relation to 'Bank', is an associative anaphor (HAWKINS 78) licensed by this RefO. The pronoun 'ihm' must refer to 'ein Mann' due to a syntactic disjoint reference constraint with 'der Angestellte' (since 'himself' would have to be used if they were coreferent), in addition to semantic and focus considerations.

(5) *Dieser Rat* gefällt ihm nicht, ...

   This advice does not please him, ...

'Rat' is licensed by 'raten' (the infinitive of 'rät') due to its being a nominalization of this verb, but with the demonstrative article the reference is made unique to its last mentioned instance. In this case, and the following, the pronoun 'ihm' refers again to 'ein Mann', but only for semantic and focus reasons. In context, it makes more sense that the advice would displease the recipient rather than the giver of the advice. A computationally more tractable factor is that if a referent was pronominalized in a previous sentence, it is the preferred referent for a pronoun in the current sentence.

(6) ..., da ihm die Rendite zu gering ist.

   ..., because the revenue is to low for him.

'Pfandbrief' licenses the relational noun 'Rendite', which is an inherent feature of it.

In this little text one can see several chains of reference:

   1. ein Mann - er - er - ihm - ihm - ihm (phrases in **bold**),
   2. 40000 DM - {die 40000 DM, das Geld, den Betrag} (phrases in *italics*),
   3. (ein Mann -) zur Bank - der Angestellte (phrases in ***bold italics***),
   4. raten - Rat (phrases in *underlined italics*),
   5. Pfandbrief - Rendite (underlined phrases),

containing pronouns as well as definite descriptions.

The basis of the formalism we use to identify such references follows the discourse representation theory (DRT) of H. Kamp (KAMP 81) with some extensions, as described by Hunze (HUNZE 88) [1].

Within this framework, the licensing referents are identified by means of syntactic constraints (HUNZE 88), semantic information and focus, as well as taxonomic information. We look first at focus.

Previous work on focus

In her classic work on the computational use of immediate focusing in discourse (SIDNER 79), Sidner proposes a very appealing focus movement mechanism, whereby focus helps determine referent resolution, and referent resolution in turn updates the focus. Despite its intuitive appeal, the approach presented there is rather complex, with both actor and discourse foci, several related data structures, and complex flowcharts indicating focus movement and referent resolution for different kinds of anaphoric reference [2]. And despite this complexity, there are a significant number of cases that are not handled correctly, either because of the difficult phenomenon of parallelism, or the dominance of semantic factors. Semantic factors are present in her model, but only in subordinate roles, their application controlled by the focus mechanism. In addition to rejecting referents proposed by the focus mechanism, semantics are used in the form of taxonomic reasoning to decide whether the referent of an anaphor is "associated with" the current focus. The taxonomic system used is left open, since it is not an integral part of the focus mechanism.

In later work (GROSZ 83, GROSZ 86), immediate focusing is renamed "centering", to avoid confusion with the more global focusing of Grosz's earlier work (GROSZ 77), and is simplified both by the discarding of the actor focus and by the replacement of the specific, complex rules with a more general description of the phenomena and a rule for the speaker (as opposed to the hearer) that if the centers of the current and the preceding utterance are the same, a pronoun should be used. While this is simpler, and possibly more correct, it is of less help for interpreting natural language input.

Our approach to focus

In general, our approach differs from these approaches in that when an anaphoric reference is to be resolved, the dialogue has already been structured in terms of "discourse representation structures" (DRSes), based on the discourse representation theory (DRT) mentioned in the introduction (KAMP 81, HUNZE 88). Within this framework, we use a special purpose taxonomic reasoner to aid in resolving definite references, and are developing a modified version of immediate focusing along with other constraints to select between alternate pronoun reference resolutions. Our approach is to use strong negative constraints such as syntactic disjoint reference constraints and semantic selectional restrictions first, followed by the application of general domain knowledge, and then, only if there is more than one alternative remaining, to apply the weaker constraints of immediate focus and semantic role parallelism to select which of the alternate resolutions to pursue.

Our version of immediate focus consists of a single type of focus, but rather than selecting exactly one discourse object as being "the" focus of a given utterance, a list of referents can appear, in order of strength of focus. The relative strength of focus will be determined by a set of simple rules. Since it may prove necessary to use a fairly large number and variety of rules, the resulting overall system may become fairly complex. This complexity will be handled by embedding the rules in a rule-based system. These focus rules will make use of the previous utterance's focus list and list of potential foci (a la Sidner (SIDNER 79)) [3], and the old focus lists of accessible DRSes (similar in function to Sidner's focus stack) to make their focus strength decisions.

For example, if several pronouns are used, or a pronoun and a definite reference, the pronouns would be present in order of the strength of their focus as determined by our focus rules, followed by any definite references, since one proposed rule is that pronoun-induced focus is significantly stronger than definite reference-induced focus. The backward center rule of Grosz et al. (GROSZ 83) is accommodated by increasing the focus strength of a pronoun resolution in the current utterance if its referent is in the focus list of the previous utterance, proportionally to its position in that list. Example (5) above is a case where this would apply: the pronoun 'ihm' in (5) could refer to either 'der Angestellte' or 'ihm' from sentence (4). The focus list for (4) is (ihm, der Angestellte, Pfandbriefen), since 'ihm' in (4) is, in turn, a pronominal reference to an entity from (3). Therefore the reference to 'ihm' in (4) makes the best use of focus.

In our system focus selects among competing reference resolutions by selecting one of a set of DRSes representing the different possible sets of resolutions. The selection is made on the basis of the best use of focus, along with role parallelism and recency. By "best use of focus" we mean that DRSes in which pronouns refer to objects in focus are better than those in which they do not, and so forth. We initially hypothesize that the recency effect reported by Sidner is intermediate in strength between definite reference-induced focus and pronoun-induced focus, so that it will dominate the former, but not the latter. Our version of role parallelism consists of matching similar roles of similar predicates from our taxonomic network.

We believe that experimentation with such a system will produce a useful system of reasonable complexity for pronoun resolution in German. Since no current system produces consistently correct pronoun resolutions, if this system can produce a high percentage of correct resolutions using a well-organized structure, it will be a significant improvement in the state of the art.

Pronoun Resolution Implementation

Since the later stages of this system have only the F-structure to work with, the LFG parser must pass on all necessary information from the C-structure in terms of F-structure attributes. In the case of pronoun resolution using our criteria, this means disjoint reference restrictions, an indication of any syntactically topicalized noun phrase, and the surface order of the noun phrases. The first is passed in an attribute called "disjoint", the second is indicated via a number of syntactic features, such as the "topic" attribute, and the last is provided by having the reference objects created for the DRS retain the surface order of their source noun phrases. The "theme" of the verb is also marked, since it is more likely to be in focus.

There are three points during the process of referent identification (HUNZE 88) where pronoun-related processing occurs. The first is during the phase that produces consistent sets of proposed reference resolutions. A function is applied to each proposed set of reference resolutions, to prune away those that are impossible. In this function, disjoint reference restrictions from the "disjoint" attribute and selectional restrictions from the taxonomic network are applied to the proposed bindings. Those bindings that would violate either of these strong negative constraints are discarded.

When there is more than one DRS alternative generated by this stage, the previously mentioned selection criteria will be used to determine which of the proposed solutions is the most likely to be correct.

Finally, whether or not pronouns are used in the current sentence, the current focus must be updated. So even when there is only one DRS produced, its discourse objects' focus strengths are calculated, as described above. A very simple rule-based system is envisioned, with minimal scheduling and conflict resolution, since the scope of the system is limited to calculating focus.

We now turn to the use of taxonomic relations.

The Taxonomic Relations Reasoner (TRR)

Generally speaking, in the following section the notion of 'equivalence' is extended in such a way that it captures not only literal identity, but also identifies the referents of definite descriptions, as shown to some extent in the first section. With respect to this, a definite description (dB) is equivalent to or licensed by the reference object (RefO), if

1. they are literally identical,
2. dB is either a synonym, a generalization (hyperonym in lexical semantics), or a specialization (hyponym in l. s.) of RefO,
3. dB is a relational notion with respect to RefO,
4. dB is an associative anaphor of RefO,

where the relationship in the first two conditions is called direct taxonomical equivalence.

This extension of equivalence is grounded in a taxonomy containing definitorial knowledge[4]. The taxonomy (TBox) is built up using QUIRK (BERGMANN 87), a member of the KL-ONE family of knowledge representation systems (BRACHMAN 85). The classifier of QUIRK takes a new piece of definitorial knowledge presented to the system and places it into the taxonomic hierarchy according to its definition and all the other definitions classified so far. Thus the TBox forms a lattice of interwoven definitions.

Hearing of KL-ONE, this notion of classification strikes one's mind. But here this association is misleading, because classifying the definite description into the taxonomy would only give its direct superconcept. In some cases this is a correct result, but not in most cases. Instead of using the built-in broad coverage classifier of QUIRK for this application, a small, restricted, special purpose taxonomic relations reasoner (TRR) [5] has been developed.

Its central part is composed of predicates for the above mentioned four conditions under which extended equivalence holds. While the first predicate is left open as an exercise for the reader, the definition of the second predicate is a direct out-growth of the classifier, where e.g. the hyponyms are the subconcepts of the notion in question. An example for this condition is

(7) Ich habe Wertpapiere gekauft. Die Aktien von Meyer Anlagenbau waren die günstigsten
     I have bought securities. The shares of Meyer Construction were the most profitable.

To define the other predicates for relational nouns and associative anaphors a closer look onto the definition of concepts in QUIRK is necessary. Besides its links to its super- and sub-concept, a QUIRK concept is defined by a number of roles consisting of a name, a number restriction, and a role restriction, which is the most general concept that can fill this role.

A dB is a relational noun with respect to the RefO if it is identical or a hyperonym to one of the role names of the RefO, as for example in

(8) Pfandbriefe sind zur Zeit recht günstig. Ihre {Laufzeit, Sicherheit, Rendite} ...
     Bonds are at the moment quite profitable. Their {term, security, yield} ...

The definition of a predicate for associative anaphor is more difficult, because the TBox establishes a strongly interwoven lattice of concepts, so that it is very easy to be related to an inappropriate concept. This predicate is defined by introducing a very general role "TEIL-VON" ("PART-OF"), which is differentiated (specialized) by all those roles that are able to license an associative anaphor. A RefO now licenses a dB iff the dB is directly taxonomically equivalent to a role restrictor of a role of RefO which differentiates "TEIL-VON". Consider for example

(9) Ich möchte mein Sparbuch auflösen. Überweisen sie bitte den Betrag auf mein Girokonto.

 I would like to close my savings account. Please transfer the amount to my checking account.

Let the concept "SPARBUCH" be defined by:

Imm.Super: GELDANLAGE

    (ROLE HAT-WERT (1 1) GELDBETRAG)

    (ROLE HAT-RENDITE (1 1) PROZENTBETRAG)

    ...,

where "HAT-WERT" ("HAS-VALUE") differentiates the role "TEIL-VON". The test whether dB is an associative anaphor of RefO first finds that "HAT-WERT" differentiates the role "TEIL-VON" and then that "BETRAG" is a superconcept of "GELDBETRAG". On the other hand, it does not relate "PROZENTBETRAG" to "SPARBUCH", so the following text contains an inadequate reference:

(10) *Ich möchte mein Sparbuch auflösen. Der Prozentbetrag ist mir zu gering.

 I would like to close my savings account. The percentage amount is too small for me.

At a first glance this approach to associative anaphors seems to be sound in the sense that no inappropriate references are identified and until now the misidentifications made are due to the taxonomy in use. A improvement in order to strengthen the soundness and to yield a greater completeness of in identifying associative anaphors is to incorporate the findings in (WINSTON 87). There the existence of a family of 'part-whole'-relations and not merely one uniform 'part-whole'-relation is stated which has consequence for the property of transitivy usually ascribed to 'part-whole'-relations. These findings will allow us to introduce the recursive application of the same subtype of 'part-whole'-relation which is prohibited in the current version of the TRR.

But misidentifications may arise due to the chosen approach under the following conditions:

Let A and B be concepts, with both having the role HAT-X among their role set, and let HAT-X differentiate TEIL-VON. If it is now inadequate to refer to B with an associative anaphor via HAT-X, while this is adequate for A, a misidentification with respect to B occurs.

A straight-forward solution is to introduce an additional role, not differentiating "TEIL-VON", thus increasing the number of roles and losing some generality in description.

Further Work

With respect to its area of application the described formalism to identify referents for definite descriptions works quite well. But at least one extension is waiting to be incorporated. Consider for example the following text

(11) *Ich besitze jetzt eine Aktie. Die Wertpapiere ... .

   I now own a share. The securities ...

A constraint derived from the number feature of RefO will discard this reference. But taxonomically based number restrictions can override the syntactic number constraint, as e.g. in

(12)   Auf unserer Wanderung kamen wir in ein Dorf. Vor {*dem Haus, einem der Häuser} machten wir Rast.
    On our walk we went into a village. In front of {*the house, one of the houses} we took a rest.

Therefore both kinds of number restrictions - the syntactic ones as well as the taxonomy based - have to be taken into consideration.

Inadequate references to superconcepts is a problem of reference identification that seems to arise in all knowledge representation systems forming hierarchies. Using the standard example of KL-ONE taxonomies

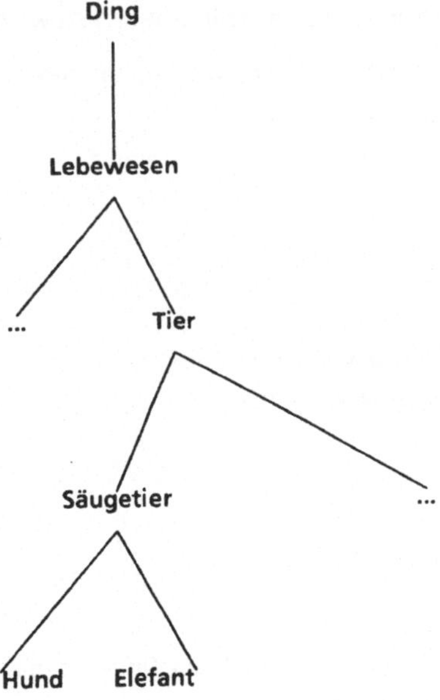

to identify the referents, one gets a misidentification in the following text :

(12)   Ein blinder Mann geht mit seinem Hund zum Park. An der Kreuzung bleibt das kluge {Tier, *Säugetier} erst einmal stehen.

A blind man is walking his dog to the park. At the crossing the clever {animal, *mammal} stops.

In analysing texts, such problems may be circumvented in many cases with the help of the discourse structure, etc., but in generation some additional mechanism, e.g. maintaining several taxonomies for different domains, may be necessary.

Notes

[1] This approach to identifying reference objects of anaphoric descriptions is being used in the WISBER Joint Project, whose task is to develop a natural language advice giving system. Its application area, from which some of the examples in this paper are taken, is advice giving in financial investment. Partners in the WISBER Project are the University of Hamburg, Nixdorf Computer Company, SCS and Siemens AG. The project is partly supported by a grant from the Federal Ministery of Research and Technology.

[2] "Anaphor" is here used in its original sense of any expression referring back to a previously introduced discourse object.

[3] Actually, in this scheme the list of potential foci is just the tail of the focus list, since they are simply the noun phrases of lower focus strength.

[4] A comparable approach is described in (HABEL 85).

[5] Using a special purpose reasoner for reference identification follows (MACGREGOR 87), where MacGregor proposes a library of domain-specific, "narrow coverage" reasoners for the Loom knowledge representation language.

References

(BERGMANN 87)

Bergmann, H., Gerlach, M., QUIRK - Implementierung einer TBox zur Repräsentation begrifflichen Wissens, WISBER-Memo 11 (2. extended Version), 1987

(BRACHMAN 85)

Brachman, R.J., Schmolze, J.G., "An Overview of the KL-ONE Knowledge Representation System", in: Cognitive Science, Vol. 9, No. 2, 1985, p. 171-217

(GROSZ 77)

Grosz, B.J., The Representation and Use of Focus in Dialogue Understanding, Technical Report 151, Artificial Intelligence Center, SRI International, 1977

(GROSZ 83)

Grosz, B.J., Joshi, A.K., and Weinstein, S., "Providing a Unified Account of Definite Noun Phrases in Discourse", in: Proceedings of the 21st Annual Meeting of the ACL, 1983, p. 44-50

(GROSZ 86)

Grosz, B.J., and Sidner, C.L., "Attention, Intentions, and the Structure of Discourse", in: Computational Linguistics, Vol. 12, No. 3, 1986, p. 175-204

(HABEL 85)

Habel, C., Prinzipien der Referentialität - Untersuchungen zur propositionalen Repräsentation von Wissen, Berlin-Heidelberg-New York, 1985

(HAWKINS 78)

Hawkins, J. A., Definiteness and Indefiniteness - A Study in Reference and Grammaticality Prediction, London, 1978

(HUNZE 88)

Hunze, R., "Resolving Anaphoric References in a DRT-based Dialogue System: Part 1: The formal discourse model", in preparation

(KAMP 81)

Kamp, H., "A Theory of Truth and Semantic Representation", in: Groenendijk, J.A.G., Janssen, T.M.V., Stokhof, M.B.J. (eds.), Formal Methods in the Study of Language, Vol. 136, 1981, p. 277-322, Amsterdam, Mathematical Centre Tracts

(MACGREGOR 87)

MacGregor, R., Bates, R. , The Loom Knowledge Representation System, USC/ISI, ms, 1987

(SIDNER 79)

Sidner, C.L., Towards a Computational Theory of Definite Anaphora Comprehension in English Discourse, Technical Report 537, Artificial Intelligence Laboratory, MIT, 1979

(WINSTON 87)

Winston, M.E., Chaffin, R., Herrmann, D., "A Taxonomy of Part-Whole Relations", in: Cognitive Science, 11 (1987), 417-444

Repräsentation von Pluralanaphern

Michael Streit

Siemens AG, München ZTI INF 322

Otto-Hahn-Ring 6 8000 München 83

Vorbemerkung

Im folgenden möchte ich einen Ansatz für eine einheitliche Repräsentation von Singular- und Pluralanaphern vorstellen, die intersententiell sind. Dabei werden Anaphern durch die explizite und selbständige Beschreibung ihrer Bedeutung repräsentiert, wie dies in grundsätzlich ähnlicher Form schon von B. L. Webber vorgeschlagen wurde (WEBBER83). Diese Bedeutungsbeschreibungen sind auf jeder Diskursebene erreichbar - im Gegensatz zu den Diskursreferenten in Hans Kamps DRT (KAMP81). Dies wird sich für die Behandlung von Pluralanaphern als wesentlich erweisen. Obwohl DRT (und die ähnliche *file change semantic* von Irene Heim - HEIM83) sich bei der Darstellung von Singularanaphern außerordentlich bewährt hat, werden hier andere Wege eingeschlagen. Dabei wird versucht,die Unterschiede zu DRT klar herauszuarbeiten.

Der hier vorgestellte Ansatz begründet sich aber nicht nur aus der bislang ungeklärten Behandlung von Pluralen im Rahmen von DRT. Es sind vielmehr auch die Eigenheiten eines Frage/Antwort-Dialogs, die es als problematisch erscheinen lassen, die Repräsentation von Diskursreferenten mehr oder weniger implizit durch die Gesamtdarstellung eines Diskurses zu leisten.

Es wird sich herausstellen, daß durch Aussagen, die im Verlauf des Dialoges falsifiziert werden, nichtsdestoweniger Diskursreferenten neu und dauerhaft eingeführt werden können, was eine unabhängige Darstellung der Referenten zumindest nahelegt. Darüberhinaus gibt es jedoch Typen von Dialogäußerungen, die wiederum Diskursreferenten neu ins Leben rufen können, denen ein Wahrheitwert aber gar nicht sinnvoll zugeordnet werden kann. Bei WH-Fragen kann man Mengen als ihre natürlichen Extension betrachten. Damit sind aber WH-Fragen als *discourse representation structures* (DRS) in Sinne von DRT - zumindest unmittelbar - nicht mehr darzustellen.

In dieser Arbeit wird eine semantische Repräsentation benutzt, in der gewisse syntaktische Funktionen kenntlich bleiben. Denn manche syntaktischen Unterscheidungen erweisen sich als wesentlich zur Determinierung der Bedeutung von Pluralanaphern.

Insbesondere möchte die Arbeit der Tatsache Rechnung tragen, daß Diskursreferenten im Verlauf des Dialogs restringiert werden können, daß über Diskursreferenten quantifiziert werden kann, und daß dadurch Diskursreferenten neu erzeugt werden. Es handelt sich hierbei um Erscheinungen, die erst in Bezug auf plurale Anaphern sinnvoll und sichtbar werden..

Die Arbeit nimmt Bezug auf das Dialogsystem für gesprochene Sprache SPICOS, von dem gegenwärtig eine Version implementiert wird, die in gewissem Umfang Singular- und Pluralanaphern behandeln kann.

Es wird die Repräsentation von intersententiellen Anaphern formal ausgearbeitet, die sich auf Nominalphrasen in JA/NEIN-Fragen des SPICOS-Systems beziehen. Die leichten Modifikationen des Verfahrens für WH-Fragen können nur angedeutet werden.

Im Gegensatz zu intrasententiellen Anaphern (die ihr Bezugselement in demselben Satz besitzen, in dem sie selbst auftreten), lassen sich für intersententielle Anaphern klare Adäquatheitskriterien aufstellen. In diesen Kriterien, der Beschränkung auf intersententielle Anaphern, sowie in der stärkeren Beachtung von syntaktischen Erscheinungen, Dialogphänomenen und Präsuppositionen, liegen, neben einer anderen Repräsentationssprache, wohl die wesentlichen Unterschiede zur Darstellung Webbers.

Auf Fragen der Anaphernresolution wird im folgenden nicht eingegangen.

Anaphernrepräsentation in DRT

Einige Grundzüge von DRT

Um die Unterschiede der hier vertretenen Aufassung zu DRT deutlich zu machen, möchte ich kurz einige Eigenschaften von DRT herausarbeiten, die in dieser Hinsicht von Interesse sind.

Diskursreferenten werden in DRT durch Individuenvariablen repräsentiert. Diese Variablen erhalten ihre Bedeutung dadurch, daß sie in einer logischen Struktur auftreten, die den gesamten Diskurs beschreibt, wobei diejenigen Ausdrücke, in denen der Diskurreferent frei auftritt, seine „conditions" bilden. Für eine ausführliche Darstellung der induktiven Definition der *discourse representation structures* (DRS) sei etwa auf GUENTHNER86 hingewiesen. Für die Darstellung hier kommt es darauf an , daß der Bezug von Anaphern auf die Diskursentitäten, auf die sie referieren, durch die Identifizierung von Individuenvariablen geleistet wird . Das Auftreten einer Anapher wird in DRT einfach durch das Wiederauftreten einer Individuenvariablen dargestellt . Die Leistung von DRT besteht nun darin, einen Formalismus zu bieten, der diese Variablenidentifikation auch über Satzgrenzen hinaus gestattet, was in der traditionellen Logik bekanntlich nicht möglich ist.

Die Darstellung von Anaphern durch Individuenvariable bringt jedoch auch gewisse Beschränkungen mit sich:

In konditionalen DRSen (damit werden in DRT Wenn-Dann-Sätze repräsentiert, aber auch Sätze, die den Quantor „jedes" enthalten) interpretiert man die Diskursreferenten wie all-quantifizierte Variable . Das heißt die Diskursreferenten stellen in Wirklichkeit viele Entitäten dar, über die sie variieren.

Sobald das Konditional beendet ist, haben diese Diskursreferenten keine Bedeutung mehr. Sie sind für anaphorische Ausdrücke aus den im Diskurs folgenden Sätzen genausowenig erreichbar wie eine allquantifizierte Variable von einer Position außerhalb des Skopus des Allquantors. Das bedeutet, daß die Skopus-„Aufweichung" in DRT sich nur auf den Existenzquantor bezieht .

Solange man sich im Bereich singularer Anaphern bewegt, ist diese - vom DRT-Formalismus notwendigerweise vorgegebene - Beschränkung weitgehend in Übereinstimmung mit den sprachlichen Gegebenheiten und im allgemeinen erwünscht.

(1)   * Pedro besitzt jeden Esel. Er schlägt ihn.

Gemäß DRT kann sich in (1) „ihn" nicht auf „Esel" beziehen. Der erste Satz des Diskurses wird nämlich als Konditional dargestellt.

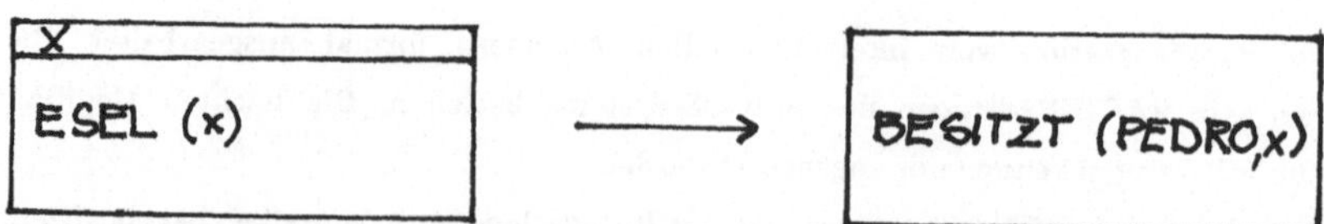

Damit ist der Diskursreferent x im weiteren Verlauf des Diskurses nicht mehr erreichbar. Und in der Tat klingt (1) abwegig, weil man - intuitiv gesprochen - nicht weiß, auf welchen Esel sich „ihn" beziehen sollte.

DRT und Pluralanaphern

Zunächst können sich Pluralanaphern sehr leicht auf Diskursentitäten beziehen, die im Sinne von DRT eingebettet und damit für den weiteren Diskurs als Bezugspunkte verloren sind.

(3)   Pedro besitzt alle Esel. Er schlägt sie.

Zwar ließe sich der propositionale Gehalt der beiden Sätze in (3) durch DRSen wiedergeben:

Aber ein solches Verfahren hätte den Nachteil, daß bereits beendete DRSen bei Hinzufügung neuer Sätze verändert werden müßten.

Außerdem kann kein Diskursreferent für „sie" gebildet werden. Diese Mängel machen sich in Beispiel (4) noch deutlicher geltend, wo über die Menge der fraglichen Esel quantifiziert wird und mit Hilfe dieser Quantifizierung sogar aus einer Diskursentität, die „alle Esel" umfaßt, eine neue gebildet wird, die aus „den Eseln, die geschlagen werden" besteht.

(4) Pedro besitzt alle Esel. Einige von ihnen schlägt er. Diese Esel laufen ihm davon.

Der Versuch, solche Strukturen durch DRSen darzustellen, würde einerseits zu progressiven Einbettungen und zu unübersichtlichen Konstruktionsverfahren für DRSen zwingen. Andererseits ist unklar wie - ohne explizite Diskursreferenten für plurale Gesamtheiten - die in (4) mittels definiter NPs ausgedrückten Existenzpräsuppositionen dargestellt werden können.

Pluralanaphern in Frage/Antwort-Dialogen

Im folgenden möchte ich die im Zusammenhang mit Pluralanaphern auftretenden - und teilweise schon angesprochenen - Phänomene anhand von Frage/Antwort-Dialogen des SPICOS-Systems zusammenstellen und verdeutlichen. Zu den Dialogen muß ich bemerken, daß die Antworten, die das System zur Zeit gibt, rein evaluierend sind. Das heißt, daß Ja/Nein-Fragen ihr Wahrheitswert, WH-Fragen ihre Extension zugeordnet wird. Diese Evaluierungsergebnisse werden (in mehr oder weniger geglückten) natürlichsprachlichen Formulierungen dargeboten. Damit werden in den Beispielen, von Individuenkonstanten abgesehen, die in den Antworten auf WH-Fragen auftreten, im wesentlichen keine neuen Diskursreferenten durch die Antworten zum Leben erweckt.

Quantifizierung

Plurale Anaphern können im Skopus eines Quantors stehen, d.h. der Quantor kann über die Elemente ihrer Extensionen laufen:

(5.1) FRAGE: Haben Mitarbeiter von Siemens Artikel über Spicos geschrieben?

(5.2) ANTWORT: Ja das ist der Fall.

(5.3a) FRAGE: Handelt einer der Artikel von Anaphern?

(5.3b) FRAGE: Wurde einer von ihnen veröffentlicht?

(5.3c) FRAGE: Wurde jeder von ihnen veröffentlicht?

Pluralanaphern verhalten sich in Bezug auf Quantoren offensichtlich in ähnlicher Weise wie *common nouns*, das heißt wie Entitäten, die i. a. durch Mengenterme oder Prädikate dargestellt werden.

Restriktion

Wenn Pluralanaphern Mengen denotieren, machen auch Restriktionen solcher Mengen Sinn. Die Restriktion von Anaphern durch Adjektive, Präpositionalphrasen oder Relativsätze scheint jedoch nur mit definiten, nicht demonstrativen NPs aufzutreten:

(6.1) FRAGE: Sind alle Vorträge von der letzten Spicossitzung an Lang geschickt worden?

(6.2) ANTWORT: Ja das ist der Fall.

(6.3a) FRAGE: Wer hat den Vortrag über Syntax verfaßt?

(6.3b) FRAGE: * Wer hat ihn/sie über Syntax verfaßt?

(6.3c) FRAGE: * Wer hat diesen Bericht/dieseBerichte über Syntax verfaßt?

Restriktionen im Zusammenhang mit Pronomen oder demonstrativen Nominalphrasen scheinen i. a. ungrammatisch oder doch sehr ungewöhnlich zu sein. Für die Repräsentation ist allerdings nur von Belang, daß mit Restriktionen im Zusammenhang mit Anaphern gerechnet werden muß. Der Ausschluß der ungrammatischen Konstruktionen (der für Speech-Systeme ein großes Problem ist) kann auf syntaktischer Ebene durchgeführt werden.

Die Einführung neuer Diskursreferenten unter Bezugnahme auf bereits bekannte Diskursentitäten

Wenn im Verlauf eines Diskurses, der nur singulare Anaphern behandelt, weitere Bedingungen an einen Diskursreferenten gestellt werden und - in DRT - als conditions in die DRS (oder in untergeordnete DRSen) eingefügt werden, dann wird dadurch kein neuer Diskursreferent erzeugt. (Allenfalls geschieht, daß die DRS durch keine Interpretation des Diskursreferenten mehr wahr gemacht werden kann.)

Ganz anders liegen die Verhältnisse bei Pluralanaphern. Der Benutzer kann etwa im Dialogbeispiel (5) nach der Frage (5.3a) und einer systemseitigen Bestätigung mit Frage (5.4) den Dialog fortsetzen:

(5.4) FRAGE: Wer hat ihn veröffentlicht?

Mit „ihn" wird aus der Menge der 'von Mitarbeitern von Siemens über Spicos geschriebenen Artikeln' derjenige herausgegriffen, der von Anaphern handelt. Es wird also, in (5.1) bis (5.4) keine zusätzliche

Bedingung an einen Diskursreferenten gestellt, sondern, vermöge einer Bedingung, aus einem mengenwertigen Diskursreferenten ein Element ausgewählt , das dann seinerseits durch Pronomen referenziert werden kann.

Es können aber aus einem mengenwertigen Diskursreferenten nicht nur einzelne Elemente, sondern gleichermaßen Teilmengen ausgesondert und als neue Diskursreferenten eingeführt werden. Wir haben diesen Vorgang schon in Beispiel (4) kennengelernt. Es lassen sich aber auch die Dialogfragmente (5) bzw. (6) leicht so variieren, daß dieser Effekt eintritt (siehe Beispiel (7)).

(7.1) FRAGE: Haben Mitarbeiter von Siemens Artikel über Spicos geschrieben?

(7.2) ANTWORT: Ja das ist der Fall.

(7.3) FRAGE: Handeln einige der Artikel von Anaphern?

(7.4) ANTWORT: Ja einige der Artikel handeln von Anaphern.

(7.5) FRAGE: Wurden sie veröffentlicht?

Am Rande möchte ich auf die Ambiguität in Beispiel (7) hinweisen. Je nach Intension von Frage (7.5) kann sich nämlich „sie" auf die größere Menge der 'Artikel von Siemens-Mitarbeitern über Spicos' oder auf die Teilmenge 'derjenigen über Anaphern' beziehen. Zur korrekten Anaphernresolution ist hier unter Umständen ein Klärungsdialog sinnvoll, wie er für die Implementierung der nächsten Systemversion auch geplant ist .

Restriktionen von Diskursreferenten vs. Bedingungen an Diskursreferenten

(8.1) FRAGE: Wer sind die Verfasser der Vorträge, die auf der letzten Spicos-Sitzung

                    gehalten wurden?

(8.2) ANTWORT: Das sind Niedermair, Thurmair, deVet und vanDeemter.

Um den Unterschied zwischen Restriktionen von Diskursreferenten und anderen Bedingungen, die im Zusammenhang mit dem Diskursreferenten auftreten, zu klären, wollen wir die beiden unterschiedlichen Fortsetzungen a) und b) des Dialoges (8) betrachten:

a)   (8.3a) FRAGE: Sind die Vorträge an Lang geschickt worden?

     (8.4a) ANTWORT: Nein, die Vorträge sind nicht an Lang geschickt worden.

     (8.5a) FRAGE: Wer sind ihre Verfasser?

     (8.6a) ANTWORT: Das sind Niedermair, Thurmair, deVet und vanDeemter.

b)   (8.3b) FRAGE: Sind die Vorträge über den dialogue handler auf der Sitzung gehalten

                          worden?

     (8.4b) ANTWORT: Ja, die Vorträge über den dialogue handler sind auf der Sitzung gehalten

                          worden.

     (8.5b) FRAGE: Wer sind ihre Verfasser?

     (8.6b) ANTWORT: Das sind deVet und vanDeemter.

Die Antworten (8.2), (8.6a) sind identisch, (8.6b) enthält nur eine Teilmenge der Verfassernamen. Die Klärung dieser Erscheinung gelingt nur, wenn man die unterschiedlichen grammatischen Funktionen , die „an Lang" und „über den dialogue handler" in den Fragen (8.4a) bzw. (8.4b) einnehmen, in Rechnung stellt. Die Bedingung, daß die Vorträge der Spicos-Sitzung an Lang geschickt wurden, beinflußt deren Extension nicht, sei die Bedingung nun erfüllt oder nicht. Wohl aber handelt es sich bei den Vorträgen mit dem Thema

Dialog nur um einen Teil der in Rede stehenden Vorträge. Denn es wird syntaktisch „an Lang" als Argument des Verbs aufgefaßt (etwa als Tiefenkasus 'Empfänger'), während „über den dialogue handler" als die (anaphorische) NP „die Vorträge" spezifizierende PP betrachtet wird. Ein Formalismus, der Pluralanaphern repräsentieren will, muß also grammatische Unterscheidungen darstellen können, die in einer rein propositionalen Betrachtungsweise normalerweise nicht getroffen werden. (Die Rede vom Verbargument ist dabei nur für Konstante im prädikatenlogischen Sinne korrekt. I. a. sind es Elemente aus der Extension der als 'Verbargument' bezeichneten NP oder PP, die im logischen Sinn Argumente des das Verb darstellenden Prädikates sind).

Präsuppositionen

Das Gebiet der Präsuppositionen kann aus Platzgründen leider nur gestreift werden.
In der Frage (8.3b) wird die Diskursentität 'Vorträge der letzten Spicos-Sitzung, die den Dialog zum Thema haben' durch eine definite NP eingeführt, wie dies häufig der Fall ist, wenn der Benutzer von der Existenz der Dinge überzeugt ist, die er beschreibt. Diese Existenzpräsupposition muß aber nicht stimmen. Falls sie verletzt ist, ist es von der Dialogführung her nicht adäquat, auf die Frage mit „Nein" zu antworten. (Abgesehen von dem Problem, daß ohne explizite Präsuppositionsbehandlung Behauptungen über nicht existierende Dinge wegen der bekannten Semantik des Konditionals unversehens wahr werden können).
Nicht nur Existenzpräsuppositionen können verletzt werden. Durch den Gebrauch von Plural oder Singular werden Präsuppositionen über Kardinalitäten ausgedrückt, die sich ebenfalls als falsch erweisen können.
Der Wunsch, diese Präsuppositionen überprüfen zu können, war ein weiterer Grund dafür, Diskursreferenten durch auswertbare Beschreibungen darzustellen. Die Sichtweise, Numerus- angaben als Kardinalitätspräsuppositionen aufzufassen, führte zu einer einheitlichen Darstellung von Singularen und Pluralen mithilfe von mengentheoretischen Ausdrücken.

Selbständigkeit der Diskursreferenten

(9.1) = (8.3b) FRAGE: Sind die Vorträge über den dialogue handler auf der Sitzung gehalten
worden?

(9.2) ANTWORT: Nein, das ist nicht der Fall.

(9.3) FRAGE: Sind sie veröffentlicht worden?

(9.4) ANTWORT: Ja, sie sind veröffentlicht worden.

Wir haben bereits gesehen, daß in (9.1) = (8.3b) ein neuer Diskursreferent eingeführt wird. Die Falsifizierung von (9.1) ändert nichts an seiner fortdauernden Existenz. Dies scheint mir ein wichtiges Argument dafür, die Darstellung der Diskursreferenten unabhängig von der Darstellung des propositionalen Gehalts der Diskursäußerungen zu gestalten.

Anaphorischer Bezug auf indefinit eingeführte Diskursreferenten

(10.1) FRAGE: Haben Mitarbeiter von Siemens Artikel über Spicos geschrieben?

(10.2) ANTWORT: Nein das ist nicht der Fall.

(10.3a) FRAGE: *Handelt einer der Artikel von Anaphern?

(10.3b) FRAGE: *Wurden sie alle veröffentlicht?

Im Unterschied zu definit eingeführten Diskursreferenten (vgl. (9)), stirbt der indefinit eingeführte Diskursreferent , wenn die Proposition, in der er eingeführt wurde, falsifiziert wird. Daß die indefinit eingeführten Diskursreferenten (im folgenden: indefiniter DR) von der gesamten Proposition abhängt, geht auch aus der intuitiven Beschreibung hervor, die man den fraglichen 'Artikeln' zuordnet:

(11)   'Artikel über Spicos, die von Mitarbeitern von Siemens geschrieben wurden'.

In der Beschreibung (11) haben wir sämtliche Prädikate (bzw. Mengen) benötigt, die in (10.1) auftreten, um diejenige Teilmenge der 'Artikel über Spicos' zu bestimmen, die dem DR entspricht. Man mag sich das mit Ersetzungstests oder Weglassungen klarmachen.

Ausgehend von diesen Beobachtungen kann man folgende zwei Adäquatheitsbedingungen für Beschreibungen indefiniter DRs formulieren:

(REF1) Der indefinite DR stellt eine Teilmenge der indefiniten NP dar, mit der er eingeführt
        wurde.

(REF2) Der indefinite DR hat genau dann nicht leere Extension , wenn die Proposition, in der
        er eingeführt wurde, wahr ist.

Die Aufgabe besteht demnach im indefiniten Fall darin, eine Restriktion der einführenden NP zu finden, die (REF2) erfüllt. Diese Restriktion werden wir durch ein geeignete Umformung der einführenden Proposition erhalten. Das eigentliche Problem dieser Umformung wird die Behandlung der Quantorenstruktur sein.

In der angegebenen Formulierung ist (REF2) nur für JA/NEIN-Fragen anwendbar. Für WH-Fragen kann (REF2) dennoch verwendet werden, wenn der WH-Frage die Existenzformel zugeordnet wird, die ausdrückt, daß die Extension der WH-Frage nicht leer ist.

Definitwerden indefiniter DRs

Wenn indefinite DRs durch eine bejahende Antwort bestätigt wurden, also nicht leer sind, kann mit anaphorischen Ausdrücken auf sie Bezug genommen werden. Durch diesen Vorgang werden sie zugleich definit und damit immun gegen die Falsifizierung der die Anapher enthaltenden Frage. Dann ist im Gegensatz zu definit eingeführten DRs auch die Existenzpräsupposition - trivialerweise - wahr.

Wie wir gesehen haben, können durch Quantifizierung und Restriktion aus definiten DRs, wiederum neue definite und indefinite DRs erzeugt werden.

Man beachte, daß auf indefinite DRs mit leerer Extension durch nichtanaphorische Ausdrücke sehr wohl Bezug genommen werden kann. Z. B.: „solche Artikel gibt es nicht".

Die Repräsentation indefiniter DRs

Zur Repräsentationssprache

Ich werde auf die verwendete Repräsentationsprache ELF nicht näher eingehen (für eine ausführliche Beschreibung siehe BUNT85). Worauf es hier ankommt ist, daß sich im Stile Montagues die syntaktischen Kategorien als logisch wohldefinierte Entitäten darstellen lassen. Für common nouns wird i.a. eine Darstellung als Mengenterm bevorzugt (gegenüber der Prädikatsdarstellung). Restriktionen mit Attributen,

PPs oder Relativsätzen werden durch die mengentheoretische Komprehension dargestellt. Aufgrund dieser Darstellungsweise ergibt sich nach der Lambda-Konversion eine Satzdarstellung, in der die Verbargumente als beschränkte Quantoren auftreten, Verben eine prädikative Darstellung erhalten.

Die Darstellung der Verbargumente als beschränkte Quantoren ist die hier wesentliche Eigenschaft, denn diese Darstellung erlaubt die Identifizierung syntaktischer Einheiten auf der semantischen Repräsentationsebene - jedenfalls in dem zur Anaphernrepräsentation nötigen Umfang.

Referenzmenge und Referenzrestriktion

Wir betrachten sogleich ein Beispiel mit relativ komplizierter Quantorenstruktur:

(12.1) FRAGE: Hat ein Mitarbeiter von Spicos an alle Projektbeteiligte Verträge geschickt?

(12.2) ANTWORT: Ja, das ist der Fall.

(12.3) FRAGE: Wer hat sie unterzeichnet?

Die (vereinfachte) ELF-Repräsentationen naheligender Lesarten der Fragen lauten:

(ELF12.1) $\exists$ x $\in$ {Mitarbeiter von Spicos} $\forall$ y $\in$ {Projektbeteiligte} $\exists$ z $\in$ {Verträge}

        schicken(x,y,z)

(ELF12.3) {x $\in$ Personen : $\exists$ y $\in$ SIE unterzeichnen (x , y) }

Die WH-Frage (12.3) wird als Menge dargestellt; denn als ihre Extension wird die Menge der Personen betrachtet, die einen der Verträge unterzeichnet hat.

Eine ausführliche Repräsentation von „{Mitarbeiter von Spicos}" würde etwa lauten:

{ x $\in$ Mitarbeiter : mitarbeitervon (x, Spicos) }.

Der Mengenterm, der die Extension eines DR beschreibt, soll als *Referenzmenge* bezeichnet werden. SIE ist hier syntaktische Variable und steht für die Referenzmenge des DR , auf den sich „sie" bezieht (kurz: Referenzmenge von „sie") .

Nach (REF1) hat SIE die Form

(13) {y $\in$ Verträge : Φ (y) }   Dabei wird Φ (y) als *Referenzrestriktion* bezeichnet

Man kann $\Phi(y)$ nun nicht dadurch erhalten, daß man in (ELF12.1) einfach den beschränkten Quantor „$\exists$ z $\in$ {Verträge}" beseitigt. Denn ein solches Vorgehen würde ergeben:

(14) SIE = { z $\in$ {Verträge} : $\exists$ x $\in$ {Mitarbeiter von Spicos} $\forall$ y $\in$ {Projektbeteiligte}

                        schicken (x,y,z) }

In (14) wird aber verlangt, daß an alle Projektbeteiligte derselbe Vertrag geschickt wurde, was gemäß (12.1) nicht der Fall sein muß. Ein Abschwächung der Referenzrestriktion aus (14) ,wie sie in (15) vorgenommen wird, hätte zur Folge, daß SIE auch dann nicht leere Extension haben kann, wenn (ELF12.1) falsifiziert worden wäre.

.(15) SIE = { z $\in$ {Verträge} : $\exists$ x $\in$ {Mitarbeiter von Spicos} $\exists$ y $\in$ {Projektbeteiligte}

                        schicken (x,y,z) }

Erst in (16) ist die Adäquatheitsbedingung (REF2) erfüllt .

(16) SIE = { z $\in$ {Verträge} : $\exists$ x $\in$ {Mitarbeiter von Spicos}

            (($\forall$ y $\in$ {Projektbeteiligte} $\exists$ z $\in$ {Verträge} schicken (x,y,z)

                &   ($\exists$y $\in$ {Projektbeteiligte} schicken (x,y,w))   )   }

Abschwächungen der Referenzrestriktion

Bei Fragen mit einfacherer Quantorenstruktur können, unter der Voraussetzung der Bestätigung der Frage, Abschwächungen der Referenzrestriktion vorgenommen werden. Denn die Voraussetzung der Wahrheit der Proposition, die den DR einführt, bedeutet eine logische Abschwächung der Adäquatsbedingung (REF2). Ich kann hier auf diese Probleme allerdings nicht näher eingehen. Die Darstellung (15) ist jedenfalls auch im „Wahrheitsfalle" zu liberal. Auch wenn (ELF12.1) bestätigt wird, kann nämlich SIE, gemäß (15) bestimmt, eine „zu weite" Extension besitzen. Denn in der durch (ELF 12.1) beschriebenen Lesart von (12.1) hat der Fragende einen Zusammenhang im Sinn, bei der ein bestimmter Bearbeiter für alle Projektbeteiligte Verträge bearbeitet hat. In (15) aber kommt eine größere Zahl von Vorgängen in Frage, was sich auch formal zeigen läßt.

Die Formationsregeln für die Referenzrestriktion

Im folgenden wird ein Schema von Formationsregeln gegeben, die die Referenzrestriktion eines DR aus der Repräsentation der ihn einführenden Spicos-Frage formal erzeugen.

Eine Repräsentation der den DR einführenden Frage sei durch (17) gegeben.

(17) $Q_1 x_1 \in ARG_1 \dots Q_i x_i \in ARG_i \dots Q_n x_n \in ARG_n \quad p (x_1 ,\dots x_i ,\dots x_n)$

„Q" ist syntaktische Variable für Existenz- und Allquantor. Die ARG_i bezeichnen Mengenterme, die durch „$Q_i x_i \in ARG_i$ bezeichneten beschränkten Quantoren, stellen die Verbargumente dar.

$p (x_1 ,\dots x_i ,\dots x_n)$ bezeichnet eine beliebige Formel mit den freien Variablen $x_1 ,\dots x_i ,\dots x_n$. (Im System Spicos handelt es sich dabei zur Zeit immer um ein nicht negiertes atomares Prädikat, das ein Verb repräsentiert, aber das ist hier nicht vorausgesetzt.) Es wird jedoch vorausgesetzt, daß allquantifizierte Verbargumente keine leere Grundmengen besitzen. Das bedeutet, daß Existenzpräsuppositionen geprüft wurden.

<u>Definition der Formationsregeln</u>

Sei $\Psi \equiv Q_1 x_1 \in ARG_1 \dots Q_i x_i \in ARG_i \dots Q_n x_n \in ARG_n \quad p (x_1 ,\dots x_i ,\dots x_n) \quad$ gemäß (17).

Wir definieren

$\Psi j (x_1 ,\dots, x_{j-1}) : \equiv Q_j x_j \in ARG_j \dots Q_n x_n \in ARG_n \, p (x_1 ,\dots x_j \dots x_n) \, (1 < j < n+1)$

Außerdem setzen wir fest: $\quad \Psi n+1 \equiv p (x_1 ,\dots x_i ,\dots x_n) \quad$ und $\quad \Psi 1 \equiv \Psi$

Die Formationsfunktoren $F_i (1 < = i < = n)$ werden definiert wie folgt:

wenn $j < i$ dann $\quad F_i (\Psi j) : \equiv$ a) $\quad Q_j x_j \in ARG_j F_i(\Psi j+1) \qquad\qquad$ wenn $Q_j \equiv \exists$

$\qquad\qquad\qquad\qquad$ b) $\quad \Psi j \,\&\, \exists x_j \in ARG_j F_i(\Psi j+1) \qquad$ wenn $Q_j \equiv \forall$

wenn $j = i$ dann $F_i (\Psi j) : \equiv \Psi j+1$

Wenn ein indefiniter DR durch das Verbargument ARG_i eingeführt wird dann gilt für die Referenzmenge, die wir mit DR-REF bezeichnen, die folgende Definitionsgleichung (FORM1). $F_i (\Psi)$ stellt dabei die Referenzrestriktion dar.

(FORM1) $\quad$ DR-REF $:= \{ x_i \in ARG_i : F_i (\Psi) \, \}$

Als Beispiel wollen wir die Referenzmenge von „sie" aus (12.3) mithilfe der Formationsregeln konstruieren. Der DR von „sie" wurde durch die indefinite NP„Verträge" eingeführt. „Verträge" bildet in der semantischen Repräsentation das dritte Verbargument, wir müssen nach (FORM1) also F_3 anwenden. Sei Ψ die Formel (ELF12.1), sei SIE-REF die Referenzmenge von „sie" und sei Φ (y) die zugehörige Referenzrestriktion. Damit ergibt sich:

SIE-REF $\equiv \{$ z $\in \{$Verträge$\}$: Φ (y) $\}$

wobei Φ (y) $\equiv F_3(\Psi) \equiv F_3(\Psi^1)$

$\equiv \exists$ x $\in \{$Mitarbeiter von Spicos$\}F_3(\Psi^2)$

$\equiv \exists$ x $\in \{$Mitarbeiter von Spicos$\}$ (Ψ^2 & ($\exists$y $\in \{$Projektbeteiligte$\}$ $F_3(\Psi^3)$))

$\equiv \exists$ x $\in \{$Mitarbeiter von Spicos$\}$ (Ψ^2 & ($\exists$y $\in\{$Projektbeteiligte$\}$ Ψ^4))

$\equiv \exists$ x $\in \{$Mitarbeiter von Spicos$\}$ (($\forall$ y $\in \{$Projektbeteiligte$\}$ $\exists$ z $\in \{$Verträge$\}$

schicken (x,y,z))

& ($\exists$y $\in \{$Projektbeteiligte$\}$ schicken (x,y,z))))

Definite DRs

Durch die Definitheit wird, wie wir gesehen haben, die Unabhängigkeit des DR von der Proposition ausgedrückt, die ihn einführt.

Wenn ein definiter DR durch das Verbargument ARG_i eingeführt wird, dann gilt demnach für die Referenzmenge DR-REF des Diskursreferenten die einfache Definitionsgleichung (FORM2).

(FORM2) DR-REF $:\equiv ARG_i$

Bei den definiten DRs liegt das eigentliche Problem einerseits in der Behandlung der Präsuppositionen, andererseits in der Entscheidung, ob tatsächlich ein definiter DR eingeführt wird, oder ob eine Anapher vorliegt. Auf beide Probleme kann hier nicht eingegangen werden.

Literatur

BUNT85 : Bunt H. , "Mass Nouns and Model Theoretic Semantics" , Cambridge University Press, 1985

GUENTHNER86 : Guenthner F. , Lehmann, H. , Schonfeld, W. ,"A Theory for the Representation of Knowledge" , in: IBM J Res Develop, vol. 30 nr. 1, pp. 35 56, 1986

HEIM83 : Heim, I. , "File Change Semantics and the Familiarity Theory of Definiteness" in: "Meaning, Use and Interpretation of Language" , Baeuerle, R. , Schwarze, Ch. , von Stechow, A. , eds. : pp. 164 -189, de Gruyter, Berlin/New York, 1983

KAMP81 : Kamp, H. ,"A Theory of Truth and Semantic Representation", in: "Formal Methods in the Study of Language", Groenendijk et al. (eds), Amsterdam, 1981

WEBBER83 : Webber, B. L. , "So What Can We Talk About Now?" , in: Computational Models of Discourse, Brady, M. , and Berwick, R. C. , eds. , ch. 6, pp. 331 - 371, The MIT Press Series in Artificial Intelligence, MIT Press, Cambridge MA, London, 1983

Functional Uncertainty and Functional Precedence in Continental West Germanic

Ronald M. Kaplan and Annie Zaenen
Xerox Palo Alto Research Center

An account of the various word order phenomena in Continental West Germanic is one of the standard challenges that a linguistic theory has to face. In this paper we will concentrate on word order in infinitival complements. In this subarea the order of the different verbal elements has received the most attention. We focus, however, on the order of the non-verbal elements. To simplify matters we will mainly look at the order of the nominal dependents of verbs. We start by reviewing the Lexical-Functional Grammar analysis of so-called crossing dependencies in Dutch as given in Bresnan et al. (1982) and amended in Johnson (1986). In Section 2, we show that another formal statement of the generalizations using functional precedence and functional uncertainty is technically possible and empirically preferable. In section 3, we summarize some facts of Zurich German discussed in Lötscher (1978) and in Haegeman and van Riemsdijk (1986) and show that these facts can only be handled assuming a version of functional precedence.

1. Crossing dependencies in Dutch

Since Evers (1975) first pointed out the properties of sentences like (1), several syntactic models have been proposed to account for them.

(1) ... dat Jan zijn zoon geneeskunde wil laten studeren.
   ... that John his son medicine wants let study.

We assume that *willen* 'want', *laten* 'let' and *studeren* 'study' have the functional subcategorization frames in (2):

(2) willen: $(\uparrow$ PRED$) = $ 'want$<(\uparrow$ SUBJ$)(\uparrow$ XCOMP$)>$'
       $(\uparrow$ SUBJ$) = (\uparrow$ XCOMP SUBJ$)$
   laten: $(\uparrow$ PRED$) = $ 'let$<(\uparrow$ SUBJ$)(\uparrow$ XCOMP$)>(\uparrow$ OBJ$)$'
       $(\uparrow$ OBJ$) = (\uparrow$ XCOMP SUBJ$)$
   studeren: $(\uparrow$ PRED$) = $ 'study$<(\uparrow$ SUBJ$)(\uparrow$ OBJ$)>$'

As these entries show, *willen* and *laten* are treated as functional control verbs, and *studeren* is a simple transitive verb. The problem is how to account for the fact that *geneeskunde* 'medicine' is interpreted as the object of *studeren*. In the transformational treatment of Evers (1975), the predicate argument structure is read off the deep structure phrase structure configuration. At that stratum, *studeren* and *geneeskunde* are adjacent, or at least within the same VP, just like a simple verb and its object are, as illustrated in (3). Verb-raising then moves the verb to its surface position.

(3) ... dat Jan geneeskunde studeert.
   ... that John studies medicine.

LFG has no movement rules and the dependency between the object and the embedded verb is established in another way. Discontinuous dependencies are, however, no problem for LFG because of the way the mapping from c-structure to f-structure is defined.

As some of the notions we want to use later crucially depend on particular characteristics of this mapping, we summarize here its relevant properties. LFG assumes there is a correspondence function ϕ from c-structure nodes to f-structure units, but this correspondence is not assumed to be one-to-one nor is it required to be onto (Kaplan and Bresnan, 1982; Kaplan, 1987). Both of these properties are illustrated by the following example of an English gerund construction:

(4)

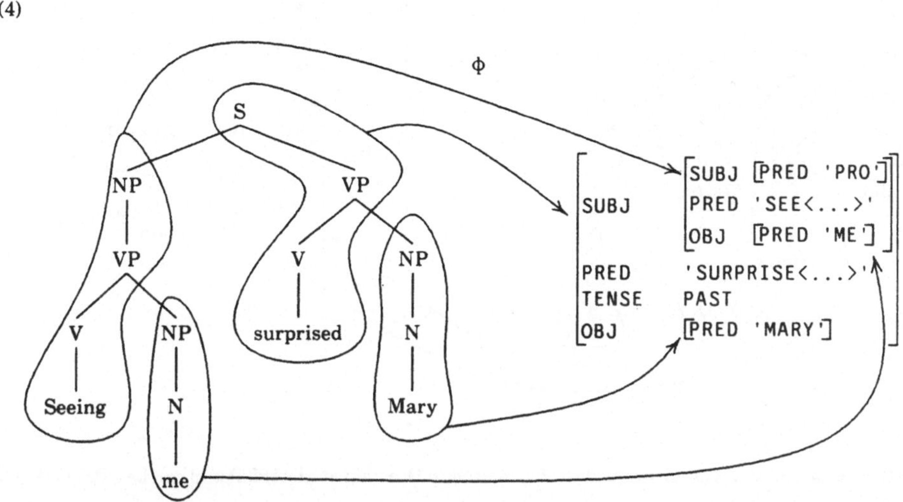

The functional annotations on the English phrase-structure rules would make all the nodes in a circled collection map to the same f-structure unit, demonstrating the many-to-one property of ϕ, and there is no node in the c-structure that maps to the pronoun subject of the predicate *see*, so that ϕ is not onto. In English nodes that map onto the same f-structure tend to stand in simple mother-daughter relations, but this is not the only possible configuration for many-to-one mappings. Bresnan et al. (1982) account for the Dutch discontinuous constituents by mapping two noncontiguous c-structure components into one f-structure. This is specified by the following two simple rules:

(5)　(a)　VP　→　　(NP)　　　　(VP)　　(V')
　　　　　　　　　($\uparrow$ OBJ)$=$$\downarrow$　　($\uparrow$ XCOMP)$=$$\downarrow$

　　　(b)　V'　→　　V　　　(V')
　　　　　　　　　　　　($\uparrow$ XCOMP)$=$$\downarrow$

The annotation on the VP preceding the V' in (5a) and the annotation on the V' expanding the V' in (5b) are the same and hence they both provide information about the shared corresponding f-structure. The main constraint on dependencies of this kind in Dutch is that all the arguments of a higher verb precede those of a lower verb; the arguments of each verb are ordered as in simple clauses and we will not discuss these orderings here (see Zaenen, in progress, for a discussion of the constraints on the order of nominal arguments in Dutch). The c-structure rules in (5) insure this ordering because the VP expands to an (optional) NP OBJect followed by an open complement VP (XCOMP). The c-structure itself thus imposes the right ordering: less embedded OBJ's always precede more embedded ones. The different parts of the more and more embedded XCOMP's link up in the right way because the XCOMP's are associated with successive expansions on both the VP and V' spines of the tree as illustrated in (6):

(6)

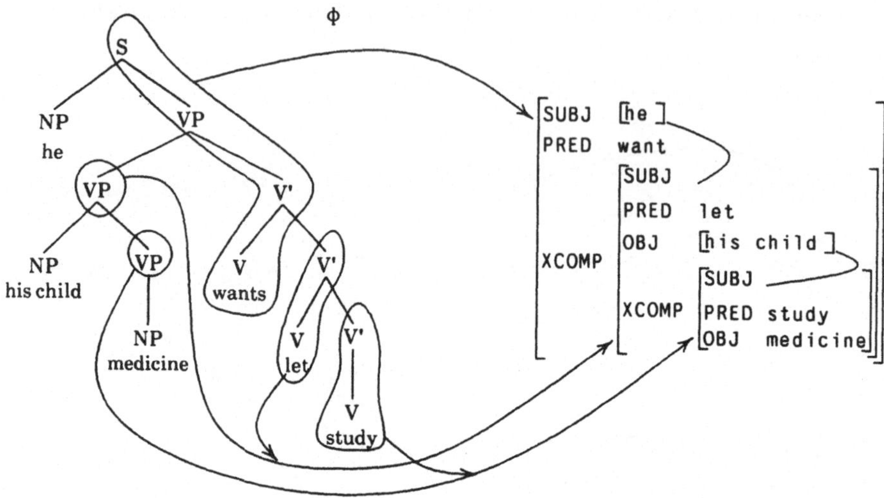

This system gives a correct description of the data considered in Bresnan et al. (1982) and can be extended in a straightforward way to cover further infinitival constructions as shown in Johnson (1986). However, it has two drawbacks, one technical and one linguistic. The technical one was pointed out in Johnson (1986) and in Netter (1987). In some cases the expansions required in these extensions violate the LFG constraint against non-branching dominance chains (Kaplan and Bresnan, 1982). According to this condition on valid c-structures, derivations of the form A $\rightarrow^*$ A, which permit an indefinite number of A nodes dominating another node of the same category, are prohibited. This restriction against non-branching dominance chains prohibits c-structure nodes that provide no information and insures that the parsing problem for LFG grammars is decidable.

The linguistic problem is that this analysis does not account for sentences like (7), which are considered perfectly grammatical by most speakers (M. Moortgat, p.c.):

(7)   ... dat Jan een liedje schreef en trachtte te verkopen.
        ... that John a song wrote and tried to sell.

Here *een liedje* 'a song' is the OBJ of *schreef* 'wrote' and of *verkopen* 'sell', but these verbs are at different levels of embedding. To be interpreted as the argument of *schreef*, *een liedje* has to be the object, but to be interpreted as an argument of *verkopen*, it has to be the object of the XCOMP. According to the LFG theory of coordination, a coordinate structure is represented formally as a set in f-structure, with the elements of the set being the f-structures corresponding to the individual conjuncts. LFG's function-application primitive is extended in a natural way to apply to sets of f-structures: a set is treated as if it were a function with the properties that are common to all its f-structure elements (see Kaplan and Maxwell (1988b) for formal details). As Bresnan, Kaplan, and Peterson (forthcoming) show, this simple extension is sufficient to provide elegant accounts for the wide variety of facts that coordinate reduction rules and across-the-board conventions attempt to handle. Given the rules in (5) and this theory of coordination, *een liedje* will not be properly distributed across the two conjuncts in (7), since it has to have a different function in each. The problem is illustrated by the disjunctive function assignments in diagram (8):

(8)

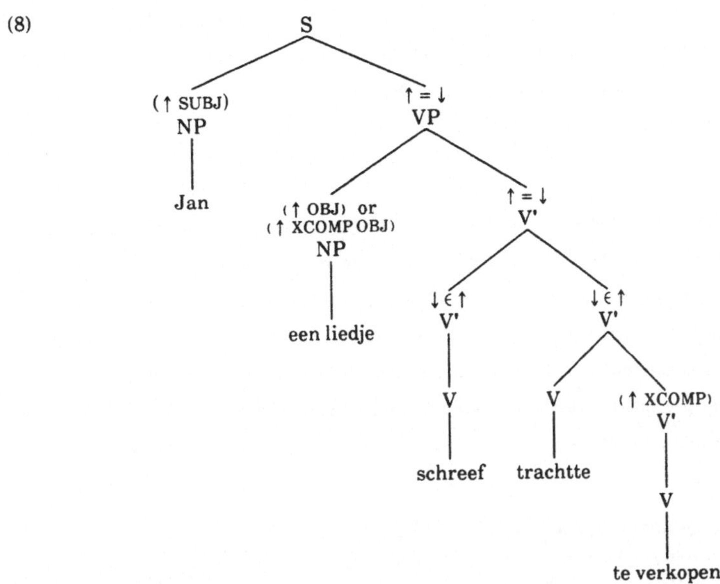

2. A New Proposal

We now propose a revision that takes care of these problems and then examine some of its other consequences. Some of the elements of this new account can also be found in Johnson (1986) and, for a different set of data, in Netter (1987).

To solve the technical problem, Johnson (1986) proposes to replace the phrase-structure rule (5a) by the one given in (9):

(9)   VP   →   (NP)   (VP)   (V')
                    (↑ OBJ) = ↓   (↑ XCOMP+) = ↓

The only difference is in the schema attached to the optional VP. This schema now uses the device of functional uncertainty that was introduced in Kaplan and Zaenen (1988) and developed further in Kaplan and Maxwell (1988a). The f-structure associated with this VP is not asserted to be the XCOMP of the V' at the corresponding level of c-structure embedding. Rather, it is asserted only that it is the value at the end of a chain of one or more XCOMP's, as denoted by the regular expression XCOMP+. This possibility obviates the need for VP expansions in which a VP exhaustively dominates another VP. Predicates and arguments will still be linked up properly because of the completeness and coherence conditions that are independently imposed on f-structure. The right word order is also maintained because the material contained in the VP following an

OBJ NP is always at least one level further embedded than the OBJ itself: the annotation is XCOMP+, not XCOMP*.

Notice, however, that the rule in (9) does not account for example (7). If the NP is generated as the OBJ of the highest VP under S, then its only function is OBJ and cannot be distributed into the second conjunct as an XCOMP OBJ. On the other hand, if it is generated under an embedded VP so that it has the proper function for the second conjunct, it cannot be a simple OBJ for the first conjunct. If we change the annotation on the VP to XCOMP*, so that the NP is properly distributed to both conjuncts, then we lose all possibility of imposing the cross-serial ordering constraints by phrase-structure encoding. One can complicate the c-structure to get the desired result in this case, but in what follows we explore a different type of solution. This solution has the advantage of generalizing in a straightforward way to account for word-order facts in other languages, as is shown in Section 3.

Functional uncertainty was originally developed to handle wh-movement constructions and to insure their proper interaction with coordination. Another formal device that was introduced into LFG theory after Bresnan et al. (1982) was published is functional precedence. This was applied to anaphoric dependencies by Bresnan (1984) and formally defined in Kaplan (1987). Precedence is a defining relation among the constituents in a c-structure, in the sense that trees with different node-orderings are interpreted as formally different trees. There is no native precedence relation among the parts of an f-structure, but the image of c-structure precedence under the mapping from c-structure to f-structure naturally induces a relation on f-structure, which we call f-precedence:

(10)   For two f-structure elements f_1 and f_2, f_1 *f-precedes* f_2 if and only if
        all the nodes that map onto f_1 c-precede all the nodes that map onto f_2; or
        $f_1 <_f f_2$ iff for all n_1 in $\phi^{-1}(f_1)$ and for all n_2 in $\phi^{-1}(f_2)$, $n_1 <_c n_2$.

Even though this relation is so directly connected to the conventional c-structure precedence, it has some surprising properties because the mapping from c-structure to f-structure is neither one-to-one nor onto. For example, if the mapping is many-to-one and f_1 and f_2 correspond to interleaved sets of c-structure nodes, then neither f_1 f-precedes f_2 nor f_2 f-precedes f_1. If the mapping is not onto so that f_1 corresponds to no node at all, then vacuously both f_1 f-precedes f_2 and f_2 f-precedes f_1 for all f_2. (This characteristic of f-precedence will not be discussed further in this paper but is exploited in the analysis of null anaphors by Bresnan, 1984 and Kameyama, forthcoming.) Technically, f-precedence is not a true ordering relation, since it is neither antisymmetric nor transitive. Its name is meant to indicate that it is a functional image of c-precedence, not that it is a precedence relation on f-structure. It also differs from c-precedence in its linguistic implications: while c-precedence restrictions can only directly order sister constituents, f-precedence constraints can implicitly restrict ordering relations among non-sister nodes by virtue of the common f-structure units they correspond to.

We use the f-precedence relation to reformulate the rules in (5). We dispense with the VP dominated subtree altogether and assume a simple succession of NP nodes. Then we add the requirement that the OBJ of a predicate's XCOMP does not f-precede the predicate's own OBJ. The revised rules are given in (11):

$$(11) \quad \text{VP} \rightarrow \quad \begin{array}{cc} \text{NP*} & \text{V'} \\ (\uparrow \text{XCOMP* OBJ}) = \downarrow & \end{array}$$

$$\text{V'} \rightarrow \quad \text{V} \quad \begin{array}{c} (\text{V'}) \\ (\uparrow \text{XCOMP}) = \downarrow \\ (\uparrow \text{XCOMP}^+ \text{OBJ}) <_f (\uparrow \text{OBJ}) \end{array}$$

These rules can be easily generalized to include the OBJ2 and OBLique functions that a larger set of data would require. This way of reformulating the constraint on order allows us to propose maximally simple c-structure expansions for Dutch infinitival constructions. A similar flat structure was rejected in Bresnan et al. (1982) for two reasons, one based on word order constraints and the other on the low acceptability of certain coordination constructions. It was thought that the VP node was necessary to account for the fact that the oblique PP arguments of an XCOMP cannot precede an OBJ on a higher level of embedding whereas in a simple clause a PP can precede its OBJ. This argument depends on the assumption that the word order condition can only be stated in c-precedence terms, an assumption which we now reject in favor of the f-precedence relation. The observed pattern of acceptability easily follows when we extend the flat c-structure rules in (11) to include PP's as well.

The unacceptable coordination is exemplified in (12) (example (20) from Bresnan et al.):

(12) ?? ... dat Jan de meisjes een treintje aan Piet en de jongens een pop aan Henk zag geven voor Marie
... that Jan the girls a toy train to Piet and the boys a doll to Henk saw gave for Marie
... 'that Jan saw the boys give a toy train to Piet and the girls give a dool to Henk for Marie.'

This is not considered ungrammatical by all speakers (W. de Geest, p.c.), but even if it were, it justifies the proposed hierarchical c-structure only on the assumption that a single constituent can be right-node raised in Dutch. This assumption is clearly incorrect: sentences like the following are completely acceptable:

(13) ... dat Annie witte en Marie bruine suiker op haar boterham wil
... that Annie white and Mary brown sugar on her bread wants.
... 'that Annie wants brown sugar on her bread and Marie white sugar.'

Here the shared material is not a constituent. While this observation does not explain the contrast noted in Bresnan et al. (1982), it does undermine their second argument in favor of the hierarchical structure of the NP sequence.

We conclude then that the use of functional uncertainty and f-precedence allows a treatment of the Dutch infinitival constructions that avoids the two problems of the Bresnan et al. account. It would be surprising, however, if the Dutch facts alone would require f-precedence and functional uncertainty as desirable ingredients in an account of the syntactic properties of infinitival constructions. In what follows we examine some facts of Zurich German that are naturally handled in terms of f-precedence.

3. Zurich German

The infinitival constructions of Zurich German are similar to the Dutch ones discussed above in that generally the verbs come in the same order (the least embedded ones precede the more embedded ones). Sentences that are grammatical in Dutch will also be acceptable in Zurich German as the sentence in (14) illustrates:

(14) ... das er sini chind mediziin wil laa studiere.
... 'that he wants to let his child study medicine.'
(translation as given in Haegeman and van Riemsdijk, 1986)

The language allows a broader range of possibilities, however. In Standard Dutch the verbs have to cluster together whereas in Zurich German NP's and PP's can be interleaved with the verbs as illustrated in (15):

(15)   ... das er wil sini chind laa mediziin studiere.
        ... das er sini chind wil laa mediziin studiere.

But not all orders are allowed. The versions in (16) are unacceptable under normal intonation and (17) is out in all circumstances:

(16)   * ... das er wil mediziin laa sini chind studiere.
           ... das er mediziin sini chind wil laa studiere.

(17)   * ... das er wil laa sini chind mediziin studiere.

This suggests two constraints on the word order in infinitival constructions in Zurich German (cf. Johnson, 1987):

(18)   (a)   The arguments of a higher verb precede those of a more deeply embedded one.

        (b)   All the nominal arguments of a particular verb precede it.

These constraints hold also in Standard Dutch, as we saw in Section 1, but for Zurich German they cannot be formulated in the same way as was done in Bresnan et al. (1982) for Dutch (5). This is because in Zurich German the NP's whose relative order has to be maintained are not adjacent. Let us consider the examples in (19) and compare them to (20):

(19)   (a)   ... das er sini chind wil mediziin laa studiere.

        (b)   * ... das er mediziin wil sini chind laa studiere.

The cause of the difference in grammaticality between (19a) and (19b) is the relative order of *sini chind* and *mediziin*, not the location of each argument with respect to its governing verb (in both cases the arguments precede their governing verb, so constraint (18b) is respected). That the distance between *mediziin* and *studiere* in (19b) in itself does not matter is shown by (20):

(20)   ... das er en arie hät wele singe.
        ... that he had wanted to sing an aria.

Here *en arie* is the object of *singe*, the lowest verb, and the level of embedding is the same as in (19b) where *mediziin* is also the object of the lowest verb. We have to allow for an expansion of the preverbal material that allows *en arie* to link up with its verb. For the sake of concreteness let us consider the phrase-structure rules in (21):

(21)   (a)   VP   →   (NP)   (VP)   (V')
                            ($\uparrow$ OBJ) = $\downarrow$ ($\uparrow$ XCOMP) = $\downarrow$

        (b)   V'   →   V   (VP)
                                ($\uparrow$ XCOMP) = $\downarrow$

These are minimally different from the Dutch rules in (5) above. The only change is that a VP instead of a V' appears in (21b) after the main verb of each expansion to allow for embedded NP's. Ignoring the problem of non-branching dominance chains, this set of rules assigns to (19a) the structure shown in (22):

(22)

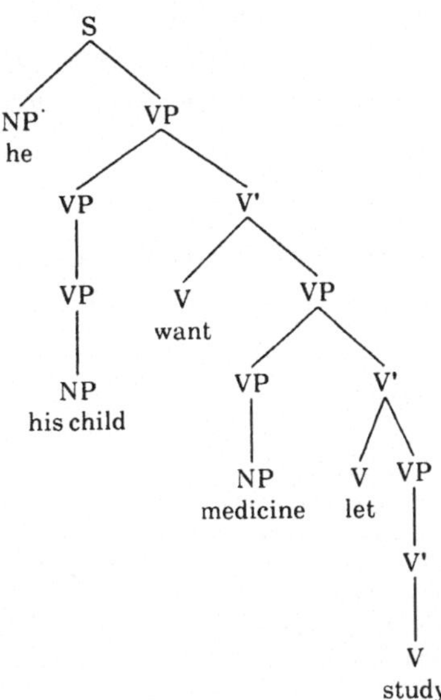

But of course these rules will accommodate (19b) as well. Given that the NP *sini chind* that should precede *mediziin* for the sentence to be correct is on a different spine, the expansions of the two VP's cannot keep track of each other's level of embedding. Any phrase-structure attempt to keep the NP's at the same level of the c-structure as the XCOMP of the preceding verb requires functional uncertainty to insure that the right level of functional and semantic embedding is eventually reached. But it is not possible to force one of the expansions of the functional uncertainty to be longer or shorter than the other, and this reintroduces the NP ordering problem. The alternative rule in (23), for example, also accomodates (19b), as shown in (24):

(23)　　VP　　→　　　　　(NP)　　　　(V)　　　(VP)
　　　　　　　　　　(↑ XCOMP* GF) = ↓　　　　(↑ XCOMP) = ↓

(24)

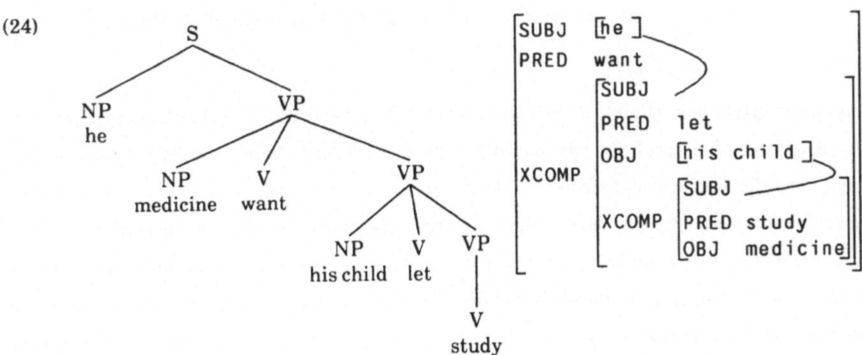

Of course, once we add an appropriate f-precedence statement, the overgeneration of the phrase-structure rules in (21) or (23) or any similar set does no harm.

Here, then, we have a case in which f-precedence, which was introduced as one way of solving the coordination problem for Dutch, plays a more essential role. The use of functional uncertainty in conjunction with f-precedence allows us to account for these data without violating the non-branching dominance constraint.

4. Conclusion

The facts discussed above are but a small sample of the various word order constraints in different, not necessarily related, languages which seem to need to be stated over similar chains of open complements. In Finnish too, word order is rather free in such chains of infinitival clauses, as illustrated by the following truth-conditionally equivalent versions of one sentence:

(25) En minä ole aikonut ruveta näissä tennistä pelaamaan.
   not I have intended to-start in-these tenis to-play.
   'I have not intended to start to play tennis in these (clothes).'

   En minä näissä ole aikonut ruveta tennistä pelaamaan.
   En minä näissä ole tennistä aikonut ruveta pelaamaan.
   En minä näissa tennistä ole aikonut ruveta pelaamaan.

Facts like these are described in detail in Vilkuna (forthcoming). To give a precise characterization of the domain in which these order variations can occur goes beyond the scope of this paper, but it can be done in a quite straightforward way (see Vilkuna (forthcoming) and Netter and Zaenen (forthcoming) for discussion).

Other phenomena that occur in open-complement infinitives and involve non-local dependencies are focus raising in Standard German as discussed in Uszkoreit (1984), extraposition in Standard German and, of course, for most variants of Standard German, wh-constructions. We have shown that the way dependencies in this domain are modeled by Bresnan et al. (1982) leads to empirical problems for Dutch coordination. Similar examples can be constructed for the other languages, e.g. for Finnish:

(26) En minä mitään peliä aio pelata ja ruveta sinulle opettamaan.
   Not I any game intend to play and to begin to teach to you.

Combinations of functional precedence and functional uncertainty give the right results in these other cases also.

The use of functional uncertainty over chains of open-complements tends to make linguists uneasy, however. Dependencies that they think of as local are treated with a device that they think should be reserved for so-called unbounded, long-distance dependencies. This sense of uneasiness seems to come from the assumption that apart from the wh-type, the taxonomy of linguistic dependencies needs to recognize only two domains: the clause, comprising a verb, all its immediate arguments, and the adjuncts pertaining to it, and an extension of this domain that includes only the subject of an immediately embedded clause. In our view, the facts discussed above show that this taxonomy is insufficient: some non-wh dependencies hold over larger domains, and functional uncertainty offers a natural account of these phenomena. What distinguishes these facts from classical wh-movement phenomena is not the length of the functional path over which the dependencies hold but that the type of functions that are allowed on that path. The functional path in the cases we have considered in this paper is very restricted: it can contain only open complement functions. When restricted in this way, functional uncertainty and functional precedence provide formal devices for constructing new intuitive models of these phenomena.

Acknowledgements

We are grateful to Mark Johnson, Lauri Karttunen, Klaus Netter, and two anonymous referees for helpful comments on a previous draft of this paper.

References

Bresnan, J. (1984) Bound Anaphora and Functional Structures. Unpublished paper given at the annual meeting of the Berkeley Linguistic Society, Berkeley, California.

Bresnan, J., R. Kaplan, S. Peters, and A. Zaenen (1982) Cross-serial dependencies in Dutch. *Linguistic Inquiry* 13, 613-635.

Bresnan, J., R. Kaplan and P. Peterson (forthcoming) Coordination in LFG. Xerox Palo Alto Research Center, Palo Alto, California.

Evers, A. (1975) *The transformational Cycle in Dutch.* Unpublished doctoral dissertation, University of Utrecht, Utrecht.

Haegeman, L. and H. van Riemsdijk (1986) VPR, Scope, and the Typology of Rules affecting Verbs. *Linguistic Inquiry,* 17, 417-466.

Johnson, M. (1986) *The LFG Treatment of Discontinuity and the Double Infinitive Construction in Dutch.* CSLI Report No. CSLI-86-65, Stanford University, Palo Alto, California.

Johnson, M. (1987) *Attribute-value logic and the theory of grammar.* Unpublished doctoral dissertation, Stanford University, Palo Alto, California.

Kameyama, M. (forthcoming) Precedence conditions on overt and zero nominals. Unpublished paper, Microelectronics and Computer Technology Corporation, Austin, Texas.

Kaplan, R. (1987) Three seductions of computational psycholinguistics. In P. Whitelock, M. M. Woods, H. L. Somers, R. Johnson, P. Bennett (eds.), *Linguistic Theory and Computer Applications.* London: Academic Press, 149-181.

Kaplan, R. and J. Bresnan (1982) Lexical-Functional Grammar: A Formal System for Grammatical Representation. In J. Bresnan (ed.), *The Mental Representation of Grammatical Relations.* Cambridge, Massachusetts: MIT Press, 173-281.

Kaplan, R. and J. Maxwell (1988a) An Algorithm for Functional Uncertainty. Proceedings of Coling '88.

Kaplan, R. and J. Maxwell (1988b) Constituent coordination in Lexical-Functional Grammar. Proceedings of Coling '88.

Kaplan, R. and A. Zaenen (1988) Long-distance Dependencies, Constituent Structure, and Functional Uncertainty. In M. Baltin and A. Kroch (eds.), *Alternative conceptions of phrase structure.* Chicago: University of Chicago Press.

Lötscher, A. (1978) Zur Verbstellung im Zürichdeutschen und in andren Varianten des Deutschen. *Zeitschrift fuer Dialektologie und Linguistik,* 45, 1-29.

Netter, K. (1987) Wortstellung und Verbalkomplex im Deutschen. In U. Klenk et al. (eds.), *Computerlinguistik une Philologische Datenverarbeitung.* Hildesheim, 98-114.

Netter, K. and A. Zaenen (in progress) Infinitival complements in German and Dutch.

Uszkoreit, H. (1984) *Word Order and Constituent Structure in German.* Unpublished doctoral dissertation, University of Texas, Austin, Texas.

Vilkuna, M. (in progress) *Word Order in Finnish.* Unpublished doctoral dissertation, University of Helsinki, Helsinki.

Zaenen, A. (in progress) Nominal arguments in Dutch and wysiwyg syntax. Xerox Palo Alto Research Center, Palo Alto, California.

Linguistisches Wissen und Strategie
in einer syntaktischen Analyse des Deutschen

Dorothee Reimann

Zentralinstitut für Sprachwissenschaft
der Akademie der Wissenschaften der DDR
Prenzlauer Promenade 149-152
DDR-1100 Berlin

Einleitung

Im Vortrag wird ein System zur syntaktischen Analyse des Deutschen vorgestellt, das bereits eine relativ lange Geschichte hat. Es beruht wesentlich auf dem von KUNZE (1975) entwickelten Modell einer Abhängigkeitsgrammatik, das mathematisch fundiert die Grundbegriffe für die Beschreibung der syntaktischen Struktur von Sätzen (auch unter Verwendung semantischer Mittel) definiert. Eine erste algorithmische Bearbeitung dieser theoretischen Grundlage in Hinblick auf ein Verfahren zur syntaktischen Analyse des Deutschen (AROLD 1976) zeigte, daß das rein deklarative Regelsystem (ohne spezielle Abarbeitungsstrategie) mit einem derart komplexen Regelformat nicht zu einem praktikablen Parser führen konnte (s. Abschnitt 1).
Es stand deshalb die Aufgabe, eine Strategiekomponente zu entwickeln, die es ermöglicht, die wesentlichen Grundlagen der Theorie beizubehalten, aber dennoch ein übersichtliches System zu gestalten, in dem die sehr komplexen Mittel in einfachere zerlegt werden und in dem auch die Analyse effektiv ablaufen kann. Das Ergebnis dieser Untersuchungen ist ein System, das bewußt mit den verschiedenen Arten von linguistischem Wissen umgeht, d.h. es ist bei jedem Analyseschritt klar, welches linguistische Wissen benötigt wird. Das Gesamtsystem ist derart angelegt, daß durch die Verwendung einfacherer Mittel zunächst das Problem reduziert wird und somit die zuletzt eingesetzten komplexen Mittel nicht mehr zu einer Explosion des Aufwandes führen können, sondern lediglich als Filter für verschiedene Lesarten dienen.

1. Abhängigkeitsgrammatik und Büschelanalyse

Grundlegende Konzepte der Abhängigkeitsgrammatik (KUNZE 1975) sind
- Unterordnungsrelationen
  Diese dienen zur Markierung der Kanten der Abhängigkeitsbäume und beschreiben dort die Beziehungen zwischen dem Teilbaum unterhalb der betrachteten Kante und dem Rest des Baumes. Sie bilden somit eine sehr komplexe Markierung, in der verschiedene Dinge vereint sind (d.h. sowohl das, was man allgemein unter syntaktischen Funktionen versteht, als auch Bedingungen an die beteiligten Knoten, Kongruenzen usw.). Das System der Unterordnungsrelationen entsteht auf der Grundlage eines Axiomensystems, dem sogenannten Differenzierungsprinzip.
- Wirkungswege
  Diese drücken Beziehungen im Satz aus, die nicht allein mit den Unterordnungskanten darstellbar sind. Dazu gehören Kongruenzen zwischen Knoten (z.B. bzgl. Numerus und Person zwischen Subjekt und finitem Verb bzw. zwischen einem Nomen und einem Reflexivpronomen – sogenannte paradigmatische Wirkungswege) und Restriktionen eines Knotens an einen anderen (z.B. selektive Einschränkung des Subjekts eines Verbs – sogenannte selektive Wirkungswege). Die Wirkungswege laufen an den Kanten des Baumes entlang bzw. bilden eine Brücke zwischen zwei Schwesterknoten und werden ebenfalls durch die Unterordnungsrelationen ausgedrückt.
- Büschel
  Diese sind in der Theorie die eigentlichen syntaktischen Regeln. Sie dienen dem Aufbau einer Etage des Abhängigkeitsbaumes, enthalten also mit einem Spitzenknoten alle ihm direkt untergeordneten Knoten mit den dazwischenliegenden Kanten und sind damit sehr komplex. Die Büschel werden gleichzeitig zur Beschreibung des Valenzverhaltens der Wortformen genutzt und haben somit ihren Platz im Lexikon bei den Eintragungen zu den Wortformen. Ein Büschel als Regel ist ein Netz von sehr vielen verschiedenen Bedingungen an die beteiligten Knoten bzw. Teilbäume. Diese Bedingungen betreffen sowohl Wortklassen, paradigmatische und selektive Forderungen aber auch Anordnungsbeziehungen.

Auf der Grundlage dieses Modells wurde ein Algorithmus für ein Verfahren zur syntaktischen Analyse erarbeitet, bei dem die Theorie unverändert verwendet wurde (AROLD 1976). Der Büschelbegriff suggeriert dabei unmittelbar eine bottom-up-Analyse, die als Mehrweganalyse angelegt wurde. Ein derartiges System hat folgende Vorteile:

- Die Büschel bilden ein deklaratives Regelsystem.
- Der Mechanismus der Regelanwendung ist einheitlich.
- Die verwendeten Datenstrukturen sind ebenfalls einheitlich, und zwar Fragmente von Abhängigkeitsbäumen, die in einem Analysegraph verbunden sind (die Kanten dieses Graphen stellen jeweils Büschelanwendungen dar).

Aber auch ohne die Erfahrung der Implementierung zeigten sich sehr schwerwiegende Nachteile:

- Die Menge der Büschel bildet eine unüberschaubare Vielfalt, da die Büschel sämtliche Kanten einer Etage im Baum enthalten, also nicht nur das, was man als Kasusrahmen bezeichnet, sondern auch jede Kombination von freien Angaben (Attribute, adverbiale Ergänzungen).
- Die Überprüfung auf Anwendbarkeit der Büschel ist ein sehr aufwendiger Prozeß (wegen der Vielfalt und Unterschiedlichkeit der zu überprüfenden Bedingungen).
- Es kommt zu einer kombinatorischen Explosion der Zahl der Analysewege.

Die weitere Arbeit an dem System mußte deshalb in zwei Richtungen gehen:

- Das Büschelkonzept war grundlegend zu verändern, um die Vielfalt und Komplexität stark herabzusetzen.
- Es mußte eine Strategie gefunden werden, die der genannten Explosion entgegenwirkt.

2. Das verwendete linguistische Wissen

Wir sind der Meinung, daß die umfassende Verwendung von zur Verfügung stehendem linguistischen Wissen für die automatische Sprachverarbeitung von wesentlicher Bedeutung ist. Hierbei muß man sich stets Klarheit verschaffen, welches Wissen für welche Aufgabe notwendig ist. Erst wenn für bestimmte Aufgaben das vorhandene Wissen nicht ausreicht, sollte auch außerlinguistisches Wissen herangezogen werden, dessen Bereitstellung und Verarbeitung zumeist wesentlich komplizierter ist.
Bei KUNZE wurde das Wissen ausschließlich durch die Wörterbucheintra-

gungen und die Büschel repräsentiert. Eine Wörterbucheintragung
enthielt
(a) eine Beschreibung der Wortklasse als Spitze eines Teilbaums (bei
    KUNZE Baumverband genannt),
(b) eine Beschreibung der flexivischen Eigenschaften der Wortform
    durch Zuordnung von Werten zu den paradigmatischen Kategorien
    Genus, Numerus, Person, Kasus, Tempus und Modus,
(c) den Deklinationstyp (bei KUNZE: Stufe) bzw. die Forderung danach
    (bei Artikeln, Adjektiven u.ä.),
(d) eine Beschreibung des selektiven Verhaltens der Wortform, d.h.
    einerseits eigene semantische Merkmale und andererseits von ande-
    ren Wortformen geforderte semantische Merkmale (über selektive
    Wirkungswege),
(e) eine Beschreibung des Dominanzverhaltens der Wortform (entspricht
    dem Valenzverhalten im Falle von Verben) in Form einer Liste von
    Büscheln, an deren Spitze die Wortform stehen kann.

Ein Büschel beschreibt
(f) die möglichen syntaktischen Beziehungen zwischen einer Wortform
    an der Spitze des Büschels und den Teilbäumen, die an den Endkno-
    ten des Büschels untergeordnet werden können (dargestellt durch
    mit Unterordnungsrelationen markierte Unterordnungskanten),
(g) die Kombinationsmöglichkeiten von Unterordnungskanten unter einer
    Wortform (Obligatheit, Abhängigkeiten der Kanten untereinander),
(h) die Kongruenzen und Restriktionen (ausgedrückt durch Wirkungswege
    und sogenannte Vorgaben - durch Unterordnungsrelationen bestimmte
    Bedingungen an einen Knoten, z.B. Kasusvorgaben für Subjekt und
    verschiedene Objekte),
(i) die Anordnungsmöglichkeiten.

Im neuen System wurden vor allem die Büschel entlastet. Dafür sind
zwei Neuerungen verantwortlich:
 - Die sehr komplexen Unterordnungsrelationen werden in syntaktische
   Funktionen und morphosyntaktische Relationen aufgegliedert, wobei
   die syntaktischen Funktionen in etwa den allgemein verwendeten
   entsprechen (z.B. SUBJ) und die morphosyntaktischen Relationen
   deren interne Repräsentation bei konkreten Instantiierungen ausdrücken (z.B. Substantivgruppe im Nominativ bei finiten Verben,
   Substantiv im Genitiv bei Substantivierungen). Das System der syntaktischen Funktionen entsteht kontrolliert aus dem System der
   Unterordnungsrelationen, d.h. es entspricht ebenfalls der zugrun-

deliegenden Theorie. Diese Aufgliederung führt dazu, daß in den Büscheln nur noch die syntaktischen Funktionen vorzukommen brauchen, um ihre Kombinierbarkeit darzustellen. Damit können gleiche Büschel für verschiedene Formen eines Wortes (z.B. finite und infinite Verbformen im Aktiv und Passiv) verwendet werden. Die Dominanzkomponente wird nun ebenfalls in zwei Teile unterteilt: Der eine Teil enthält alle möglichen unterordenbaren Kanten unter die Wortformen als einfache Listen von syntaktischen Funktionen mit ihren jeweiligen Realisierungsmöglichkeiten in Form von morphosyntaktischen Relationen, der andere Teil eine Liste von Büscheln als Ausdrücke in syntaktischen Funktionen zur Darstellung ihrer Kombinationsmöglichkeiten. Die Liste von Büscheln ist allerdings nur dann im Wörterbuch anzugeben, wenn echte Einschränkungen ausgedrückt bzw. wenn mehrere Bedeutungen von Wortformen dadurch unterschieden werden sollen (REIMANN 1987 und 1988).

- Die Beschreibung der möglichen Anordnungen wurde völlig aus dem deklarativen Teil des Systems herausgenommen. Sie erfolgt durch ein ATN in einer sequentiellen Voranalyse bzw. eine ATN-ähnliche Prozedur in der sogenannten lokalen Analyse. Außerdem wird die interne Struktur der Verbgruppen durch programmierte Regeln und eine gewisse Merkmalisierung in der Verbgruppenanalyse beschrieben (s. Abschnitt 3).

Die Wörterbucheintragungen bleiben bis auf die genannte Änderung der Dominanzkomponente im wesentlichen gleich. Interessant ist hier noch eine Erweiterung des semantischen Merkmalssatzes, der üblicherweise für selektive Beziehungen verwendet wird. Hier handelt es sich meist nur um deskriptive Merkmale wie KONKRET, MENSCH usw. Zur Behandlung von Präpositionalgruppen als adverbiale Bestimmungen wird jetzt auch ein Merkmalssatz einbezogen, der den möglichen Funktionen solcher Gruppen entspricht. Diese Merkmale nennen wir funktionale Merkmale, sie werden sowohl den Präpositionen als auch Klassen von Substantiven zugeordnet.

3. Die Strategie der syntaktischen Analyse

Das derzeitige System zur syntaktischen Analyse (REIMANN u.a. 1987) enthält drei klar voneinander abgegrenzte Analyseschritte, die ein starres sequentielles System bilden. Die Starrheit ist dabei durch die Verwendung unterschiedlicher Methoden und Strukturen in den einzelnen Schritten bedingt, so daß ein Scheitern der Analyse in einem Schritt zum Abbruch führt. Diese Starrheit ist sicher sehr nachteilig, und es ist unbedingt notwendig, hier Abhilfe zu schaffen, z.B. durch die Möglichkeit der weiteren Verarbeitung von unfertigen Strukturen. Ein stratifiziertes System hat aber auch wesentliche Vorteile, die man bei der Bewältigung einer so komplexen Aufgabe unter Verwendung von sehr heterogenen Mitteln (das notwendige linguistische Wissen) nicht unterschätzen sollte:

- Die Modularität erlaubt eine selbständige Erarbeitung der einzelnen Schritte sowie Änderungen, deren Auswirkungen auf die übrigen Stufen des Systems kontrollierbar sind.
- In den ersten Schritten können unter Verwendung klar abgrenzbaren Wissens relativ einfache Entscheidungen schnell gefällt werden. Damit ist das Gesamtproblem stark reduziert, so daß die eigentliche Büschelanalyse im dritten Schritt nicht mehr zu einer Explosion des Aufwandes führt.

Das System wurde in seiner ersten Version nur für koordinations- und ellipsenfreie deutsche Sätze implementiert. In letzter Zeit wurde jedoch der erste Schritt erweitert, um hier auch koordinierte Sätze (sowohl nominale als auch Satzkoordination) verarbeiten zu können.

3.1. Die sequentielle Voranalyse

Die sequentielle Voranalyse wird durch ein ATN realisiert, das wesentlich durch eine sehr präzise Verbgruppenanalyse erweitert wurde. Im ATN wird folgendes Wissen verwendet:
- die Wortklassen (a),
- Teile der paradigmatischen Eigenschaften (b),
- die Deklinationstypen (c),
- Anordnung von einfachen nominalen Gruppen (Substantiv-, Präpositional-, Adverbialgruppen) ohne rechtsseitige Erweiterungen,
- Rahmenbildung in deutschen Sätzen (Stellung von einzelnen Bestandteilen der Verbgruppen, Konjunktionen, Relativpronomen etc.),
- Zeichensetzung (Sie wird als korrekt vorausgesetzt, insbesondere bei der Bearbeitung koordinierter Sätze.),

- der Aufbau und die Anordnung deutscher Verbgruppen.

Das Ergebnis der ATN-Analyse ist ein Konstituentenbaum, dessen nicht-terminale Knoten jeweils die Struktur der untergeordneten Gruppe beschreibt (z.B. Nominalgruppe, relativpronomenhaltige Präpositional-gruppe). Es werden noch keine syntaktischen Funktionen ermittelt. Im Ergebnis der ATN-Analyse eines Satzes wurde folgendes erkannt:
  - die Gliederung des Satzes in Haupt- und Nebensätze,
  - die einfachen nominalen Gruppen (ohne Unterordnung untereinander),
  - die Struktur der Verbgruppen der einzelnen Gliedsätze.

Die Verbgruppenanalyse (KUSTNER 1987) arbeitet auf der Grundlage von Listen der Verbformen, die im ATN gefunden wurden. Wesentlich sind hierbei vor allem Wortklassenmerkmale und die Anordnung in den Grup-pen. Die Verbgruppenanalyse dient einerseits als Test für die ATN-Analyse, der entscheidet, ob ein Gliedsatz richtig analysiert wurde. Andererseits untersucht sie die einzelnen Bestandteile der Verbgruppen und synthetisiert sogenannte einfache Verbgruppen zu einem Knoten. Einfache Verbgruppen sind:
  - einfache finite Formen von Voll- und Modalverben,
  - Perfekt- und Futurformen von Voll- und Modalverben,
  - Passivformen der genannten Gruppen,
  - Infinitive mit "zu".
Komplexe Verbgruppen setzen sich aus einfachen Verbgruppen zusammen, also
  - modale Konstruktionen   ("kann arbeiten")
  - quasimodale Konstruktionen   ("hat zu arbeiten")
  - AcI   ("sieht ihn arbeiten")
  - Vollverb mit Infinitiv   ("geht arbeiten")
Im Ergebnis bilden die Verbgruppen die Spitze der Gliedsätze, ihre Stellung innerhalb der Sätze wird jedoch durch Platzhalter in der Konstituentenliste markiert, um die lineare Anordnung im 2. Schritt noch nutzen zu können.

Die Bearbeitung koordinierter Sätze mit einem stark erweiterten ATN führt zu erstaunlich guten Ergebnissen (HESSE 1988). Erkauft werden diese allerdings durch einen erhöhten Aufwand, der auch die normaler-weise schnelle Analyse einfacher Sätze sehr verlangsamt. Welche heuri-stischen Kriterien hier eventuell Abhilfe schaffen können, muß noch untersucht werden.
Das derzeit genutzte ATN ist in der Lage, sehr komplizierte koordi-

nierte Sätze richtig zu analysieren, wozu häufig auch die Verbgruppenanalyse wesentlich beiträgt, z.B. in dem Satz
>   Er   kann   heute und morgen   fotografiert
>   und   übermorgen gefilmt werden.

3.2. Die lokale Analyse

Die lokale Analyse als zweite Stufe hat die Aufgabe, die Unterordnungsmöglichkeiten für jeden einzelnen Knoten zu bestimmen, d.h. es
wird ermittelt, ob ein Knoten einem anderen untergeordnet werden
könnte, und zwar mit Hilfe welcher syntaktischen Funktion, zu deren
Ermittlung wiederum die morphosyntaktischen Relationen herangezogen
werden. Verwendet wird hierbei das folgende Wissen:
- die Konstituentenstruktur (Ergebnis der ATN-Analyse),
- die Wortklassen (a),
- die paradigmatische Eigenschaften (b),
- gewisse selektive Eigenschaften (z.B. für adverbiale Glieder) aus
  (d),
- der erste Teil der Dominanzkomponente (e) (Liste von syntaktischen
  Funktionen mit morphosyntaktischen Relationen),
- Anordnungseigenschaften von komplexen nominalen Gruppen,
- Anordnungseigenschaften von nominalen Gruppen in Bezug auf überge-
  ordnete Verben.
Die Anordnungseigenschaften werden durch ATN-ähnliche Netze dargestellt, die auf dem Ergebnis des ersten Analyseschrittes operieren
(also auf einem Baum und nicht auf einer linearen Kette). Dabei sind
beliebige Bewegungen im Baum (LEFT, RIGHT, DOWN, UP) sowie iterative
Operationen (durch eine Art LOOP) möglich.

Das Ergebnis dieser lokalen Analyse ist ein Graph von Unterordnungsmöglichkeiten, der i.allg. noch viele falsche Unterordnungen enthält.
Beispiel: Der Fuchs mit dem buschigen Schwanz, der die
>   Gans gestohlen hat, ist in den Garten gelaufen.

Hier haben wir noch folgende falsche Unterordnungen:
(1) Antezedent zum Relativpronomen "der" kann sowohl "Fuchs" als auch
    "Schwanz" sein, da in der lokalen Analyse lediglich paradigmati-
    sche Kongruenzen ausgenutzt werden.
(2) Das Relativpronomen "der" kann sowohl Subjekt als auch Dativob-

jekt sein, da "der" paradigmatisch mehrdeutig ist und die Beziehungen zu anderen Kanten nicht überprüft werden.

(3) "die Gans" kann Subjekt und Akkusativobjekt sein.

(4) "in" ist noch als Lokal- und als Richtungsbestimmung untergeordnet, da eine weitere Vererbung der Kasus noch nicht vorgenommen wurde.

Diese rein lokale Arbeitsweise ist ebenfalls relativ einfach, führt aber - wie im Beispiel - noch zu einer Reihe von Mehrdeutigkeiten.

3.3. Die globale Büschelanalyse

In der globalen Büschelanalyse werden aus dem Graphen der Unterordnungsmöglichkeiten die falschen Kanten herausgestrichen, d.h. es werden zunächst die innerhalb des Graphen vorliegenden Lesarten gebildet, aus denen die falschen herausgefiltert werden. Dazu werden folgende Kriterien verwendet:

 - Eine richtige Lesart muß ein Baum sein.
 - Jede Etage des Baumes muß einem Büschel des Spitzenknoten entsprechen, d.h. daß die Kanten in dieser Weise kombinierbar sind und daß alle obligatorischen Kanten vorhanden sind.
 - Alle Bedingungen, die durch Wirkungswege gefordert werden, müssen im gesamten Baum erfüllt sein.

Mit dem für die globale Büschelanalyse entwickelten Graphentransformationssystem GRACOLI (Henschel 1986a,b), das auch für andere Anwendungen in der automatischen Sprachverarbeitung einsetzbar ist, ist es möglich, die notwendigen Tests und Operationen innerhalb des Graphen auszuführen, so daß der erforderliche Aufwand begrenzt bleibt.

Die Mehrdeutigkeiten, die im obigen Beispielsatz nach der lokalen Analyse noch bestehen, werden in der globalen Büschelanalyse vollständig gelöst:

 (1): Es werden die selektiven Wirkungswege innerhalb des Relativsatzes sowie zwischen Antezedent und Relativpronomen ausgewertet.

 (2),(3): Das Subjekt von "stehlen" ist obligatorisch, das Vorhandensein des Dativobjekts erfordert das Vorhandensein eines Akkusativobjekts (im Büschel ausgedrückt).

 (4): Die Vererbung paradigmatischer Merkmale wird vollständig ausgeführt, so daß hier wegen des Kasus von "den Garten" nur eine Richtungsbestimmung vorliegen kann.

Literatur

Arold, Dorothee: Der logische Teil einer automatischen syntaktischen
    Analyse deutscher Sätze. Sonderheft Linguistische Studien,
    ZI für Sprachwissenschaft der AdW der DDR, Berlin, 1976.
Henschel, Renate: Ein Filter für die automatische syntaktische Analyse
    als Graphentransformationssystem. Dissertation A, ZI für
    Sprachwissenschaft der AdW der DDR, Berlin, 1986.
Henschel, Renate: Das Graphen-Transformationssystem GRACOLI. Mittei-
    lungen zur automatischen Sprachverarbeitung, AdW der DDR,
    Berlin, 1986.
Hesse, Harald. ATN-Analyse koordinierter Sätze. Interner Bericht, ZI
    für Sprachwissenschaft der AdW der DDR, Berlin, 1988.
Kunze, Jürgen: Abhängigkeitsgrammatik. Studia Grammatica XII,
    Akademie-Verlag, Berlin, 1975.
Küstner, Andreas: Ein Verfahren zur Analyse deutscher Verbgruppen.
    Mitteilungen zur automatischen Sprachverarbeitung, AdW der
    DDR, Berlin, 1987.
Reimann, Dorothee, Renate Henschel, Harald Hesse und Andreas Küstner:
    Syntactic Analysis. In: Mitteilungen zur automatischen
    Sprachverarbeitung, AdW der DDR, Berlin, 1987.
Reimann, Dorothee: Lexical Information for Syntactic Analysis. In:
    Mitteilungen zur automatischen Sprachverarbeitung, AdW der
    DDR, Berlin, 1987.
Reimann, Dorothee: Die Dominanzkomponente als wesentlicher Bestandteil
    der Lexikoninformationen für die syntaktische Analyse. Zeit-
    schrift für Phonetik, Sprachwissenschaft und Kommunikations-
    forschung, Berlin, 1988 (in Druck).

Die Kontrollbeziehung bei Nomen mit abhängigem zu-Infinitiv

Bettina Harriehausen
Wiss. Zentrum Heidelberg

Sabine Reinhard
Universität Trier *

* Die zugrundeliegenden Untersuchungen wurden während Sabine Reinhards Werkstudententätigkeit am Wissenschaftlichen Zentrum Heidelberg der IBM Deutschland GmbH durchgeführt.

Abstraktum

Bei der Betrachtung der abhängigen zu-Infinitive im Deutschen treffen wir auf das Problem, daß die Kontrollbeziehung zwischen dem Subjekt des zu-Infinitiv-Komplements und der kontrollierenden NP des Hauptsatzes (im folgenden 'Kontrolleur' genannt) starke Unregelmäßigkeiten aufweist. So scheint es zunächst nicht von vornherein festlegbar zu sein, welche NP des Hauptsatzes die Funktion der kontrollierenden Instanz übernimmt.

Bsp.

    (1a) Pauls Chance, das Lied zu singen....(Paul singt)
    (1b) Pauls Befehl, das Lied zu singen.... (J[1] singt)
    (1c) Pauls Erlaubnis, das Lied zu singen....(Paul / J singt)

Unser Ziel war es, das unterschiedliche Kontrollverhalten zu schematisieren, zu erklären und dabei Kriterien herauszuarbeiten, anhand derer es möglich ist, das Kontrollverhalten der einzelnen Nomen für die maschinelle Verarbeitung zu kodieren.

Eine empirische Untersuchung der syntakto-semantischen Verhältnisse führte uns zu einer Unterteilung der Nomen bzgl. ihres Kontrollverhaltens in 23 Gruppen.

Das Kontrollverhalten bzw. die möglichen Kontrolleure eines Nomens stellte sich als Eigenschaft des jeweiligen Nomens heraus, anhand derer die Nomina differenziert werden können. Dieses Ergebnis erlaubt es, das jewei-

---

1 J = nicht explizite NP fungiert als Kontrolleur

lige Kontrollverhalten als Merkmal zu kodieren, wobei ein Merkmal als Menge der jeweils möglichen Kontrolleure (des betreffenden Nomens) zu verstehen ist.

0. Einleitung

Am Wissenschaftlichen Zentrum der IBM Deutschland in Heidelberg arbeitet eine Gruppe auf dem Gebiet der natürlichsprachlichen Datenverarbeitung. Im Rahmen des LEX Projekts (ALSCHWEE et al. 1985) zur Entwicklung eines Prototyps eines natürlichsprachlichen juristischen Expertensystems, wurde ein derzeit ca. 20.000 Einträge (Nomen, Adjektive und Verben) umfassendes Lexikon erstellt, welches in einer relationalen Datenbank (SQL/DS (IBM 1983)) gespeichert ist. Zu jedem lexikalischen Eintrag werden in mehreren Spalten primär morphologische und syntaktische Merkmale kodiert (BARNETT et al. 1986).
Dieses Lexikon legten wir unserer Untersuchung zugrunde, mit dem Ziel, die Problematik der Kontrollbeziehung bei Nomen mit abhängigem zu-Infinitiv zu erfassen und Kriterien herauszuarbeiten, anhand derer es möglich ist, das Kontrollverhalten der einzelnen Nomen für die maschinelle Verarbeitung zu kodieren.

1. Vorgehensweise

Um die Problematik zu erfassen, mußten der empirischen Untersuchung folgende Überlegungen vorangestellt werden:
1. Bei *Verben* ist der Kontrolleur
    a) ein Valenzelement des Matrixverbs
    b) logischerweise <u>nicht</u> das Element, das durch den zu-Infinitiv-Satz vertreten ist
    c) in seltenen Fällen ist der Kontolleur <u>kein</u> Valenzelement des Matrixverbs, d.h. kann generell nicht natürlich in den Matrixsatz eingeführt werden: Bsp. <u>anordnen</u> (Kontolleur = J)

2. *Adjektive* haben immer die Valenz N, d.h. das 'head' Nomen oder das Subjekt der Kopula bei prädikativer Stellung.
Der Kontrolleur ist
    a) das 'head' Nomen bzw. das Subjekt der Kopula bei prädikativen Adjektiven (SINF = NZ)[2]
    (2) Paul ist verantwortlich (dafür), Maria zu benachrichtigen.
    IZU = P(für), SINF = N (Paul)
    b) logischerweise <u>nicht</u> das durch den zu-Infinitiv vertretene Element. Folge: IZU = NZ, SINF = J.[3]

3. Im Gegensatz zu Verben und Adjektiven ist der Kontrolleur bei *Nomen* nicht eindeutig zu bestimmen.

---

2 SINF = Subjekt des zu-Infinitivs
3 IZU = das Valenzelement, das durch den Infinitivsatz vertreten wird

Jedes Nomen hat die Valenz N, d.h. die Menge der Referenten des Nomens selbst.

Als mögliche SINF treten auf:

    a) die Valenzelemente des Nomens

    b) das Nomen selbst

    c) freie Angaben zum Nomen (z.B. die von-PP)

    d) Schwestern des Nomens im Matrixsatz, d.h. Valenzelemente des Matrixverbs / freie Angaben des Matrixverbs.

In diesem Zusammenhang stellen sich folgende Fragen:

    a) Ist der Kontrolleur eine Eigenschaft des Nomens generell, d.h. ist er für alle Nomen gleich?

    b) Ist der Kontrolleur eine individuelle Eigenschaft des Nomens, d.h. lassen sich die Nomina klassifizieren?

    c) Gibt es eine reguläre Zuordnung?

    d) Wie "fest" ist die Zuordnung bei von Nomen abhängigen Kontrolleuren, d.h. wenn das SINF-Element nicht vorhanden ist, ist SINF elliptisch oder übernimmt ein anderes Element die Funktion?

    e) Falls ein Genitivattribut in Frage kommt: Verhalten sich alle strukturellen Varianten der Assoziationsbeziehung ('abstraktes' Genitivattribut) gleich? (Genitiv vorangestellt, Genitiv nachgestellt, von PP, Nominativ von 'haben')

    f) Spielen Genitive / von PPs eine Rolle, die _nicht_ die Assoziationsbeziehung ausdrücken, sondern die als Neutralisierung expliziter Valenzen des Nomens oder als Genitivvalenzen aufzufassen sind? (Bsp. die Bedingung der Möglichkeit für...; die Anklage des Mordes, das Programm des letzten Jahres)

    g) Spielen Varianten des Genitivus subiectivus durch PP eine Rolle? (Bsp. der Verkauf des Hauses durch Peter)

    h) Wenn Schwestern im Matrixsatz kontrollieren können: Ist der Kontrolleur immer derselbe, d.h. syntaktisch bestimmt, oder bei verschiedenen Matrixverben verschieden, also eine Eigenschaft des Matrixverbs, oder eine Eigenschaft des Nomens selbst?

    i) Wie "fest" ist die Zuordnung bei Schwestern des Nomens?

    j) Bei Deverbativa: Steht die SINF-Klasse des Nomens in Beziehung zur SINF-Klasse des Verbs, von der es abgeleitet wird? (vgl. STEINER 1986)

Um alle diese Einflußgrößen zu untersuchen, betrachteten wir Textkontexte, in denen verschiedene von Nomen abhängige Elemente (vorgestellter Genitiv, nachgestellter Genitiv, von PP, durch PP), Valenzelemente des Nomens (an) und Satzzusammenhänge mit verschiedenen Verben ((h), (i)) auftreten. Da nicht alle Verben untersucht werden konnten, betrachteten wir zunächst _geben_ , _bekommen_ , _sein_ und das transitive Verb _lieben_ , um zu sehen, ob die Art des Verbs eine Rolle spielt.

Haben und _sein_ verhalten sich oft anders als andere Verben; _geben_ und _bekommen_ stehen in einer Bedeutungsbeziehung, korrelierend mit einer Beziehung zwischen Valenzelementen , die sie geeignet erscheinen ließ, Einflußgrößen wie Adressaten (als Zielgrößen des Transfervorganges) zu untersuchen:

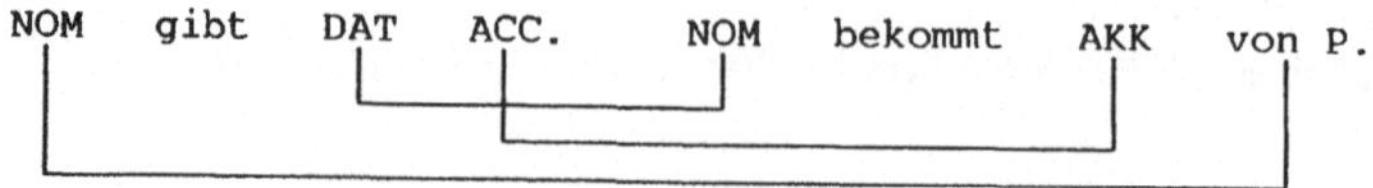

Das untersuchte Korpus bestand aus 423 Nomen, die mit Hilfe der Benutzerschnittstelle QMF (IBM 1983, 1984) aus o.g. Lexikon extrahiert wurden, da sie auf die Möglichkeit hin kodiert sind, ein zu-Infinitiv-Komplement zu regieren.

Der empirische Teil der Arbeit bestand in der Festlegung der Kontrollbeziehung aller Nomen in zehn Satzrahmen. Das Ergebnis wurde in einer Liste (Auszüge davon, siehe Abb. 1) festgehalten, die im folgenden detailliert dargestellt wird.
Aus dieser Liste zeichneten sich 23 Klassen ab, welche wir unter syntakto-semantischen Aspekten betrachteten. Die Untersuchung führte zu dem Ergebnis, daß eine Kategorisierung der verschiedenen Nomen bezüglich ihres Verhaltens in den verschiedenen Satzrahmen möglich ist. Ferner kann mittels einer Berücksichtigung der Kasusrollen der Kontrollinstanz und ihres semantischen Gehalts ein gruppenspezifisches Verhalten erklärt werden.

2. Grundannahme

Syntakto-semantische Verhältnisse spielen eine Rolle. Die Betrachtung der Struktur wird durch die Betrachtung der strukturellen Bedeutung ergänzt. Dadurch gruppieren sich verschiedene Strukturen zu einer Bedeutung und gleiche Strukturen zu verschiedenen Bedeutungen. Falls die Menge der möglichen Kontrolleure sich als Eigenschaft des jeweiligen Nomens herausstellt, d.h. eine Eigenschaft, die im Merkmal SINF zu kodieren wäre, wird das Merkmal als Notation für die Menge der möglichen Kontrolleure verstanden.

3. Die Kontrollbeziehungen

Um die Kontrollbeziehungen darzustellen, sollen die zehn Satzrahmen, die als Testumgebung gewählt wurden, skizziert werden:

SATZRAHMEN I: P's (Genitiv vorangestellt):
Kategorie 1-9: (3a) Pauls Hoffnung, den Kuchen zu essen...
Kontrolleur: GEN (= Paul ißt)
Kategorie 10-14: (3b) Pauls Gebot, den Kuchen zu backen,...
Kontrolleur: J (= J backt)
Kategorie 15-18: (3c) Pauls Erlaubnis, das Auto zu kaufen,...
Kontrolleur: GEN / J (= Paul oder J kauft)
Kategorie 19-20: (3d) Pauls Diskussion (mit J), das Auto zu kaufen,...
Kontrolleur: GEN + J(mit) (= Paul und J kaufen)
Kategorie 21: (3e) Pauls Bedenken, den Vertrag abzuschließen ,...
Kontrolleur: GEN + / J (= Paul / Paul und J / J schließt ab)
Kategorie 22:(3f) Pauls Beschluß, ein Auto zu kaufen,...

Kontrolleur GEN / + J (= Paul / Paul und J kaufen)

Kategorie 23:(3g) Des Kaisers Gesetz, Steuern zu sparen,...

Kontrolleur: JZ^4 (= jeder/alle sparen)

SATZRAHMEN II: X des P (Genitiv nachgestellt):

Die Kontrollbeziehungen verhalten sich entsprechend Satzrahmen I. Zur Illustration dient ein Beispiel der Kategorien 1-9:

Kategorie 1-9: (4a) Die Hoffnung des Paul, den Kuchen zu essen,...

Kontrolleur: GEN (= Paul ißt)

SATZRAHMEN III: X von P (von-Genitiv nachgestellt):

Die Kontrollbeziehungen verhalten sich entsprechend Satzrahmen I. Zur Illustration dient ein Beispiel der Kategorien 1-9:

Kategorie 1-9: (5a) Die Hoffnung von Paul, den Kuchen zu essen,...

Kontrolleur: GEN (= Paul ißt)

SATZRAHMEN IV: X an P (an PP):

Kategorie 2,10,13,14,16,17: (6a) Der Appell an Paul, einen Kuchen zu backen,...

Kontrolleur: an-AKK (= Paul backt)

Kategorie 7: (6b) Das Geständnis an Paul, einen Teller zerbrochen zu haben,...

Kontrolleur: J-GEN (= J hat den Teller zerschlagen)

Kategorie 18: (6c) Das Angebot an Paul, einen Vertrag abzuschließen,...

Kontrolleur: J-GEN / an-AKK (= J / P schließt ab)

SATZRAHMEN V: P hat X:

Kategorie 1-5,9-10,13,15-18: (7a) Paul hat die Möglichkeit, ein Haus zu kaufen.

Kontrolleur: SBJ (= Paul kauft)

Kategorie 12: (7b) Paul hat Verständnis (dafür), ein Geschenk zu kaufen.

Kontrolleur: J (= J kauft)

Kategorie 19: (7c) Paul hat eine Vereinbarung (mit J), einen Vertrag abzuschließen.

Kontrolleur: SBJ + J(mit) (Paul + J schließen ab)

Kategorie 21: (7d) Paul hat Bedenken, Fußball zu spielen.

Kontrolleur: SBJ + / J (= Paul / Paul + J spielen)

SATZRAHMEN VI: P liebt X (transitive Verben)

Kategorie 1-23: (8) Paul liebt die Idee, Fußball zu spielen.

Kontrolleur: 0

Die Gruppe der Nomen, die einen zu-Infinitiv regieren können, können als vorwiegend abstrakte Nomen nur die Objekts-Argumentstelle abstrakter Verben besetzen (Bsp.: lieben , hassen , verabscheuen , bevorzugen). Aus diesem Grund wird einzig die Einstellung einer bestimmten Sache oder Aktion (= AKK) ausgedrückt.

---

4 JZ = nicht overter und nicht spezifisch angesprochener Adressat, sondern allgemeine Menge

Nur wenige nicht-abstrakte Verben können mit derartigen Nomen auftreten und dabei eine Kontrollbeziehung ausüben (Bsp.: abwägen , bedenken). Der zu-Infinitiv hat in diesen Konstruktionen im Matrixsatz keinen Kontrolleur.

SATZRAHMEN VII: P bekommt X:

Kategorie 1-4,9-18: (9a) Paul bekommt den Befehl, einen Kuchen zu backen.

Kontrolleur: SBJ (= Paul backt)

Kategorie 7-8: (9b) Paul bekommt das Versprechen, einen Kuchen zu backen.

Kontrolleur: von-J (= von-J backt)

Kategorie 21: (9c) Paul bekommt Bedenken, Fußball zu spielen.

Kontrolleur: SBJ + / J (= Paul / J / Paul + J spielen)

Kategorie 22: (9d) Paul bekommt eine Erklärung dafür, nach Hause zu gehen.

Kontrolleur: SBJ / + J (= Paul / Paul + J gehen)

SATZRAHMEN VIII: P bekommt X von Maria

Kategorie 1-3,10-17: (10a) Paul bekommt von Maria den Befehl, einkaufen zu gehen.

Kontrolleur: SBJ (Paul geht einkaufen)

Kategorie 7-8: (10b) Paul bekommt von Maria das Geständnis, das Auto kaputtgefahren zu haben.

Kontrolleur: von-GEN (= Maria hat das Auto kaputtgefahren)

Kategorie 9,18: (10c) Paul bekommt von Maria einen Beweis dafür, schön zu sein.

Kontrolleur: SBJ / von-GEN (= Paul / Maria ist schön)

Kategorie 21: (10d) Paul bekommt Bedenken, Fußball zu spielen.

Kontrolleur: SBJ + / von-J (= Paul / J / Paul und J spielen Fußball)

Kategorie 22: (10e) Paul bekommt die Erklärung, nach Hause zu gehen.

Kontrolleur: SBJ / + von-J (= Paul / Paul und J gehen nach Hause)

SATZRAHMEN IX: P gibt X:

Kategorie 1,2,11,13,15-17: (11a) Paul gibt den Befehl, einen Kuchen zu backen.

Kontrolleur: J-DAT (J backt)

Kategorie 8,9: (11b) Paul gibt das Versprechen, einen Kuchen zu backen.

Kontrolleur: SBJ (= Paul backt)

Kategorie 22: (11c) Paul gibt eine Erklärung (dafür), das Haus abzuschließen.

Kontrolleur: SBJ / + J-DAT (= Paul/ Paul und J geben eine Erklärung ab)

SATZRAHMEN X: P gibt X + DAT:

Kategorie 1,2,11,13,15-17: (12a) Paul gibt Maria den Befehl, einen Kuchen zu backen.

Kontrolleur: DAT (Maria backt)

Kategorie 7,8: (12b) Paul gibt Maria das Versprechen, einen Kuchen zu backen.

Kontrolleur: SBJ (= Paul backt)

Kategorie 9: (12c) Paul gibt Maria die Gewißheit, einen Job zu bekommen.

Kontrolleur: SBJ / DAT (= Paul / Maria bekommt einen Job)

Kategorie 21: (12d) Paul gibt (äußert gegenüber) Maria Bedenken, ein Auto zu kaufen.

Kontrolleur: SBJ + / DAT (= Paul / Maria / Paul + Maria kaufen)

4. Kodierung der Klassen

4.1 Syntaktische Überlegungen

Nach ausführlicher Darstellung der Problemfälle fällt auf, daß, bis auf wenige Nomen, alle Ausnahmen Deverbativa sind. Da im Lexikon die SINF-Kodierung der Verben abgeschlossen ist, verglichen wir als ersten Schritt einer möglichen Klassifizierung das SINF- Verhalten der Nomina mit dem der korrelierenden Verben, mit dem Ziel, die Kodierung der Verben als Hilfe für die SINF-Kodierung der Substantive zu verwenden, d.h. sie im Idealfall übertragen zu können.

Wir schauten uns vergleichend folgende Kriterien an:

a) SINF-Verhalten der Deverbativa

b) SINF-Kodierung der korrelierenden Verben

c) Valenzrahmen der korrelierenden Verben

Es zeichnete sich das nachstehende Kontrollverhalten ab:

Valenzrahmen der Verben, die mit den Nomen der Kategorie 1–6,19–23 korrelieren	SINF der Verben
Nom Dat Acc Nom Acc Gen Nom Acc (Acc) Nom Acc PP Nom Acc PP PP Nom PP	Dat Nom Acc Acc Nom Acc PP Nom Nom Nom

Bei Betrachtung dieser Tabelle wird deutlich, daß die SINF-Kodierung der Verben nicht als Kodierhilfe verwendet werden kann, da sich keine regelhaften Parallelen abzeichnen.

Valenzrahmen der Verben, die mit den Nomen der Kategorie 10–18 korrelieren	SINF der Verben
Nom Dat Acc Nom Acc Gen Nom Acc (Acc) Nom Acc PP	Dat Acc Acc Acc/PP

Innerhalb der Valenzrahmen ergeben sich zwar einzelne Regelhaftigkeiten (beispielsweise wird die Rolle des SINF bei Nom-Dat-Acc-kodierten Verben vom Dativ übernommen); jedoch sind die Ausnahmen zu zahlreich, um sie, beim Versuch, eindeutige Beziehungen zwischen Valenzrahmen der Verben und ihrer SINF-Kodierung herzustellen, als Kodierhilfe zu verwenden; d.h. eine generelle Vererbung ist nicht möglich.

Valenzrahmen der Verben, die mit den Nomen der Kategorie 7–9 korrelieren	SINF der Verben
Nom Acc PP PP	Nom
Nom Acc Acc	Nom
Nom Dat Acc	Nom
Nom PP	Nom
Nom Acc PP PP	Nom
Nom Acc PP	Nom

Bei Verben, die mit den Nomen der Kategorien 7-9 korrelieren, fällt auf, daß ihr SINF immer Nominativ[5] ist. Damit grenzen sie sich zwar eindeutig von den Kategorien 10-18 ab, jedoch grenzen sich weder die Kategorien 7-9 noch die Kategorien 10-18 von den Kategorien 1-6 bzw. 19-23 ab, denn bei 1-6 und 19-23, kann der zu-Infinitiv von allen Kasus kontrolliert.

Somit kann über die SINF-Kodierung der Verben lediglich festgelegt werden, ob ein Deverbativum entweder in 1-6/19-23 oder 10-18 fällt oder ob es in 1-6/19-23 oder 7-9 fällt. Lediglich für die Kategorien 7-9 gilt, daß die SINF-Kodierung eine Kordierhilfe darstellt.

4.2 Tiefenkasus

Ein weiterführender Ansatz zielte dahin, eine Kategorisierung der Nomen über deren Tiefenkasus vorzunehmen. (FILLMORE 1968, 1977).

Die Nomen der Kategorien 1-6 zeigen, daß der GEN die Rolle des *EXPERIENCERS* übernimmt und zum *AGENS* des zu-Infinitivs wird:

Nomen der Kategorien 1-6

Satzrahmen I: (13a) Pauls (*EXP - > AGENS*) Aufgabe (*GOAL*) , den Brief zu schreiben...

Satzrahmen II: (13b) Die Aufgabe (*GOAL*) des Paul (*EXP - > AGENS*), den Brief zu schreiben...

Satzrahmen III: (13c) Die Aufgabe (*GOAL*) von Paul (*EXP - > AGENS*), den Brief zu schreiben...

Satzrahmen IV: (13d) Die Aufgabe(*GOAL*) an Paul (*EXP - > AGENS*), den Brief zu schreiben...

Satzrahmen V: (13e) Paul (*EXP - > AGENS*) hat die Aufgabe (*GOAL*), den Brief zu schreiben.

Satzrahmen VI: (13f) Paul (*EXP - > 0*) liebt die Aufgabe, den Brief zu schreiben

Satzrahmen VII: (13g) Paul (*EXP - > AGENS*) bekommt die Aufgabe (*GOAL*), den Brief zu schreiben.

Satzrahmen VIII: (13h) Paul (*EXP - > AGENS*) bekommt die Aufgabe (*GOAL*) von Maria (*SOURCE*) , den Brief zu schreiben.

Satzrahmen IX: (13i) Paul (*AGENS*) gibt (DAT (*EXP - > AGENS*)) die Aufgabe (*GOAL*), den Brief zu schreiben.

Satzrahmen X: (13j) Paul (*AGENS*) gibt Maria (*EXP - > AGENS*) die Aufgabe (*GOAL*), den Brief zu schreiben.

---

5 Bisher wurde nur eine Ausnahme gefunden: der SINF des Verbs 'zugestehen' wird vom Dativ regiert.

Es ist bemerkenswert, daß in allen Fällen der *EXPERIENCER* zum *AGENS* (Kontrolleur) des zu-Infinitivs wird, auch wenn (wie in h) und i)) ein AGENS vorhanden ist. Dennoch wird der (nicht-)explizite *EXPERIENCER* zum Subjekt des zu-Infinitivs.

Wir müssen uns die Frage stellen, ob die Tiefenkasusrollen der anderen Kategorien ein abweichendes Verhalten zeigen (die folgenden Illustrationen werden - aus Platzgründen - nur noch exemplarische Satzrahmen gewählt):

Nomen der Kategorien 10-18:

Satzrahmen I: (14a) Pauls (*SOURCE*) Empfehlung (*GOAL*) (anAKK (*EXP -> AGENS*)), den Brief zu schreiben ...

Satzrahmen II: (14b) Die Empfehlung (*GOAL*) des Paul (*SOURCE*) (anAKK (*EXP -> AGENS*)), den Brief zu schreiben ...

Satzrahmen I: (14c) Pauls (*SOURCE*) Auftrag (*GOAL*) (anAKK (*EXP -> AGENS*)), die Hände zu waschen ...

Satzrahmen II: (14d) Die Ermahnung (*GOAL*) des Paul (*SOURCE*) (anAKK (*EXP -> AGENS*)), die Hände zu waschen ...

   <u>alternativ</u>:

   Die Ermahnung (*GOAL*) des Paul (*EXP -> AGENS*), die Hände zu waschen ...

Satzrahmen I: (14e) Pauls (*SOURCE*) Auftrag (*GOAL*) (anAKK (*EXP -> AGENS*)), die Fenster zu putzen ...

   <u>alternativ</u>:

   Pauls (*EXP -> AGENS*) Auftrag (GOAL), die Fenster zu putzen ...

Satzrahmen II: (14f) Der Auftrag (*GOAL*) des Paul (*SOURCE*) (anAKK (*EXP -> AGENS*)), die Fenster zu putzen ...

   <u>alternativ</u>:

   Der Auftrag (*GOAL*) des Paul (*EXP -> AGENS*), die Fenster zu putzen ...

Bei den Nomen der Kategorien 10-18 wird immer der *EXPERIENCER*, der implizit oder in Alternativfällen auch overt vorhanden ist, zum Subjekt des zu-Infinitivs, d.h zum *AGENS*. Dies gilt unabhängig von der Interpretation, d.h. spielt der GEN die Rolle der *SOURCE*, dann ist ein *EXPERIENCER*, der zum *AGENS* wird, mindestens implizit vorhanden.

Nomen der Kategorien 7-9 (repräsentative Beispiele):

Satzrahmen IV: (15a) Das Geständnis (*GOAL*) (vonJ (*SOURCE -> AGENS*)) an Paul (*EXP*), zu lügen ...

Satzrahmen VI: (15b) Paul (*EXP*) bekommt das Geständnis (*GOAL*) (von J (*SOURCE -> AGENS*)), zu lügen ...

Satzrahmen VIII: (15c) Paul (*SOURCE -> AGENS*) gibt das Versprechen (*GOAL*), den Brief zu schreiben.

Satzrahmen IX: (15d) Paul (*SOURCE -> AGENS*) gibt Maria (*EXP*) das Versprechen (*GOAL*), den Brief zu schreiben.

Satzrahmen IV: (15e) Die Zusage (*GOAL*) (vonJ (*SOURCE -> AGENS*)) an Paul (*EXP*), ins Schwimmbad zu gehen ...

<u>alternativ</u>:
Die Zusage (*GOAL*) an Paul(*EXP -> AGENS*), ins Schwimmbad zu gehen ...

Bei den Nomen der Kategorien 7-9 wird die *SOURCE*-NP, bzw. - je nach Interpretation - der *EXPERIEN-CER* zum *AGENS*. Betrachten wir zur Illustration das Bsp. (15e):
Hat die *SOURCE*-NP (J, als der implizite GEN) interpretativen Vorrang, wird die *SOURCE*-NP zum Subjekt des zu-Infinitivs, d.h. J wird zum *AGENS*. Überwiegt auf der anderen Seite die Interpretation, daß die *SOURCE* (d.h. J als impliziter GEN) die 'Begründung' mit einer solchen Erwartungshaltung an 'Paul' gibt, daß dieser (als *EXPERIENCER*) die Handlung ausführt; d.h. 'Paul' wird als *EXPERIENCER* zum *AGENS*.

Somit können die Interpretationen über die Tiefenkasus differenziert werden.

Die Kategorien 19-23 stellen insofern Sonderfälle dar, als daß in den Kategorien 19-20 der "mitJ" den gleichen Status, d.h. Tiefenkasus, hat wie das SBJ des Matrixsatzes, und in den Kategorien 21-22 impliziert das Nomen, daß alternative Kontrollbeziehungen auftreten können. Entweder fungiert der *EXPERIENCER* (Paul) alleine als *AGENS* oder es fungieren die *SOURCE* (Paul) und der *EXPERIENCER* (J) zusammen als *AGENS*, oder es haben beide den Status eines *EXPERIENCERs* der zum *AGENS* wird. In der Kategorie 23 wird der JZ (*EXPERIENCER*) zum *AGENS*.

4.3 Semantische Differenzierung der Kategorien

Dieser Interpretationsunterschied, der über die Tiefenkasus Auswirkungen auf den Kontrolleur hat, veranlaßte uns zu der Vermutung, daß die aufgezeigten Besonderheiten auf Differenzen in den semantischen Klassen der Nomen zurückzuführen sind.
Daraufhin betrachteten wir die Nomen im Hinblick auf ihre semantische Implikation und kamen zu folgendem Schluß:

Kategorien 10-18:
Der GEN suggeriert dem Adressaten seine Erwartungshaltung, der nachgekommen werden soll (Pauls Befehl, etw. zu tun), oder der GEN beurteilt im nachhinein eine Handlung (Pauls Rüge, ...).
In beiden Fällen besteht eine hierarchische Beziehung zwischen dem GEN und dem Adressaten, d.h. der GEN handelt als Dominierender und der Adressat befindet sich in der Rolle des Betroffenen/Ausführenden. In Fällen, bei denen das Dominanzverhältnis unklarer ist, z.Bsp. 'Einladung', liegt die Möglichkeit der Entscheidung ebenso beim GEN, d.h. eine Kompetenzdifferenz liegt in allen Beispielen vor.

Kategorien 7-9:
Die Nomen der Kategorien 7-9 lassen sich nicht durch o.g. Dominanzverhalten beschreiben.
Die Richtung, die über die Deixis der Verben <u>bekommen</u> und <u>geben</u> impliziert ist, d.h. bei <u>bekommen</u> ("Ich bekomme den Befehl.") ist das SBJ die kontrollierende Instanz und bei <u>geben</u> ("Ich gebe den Befehl.") ist es der Adressat. Bei Nomen der Kategorien 7-9 ist diese deiktische Implikation umgedreht, d.h.:
Ich gebe das Versprechen (SBJ= Kontrolleur)
Ich bekomme das Versprechen. (DAT= Kontrolleur)

Die Kategorien 1-6 und 19-23 zeichnen sich nicht durch derartige Merkmale aus.

Wir schlagen vor, daß sich die Nomen im Deutschen bezüglich ihres Kontrollverhaltens bei zu-Infinitiven in 23 Gruppen (3 Großgruppen) einteilen lassen:

A) Kategorien 1-6, (19-23)
B) Kategorien 10-18
C) Kategorien 7-9

B) grenzt sich von A) insoweit ab, als daß der implizite *EXPERIENCER* die Kontrolle übernehmen kann;
C) grenzt sich von A) über die Kasusrolle des Subjekts des zu-Infinitivs ab;
B) und C) grenzen sich untereinander semantisch-hierarchisch ab.

Um die jeweilige Klasse, der ein Nomen zuzuordnen ist, festlegen zu können, kann nach folgendem Flußdiagramm vorgegangen werden:

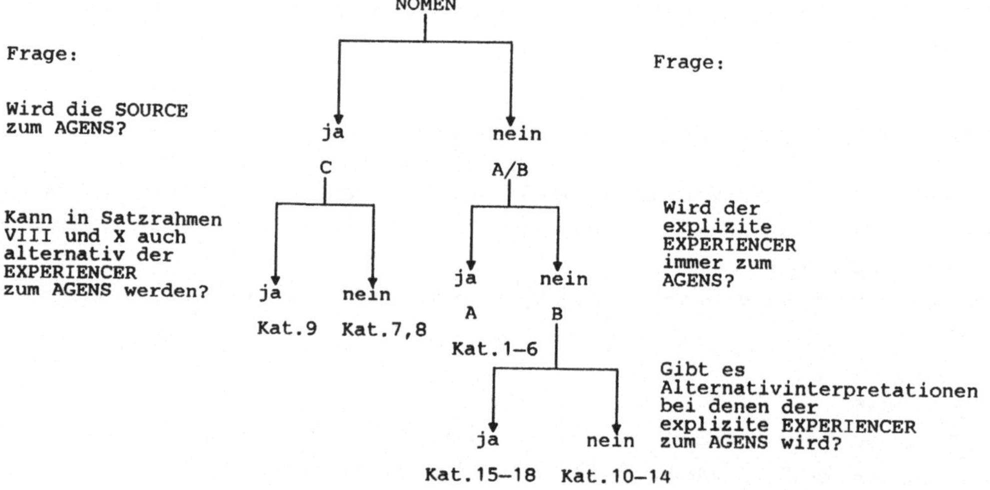

Dieses Flußdiagramm soll dazu dienen, gruppenspezifische Kontrollverhalten, d.h. die Kasusrollen der Kontrolleure - unabhängig von deren syntaktischen Funktionen - zu verdeutlichen. Zur Kodierung der einzelnen Nomen reicht diese Grobklassifizierung nicht aus, und es muß auf o.g. 23 Klassen zurückgegriffen werden.

5. Fazit

Die einzelnen Kategorien kennzeichnen sich durch ihr Satzrahmen- spezifisches Kontrollverhalten. kategorienübergreifend können die Kategorien 1-6, 7-9, 10-18 und 19-23 aufgrund ihrer Tiefenkasusrelationen und ihres semantischen Gehalts beschrieben werden. Diese kategorienübergreifende Information kann jedoch nicht als Kodierhilfe sondern ausschließlich als zusätzliche Information verstanden werden. Nur eine Differenzierung in die vorgestellten 23 Kategorien ermöglicht eine Zuordnung bestimmter Merkmalsbündel und damit eine Kodierung zur maschinellen Verarbeitung.

An dieser Stelle möchten wir Magdalena Zoeppritz für die Aufgabenstellung, den Ansatz und ihre hilfreichen Beiträge danken.

Literatur

Alschwee. B, A. Blaser, He. und Hu. Lehmann, W Schönfeld (1985): "Ein juristisches Expertensystem mit natürlichsprachlichem Dialog - ein Projektbericht", Proceedings of the International GI Congress '85, Munich, W. Brauer, B. Radig (eds.): Wissensbasierte Systeme, Informatikfachberichte 112, Springer Verlag, Berlin Heidelberg New York Tokyo.

Barnett et.al. (1986):" A Word Database for Natural Language Processing". in: COLING proceeding 1986. Universität Bonn. 435-440.

Fillmore, C.F. (1968). The case for case. in: Bach/Harms (eds.). Universals in linguistic theory. New York: Holt, Rinehart & Winston. 1-88.

Fillmore, C.F. (1977). The case for case reopened. in: Cole/ Saddock (eds.). Syntax and Semantics, Vol.8. New York: Academic Press. 59-81.

IBM (1983): SQL Data System, General Information, GH24-5013. International Business Machines Corporation, Endicott, New York.

IBM (1983, 1984): Query Management Facility, General Information, GC26-4071, International Business Machines Corporation, San Jose, California.

Steiner, E. (1986): "Generating semantic structures in EUROTRA-D." in: COLING proceedings 1986. Universität Bonn. 304-307.

<table>
<tr><td rowspan="3"></td><td colspan="10" align="center">S a t z r a h m e n</td></tr>
<tr><td>I — III</td><td>IV</td><td>V</td><td>VI</td><td>VII</td><td>VIII</td><td></td><td>IX</td><td>X</td></tr>
<tr><td>Nomen:</td><td>Genitive</td><td>X an P</td><td>P hat X</td><td>P liebt X</td><td>P bekommt X</td><td>VI + von M</td><td>P gibt X</td><td>VIII+DAT</td></tr>
<tr><td>13

.2%</td><td>Appell
Empfehlung
Ratschlag</td><td>J(an)
J(an)
J(an)</td><td>an—AKK
an—AKK
an—AKK</td><td>SBJ
SBJ
(SBJ)</td><td>0
0
0</td><td>SBJ
SBJ
SBJ</td><td>SBJ
SBJ
SBJ</td><td>J—DAT
J—DAT
J—DAT</td><td>DAT
DAT
DAT</td></tr>
<tr><td>14

.2%</td><td>Bitte
Forderung
Glückwunsch</td><td>J(an)
J(an)
J(an)</td><td>an—AKK
an—AKK
an—AKK</td><td>—
—
—</td><td>0
0
—</td><td>SBJ
SBJ
SBJ</td><td>SBJ
SBJ
SBJ</td><td>—
—
J—DAT
(J—DAT)</td><td>—
DAT
(DAT)</td></tr>
<tr><td>15

.2%</td><td>Erlaubnis
Strafe
Veranlassung</td><td>GEN/J
GEN/J
GEN/J</td><td>—
—
—</td><td>SBJ
SBJ
SBJ</td><td>0
0
0</td><td>SBJ
SBJ
(SBJ)</td><td>SBJ
SBJ
(SBJ)</td><td>J—DAT
J—DAT
J—DAT</td><td>DAT
DAT
DAT</td></tr>
<tr><td>16

.1%</td><td>Genehmigung
Order
Weisung</td><td>GEN/J
GEN/J
GEN/J</td><td>an—AKK
an—AKK
an—AKK</td><td>SBJ
SBJ
SBJ</td><td>0
0
0</td><td>SBJ
SBJ
SBJ</td><td>SBJ
SBJ
SBJ</td><td>J—DAT
J—DAT
J—DAT</td><td>DAT
DAT
DAT</td></tr>
<tr><td>17

.2%</td><td>Ansporn
Auftrag
Befehl</td><td>GEN/J(an)
GEN/J(an)
GEN/J(an)</td><td>an—AKK
an—AKK
an—AKK</td><td>SBJ
SBJ
SBJ</td><td>0
0
0</td><td>SBJ
SBJ
SBJ</td><td>SBJ
SBJ
SBJ</td><td>J—DAT
J—DAT
J—DAT</td><td>DAT
DAT
DAT</td></tr>
<tr><td>18

.1%</td><td>Angabe
Angebot
Offerte</td><td>GEN/J(an)
GEN/J(an)
GEN/J(an)</td><td>(JGEN/anAKK)
(JGEN/anAKK)
J—GEN/anAKK</td><td>SBJ
SBJ
SBJ</td><td>0
0
0</td><td>SBJ
SBJ
SBJ</td><td>SBJ/vonGEN
SBJ/vonGEN
SBJ/vonGEN</td><td>—
—
—</td><td>—
—
—</td></tr>
<tr><td>19

.4%</td><td>Abkommen
Diskussion
Vereinbarung</td><td>GEN + J(mit)
GEN + J(mit)
GEN + J(mit)</td><td>—
—
—</td><td>SBJ+J(mit)
SBJ+J(mit)
SBJ+J(mit)</td><td>0
0
0</td><td>—
—
—</td><td>—
—
—</td><td>—
—
—</td><td>—
—
—</td></tr>
<tr><td>20

.1%</td><td>Übereinkunft
Übereinstimmung
Abstimmung</td><td>GEN + J(mit)
GEN + J(mit)
GEN + J(mit)</td><td>—
—
—</td><td>—
—
—</td><td>0
0
0</td><td>—
—
—</td><td>—
—
—</td><td>—
—
—</td><td>—
—
—</td></tr>
<tr><td>21

.1%</td><td>Bedenken
Einspruch</td><td>GEN +/ J
GEN +/ J</td><td>—
—</td><td>SBJ +/ J
SBJ +/ J</td><td>0
0</td><td>SBJ+/vJ—GEN
SBJ+/vJ—GEN</td><td>SBJ+/vonGEN
SBJ+/vonGEN</td><td>—
—</td><td>SBJ+/J
(SBJ+/J)</td></tr>
<tr><td>22

.1%</td><td>Beschluß
Erklärung</td><td>GEN /+ J
GEN /+ J</td><td>—
—</td><td>—
SBJ /+ J</td><td>0
0</td><td>SBJ/+vJ—GEN
SBJ/+vJ—GEN</td><td>SBJ /+ J
SBJ /+ J</td><td>SBJ/+J—DAT
SBJ/+J—DAT</td><td>SBJ/+DAT
SBJ/+DAT</td></tr>
<tr><td>23

.3%</td><td>Gesetz
Klausel
Lehre</td><td>JZ
JZ
JZ</td><td>—
—
—</td><td>—
—
—</td><td>0
0
0</td><td>—
—
—</td><td>—
—
—</td><td>—
—
—</td><td>—
—
—</td></tr>
</table>

Abb. 1

Anm.: Die Prozentzahlen beziehen sich auf die Verteilung der Nomen der Einzelkategorien auf das gesamte Testkorpus

Legende: — = Konstruktion nicht möglich   (Kontrolleur) = nur bedingt möglich
          / = a oder b   (Präp)   = PP als Kontrolleur
        /+ = entweder a oder a + b   J   = nicht expliziter Kontrolleur
        +/ = a + b oder a oder b   0   = Kontrolleur in einem abstrakten Konzept

		Satzrahmen							
		I – III	IV	V	VI	VII	VIII	IX	X
	Nomen:	Genitiv	X an P	P hat X	P liebt X	P bekommt X	VI + von M	P gibt X	VIII+DAT
1	Chance	GEN	–	SBJ	0	SBJ	SBJ	J—DAT	DAT
	Hoffnung	GEN	–	SBJ	0	SBJ	SBJ	(J—DAT)	DAT
11%	Möglichkeit	GEN	–	SBJ	0	SBJ	SBJ	J—DAT	DAT
2	Anspruch	GEN	an—AKK	SBJ	0	SBJ	SBJ	(J—DAT)	(DAT)
	Antrieb	GEN	an—AKK	SBJ	(0)	SBJ	SBJ	J—DAT	DAT
.2%	Aufgabe	GEN	an—AKK	SBJ	0	SBJ	SBJ	J—DAT	DAT
3	Arbeitsziel	GEN	–	SBJ	0	SBJ	SBJ	–	–
	Pflicht	GEN	–	SBJ	0	SBJ	SBJ	–	–
.2%	Zielsetzung	GEN	–	SBJ	0	SBJ	SBJ	–	–
4	Absicht	GEN	–	SBJ	0	SBJ	–	–	–
	Bedürfnis	GEN	–	SBJ	0	SBJ	–	–	–
16%	Wunsch	GEN	–	SBJ	0	SBJ	–	–	–
5	Bereitschaft	GEN	–	SBJ	(0)	–	–	–	–
	Vorhaben	GEN	–	SBJ	0	–	–	–	–
25%	Ziel	GEN	–	SBJ	0	–	–	–	–
6	Behauptung	GEN	–	–	0	–	–	–	–
	Bemühung	GEN	–	–	0	–	–	–	–
18%	Entscheidung	GEN	–	–	0	–	–	–	–
7	Geständnis	GEN	J—GEN	–	0	(vonJ—GEN)	vonGEN	–	–
	Versprechen	GEN	J—GEN	–	0	vonJ—GEN	vonGEN	SBJ	SBJ
.3%	Zusage	GEN	J—GEN	–	0	(vonJ—GEN)	vonGEN	SBJ	SBJ
8	Einwilligung	GEN	–	–	0	(vonJ—GEN)	vonGEN	SBJ	SBJ
	Entschuldigung	GEN	–	–	0	(vonJ—GEN)	vonGEN	(SBJ)	(SBJ)
.3%	Weigerung	GEN	–	–	0	(vonJ—GEN)	vonGEN	–	–
9	Beweis	GEN	–	SBJ	0	SBJ	SBJ/vonGEN	SBJ	SBJ/DAT
	Gewißheit	GEN	–	SBJ	0	SBJ	SBJ/vonGEN	SBJ	SBJ/DAT
.1%									
10	Einladung	J	an—AKK	SBJ	0	SBJ	SBJ	–	–
	Gebot	J	–	SBJ	0	SBJ	SBJ	–	–
.2%	Verordnung	J	–	SBJ	0	SBJ	SBJ	–	–
11	Lob	J	–	–	0	SBJ	SBJ	(J—DAT)	(DAT)
	Tadel	J	–	–	0	SBJ	SBJ	J—DAT	DAT
.2%	Vorwurf	J	–	–	0	SBJ	SBJ	–	–
12	Verständnis	J	–	J	0	SBJ	SBJ	–	–
.1%									

Zur Behandlung von Funktionsverbgefügen
im Deutschen
I. Starke
Zentralinstitut für Sprachwissenschaft
der AdW der DDR

Problemstellung

Funktionsverbgefüge (FVG) sind häufig auftretende Erscheinungen sowohl im Deutschen als auch in anderen Sprachen. Sie sind eine viel-
schichtige Erscheinung und lassen bei ihrer Untersuchung verschiedene Probleme hervortreten. Das betrifft die Struktur ihrer Bedeutung und die Struktur der ihnen entsprechenden Vollverben, die Form
der Darstellung der semantischen Struktur, das Verhältnis zur syntaktischen Struktur, Fragen der Nominalisierung und damit verbunde-
ner Fortfall von Aktanten, Probleme der Mehrdeutigkeit und auch
Fragen der Abgrenzung sowohl zu den Idiomen als auch zu freien syntaktischen Verbindungen.

Funktionsverbgefüge stellen einen speziellen Typ von Prädikaten dar.
Es handelt sich um analytische Formen, die semantisch eine Einheit
bilden, dies jedoch in unterschiedlichem Maße, abhängig vom Grad
ihrer Festgefügtheit. FVG lassen sich nicht auf nur eine einzige
Art interpretieren. Abhängig von den an ihnen beteiligten Elementen
und der Festigkeit ihrer Fügung bilden sie verschiedene Klassen von
Prädikaten. Bei der Analyse der FVG, vor allem auch mit der Zielstellung einer automatischen Analyse, ist es erforderlich, bis zu
einem gewissen Grade etwas über ihre Bedeutungsstruktur zu wissen.
Auch bei einer syntaktisch orientierten Analyse kann man sich nicht
auf die Oberflächenstruktur beschränken, denn um die syntaktische
Funktion zu bestimmen, muß man die Bedeutungsstruktur bis zu einem
gewissen Grade erkennen. Inwieweit dies erforderlich ist, hängt wesentlich von der Zielstellung der Analyse ab. Reicht es aus, das
analytische Prädikat als eine Einheit zu erkennen oder ist eine weitere semantische Zerlegung erforderlich? Es ist abzuwägen, wie
w e i t   eine Zerlegung zu treiben ist. Sollen die Analyseergebnisse im Rahmen eines Verfahrens für automatische Übersetzung verwendet
werden, ist man mit diesem Problem ebenso konfrontiert. Hinzu kommt
hier die Notwendigkeit, die Analyseergebnisse der Quellensprache
durch entsprechende Äquivalente der Zielsprache zu ersetzen. Man muß

wissen, ob die Zielsprache direkte Entsprechungen bereitstellt oder
ob eine andere Prädikatform zu wählen ist. Je elementarer eine Be-
deutungskomponente der untersuchten Konstruktion ist, desto eher
läßt sich ein Lexem finden, das dieser Komponente in einer anderen
Sprache entspricht. Wieweit man in der Zerlegung gehen sollte, hängt
dabei sicher auch von der zu bearbeitenden Quellen- bzw. Zielsprache ab.

Die Zielstellung der Untersuchung war, eine Differenzierung der verschiedenen Gruppen und Bedeutungen der FVG vorzunehmen. Dazu war es
notwendig, die komplexe Prädikatbedeutung in weniger komplexe Einheiten, in sog. "Elementar-" oder Basisprädikate zu zerlegen. Die
Darstellung erfolgt in Form logisch-semantischer Prädikate. Dabei
ist ebenfalls die Bedeutung des Funktionsverbs als Träger der morphologischen Kategorien des Prädikats und auch als Träger semantischer Klassifikationsmerkmale einschließlich spezifizierender Merkmale zu berücksichtigen. Daraus ergibt sich die resultierende Bedeutung der gesamten Konstruktion "FVG", die nicht immer allein als
Summe der Bedeutung ihrer einzelnen Komponenten erscheint.

Die Rolle der Funktionsverben

Bei der Identifizierung der FVG als Prädikat ergeben sich Schwierigkeiten, da es in der Maske einer syntaktischen Konstruktion mit einem
Vollverb auftritt. Auf Grund ihrer ursprünglichen Vollverbfunktion
bieten die Funktionsverben den syntaktischen Rahmen für die FVG-Konstruktionen:

Die Funktionsverben, die sich meist aus dem Bestand der Vollverben re-
krutieren (Konstruktionen mit den Hilfsverben "sein", "haben" sind allerdings ebenfalls in die FVG-Behandlung eingeschlossen), besitzen
nicht mehr alle spezifischen Bedeutungskomponenten der Vollverben.
Sie bringen Merkmale ein, die durch eine Bedeutungsveränderung der
Verben bedingt sind. Es handelt sich hier um einen Grammatikalisierungsprozeß, bei dem spezifische Merkmale, die sie in ihrer Vollverbfunktion besaßen, zu generellen Merkmalen umfunktioniert wurden; z. B.:

- Ruhekomponente — Merkmal "statisch" bei FV wie "liegen, stehen",
- Bewegungskomponente "Richtung" — Merkmal "nichtstatisch" bei FV
  wie "kommen zu/in, gelangen zu/in, ..."
- Tun-Komponente — Merkmal "handelnd" (bewußt, absichtlich) bei FV
  wie "machen"
- Orts-, Lageveränderung, gekoppelt mit der Tun-Komponente — Merkmal
  "kausierend" (CAUS) bei FV wie "stellen, setzen, bringen" und Präposition "in/zu"

- passivischer Besitzwechsel — Merkmal "nicht selbsttätig" bei FV
  wie "bekommen, erhalten". (Eigentlich handelt es sich hier um einen
  Empfänger in weiterem Sinne.)

Diese Komponenten werden als generelle Merkmale in die Bedeutung der
FVG eingebracht und ergeben eine weitere Klassifizierung der Prädikate. Es ist hier ein Übergang zum Ausdruck grammatischer Kategorien
zu vermerken (STEINITZ 1977).

Zur Festigkeit der FVG; ihre spezielle Rolle im Vergleich zu Verbformen

Der Grammatikalisierungsprozeß bewegt sich zwischen den freien syntaktischen und den phraseologischen Verbindungen. Die FVG befinden sich
innerhalb dieser Grenzen und tendieren sowohl in die eine als auch in
die andere Richtung, abhängig von den einzelnen FVG, die man auch
wieder unterscheiden muß:

Produktive FVG: kommen + in/zu, bringen + in/zu u. a. mit einer relativ freien Verbindbarkeit im Rahmen bestimmter semantischer Klassen.

Bereits feste Fügungen: in Lösung gehen, Widerstand leisten u. a.

FVG mit Funktionsverben, die außer ihren klassenbildenden Merkmalen
noch zusätzlich spezifizierende haben: in Angst, Verzweiflung, ...
stürzen u. a.

Die Bedeutungskomponenten der FVG verteilen sich auf die einzelnen an
der Konstruktion beteiligten Lexeme. Ihre Bedeutung scheint dadurch
in gewisser Weise transparenter zu sein als dies z. B. bei den Verben
der Fall ist. Das trifft jedoch nicht immer zu. Ein Funktionsverbgefüge kann oft nicht voll mit entsprechend vorhandenen Verbformen
gleichgesetzt werden. Es gibt eine Reihe von Spezifizierungen und Unterschieden. Zwischen den Verbformen und den FVG besteht keine vollständige semantische Äquivalenz. Einzelne Komponenten der FVG lassen
bestimmte Bedeutungsanteile stärker hervortreten bzw. ermöglichen den
Zugang zu bestimmten Bedeutungskomponenten. Andererseits verfügen die
FVG über ein spezielles Ausdrucksmittel, das in der Möglichkeit des
Weglassens von Aktanten besteht, da die Sättigung einer Aktantenstel-
le des Funktionsverbs durch den prädikativen Komplex bereits erfolgt
ist:

(1) Er gibt einen Rat. - Er rät (wem wozu)
(2) Sie gibt eine Information. - Sie informiert (wen worüber).

Das in Objektposition stehende Nomen ist beim FVG in das Prädikat in-
korporiert.

Zur Frage der Mehrdeutigkeit der FVG-Konstruktionen sei nur soviel gesagt, daß es in einer Reihe von Fällen die Möglichkeit gibt, sie durch Selektionsbeschränkungen aufzulösen. Dazu ein Beispiel:

(3) x kommt zur Versteigerung.

Kriterium: Handelt es sich bei x um einen Menschen /H.B./, ist die Präpositionalgruppe eine Richtungsbestimmung (Der Fall, daß x = Sklave soll ausgeschlossen sein). Für alle anderen x = /KONKRET/ gilt: Es handelt sich um ein FVG, das einen passivischen Vorgang bezeichnet:

(3') x wird versteigert.

Prädikatsklassen

Es wurde angestrebt, die FVG nicht isoliert als besonderes grammatisches Phänomen zu behandeln, sondern eine Beschreibungsgrundlage zu schaffen, die einen Vergleich mit anderen entsprechenden Formen syntaktischer Prädikate, vor allem mit Verbformen gestattet.

Die Nominal- bzw. Präpositionalgruppe in Objektposition stellt den Hauptbedeutungsträger der FVG dar und bildet zusammen mit dem Funktionsverb (FV) das Prädikat. Beim Substantiv in Subjektposition handelt es sich um Eigenschaftsträger, Zustandsträger, Prozeßträger, Handlungsträger, je nachdem, welche Art von Prädikat vorliegt. Bei der syntaktischen Analyse kann nicht darauf verzichtet werden, bereits festzustellen, daß es sich um einen prädikativen Komplex besonderer Art handelt. Abgesehen von der Deklarierung der Verben im Lexikon als Funktionsverben mit einer speziellen Dominanz- und selektiven Komponente (obligatorisches Nomen im Nominativ, obligatorisches Nomen im Akkusativ/Dativ/Genitiv oder obligatorische Präposition; Forderung, daß es sich bei den Nomina in Objektposition um Abstrakta handelt), kann man für die Hauptbedeutungsträger bestimmte Klassen von Prädikaten ermitteln, wobei keine komplette Komponentenstrukturanalyse angestrebt wird. Die Zerlegung erfolgt bis zu einem Grade, der es erlaubt, Klassen semantischer Prädikate zu bilden, die vor allem auf der Grundlage bestimmter Merkmale der Abstrakta ermittelt werden:

"statisch" /±STAT/, "inhärent" /±INHÄR/,
"selbsttätig" /±SELBSTTÄT/, "bewußt" /±BEW/,
"absichtlich" /±ABS/, "sichgerichtet" /±SICH/.

Die Merkmale sind hierarchisch angeordnet und binär. Die Binarität läßt sich bis zu einem gewissen Grade durchhalten, da es sich um generelle Merkmale handelt, nach denen die Prädikatsklassen gebildet werden. Wird eine feinere Beschreibung der Bedeutung bis hin zu einer

vollständigen Beschreibung einzelner Sememe angestrebt, läßt sich eine
solche Merkmalsopposition sicher nicht fortsetzen. Weitere spezifische
Merkmale sind dann positiv festzulegen.

Auf Grund der genannten Merkmale erhält man Prädikatsklassen wie
"Eigenschaft", "Zustand", "Prozeß", "Handlung", wobei diese noch
weiter unterteilbar sind.

Auf der Grundlage der o. g. Merkmale ergeben sich folgende Klassen von
Prädikaten, die jeweils wiederum in sich untergliedert sind. Für die
einzelnen Hauptgruppen werden hier nur typische Beispiele von FVG angeführt. Alle einzelnen Untergruppen zu nennen, wäre zu umfangreich.
Siehe dazu STARKE (in Vorbereitung). Als zwei Hauptgruppen werden statische von nicht statischen Prädikaten (= Vorgangsprädikate) unterschieden.

1. Eigenschaften /+STAT/, /–INHÄR/, EIG(x):
   Begabung haben, ein ... Gehör haben, eine Rundung haben,
   von Nutzen/Schaden sein, ... Es handelt sich um psychische, phy-
   siche, Form-, Maß-, Benefiz-, Malefizeigenschaften u. a.

2. Zustände /+STAT/, /–INHÄR/ mit einem Argument, ZUST(x) oder mit
   mehr als einem Argument, ZUST(x,y). Bei den Zuständen werden vor
   allem Qualifikationszustände (allgemeine und spezielle) und resul-
   tative Zustände unterschieden. Letztere sind das Ergebnis vor sich
   gegangener Prozesse oder Handlungen:
   $ZUST^{QUAL}$: von ... Sauberkeit sein; $ZUST^{PSYCH}$: Furcht haben, ...
   $ZUSTRES^{PROZ}$: eine Erkältung haben; $ZUSTRES^{PASS}$: eine Beschädigung
   haben
   $ZUST^{REL}$: x ist in Verbindung/Beziehung mit/zu y;
   $ZUST^{BEFUG}$: x hat/trägt Verantwortung für y.

   Zustände mit zwei Argumenten setzen diese miteinander in Beziehung.
   Bei den Verben handelt es sich in der Regel um solche mit stati-
   scher Bedeutung (sein, haben).
   Die folgenden Klassen sind Vorgänge, die auf der Grundlage stati-
   scher Prädikate und entsprechender Funktionsverben, meist nichtsta-
   tischer Art, gebildet werden: Es gibt Ausnahmen, bei denen Vorgangsprädikate mit statischen Verben gebildet werden, so z. B. die folgende Gruppe:

3. Passivische Vorgänge /–STAT/, /–SELBSTTÄT/, PASSVORG(x):
   unter Kontrolle stehen, unter Aufsicht sein, im Verkauf sein, ...
   Durch das statische FV wird eine Komponente eingebracht, die eine
   Tendenz zu den Zustandsprädikaten zeigt.

Ähnliches gibt es auch bei anderen Vorgängen (Prozessen, Handlungen): im Reifen sein, im Laufen sein. Hier wird nur ein Ausschnitt des gesamten Vorgangs herausgegriffen und beschrieben.

Durch nichtstatische FV wie "kommen, geraten" wird der Beginn des Vorgangs ausgedrückt: unter Kontrolle kommen, zum Reifen kommen.

Häufig treten bei passivischen Vorgängen auch Bildungen mit FV wie "bekommen, erleiden" auf, da sie auf Grund ihrer ehemaligen Vollverbsemantik die passivische Komponente unterstreichen: eine Verletzung bekommen/erleiden. Manchmal handelt es sich bei den FVG auch um einen Ersatz für nicht vorhandene Passivformen: etwas kommt zur Kenntnis.

Bei den Prozessen werden psychische von anderen Arten von Prozessen unterschieden; PROZ(x):

4. Physiologische, physikalische, chemische u. ä. /-STAT/, /+SELBSTTÄT/, /-BEW/ und

5. psychische Prozesse /-STAT/, /+SELBSTTÄT/, /BEW/
   (Das Merkmal /BEW/ bedeutet: "Prozeß wird im Bewußtsein reflektiert".)

Zu den Prozessen werden nicht nur Zustandsänderungsprozesse gezählt, sondern auch solche, die man als zustandserhaltende Prozesse ansehen kann wie z. B.: im Blühen sein, im Kochen sein, also DUR(ZUST(x)) = PROZDUR(x).

Sehr produktiv sind FVG zum Ausdruck von Zustandsänderungsprozessen, BECOME(ZUST(x)) = PROZTRANSF(x). Wie jeder Vorgang besteht der Zustandsänderungsprozeß aus mehreren Phasen (Beginn, Verlauf, Ende), wobei hier noch die Dimension "Zustandsänderung" hinzukommt. Sprachlich kann dies auf verschiedene Weise realisiert werden. Die Darstellung des vollständigen Ablaufs mit allen seinen Phasen einschließlich Vor- und Nachzustand läßt sich nicht durch e i n Lexem beschreiben. Meist wird der Beginn mit sich anschließendem Verlauf oder häufiger noch der Verlauf der Zustandsänderung mit dem erzielten Resultat ausgedrückt. Es kann auch der Verlauf allein zum Ausdruck kommen. Funktionsverbgefüge sind ein besonders gut geeignetes Ausdrucksmittel, um bestimmte Phasen miteinander zu koppeln bzw. hervorzuheben. So läßt sich durch FVG wie "zum Kochen kommen" eine Vorbereitungsphase einschließlich des Beginns des Prozesses ausdrücken oder durch FVG wie "zur Reife kommen" der Ablauf der Zustandsänderung "reifer werden" einschließlich des Resultats "reif" beschreiben.

Der Ausdruck für den Beginn eines Vorgangs, meist mit den FV "kommen, geraten" gebildet, kann ebenso bei Handlungs-FVG verwendet werden. Dabei erfolgt gleichzeitig eine Bedeutungsmodifizierung durch zusätzliche Komponenten "unbeabsichtigt" und "Anwachsen der Intensität des Vorgangs": ins Laufen kommen/geraten. Dadurch erhält der Vorgang eher die Bedeutung eines Prozesses als einer Handlung.

Zu den Handlungsprädikaten zählen wir die sog. Elementarhandlungen, selbstkausierende Handlungen und Kausalhandlungen:

6. "Elementar"handlungen /-STAT/, /+SELBSTTÄT/, /+BEW/, /+ABS/, EHANDL(x):

   Sie sind nur in dem Sinne als elementar aufzufassen, als daß sie im Vergleich zu den selbstkausierenden und Kausalhandlungen weniger komplex strukturiert sind. Es handelt sich um Aktivitäten eines Agens, die sich auf das Agens selbst beziehen. "essen, laufen, ..." bzw. FVG wie:"beim Essen sein, im Laufen sein".Eine Besonderheit soll hier angeführt werden. In Verbindung mit FV "stellen, machen, führen, geben", die besonders häufig vertreten sind, können bestimmte semantische Gruppen der abstrakten Nomina (Handlung der Fortbewegung, Mitteilung) durch Funktionsverbgefüge das Hinstreben zu einem Resultat ausdrücken: eine Reise, Fahrt, ... machen, eine Mitteilung machen, eine Frage stellen.

7. Selbstkausierende Handlungen /-STAT, +SELBSTTÄT/, /+BEW/, /+ABS/, /+SICH/ sind z. B.: Kenntnis nehmen, in Besitz nehmen: CAUS(x, BECOME(ZUST(x))).

8. Kausalhandlungen /-STAT/, /+SELBSTTÄT/, /+BEW/, /+ABS/, /-SICH/: Ebenso wie für die vorangehenden Gruppen jeweils nur einige Beispiele und Probleme genannt werden konnten, kann die komplizierte Frage der Kausalhandlungen nur kurz skizziert werden. Die kausativen Verben lassen sich nicht auf ein Verursachen des Agens reduzieren, sondern implizieren ein Tun eines x (=Agens) als Ursache des Werdens bzw. Veränderns von y, wobei die Handlung von x durch das angestrebte Resultat bestimmt ist (etwas säubern, jemanden begeistern): CAUSDO(x, BECOME(ZUST(x))). Entsprechende FVG wie "jemanden in Begeisterung versetzen, zur Ruhe bringen" und andere sind entsprechende kausative Konstruktionen, d. h. die eigentlichen kausativen FVG. Durch FVG kann auch die Verursachung eines passivischen Vorgangs ausgedrückt werden:
   etwas zur Verhandlung bringen,
   etwas zur Aufführung bringen.
   Hier kann das Argument x auch nur Initiator einer Handlung sein:

"x initiiert, daß über y verhandelt wird" bzw. "..., daß y aufgeführt wird".

Konstruktionen wie "jemanden zum Arbeiten, Essen, Lachen, ... bringen" werden häufig aus der Behandlung der FVG ausgeklammert. Wir
wollen sie dennoch in unsere Betrachtung einbeziehen, wobei wir
uns dessen bewußt sind, daß es sich hier nicht um eigentliche kausative Handlungen eines x handelt, sondern um eine initiierende
Handlung von x, die einen an y bewußt ablaufenden Prozeß oder eine
Handlung von y hervorbringt: $INIT(x, PROZ^{BEW}(y)/HANDL(y))$. Hierbei
ist es allerdings schwierig, die Grenze zwischen bewußten und un-
bewußt ablaufenden Prozessen zu ziehen. Die Frage wäre z. B., wie
"hoffen" hier einzuordnen wäre.

Literatur:

Persson, Ingmar, Das System der kausativen Funktionsverbgefüge,
        Lunder Germanistische Forschungen 42, CWK Gleerup 1975.

Starke, Ingrid, Functional Verb Complexes. In: Mitteilungen zur
        automatischen Sprachverarbeitung, Akademie der Wissenschaf-
        ten der DDR, Berlin, Juni 1987.

Starke, Ingrid, Untersuchungen zur syntaktisch-semantischen Leistung
        von Funktionsverbgefügen im Deutschen (als Grundlage für
        eine automatische Analyse). In: Studia Grammatica XXX,
        Sammelband. Akademie-Verlag Berlin (in Vorbereitung).

Starke, Ingrid, Machen Funktionsverbgefüge die semantische Struktur
        transparenter? Vortrag auf dem XIV. Internationalen
        Linguistenkongreß, Berlin 1987.

Steinitz, Renate, Zur Semantik und Syntax durativer, inchoativer
        und kausativer Verben. In: Linguistische Studien (A),
        Berlin 1977.

Überlegungen zu einer Two-level Morphologie
für das Deutsche

Martin Emele

Projekt SEMSYN, Institut für Informatik
Universität Stuttgart, Herdweg 51
7000 Stuttgart 1

1 Einleitung

Seit der Einführung der Two-level Morphologie durch Koskenniemi [Koskenniemi 83] entstanden darauf aufbauend eine Reihe von Implementierungen.[1] Als besonderer Vorteil der Two-level Morphologie wird angesehen, daß zwischen der Beschreibung und der tatsächlichen Implementierung der phonologischen Regeln und der Morphosyntax getrennt wird. So lassen sich die morphologischen Regeln und die Strukturierung des Lexikons in gleichem Maße sowohl für die Analyse als auch für die Generierung einsetzen. Als einer der Nachteile dieses Formalismus wurde angeführt, daß bestimmte linguistische Generalisierungen nicht adäquat ausgedrückt werden können. Beispielsweise können phonologische Prozesse, die nur bei bestimmten Wortklassen auftreten, oder lexikalische Idiosynkrasien nur mit Hilfe von unmotiviert eingeführten diakritischen Zeichen auf der lexikalischen Ebene beschrieben werden.[2] Ebenso wurde schon sehr frühzeitig bemerkt, daß die Charakterisierung von Kombinationsrestriktionen zwischen den einzelnen Morphemen mit Hilfe von Fortsetzungsklassen nicht ausreicht, um beispielsweise diskontinuierliche Morpheme oder Derivationsprozesse, die nur für Untermengen einer ganzen Wortklasse produktiv sind, adäquat zu beschreiben.[3] Neuere Ansätze schlagen deshalb für die Beschreibung der Morphosyntax die Verwendung von annotierten kontextfreien Phrasenstrukturregeln vor (etwa im Sinne von PATR-II– Regeln [Bear 86,Bear 88a] oder in Form von kategorialen Regeln [Karttunen 87]).

Im ersten Teil dieses Beitrags sollen exemplarisch Two-level Regeln vorgestellt werden, die orthographische Phänomene des Deutschen beschreiben.[4]

Anhand dieser Regeln sollen spezifische Probleme, die bei der Beschreibung der deutschen Morphologie auftreten, aufgezeigt werden. Diese Probleme sind jedoch nicht grundsätzlich auf das Deutsche beschränkt, ähnlich gelagerte Probleme finden sich auch in anderen Sprachen.[5]

Im letzten Teil sollen Vorschläge und Ansätze zur Überwindung dieser Schwierigkeiten vorgestellt und diskutiert werden.

---

[1] vgl. die Arbeiten von [Karttunen 83],[Bear 86] und [Genikomsidis 88]

[2] vgl. die Diskussion dieser Problematik in [Bear 88a]

[3] siehe hierzu [Karttunen/Wittenburg 83] und [Bear 86]

[4] Die Regeln wurde mit Hilfe des von L. Karttunen, K. Koskenniemi und R. Kaplan entwickelten und implementierten Two-Level-Compiler (TWOL) [Karttunen/Koskenniemi/Kaplan 87] erstellt und getestet.

[5] siehe hierzu [Delogu 86], die ebenfalls Beispiele für kategorieabhängige Regeln im Italienischen anführt.

2 Der Two-level Formalismus

Das Two-level Modell besitzt zwei Ebenen zur Repräsentation eines Wortes: Eine lexikalische Ebene und eine Oberflächenebene. Auf der Oberfläche sind die Wörter so dargestellt, wie sie in Texten auftreten. Auf der lexikalischen Ebene bestehen die Wörter aus einer Sequenz von Stämmen, Affixen, diakritischen Zeichen und Morphemgrenzen. Werden Morpheme aus dem Lexikon aneinandergehängt, um Wortformen oder neue Wörter zu bilden, kann es vorkommen, daß Änderungen der Aussprache bzw. der Schreibung auftreten.

Jedem Zeichen auf der lexikalischen Ebene ist ein Zeichen auf der Oberfläche zugeordnet. Die Liste aller erlaubten Korrespondenzpaare ergibt alle möglichen Abbildungen zwischen der lexikalischen Zeichenkette und der Oberflächenkette. Defaultmäßig entspricht jedem lexikalischen Alphabetzeichen das gleiche Zeichen auf der Oberfläche ($a{:}a - z{:}z$), während diakritische Zeichen dem Nullzeichen (0) entsprechen.

Two-level Regeln stellen eine weitere Quelle von möglichen Abbildungen zwischen lexikalischer Ebene und Oberflächenebene dar. Dabei sind die Regeln aufzufassen als Bedingungen, in welchen Kontexten ein lexikalisches Zeichen auf der Oberfläche als ein bestimmtes Zeichen vorkommen darf und/oder vorkommen muß (in Abhängigkeit vom gewählten Operator). Die einzelnen Regeln bestehen aus einem Korrespondenzpaar, einem Operator, sowie aus einem Links- und Rechtskontext, und haben folgende Gestalt[6]:

$$a{:}b \ \texttt{<=>} \ \alpha \ \_ \ \beta$$

Das lexikalische Zeichen a, dem eine Sequenz von Zeichenpaaren α vorausgeht, und das gefolgt wird von einer Sequenz von Zeichenpaaren β, muß auf der Oberfläche dem Zeichen b entsprechen (und umgekehrt).[7]

3 Regeln für das Deutsche

Im Folgenden wird anhand von Beispielen erläutert, welcher Art die zu behandelnden Phänome sind, und wie mögliche Two-level Regeln hierfür aussehen könnten.

3.1 Umlautung

Umlautung kennzeichnet im Deutschen morphologische Oppositionen, wie z.B. Singular vs. Plural bei Substantiven, bzw. Positiv vs. Komparativ bei Adjektiven. Dieser Prozeß tritt aber nicht systematisch für alle Substantive und Adjektive auf. Stattdessen ist für alle Stämme mit einen umlautfähigen Vokal (a, o, u) lexikalisch festgelegt, ob umgelautet wird oder nicht. Unter den als regelmäßig zu betrachenden Pluralendungen $+0$, $+e$, $+er$, $+(e)n$ und $+s$, tritt eine Umlautung nur bei den Typen $+0$, $+e$, $+er$ auf.

---

[6]Für die genaue Definition des Regelformats und der Lexikoneinträge sei auf die Beschreibung des Two-level-Compiler (TWOL) und des KIMMO Systems verwiesen ([Karttunen/Koskenniemi/Kaplan 87]).

[7]Der Doppelpunkt (:) trennt die Zeichen eines Paares, der Unterstreichstrich (_) kennzeichnet die Position des Korrespondenzpaares im Kontext.

Betrachten wir zunächst einige Beispiele von Substantiven verschiedener Genera mit und ohne Umlautung:

Plural *+0* **mit** Umlaut:
    der Apfel, Apfel+0 ↔ Äpfel
    der Faden, Faden+0 ↔ Fäden
    der Acker, Acker+0 ↔ Äcker
    das Kloster, Kloster+0 ↔ Klöster
    die Tochter, Tochter+0 ↔ Töchter

Plural *+0* **ohne** Umlaut:
    der Balken, Balken+0 ↔ Balken
    der Anker, Anker+0 ↔ Anker
    das Kabel, Kabel+0 ↔ Kabel

Plural *+e* **mit** Umlaut:
    der Schlag, Schlag+e ↔ Schläge
    der Einwand, Einwand+e ↔ Einwände
    die Hand, Hand+e ↔ Hände
    die Ausflucht, Ausflucht+e ↔ Ausflüchte
    das Floß, Floß+e ↔ Flöße

Plural *+e* **ohne** Umlaut:
    der Tag, Tag+e ↔ Tage
    der Monat, Monat+e ↔ Monate

Plural *+er* **mit** Umlaut:
    der Mann, Mann+er ↔ Männer
    der Irrtum, Irtum+er ↔ Irrtümer
    das Haus, Haus+er ↔ Häuser
    das Buch, Buch+er ↔ Bücher

Plural *+er* **ohne** Umlaut:
    keine Beispiele mit umlautfähigem Vokal existent

Die Parallelität hinsichtlich der Stellung des umlautbaren Vokals, der Stammendungen sowie der Pluralendung (vgl. z.B. *Schlag* und *Tag*) erfordert eine lexikalische Markierung des Stammes, ob Umlautung vorliegt oder nicht. Ebenso ist eine Kennzeichnung der Pluralendungen notwendig, da homographe Flexionsendungen wie *-0* und *-e* sowohl Singular, als auch Plural bezeichnen können.

Nachfolgend ist eine vereinfachte Regel für die Umlautbildung anhand des umlautbaren Vokals *a* aufgeführt. Entsprechende Regeln sind für die restlichen umlautfähigen Vokale anzugeben. Im Rahmen des TWOL Formalismus lassen sich die einzelnen Regeln durch die Einführung von Variablen zu einer einzigen Regel zusammenfassen, worauf aus Darstellungsgründen verzichtet wurde.

    Umlaut *a*   `A:ä <=> _ =* +: %:`

Von dieser Regel werden folgende Paarungen von Zeichenketten auf der lexikalischen Ebene und der Oberflächenebene akzeptiert[8]:

```
Acker+0      Acker+%0      anker+0      anker+%0
acker00      äcker000      anker00      anker000

schlAg+0     schlAg+%e     tag+0        tag+%0
schlag00     schläg00e     tag00        tag00e
```

Das Archiphonem *A* besitzt hierbei eine Doppelfunktion: Es markiert sowohl den Stamm als umlautbar als auch die Position des umzulautenden Vokals. Defaultmäßig werden die Archiphoneme *A, O, U* auf der Oberfläche als *a, o, u* realisiert.

Die Umlautregel läßt sich dann folgendermaßen paraphrasieren: Dem Archiphonem *A* auf der lexikalischen Ebene entspricht der Umlaut *ä* auf der Oberfläche, falls eine Sequenz von beliebigen Zeichen[9], die den

---

[8] Nullzeichen auf der Oberfläche werden bei der Ausgabe unterdrückt.

[9] Das Gleichzeitszeichen steht stellvertretend für alle erlaubten Paare, die entweder implizit durch das Alphabet oder explizit durch eine Regel eingeführt wurden. Das nachfolgende Sternzeichen (*) denotiert den Kleenestar-Operator.

Rest des Stammes ausmachen, gefolgt wird von der Morphemgrenze + und dem Prozentzeichen %. Die Verwendung des Prozentzeichens als diakritisches Zeichen stellt im bestehenden Formalismus die einzige Möglichkeit dar, auf bestimmte Merkmale zu testen; in diesem Fall auf Vorliegen einer Pluralendung. In allen anderen Kontexten entspricht das Archiphonem gemäß der Standardpaarung im Alphabet dem Vokal *a*.

3.2 Elision

Mit Elision wird der Ausfall des unbetonten *e*-Lauts, der auch Murmelvokal oder Schwa-Laut genannt wird, bezeichnet. Dabei ist der Ausfall im Stammauslaut zu unterscheiden von der Tilgung im Suffix. So entfällt das *e* in der unbetonten Flexionsendung bei Substantiven, die ihren Plural mit *+(e)n* bilden, falls der Stamm auf *-e*, *-el* oder *-er* endet. Ebenso wird das *e* der unbetonten Endung *+en* (Infinitiv, Ind. Präs. 1. & 3. Plural) bei Verben getilgt, deren Stammendung *-el* bzw. *-er* lautet.

Substantive auf *-e*, *-el*, *-er* und Plural *+(e)n*:
    die Gabe, Gabe+en ↔ Gaben
    der See, See+en ↔ Seen
    die Tafel, Tafel+en ↔ Tafeln
    der Muskel, Muskel+en ↔ Muskeln
    die Steuer, Steuer+en ↔ Steuern
    der Vetter, Vetter+en ↔ Vettern

aber **nicht** Substantive auf Diphthong *-au*, *-ei*:
    die Frau, Frau+en ↔ Frauen
    der Pfau, Pfau+en ↔ Pfauen
    die Grübelei, Grübelei+en ↔ Grübeleien

Verben mit Stamm auf *-el*, *-er* und Suffix *+en* (Infinitiv, Ind. Präs. 1. & 3. Plural):
    handeln, handel+en ↔ handeln
    erneuern, erneuer+en ↔ erneuern
    versauern, versauer+en ↔ versauern
    bewundern, bewunder+en ↔ bewundern

Dazu die entsprechende Regel (der senkrechte Strich | dient zur Abtrennung von Alternativen):

    Suffix Schwa Tilgung   `e:0 <=> [e|el|er] +: _ n`

Im Gegensatz zum vorhergehenden Ausfall in der Flexionsendung wird bei Verben das unbetonte *e* des Stammauslauts *-el* bzw. *-er* getilgt, falls die Endung *+e* angehängt wird (vgl. die folgenden Beispiele):

Verben mit Stamm auf *-el*, *-er* und Suffix *+e* (Imperativ Sing., Ind. Präs. 1. Sing.):
    handeln, handel+e ↔ handle
    erneuern, erneuer+e ↔ erneure
    versauern, versauer+e ↔ versaure
    bewundern, bewunder+e ↔ bewund(e)re

Bei Adjektiven auf *-el*, *-er*, die mit einer der möglichen Flexionsendungen *+e*, *+en*, *+er*, *+es* oder *+em* versehen sind, entfällt generell das *-e* des Stammauslauts.

Adjektive auf *-el*, *-er*:
    dunkel, dunkel+en ↔dunklen, dunkel+er ↔dunkler, dunkel+sten ↔dunkelsten
    heikel, heikel+e ↔heikle, heikel+es ↔heikles
    sauer, sauer+e ↔saure, sauer+en ↔sauren
    neuer, neuer+e ↔neu(e)re, neuer+en ↔neu(e)ren
    integer, integer+er ↔integrer
    heiter, heiter+es ↔heit(e)res

Die folgende vorläufige Regel berücksichtigt obige Daten:

Root Schwa Tilgung   e:0 <=>   _ l +: e
                                   [eu|au] _ r +: e

Stämme auf *-el* verlieren bei der Flexion immer den unbetonten Vokal, während bei Stämmen auf *-er* nur mit vorausgehendem Diphthong *au*, *eu* oder bei Fremdwörtern (z.B. *integer*) der Ausfall die Regel ist. Bei allen anderen Stämmen auf *-er* ist die Tilgung als umgangssprachlich und optional zu bezeichnen. Die nachfolgende Regel berücksichtigt diesen Tatbestand durch die Verwendung eines nach rechts gerichteten Pfeils =>, der besagt, daß im Kontext *r+e* das vorangehende *e* auf der Oberfläche getilgt sein darf, aber nicht gelöscht zu sein braucht. Ein zusätzlicher Pfeil nach links <= würde letzteres fordern, nämlich, daß im vorliegenden Kontext das *e* immer getilgt werden muß.

Optional Root Schwa Tilgung   e:0 => _ r +: e

Die jetzige Form der Tilgungsregeln berücksichtigt nicht, daß für die Flexionsendung *+en* beide Regeln, gemäß dem Kontext, anwendbar sind. Abhängig von der Wortklasse ist aber nur die Anwendung einer der beiden Regeln korrekt. Daß beide Regeln gleichzeitig zur Anwendung gelangen, ist durch die interagierenden Kontexte ausgeschlossen, da für das im Kontext auftretende *e* (Kurzform für *e:e*) explizit gefordert wird, daß es auf der Oberfläche realisiert ist (vgl. jeweils die beiden akzeptierten Paarungen, von denen eine nicht korrekt ist, und die dritte nicht akzeptierte Paarung):

```
mogel+en          mogel+en          mogel+en
mog010en          mogel00n          mog0100n

heikel+en         heikel+en         heikel+en
heik010en         heikel00n         heik0100n
```

Da die entscheidende Information über die Zugehörigkeit eines Lexems zu einer Wortklasse auf der Regelebene nicht zur Verfügung steht, verbleibt als einzige Alternative die Einführung eines diakritischen Zeichens ($), das die Unterscheidung zwischen Adjektiv- und Verbendung bzw. Substantivendung kodiert. Damit erhalten wir die folgende Zusammenfassung der beiden vorläufigen Regeln zu einer Elisions-Regel:

Elision   e:0 <=>   [e|el|er] +:   _ n $:
                                       _ l +: $: e
                            [eu|au] _ r +: $: e

4 Erweiterungen des bestehenden Formalismus

Die Formulierung der Regeln im vorherigen Abschnitt offenbart eine Reihe von Schwächen, die durch die Beschränkungen des bestehenden Formalismus bedingt sind.

So bedeutet die Verwendung von diakritischen Zeichen zur Kennzeichnung von Merkmalen auf der lexikalischen Ebene redundante Information, da jedem Morphem bereits im Lexikon Merkmalsbeschreibungen zugeordnet sind, die aber für die Regeln nicht zugänglich sind. Ein weiterer Nachteil liegt darin, daß unterschiedliche Beschreibungsebenen vermischt werden: Einerseits die lexikalische Ebene, die zur Repräsentation der phonologischen oder graphemischen Einheiten dient, andererseits die Merkmalsebene, die in Form von Attribut/Wert-Paaren die inhärenten Merkmale der einzelnen Morpheme beschreibt. Damit werden die diakritischen Zeichen, die ursprünglich zur Kennzeichnung der besonderen Aussprache von einzelnen Grundzeichen dienten (z.B. als Angabe der Länge eines Vokals /a:/) dazu mißbraucht, Eigenschaften, die mit dem Morphem assoziiert sind, zu kodieren. Darüberhinaus erschwert die Verwendung von Archiphonemen im Stamm die Erstellung eines Stammformenlexikons, da der Lexikograph die speziellen Kodierungskonventionen auf der lexikalischen Ebene berücksichtigen muß, was nicht ohne Rückgriff auf die vorhandenen morphologischen Regeln möglich ist (z.B. muß bekannt sein, daß umlautbare Vokale durch Großbuchstaben kodiert werden). Als letzter Punkt sei angeführt, daß Ausnahmen bei der Regelanwendung, die idiosynkratisch bei einzelnen Lexemen vorkommen, wiederum nur durch unmotiviert eingeführte diakritische Zeichen behandelt werden können (vgl. den weiter oben diskutierten Unterschied bei der Elision, abhängig davon, ob es sich bei dem Stamm auf -er um ein Fremdwort handelt oder nicht).[10]

Im Folgenden soll versucht werden, durch die Erweiterung des Regelformats um Bedingungen über Merkmalsbeschreibungen, die den Geltungsbereich der Regel einschränken, die bestehenden Nachteile zu überwinden. Mit diesem neuen Regelformat lassen sich die gewünschten Generalisierungen einfach und adäquat beschreiben.

Betrachten wir die neu formulierte Umlaut-Regel:

New Umlaut *a*

$$if \begin{bmatrix} \text{umlaut} & + \\ \text{number} & \text{pl} \end{bmatrix} then \quad \text{a:ä <=> \_ (u) Cons* ([el|er|en]) +:}$$

Unter der Voraussetzung, daß ein umlautbarer Stamm vorliegt (der Lexikoneintrag enthält das Attribut/Wert-Paar [umlaut +]) und Numerus Plural ([number pl]) für die Generierung vorgegeben ist oder aufgrund der Pluralendung analysiert wird, entspricht dem umlautbaren Vokal *a* der Haupttonsilbe der Umlaut *ä*. Der Rechtskontext dieser Regel spezifiziert die Position des umzulautenden Vokals, da mehrere umlautbare Vokale innerhalb eines Stammes vorkommen können und keiner davon besonders gekennzeichnet ist. Die mögliche Generalisierung lautet: Es wird immer der zuletzt vorkommende umlautfähige Vokal

---

[10]siehe hierzu [Bear 88a], der negierte Merkmale für die Nichtanwendbarkeit von Regeln vorsieht.

oder Diphthong *au* umgelautet. Danach kann eine Sequenz von Konsonanten sowohl die Silbe, als auch bei mehrsilbigen Stämmen eine der unbetonten Endungen *-el*, *-er* und *-en* den Stamm abschließen.

Entsprechend wurden komplexe Bedingungen in die folgenden Tilgungsregeln integriert:

Suffix Schwa Tilgung

$$if \left\{ \begin{bmatrix} \text{cat} & \text{Noun} \\ \text{cat} & \text{Verb} \end{bmatrix} \right\} then \quad \text{e:0 <=> [e|el|er] +: \_ n}$$

Root Schwa Tilgung

$$if \left\{ \begin{bmatrix} \text{cat} & \text{Adj} \\ \text{cat} & \text{Verb} \\ \text{mood} & \text{imp} \\ \text{number} & \text{sg} \\ \text{cat} & \text{Verb} \\ \text{tense} & \text{pres} \\ \text{number} & \text{sg} \\ \text{person} & \text{1.} \end{bmatrix} \right\} then \quad \text{e:0 <=> \_ [l|r] +: e}$$

Die Angabe der Wortklasse reicht bei Substantiven und Adjektiven als Bedingung aus, um zwischen Schwa-Tilgung im Stamm und in der Endung unterscheiden zu können. Bei Verben sind zusätzliche Merkmale anzugeben, die den Unterschied zwischen dem Suffix *+e* und *+en* charakterisieren. Ansonsten entsprechen die Regelkörper den weiter oben als vorläufige Regeln formulierten Darstellungen ohne diakritische Zeichen.

5 Zusammenfassung

In diesem Beitrag wurden beispielhaft orthographische Two-level Regeln für das Deutsche präsentiert. Es konnte gezeigt werden, daß der Two-level Formalismus in seiner bisherigen Form nicht ausreicht, um linguistische Generalisierungen, die bei der Behandlung der deutschen Morphologie zu berücksichtigen sind, einfach und adäquat zu beschreiben. Dazu gehört vor allem die Tatsache, daß bestimmte Regeln nur im Bezug auf einzelne Wortklassen Gültigkeit besitzen. Die Verwendung von diakritischen Zeichen zur Lösung dieses Problems kann nur als notationeller Trick verstanden werden. Vorschläge zur Erweiterung des Regelformats um Merkmalsbeschreibungen wurden vorgestellt und diskutiert. Eine Implementierung der vorgeschlagenen Erweiterungen steht noch aus, es wurden aber bereits Vorstudien zu einer Integration dieser Arbeiten in einen objektorientierten Ansatz durchgeführt. Anstelle der parallelen Bearbeitung aller Regeln werden die Regeln zu einzelnen Regelpaketen aufgeteilt und bestimmten Wortklassen innerhalb einer Wortklassenheterarchie zugeordnet. Sie unterliegen damit denselben Vererbungsmechanismen, die auch bei der Vererbung von Merkmalsbeschreibungen zur Anwendung gelangen (siehe hierzu [Emele 86]).

Literatur

[Bear 86] John Bear: "A Morphological Recognizer with Syntactic and Phonological Rules", in: *Proceedings of COLING 1986*, IKP, Bonn, 1986.

[Bear 88a] John Bear: "Morphology with Two-level Rules and Negative Rule Features", erscheint in: *Proceedings of COLING 1988*, Budapest, 1988.

[Bear 88b] John Bear: "Generation and Recognition of Inflectional Morphology", erscheint in: *Proceedings of WWWS 1988*, Wien, 1988.

[Dalrymple et al. 87] Mary Dalrymple, Ronald M. Kaplan, Lauri Karttunen, Kimmo Koskenniemi, Sami Shaio & Michael Wescoat: *"Tools for Morphological Analysis"*, CSLI Report 108, Center for the Study of Language and Information, Stanford University, Stanford, CA 1987.

[Delogu 86] Cristina Delogu: *"Morfofonemi in un lessico morfologico"*, Fondazione Ugo Bordoni, Rom, 1986.

[Emele 86] Martin Emele: *"FREGE – Entwicklung und Implementierung eines objektorientierten FRont-End-GEnerators für das Deutsche"*, Diplomarbeit, Institut für Informatik, Universität Stuttgart, Stuttgart, 1986.

[Genikomsidis 88] Dimitrios Genikomsidis: *"Eine französische Two-Level-Morphologie"*, Studienarbeit Nr. 655, Institut für Informatik, Universität Stuttgart, Stuttgart, 1988.

[Helbig/Buscha 86] Gerhard Helbig & Joachim Buscha: *Deutsche Grammatik: ein Handbuch für den Ausländerunterricht.* 9. Aufl., Leipzig: Enzyklopädie, 1972.

[Karttunen 83] Lauri Karttunen: "Kimmo: A General Morphological Processor", in: Dalrymple et al. (Eds.), *Texas Linguistic Forum #22*, Linguistics Department, University of Texas, Austin, Texas, 1983.

[Karttunen 87] Lauri Karttunen: "Definitions for a Categorial Lexicon", distributed at the 1987 Summer Linguistic Institute at Stanford University, Stanford, California, 1987.

[Karttunen/Wittenburg 83] Lauri Karttunen & Kent Wittenburg: "A Two-level Morphological Analysis of English", in: Dalrymple et al. (Eds.), *Texas Linguistic Forum #22*, Linguistics Department, University of Texas, Austin, Texas, 1983.

[Karttunen/Koskenniemi/Kaplan 87] Lauri Karttunen, Kimmo Koskenniemi & Ronald Kaplan: "TWOL: A Compiler for Two-level Phonological Rules", in: Dalrymple et al. (Eds.), *"Tools for Morphological Analysis"*, CSLI Report 108, Center for the Study of Language and Information, Stanford University, Stanford, CA 1987.

[Koskenniemi 83] Kimmo Koskenniemi: *"Two-level Morphology: A General Computational Model for Word-form Recognition and Production*, Publication No. 11 of the University of Helsinki department of General Linguistics, Helsinki, Finland, 1983.

Zum Lexikonzugriff bei der Generierung mit GPSG

Stephan Busemann

Technische Universität Berlin
Fachbereich Informatik
ISTI, Sekr. FR 5-12
Franklinstr. 28/29, D-1000 Berlin 10
E-mail: busemann@db0tui11.bitnet

Zusammenfassung [1]

Vor dem Hintergrund einer strikten Trennung von Generierungsverfahren, universellem sprachlichen und einzelsprachspezifischem Wissen bei der Generierung mit GPSG werden zwei Arten von Abhängigkeiten zwischen diesen Komponenten bei der Einfügung lexikalischer Elemente in die syntaktische Struktur aufgezeigt. Eine Gruppe von Phänomenen, paradigmatische Lücken, wird kritisch bei der Verwendung eines Stammformenlexikons und einer separaten Flexionskomponente zur Erzeugung von Vollformen. Eine zweites Problem stellt die Auswahl von Perfekt-Hilfsverben im Deutschen dar.

1 Einleitung

Bei der Generierung der sprachlichen Form einer Äußerung ist die Trennung zwischen Generierungsalgorithmus und sprachlichem Wissen umstritten. Generierungssysteme, die mit syntaktischen Unifikationsgrammatiken arbeiten, benutzen eine separat und deklarativ repräsentierte Menge von Regeln; sie müssen aber sprachliche Entscheidungen treffen, die nicht durch die Grammatik gestützt oder widerlegt werden. Dies betrifft z.B. die Informationsverteilung auf syntaktische Konstituenten, die Wortwahl, die Wahl des Satzbaus oder die Fokusrealisierung. Aufgrund der Grammatik entstehen dann u.a. eine Wortfolge, die Kongruenzbeziehungen und flektierte Formen. Die Grammatik verhindert außerdem die Produktion inakzeptabler Sätze. Diesen Aufgaben sind universelle und einzelsprachspezifische Aspekte eigen, die anhand geeigneter linguistischer Theorien expliziert werden können. In der dieser Arbeit zugrundeliegenden Theorie der Generalisierten Phrasenstruktur-Grammatiken (GPSG) (Gazdar et al. 1985; im folgenden GKPS) regeln universelle Prinzipien die Verteilung von Merkmalspezifikationen in syntaktischen Strukturen, die durch einzelsprachliche

[1] Das diesem Bericht zugrundeliegende Vorhaben wurde mit Mitteln des Bundesministers für Forschung und Technologie unter dem Förderkennzeichen 1013211 gefördert. Die Verantwortung für den Inhalt des Berichts liegt beim Autor.

Regelsysteme definiert sind. Ein Grundbaustein dafür sind komplexe syntaktische Kategorien, die, vereinfacht gesagt, aus Mengen von Merkmal-Wert-Paaren bestehen.

Für ein GPSG-basiertes Generierungsverfahren ergeben sich folgende Grundlagen: Die grammatik-externen generierungsspezifischen Entscheidungen über die Form der Äußerung sind vorauszusetzen; sie manifestieren sich in Form und Inhalt der Ausgangsstruktur des Generators. Die universellen Prinzipien der GPSG und die einzelsprachspezifische Grammatik werden getrennt repräsentiert. Von beiden ist das Generierungsverfahren unabhängig; es besteht im wesentlichen aus einem der typischen Baumkonstruktionsalgorithmen.

Im Berliner GPSG-System (Hauenschild/Busemann 1988, Busemann/Hauenschild 1988) stellt eine solche Modularisierung eine Voraussetzung für maschinelle Übersetzung dar. Die universellen Prinzipien werden vom Generator und dem Parser gleichermaßen benutzt, und der Generator (wie auch der Parser) kann eine anderes Sprachfragment verarbeiten, indem einfach die GPS-Grammatik ausgetauscht wird.

So elegant dies klingt, müssen doch Abhängigkeiten zwischen dem Generierungs- algorithmus, dem operationalisierten Grammatikformalismus und den deklarativ repräsentierten Grammatikregeln berücksichtigt werden. Dieser Beitrag betrachtet exemplarisch zwei Probleme bei der Einfügung lexikalischer Elemente in die syntaktische Struktur (Abschnitte 4 und 5). Ganz ähnliche Fragestellungen ergeben sich bei bidirektionaler Verwendung von Grammatiken (siehe hierzu Appelt 1987, Hauenschild/Busemann 1988).

Zunächst jedoch wird der Aufbau des Lexikons beschrieben (Abschnitt 2) und das Generierungsverfahren skizziert (Abschnitt 3).

2 Das Wortlexikon

In GKPS wird wenig über das Lexikon ausgesagt. Für jede Wortform gibt es mindestens einen Eintrag bestehend aus phonologischer Form, syntaktischer Kategorie, eventuellen morphologischen Irregularitäten und einer Bedeutungsrepräsentation. Trotz gegenteiliger Indizien (vgl. GKPS:34) benötigt GPSG ein Vollformenlexikon (VFL): die Wortformen in Syntaxbäumen werden durch präterminale Kategorien beschrieben, die mit lexikalischen Kategorien *identisch* sein müssen. Identität wird auch gefordert, wenn lokale Bäume, d.h. solche der Tiefe 1 (die die Grundbausteine syntaktischer Strukturen bilden), zu komplexeren Bäumen zusammengefügt werden sollen. Insofern ist der Lexikonzugriff in GKPS nichts anderes als die Auswahl unter einer Menge von unären lokalen Bäumen, deren Mütter präterminale Kategorien und deren Töchter Wortformen sind.

Für stark flektierende Sprachen wie das Deutsche ist die Verwendung eines VFL in einem natürlichsprachlichen System unökonomisch. Im Berliner GPSG-System wird daher für das Deutsche ein Stammformenlexikon (SFL) benutzt. Den Übergang von der Stammform zum Wort leistet eine separate Flexionskomponente. Jeder Eintrag besteht aus:

- einem Wortstamm (i.a. der längsten Zeichenkette, die allen flektierten Formen gemeinsam ist),
- einer syntaktischen Kategorie, die nicht in allen Merkmalen spezifiziert ist (und die somit die

syntaktischen Kategorien aller flektierten Formen als Extension hat) und

- morphologischen Charakterisierungen (Umlautfähigkeit, abgelautete Formen, Flexionsklassen usw.)

Außerdem enthält das SFL Bedeutungsrepräsentationen, auf die hier aber nicht eingegangen wird. Die beiden ersten Punkte lassen sich zu Regeln des Typs 'Kategorie → Stamm' zusammenfassen. Diese Regeln werden von der Syntax zur Terminierung der Bäume benötigt. Die morphologischen Charakterisierungen werden ausschließlich von der nachgeschalteten Flexionskomponente benutzt. Für das Verb *bitten* ergibt sich z.B. folgender Eintrag:

Lexikonregel: {<v, +>, <n, ->, <bar, 0>, <sub, 6>, <paux, hab>} → *bitt*
Morph. Char.: Grundform C: *bat*
Grundform D: *baete*
Passiv/Perfekt: *gebeten*
Konjugation: Typ4

Der Stamm wird für die Flexion der regulär gebildeten Formen benutzt; alle anderen flektieren aufgrund der abgelauteten Grundformen C und D (vgl. Busemann 1984). Dabei bestimmt der Konjugationstyp, welche Formen mit welchem Stamm gebildet werden. Die syntaktische Kategorie beschreibt ein transitives Verb, dessen perfektive Formen mit *haben* gebildet werden (Kurzbezeichnung: V[6, paux:hab]). Die Kategorie ist unspezifiziert u.a. für Person, Numerus und Verbform; sie subsumiert also alle möglichen Kombinationen dieser Merkmale.

Die Subkategorisierung beschreibt syntaktische Kontexte als obligatorisch. Dies bedeutet, daß es für jede Subkategorisierung eine eigene Lexikonregel gibt; z.B. besitzt *bitten* bei agenslosem Passiv die Subkategorisierung intransitiver Verben.

3 Generierung mit Stammformenlexika

Die Generierung im Berliner GPSG-System (siehe Busemann 1987) geht von oberflächen-nahen semantischen Strukturen aus, die u.a. die zu verbalisierenden lexikalischen Elemente in Form von eindeutigen Zeigern auf Lexikoneinträge enthalten. Zunächst wird eine syntaktische Struktur aufgrund der verwendeten Regeln aufgebaut (top-down). Dabei werden u.a. präterminale Kategorien erzeugt, die mit der Kategorie eines lexikalischen Elements *unifizieren* müssen: Unifikation (anstelle von Identität wie in GKPS; siehe oben) ist generell die Bedingung für die Kombination lokaler Bäume zu komplexeren Strukturen.

Wie die lexikalischen Kategorien sind auch die Kategorien im Baum zu diesem Zeitpunkt erst teilweise spezifiziert, denn die verwendeten Regeln beschreiben gemäß der GPSG-Philosophie einzelsprachliche Verhältnisse in allgemeiner Form. So stehen z.B. Person und Numerus in der Kategorie eines zu verbalisierenden Verbs noch nicht fest, denn die zugrundeliegende Grammatikregel definiert identische Strukturen für sämtliche Kombinationen dieser Merkmale. Die notwendige vollständige Spezifikation erfolgt bottom-up in einem zweiten Schritt durch universelle Instanziierungsprinzipien, die Merkmalwerte u.a. für Numerus und Person über die vorher erzeugte syntaktische Struktur auch an die präterminalen Kategorien transportiert, wo sie z.B. zur Realisierung von Kongruenzrelationen benötigt werden.

An dieser Stelle ist eine technische Randbemerkung zum Verständnis wichtig: Die Richtung, in der Merkmalwerte transportiert werden, ist unabhängig von der Verarbeitungsrichtung (bottom-up), denn die noch unspezifizierten Merkmale können von den Instanziierungsprinzipien *kospezifiziert* werden, d.h. sie erhalten denselben Wert, sobald eines von ihnen instanziiert wird.

Letztendlich sind an den präterminalen Kategorien alle Informationen angesammelt, die für die Flexion des Wortstammes durch die nachgeschaltete Morphologiekomponente erforderlich sind. Diese benutzt dann die Stammform und die morphologischen Einträge des Lexikons zur Erzeugung einer flektierten Wortform.

Diese *Konstruktion* von vollständig spezifizierten Kategorien (im Gegensatz dazu beschreiben GKPS eine *Selektion* aus der Menge aller möglichen Kategorien; vgl. Busemann/Hauenschild 1988) kann erst durch die Verwendung eines SFL effizient realisiert werden; aus einem VFL könnte der Generator nicht eindeutig einen Eintrag auswählen, da zu dem Zeitpunkt, zu dem ein lexikalisches Element in die syntaktische Struktur eingefügt wird, dessen Kategorie gewöhnlich noch zu wenig spezifiziert ist. Solange der Generierungsprozeß nicht abgeschlossen ist, könnten jederzeit Merkmalspezifikationen an die Kategorie gelangen und die Auswahl eines anderen Eintrags des VFL erzwingen.

Durch die Verwendung eines SFL kann das dann notwendige Backtracking vermieden werden. Die folgenden Abschnitte geben hinreichende Bedingungen dafür an.

4 Paradigmatische Lücken

Die naheliegende Gleichung 'VFL = SFL + Flexionsprozesse' ist falsch. Ein SFL erlaubt es, alle möglichen Extensionen der lexikalischen Kategorien zu generieren; d.h. die Lexikonregeln in einem SFL umfassen das komplette durch die Definition der möglichen Merkmalkombinationen definierte Paradigma. Hingegen kann ein VFL die Verwendung bestimmter Kategorien ausschließen, indem die entsprechenden Einträge einfach fehlen. Damit können die zahllosen paradigmatischen Lücken, d.h. das Fehlen von bestimmten Formen einzelner Wörter, auf einfache, aber implizite Weise erfaßt werden (z.B. bildet das Futur-Hilfsverb *werden* kein Imperfekt, *bekommen* kein Passiv etc.). Diese restriktive Eigenschaft des VFL muß bei einem SFL nachgespielt werden. Doch zunächst ein Beispiel.

In Abbildung 1 erlauben die Syntaxregeln (1)-(4) (vgl. Uszkoreit 1984) die Generierung der Bäume *s1* und *s2*. Dabei stellt V[1] ein Perfekt-Hilfsverb, V[3] das Passiv-Hilfsverb und V[5] ein intransitiv subkategorisiertes Verb dar. Der Merkmaltransport erzeugt die Spezifikationen des Merkmals 'verbform' an den präterminalen V-Knoten (fin = finit, pas = Passiv-Partizip, psp = Perfekt-Partizip). Wie ersichtlich, verlangt die markierte Kategorie V[1, pas] in *s2*, ein Passiv-Partizip des Perfekt-Hilfsverbs zu bilden, was die lexikalische Kategorie von *sein* im SFL nicht verbietet (sie ist ja unspezifiziert in Bezug auf 'verbform').

In einem VFL würde ein Eintrag für V[1, pas] einfach fehlen und der markierte Teilbaum im

Verlauf der syntaktischen Generierung als unzulässig erkannt werden. Bei einem SFL hingegen ist der Ausschluß von *s2* auf der syntaktischen Ebene nicht möglich. Dann allerdings muß die Morphologiekomponente feststellen, daß V[1] kein Passiv-Partizip besitzt: im morphologischen Lexikoneintrag fehlt das Merkmal 'passiv/perfekt'; stattdessen gibt es ein Merkmal 'perfekt' mit dem Partizip als Wert. Somit resultiert als Ergebnis der gewählten Modularisierung des Generierungsverfahrens mit *s2* eine syntaktisch wohlgeformte Struktur ohne Endkette. Eine zusätzliche Aufgabe der Morphologiekomponente ist hierbei, nicht legale Merkmal-kombinationen zu erkennen und die Generierung der Endkette abzubrechen.

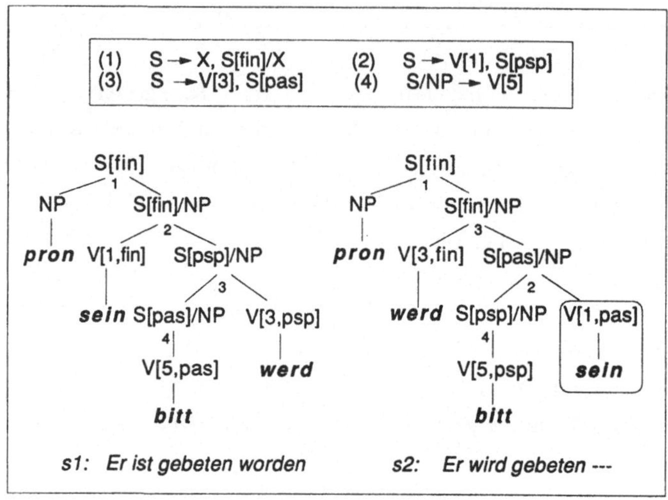

Abb. 1: Zur lexikalischen Beschränkung syntaktischer Strukturen

Neben dieser im Berliner GPSG-System realisierten Methode kann man dem Problem auch innerhalb der Syntaxkomponente beikommen, indem man ein zusätzliches binäres Merkmal 'passive' verwendet, dessen Wert für alle Verben lexikalisch angibt, ob sie ein Passiv bilden. Um im Verlauf der Generierung die erforderliche Relation zwischen 'verbform'- und 'passive'-Spezifikationen herzustellen, benutzt man den Mechanismus der Feature Co-occurrence Restrictions (FCRs) aus der GPSG-Theorie. FCRs definieren die Kategorien, die in syntaktischen Strukturen vorkommen dürfen. Eine FCR hat die Form 'Kat1 ⊃ Kat2' und besagt, daß jede Kategorie, die eine Extension der linken Seite ist, auch eine Extension der rechten Seite sein muß; sonst wird der Teilbaum mit der inkriminierten Kategorie zurückgewiesen. Man definiert die FCR '[pas] ⊃ [+passive]' und erzwingt somit den Ausschluß von *s2*, da ihr die Kategorie V[1, pas, -passive] widerspricht.

Ein wesentlicher Nachteil bei dieser Vorgehensweise ist, daß für jedes analoge Phänomen ein neues Merkmal eingeführt werden muß, was auf die Dauer die Komplexität der Kategorien in der Grammatik beträchtlich erhöht.

5 Die Generierung von Perfekt-Hilfsverben im Deutschen

Um Backtracking bei der Auswahl von Lexikoneinträgen zu vermeiden, verlangt der Generierungsalgorithmus, daß Zeiger aus der Ausgangsstruktur auf nicht mehr als einen Eintrag des SFL verweisen. Diese Forderung scheint zunächst unbequem, denn bei der Generierung von Perfektkomplexen im Deutschen spricht vieles dafür, dem Generator nur den Auftrag 'Generiere Perfekt!' zu geben, ohne z.B. auf semantischer Ebene zu spezifizieren, mit welchem Wortstamm dies geschehen soll [2]. Dieser Auftrag wird einfach durch einen Zeiger in der Ausgangsstruktur auf die Lexikoneinträge für Perfekt-Hilfsverben repräsentiert.

Bei einem SFL liegt es dennoch auf den ersten Blick nahe, für *sein* und *haben* V[1]-Einträge vorzusehen, auf die mit demselben Zeiger verwiesen wird. Die Instanziierungsprinzipien erfüllen die Aufgabe, den Wert des lexikalisch für Verben spezifizierten Merkmals 'paux' vom Hauptverb (z.B. V[5] in *sl*; vgl. Abb. 1) zur präterminalen Kategorie V[1] zu transportieren. Diese ist dann ausreichend spezifiziert für die eindeutige Entscheidung zwischen *haben* oder *sein* denn beim Lexikonzugriff müssen u.a. die 'paux'-Spezifikationen miteinander unifizieren (hierbei wird ausgenutzt, daß die perfektiven Formen von *sein* mit *sein* und die von *haben* mit *haben* gebildet werden; wäre das anders, müßte man ein zusätzliches Merkmal einführen).

Da jedoch das Generierungsverfahren den V[1]-Stamm in die syntaktische Struktur einfügt, *bevor* die Instanziierungsprinzipien den Transport durchführen können, ist keine fundierte Entscheidung möglich. Wird der 'falsche' Stamm genommen, entsteht beim Merkmaltransport ein Konflikt, da die 'paux'-Spezifikationen des Vollverbs und an V[1] nicht übereinstimmen. Dieser Konflikt führt im günstigstem Fall zu eben dem Backtracking, das vermieden werden sollte; infolge einer unabhängig motivierten, 'liberalen' Definition des Instanziierungsprinzips Head Feature Convention im Berliner GPSG-System wird die Struktur jedoch nicht zurückgewiesen, sondern der Transportversuch erfolglos abgebrochen und der falsche V[1]-Stamm generiert. Der skizzierte Ansatz ist daher untauglich für das verwendete Generierungsverfahren.

Die Entscheidung muß stattdessen ebenfalls in die Morphologiekomponente hinein verschoben werden. Im SFL sieht man nur einen V[1]-Eintrag vor, der einen Dummy-Wortstamm hat und für 'paux' unspezifiziert ist. So kann in der syntaktischen Struktur die 'paux'-Spezifikation des Vollverbs ungehindert an die präterminale Kategorie V[1] gelangen. Der Wortstamm des Perfekt-Hilfsverbs wird erst im Zuge der nachgeschalteten Flexion anhand von 'paux' bestimmt.

Die Wahl des Perfekt-Hilfsverbs verläuft dann völlig analog zur Wahl von Suppletivstämmen, wie sie z.B. in der morphologischen Charakterisierung deutscher Verben ohnehin angelegt ist. Die Verlagerung des Problems in die Morphologiekomponente stellt somit eine 'harmonische' Lösung dar.

---

[2] Daß z.B. Verben der Bewegung je nach lokaler oder temporaler Sehweise verschiedene Perfekt-Hilfsverben fordern, spricht nicht dagegen; *dies ist ein semantischer Unterschied* und stellt ein Wortwahlproblem dar.

6 Schluß

Obwohl die beiden beschriebenen Probleme zu einem gewissen Grad theorie- und systembedingt sind, lassen sich einige wichtige Generalisierungen festhalten.

Paradigmatische Lücken werden zu einem Problem, wenn die rein deklarative Repräsentation des VFL durch eine zum Teil prozedurale Repräsentation mit einem SFL ersetzt wird.

Das Problem mit den Perfekt-Hilfsverben tritt nicht auf, wenn eine rein deklarative Definition des Merkmaltransports und der Strukturbildung verwendet würde, wie etwa bei GKPS. Generierung ist jedoch als Prozeß zu betrachten und erfordert somit eine Abarbeitungsreihenfolge, die in die faktische Ausgabe einer Endkette mündet. Daher war über die Reihenfolge von Lexikonzugriff und Merkmalsinstanziierung zu entscheiden.

Der Einwand, daß die GPSG-Theorie diese Entscheidung nicht vorschreibt und sie auch anders herum hätte ausfallen können, stößt auf Effizienzprobleme: jede Algorithmisierung der in GKPS vorgeschlagenen Version der GPSG muß die kombinatorische Explosion der Anzahl zu betrachtender Kategorien vermeiden. Im Berliner GPSG-System wurden daher unterspezifizierte Kategorien eingeführt, die während der Generierung nach und nach weitere Merkmalwerte aufnehmen können (vgl. Hauenschild/Busemann 1988). Da sichergestellt sein muß, daß die syntaktischen Kategorien ausreichend spezifiziert sind, damit die Instanziierungsprinzipien und FCRs ansetzen können, erfolgt der Lexikonzugriff mit dem damit verbundenen Informationsgewinn zuerst.

Beide Probleme sind Konsequenzen der effizienten Algorithmisierung einer rein deklarativ formulierten linguistischen Theorie.

7 Literaturhinweise

Appelt, Douglas E. (1987), 'Bidirectional Grammars and the Design of Natural Language Generation Systems', in *Procs. Theoretical Issues in Natural Language Processing III*, 1987, 185-190.

Busemann, Stephan (1984), 'Surface Transformations During the Generation of Written German Sentences', in D.D. McDonald und L. Bolc (Hg.), *Natural Language Generation Systems*, Berlin, New York, Springer (Symbolic Computation), 1988, 98-165.

Busemann, Stephan (1987), 'Generierung mit GPSG', in K. Morik (Hg.), *Procs. 11th German Workshop on Artificial Intelligence*, Berlin, New York, Springer, 1987, 355-364.

Busemann, Stephan; und Hauenschild, Christa (1988), 'A Constructive View of GPSG or How to Make it Work', in *Procs. 12th International Conference on Computational Linguistics* (*COLING-88*), Budapest.

Gazdar, Gerald; Klein, Ewan; Pullum, Geoffrey; und Sag, Ivan (1985), *Generalized Phrase Structure Grammar*, Oxford, Blackwell.

Hauenschild, Christa; und Busemann, Stephan (1988), 'A Constructive Version of GPSG for Machine Translation', in E. Steiner, P. Schmidt und C. Zelinsky-Wibbelt (Hg.), *From Syntax to Semantics - Insights From Machine Translation*, London, Frances Pinter, 1988, 216-238.

Uszkoreit, Hans (1984), *Word Order and Constituent Structure in German*, Ph.D. Dissertation, University of Texas, Austin.

ANWENDBARKEIT VON UNIFIKATIONSGRAMMATIKEN FÜR EFFIZIENTES GENERIEREN

Helmut Horacek
Projekt WISBER
Universität Hamburg
Fachbereich Informatik
Jungiusstraße 6
D-2000 Hamburg 36
B.R.D.

Claudius Pyka
Projekt LOKI
Universität Hamburg
Fachbereich Informatik
Bodenstedtstraße 16
D-2000 Hamburg 50
B.R.D.

Zusammenfassung

Die prinzipielle Anwendbarkeit von Unifikationsgrammatiken für die Generierung ist mehrfach gezeigt worden, wobei jedoch das Problem der Effizienz meist nicht untersucht wurde. In diesem Papier soll anhand einiger einfacher und für das Deutsche typischer Beispiele die Eignung bzw. Ungeeignetheit von Unifikationsgrammatiken zur effizienten Bearbeitung der gewählten Phänomene demonstriert werden. Abschließend wird auch versucht, die typischen Eigenschaften der untersuchten Phänomene zu beschreiben, um aus den gewonnenen Erfahrungen (gewisse) Richtlinien für den effizienten Einsatz von Unifikationsgrammatiken zu erhalten.

1. Einleitung

Ende der siebziger Jahre sind Unifikationsgrammatiken für die Beschreibung der Syntax von natürlichen Sprachen konzipiert worden. Solche Grammatiken wurden zunächst erfolgreich für die Analyse eingesetzt. Die spätere Anwendung bei der Generierung (zum Beispiel [2]) erwies sich zwar als möglich, die Effizienz ließ jedoch stark zu wünschen übrig (siehe eine ausführliche Betrachtung in [1]).

Dennoch stellt die Entwicklung einer für Parsing und Generierung einheitlichen Grammatik sicherlich ein erstrebenswertes Ziel dar (einen frühen Ansatz findet man in [5]):

- Die syntaktische Kompetenz ist explizit und transparent dargestellt (und unabhängig von der Interpretationsrichtung), und ein kontinuierlicher Ausbau kann gleichmäßig erfolgen.

- Bei den Prozessen Parsing und Generierung können interpretationsrichtungsspezifische Effizienzverbesserungen explizit herausgearbeitet werden (das ist beim Parsing schwieriger, weil viele Ambiguitäten, vor allem auch lokale, möglich sind).

2. Eine Methodik für effiziente Anwendung von Unifikationsgrammatiken

Angesichts des Effizienzdefizits wurde im ESPRIT-Projekt LOKI ein Verfahren entwickelt, bei dem aus einer kompakt repräsentierten 'Kompetenzgrammatik' mittels eines Compilers wahlweise eine Parsing- bzw. eine Generierungsgrammatik ('Performanzgrammatiken') erzeugt werden kann [4]. Dabei werden sprachliche Regelmäßigkeiten durch nicht standardmäßige Konstrukte wie Metavariable (siehe [6]) und reguläre Ausdrücke in der Kompetenzgrammatik kompakt dargestellt. Ebenso unterstützen redundante Bedingungen eine adäquate Vorgangsweise für die potentielle bi-direktionale Interpretation der Regeln. Der Compiler besorgt im wesentlichen eine geeignete Gruppierung der neuen Regeln, die beim Splitten der regulären Ausdrücke entstehen, sowie eine der Interpretationsrichtung der Regeln angepaßte Sortierung der Gleichungen. Die Ergebnisse aus der Generierungssicht wurden bereits in [3] vorgestellt.

Syntaktische Verarbeitung wird in diesem Zusammenhang gesehen als die Zuordnung von einem Oberflächensatz auf die den strukturell verschiedenen Lesarten entsprechenden, voll spezifizierten funktionalen Beschreibungen. Damit wird unter anderem die Auflösung und die Generierung von Referenzen ausgeklammert. Weiters muß auch eine vom Standard abweichende Wortstellung (mit der etwa eine Topikalisierung erreicht wird) durch entsprechende Merkmale ausgedrückt sein. Die Generierung liefert unter diesem Paradigma eine eindeutige Lösung und sollte daher eigentlich ziemlich effizient erfolgen können.

Diese Methode wurde bisher an relativ einfachen syntaktischen Konstruktionen erprobt. Im Rahmen dieses Workshops soll ihre Eignung (und damit auch die von Unifikations-grammatiken an sich) für einige praktisch relevante Eigenheiten des Deutschen untersucht werden.

3. Die Generierung einiger syntaktischer Eigenheiten des Deutschen

Die besonderen Schwierigkeiten des Deutschen werden etwa dort besonders augenfällig, wo eine unterschiedliche Anzahl von Wörtern für vergleichbare funktionale Strukturen erzeugt werden muß. Solche Fälle liegen vor

- bei Verben mit abtrennbarem Partikel (z.B. 'vorschlagen', im Präsens: 'ich schlage vor'); das ergibt zwei Wörter anstatt einem, sowie

- bei Zusammenziehungen von Präpositionen mit den Partikeln wo-, da- (z.B. 'wodurch', 'davor') bzw. Präpositionen mit (definiten) Artikeln (z.B. 'am', 'im'); das ergibt ein Wort anstatt zweier.

3.1 Partikelabtrennung

Bei der Partikelabtrennung entsteht eine Diskontinuität zwischen dem finiten Verbteil und dem Partikel, wodurch sich einige Schwierigkeiten bei der Verarbeitung ergeben. Beim Parsing liegen außerdem Ambiguitäten vor, da der Verbstamm selbst (ohne Partikel) üblicherweise als Verb mit völlig anderer Bedeutung (und oft auch anderem Kasusrahmen) existiert (etwa 'vorschlagen', 'schlagen'). Dieses Analyseproblem ist nicht zu umgehen, da das

Vorhandensein eines abgetrennten Verbpartikels erst deutlich nach der Analyse des finiten Verbs erkannt werden kann (das trifft in jedem Fall bei left-to-right Parsing, der am weitesten verbreiteten Strategie, zu). Der zusätzliche Aufwand kann nur durch Einsatz einer geeigneten Methode möglichst gering gehalten werden.

Bei der Generierung hingegen sollte eigentlich auf Grund der bereits getroffenen Wortwahl sowie der Festlegung von Zeit und Form klar sein, ob eine Partikelabspaltung zu erfolgen hat oder nicht und wo das eventuell abzutrennende Partikel eingefügt werden muß. Dies ist im Präsens und im Imperfekt aktiv sowie im Imperativ der Fall, in allen anderen (den zusammengesetzten Zeiten) erfolgt keine Partikelabspaltung. In den kritischen Fällen (der Imperativ ist hier nicht behandelt) kann die Unterscheidung für die Verbphrase (VP) mittels zweier (an den LFG-Formalismus angelehnten) Grammatikregeln folgendermaßen ausgedrückt werden:

<u>Regel 1:</u>

$$
\begin{array}{lll}
\text{VP} \rightarrow & \text{VFIN} & \text{NPP*} \\
& \{\ \uparrow\text{TENSE} =_c \text{PRES} \ \lor \ \uparrow\text{TENSE} =_c \text{PAST}\ \} & \uparrow = \downarrow \\
& \ \ \uparrow\text{TENSE} = \uparrow\text{STENSE} & \\
& \{\ \uparrow\text{STENSE} = \text{PRES} \ \lor \ \uparrow\text{STENSE} = \text{PAST}\ \} & \\
& \ \ \uparrow\text{VOICE} = \text{ACTIVE} & \\
& \neg\ (\uparrow\text{PART}) &
\end{array}
$$

<u>Regel 2:</u>

$$
\begin{array}{llll}
\text{VP} \rightarrow & \text{VFIN} & \text{NPP*} & \text{PART} \\
& \{\ \uparrow\text{TENSE} =_c \text{PRES} \ \lor \ \uparrow\text{TENSE} =_c \text{PAST}\ \} & \uparrow = \downarrow & \uparrow\text{PART} = \downarrow\text{PART} \\
& \ \ \uparrow\text{TENSE} = \uparrow\text{STENSE} & & \\
& \{\ \uparrow\text{STENSE} = \text{PRES} \ \lor \ \uparrow\text{STENSE} = \text{PAST}\ \} & & \\
& \ \ \uparrow\text{VOICE} = \text{ACTIVE} & & \\
& \ \ (\uparrow\text{PART}) & &
\end{array}
$$

Dabei bezeichnet 'VFIN' ein finites Verb (in der Verwendung als Vollverb, das heißt semantisch relevant im Gegensatz etwa zu 'AUXFIN') mit den üblichen Merkmalen 'TENSE', 'NUM', 'PERS' und 'PRED'. 'PART' wird sowohl für die Bezeichnung der Kategorie Partikel verwendet als auch für das gleichnamige Merkmal. Dieses tritt sowohl bei dem Partikel selbst als auch bei einem Vollverb mit abspaltbarem Partikel auf, der Wert ist das Partikel selbst. 'STENSE' steht für die Zeit im Satz, die sich aus der temporalen Interpretation der gesamten Verbgruppe ergibt. Die vierte bzw. fünfte Gleichung ($\uparrow$STENSE = PRES $\lor$ $\uparrow$STENSE = PAST) ist redundant, ihre Verwendung ist aber für die Generierung geeigneter als die sonst übliche erste bzw. zweite Gleichung ($\uparrow$TENSE $=_c$ PRES $\lor$ $\uparrow$TENSE $=_c$ PAST), weil die Zeit im Satz bei der Generierung schon feststeht und daher eine Nichtanwendbarkeit der Regel, etwa bei $\uparrow$STENSE = PERFECT, sofort erkannt werden kann. Das Mittelfeld wird durch 'NPP*' dargestellt (das bedeutet keine bis beliebig viele Konstituenten des Typs NP oder PP), worauf jedoch in diesem Zusammenhang nicht näher eingegangen wird. Nach der Bearbeitung durch den

Compiler ergeben sich folgende Gleichungen für die Präsensvariante (Gleichungen der Form ' ↑ Pfad = Konstante' werden bei der Generierung nach vorne gestellt):

Regel 3:

```
VP   ->              VFIN                          NPP*

          ↑ STENSE   = PRES                        ↑ = ↓
          ↑ VOICE    = ACTIVE
       ¬ ( ↑ PART)
          ↑ TENSE    =   ↑ STENSE
          ↑ TENSE    = c PRES
```

Regel 4:

```
VP   ->              VFIN                  NPP*        PART

          ↑ STENSE   = PRES               ↑ = ↓     ↑ PART = ↓ PART
          ↑ VOICE    = ACTIVE
         ( ↑ PART)
          ↑ TENSE    =   ↑ STENSE
          ↑ TENSE    = c PRES
```

Durch diese Sortierung ergibt sich, daß bei jeder VP-Regel (die VP-Regeln für die zusammengesetzten Zeiten sind hinsichtlich der Gleichungen im finiten Verbteil ähnlich strukturiert) nur drei Gleichungen ausgewertet werden müssen, um die richtige Regel zu selektieren. Bei einigen Verben, bei denen unterschiedliche Bedeutungen durch die Verwendung von 'haben' bzw. 'sein' für die Perfektbildung ausgedrückt wird (z.B. 'fahren', 'erschrecken'), sollte zusätzlich das der gewünschten Bedeutung entsprechende Auxiliar spezifiziert sein.

Die Auswertung der Gleichungen mit 'STENSE', 'VOICE' und fallweise 'PART' bewirkt also die nötige Fallunterscheidung, um die zur erfolgreichen Expansion geeignete Regel zu selektieren. Falls hingegen der Test (¬) (↑ PART) erst zu einem späteren Zeitpunkt ausgewertet wird (oder überhaupt fehlt), kann es passieren, daß das gesamte Mittelfeld (NPP*) expandiert wird, bevor die Inadequatheit der Regel für das entsprechende Verb erkannt wird. Bei einem passenden Regeldesign und geschickter Sortierung der Gleichungen aber erweist sich eine Unifikationsgrammatik in solchen Fällen als ziemlich effizient.

3.2 Zusammenziehungen mit Präpositionen

Eine weitere Eigenheit des Deutschen besteht in der Verschmelzungsmöglichkeit einiger Präpositionen mit den Partikeln wo-, da- bzw. Artikeln. Die Unterscheidung zwischen Nominal- und Präpositionalphrase 'normaler' Bauart kann sehr kompakt mittels zweier Regeln (5 und 6) ausgedrückt werden (aus der Sicht der Generierung muß nur eine Gleichung ausgewertet werden, um die richtige Regel zu selektieren); diese werden jedoch den Verschmelzungen nicht gerecht. Es müßte also möglich sein, 'daran', 'am Workshop' und 'an *dem* (betont) Workshop' mit geeigneten Regeln abzuleiten, je nachdem, ob der Wert des

PRED-feature 'PRO' oder 'Workshop' ist und ob eine Betonung des Definitartikels (Demonstrativgebrauch) vorliegt oder nicht.

<u>Regel 5:</u>

NPP   ->   PREP   NP
                    ↑PTYPE = ↓PTYPE   ↑ = ↓

<u>Regel 6:</u>

NPP   ->   NP
               ¬ (↑PTYPE)
                 ↑   = ↓

<u>Regel 7:</u>

NPP   ->   PREPADV
                  (↑PTYPE)
                  ↑PRED   = PRO
                  ↑PERSON = -
              {   ↑SPEC   = DEF   ∨   ↑SPEC   = WH   }

Die Kategorie 'PREP' bezeichnet Präpositionen mit dem Merkmal 'PTYPE', dessen Wert die Präposition selbst ist. Regel 7 zeigt eine (einfache) Erweiterung zu Regel 5. Damit können zusätzlich Präpositionaladverbien ('PREPADV', z.B. 'wodurch', 'dadurch') verarbeitet werden, jedoch mit gegenüber dem ersten Ansatz gestiegenem Aufwand: Die drei zusätzlichen Gleichungen müssen in negierter Form bei Regel 5 eingefügt werden und bei jeder zu generierenden Präpositionalphrase ausgewertet werden. Damit ist jedoch erst ein kleiner Teil des Phänomens abgedeckt.

<u>Regel 8:</u>

NPP   ->   PREPDET   NPDEFohneDET
                ¬ (↑PRED   = PRO)   ↑ = ↓
                  ↑SPEC   = DEF
                  ↑NUM   = SG
                  ↑DEMO   = -
              (↑PTYPE   = zu   ∨
              {   ↑KASUS   = DATIV   ∧
              {   ↑GENUS   = MASC ∨ ↑GENUS = NEUT } ∧
              {   ↑PTYPE   = an   ∨ ↑PTYPE = ...   }) ∨ ...)

Die Komplexität der zu überprüfenden Bedingungen nimmt bei der Beschreibung der Verschmelzung von Präposition und Artikel (hier als Kategorie 'PREPDET' bezeichnet) stark zu. Regel 8 stellt ansatzweise einen (unvollständigen) Versuch dar. Die Präpositionen, mit denen eine Verschmelzung erfolgen kann, müssen explizit aufgeführt werden (durch die Punkte angedeutet). Außerdem gibt es Präpositionen, die nur bei Genus masculin und neutrum eine Verschmelzung zulassen ('am', aber 'an die'), andere jedoch auch bei Genus feminin ('zum', 'zur'). Zusätzlich kann die Verschmelzungsmöglichkeit noch vom Kasus abhängen, falls die Präposition mehrere zuläßt ('im', 'in der', 'im'; aber 'in den', 'in die', 'ins'). Die Gleichungen mit 'PTYPE', 'GENUS' und 'KASUS' können zwar auch (was eigentlich, speziell aus der Sicht des Parsing, üblicher ist) im Lexikon vorhanden sein, dadurch erhöht sich aber der Aufwand bei der Generierung wegen der zusätzlichen Lexikonsuche und der Möglichkeit, daß die Anwendung der Regel zurückgenommen werden muß.

Obendrein ergeben sich weitere Auswirkungen auf Regel 5 und auf die eigentliche NP-Regel ('NPDEFohneDET' muß eingeführt und angepaßt werden). Diese Ausführungen sollten genügen, um die Komplexität der hier auftretenden Fälle einschätzen zu können.

4. Schlußfolgerungen

Die Erfahrungen haben gezeigt, daß sich Unifikationsgrammatiken bei Befolgung gewisser Richtlinien gut zur effizienten Linearisierung einer (nicht zu komplexen) funktionalen Beschreibung eignen. Dies wurde hier anhand der Partikelabspaltung für diskontinuierliche Konstituenten gezeigt.

Die Voraussetzung für eine effiziente Verarbeitung besteht unter anderem darin, daß jene Gleichungen nicht zu komplex werden, die 'Verzweigungsbedingungen' ausdrücken. Damit ist eine Menge von Gleichungen gemeint, die die Anwendbarkeit einer Regel festlegt; leicht modifizierte Mengen von Gleichungen wiederum beschreiben die Anwendbarkeit ähnlicher Regeln (siehe etwa die Gleichungen mit 'STENSE' und 'VOICE' bei den VP-Regeln). Dann kann die Stärke einer Unifikationsgrammatik (das Expandieren von Konstituenten und gleichzeitiges Vererben von Eigenschaften) ausgenutzt werden, ohne daß die Schwäche zu stark ins Gewicht fällt (bestimmte Gleichungen in 'Verzweigungsbedingungen' müssen mehrfach ausgewertet werden, je nachdem wie viele der sie enthaltenden Regeln untersucht werden müssen).

Besonders drastisch tritt diese Schwäche bei den untersuchten Verschmelzungsmöglichkeiten auf. Ähnliche Verhältnisse liegen auch bei der Beeinflussungsstufe von Adjektiven und adjektivisch flektierenden Wörtern vor (z.B. 'der Angestellte', aber 'ein Angestellter'). Das ist eine weitere Eigenheit des Deutschen, bei der ziemlich komplexe Fälle auftreten, vor allem bei mehreren aufeinanderfolgenden indefiniten Numeralia. Eine Verarbeitung dieser Phänomene mit einer Unifikationsgrammatik ist zwar möglich, der Aufwand steht jedoch in keinem Verhältnis zu der an sich leichten Aufgabe. Beides sind nämlich 'lokale' Phänomene, das heißt, daß nur jeweils benachbarte Worte davon betroffen sind. Eine Verlagerung der Verarbeitung in die Morphologiekomponente (die dann allerdings auch das jeweils nächste Wort berücksichtigen müßte) scheint uns hier eine geeignetere Methode zu sein.

Am schwierigsten dürften jedoch jene Phänomene zu behandeln sein, die sowohl komplex sind als auch nicht lokale Abhängigkeiten beinhalten, etwa Nominalphrasen mit mehreren Attributen oder Adjektivphrasen, speziell solche im Komparativ. Nicht ohne Grund werden diese Phrasentypen in der Standardliteratur über Unifikationsgrammatiken eher spärlich und stark vereinfacht abgehandelt.

Literatur

1. R. Block, 'LFG and Natural Language Generation', WISBER Bericht Nr. 10, Verbund-vorhaben WISBER, Universität Hamburg, 1986.
2. S. Busemann, 'Generierung mit GPSG', K. Morik (ed.), GWAI-87, Eringerfeld bei Geseke, Springer-Verlag, Berlin, pp. 355-364, 1987.
3. H. Horacek, 'The Application of Unification For Syntactic Generation in German', erscheint in: ADVANCES IN NATURAL LANGUAGE GENERATION: an Interdisciplinary Perspective, M. Zock, G. Sabah (eds.), Ablex, New Jersey & Pinter, London, 1988.
4. H. Horacek, C. Pyka, 'Facets of Knowledge about Natural Language Syntax - Representation and Use in Parsing and Generation', erscheint in W. Hoeppner (ed.), GWAI-88, Eringerfeld bei Geseke, Springer-Verlag, Berlin, 1988.
5. J.-M. Lancel, F. Rousselot, N. Simonin, 'A Grammar Used For Parsing and Generation', COLING-86, Bonn, pp. 536-539, 1986.
6. K. Netter, 'An LFG-Proposal for the Treatment of German Word Order', Coling, Bonn, pp. 494-496, 1986.

Die Übertragung des MUMBLE-Generators für die Generierung von Deutsch

Daniel Jacob, Elisabeth Maier

Projekt GENESIS
GMD, F4
Dolivostr. 15
D-6100 Darmstadt

maier@ipsi.darmstadt.gmd.dbp.de

1. Einleitung

Im Rahmen des Text-Generierungsprojekts GENESIS wurde der MUMBLE-Generator ([Meteer (et al.) 87])[1] daraufhin untersucht, welche Änderungen vorgenommen werden müssen, um eine weitere Zielsprache, in unserem Fall Deutsch, zu erzeugen. Ziel dieser Arbeiten war, die Stellen aufzuspüren, in denen MUMBLE Strukturen aufweist, die an das Englische gebunden sind und damit Aufschlüsse zu gewinnen über die Anforderungen, die an ein multilinguales System zu stellen sind. Das Interesse an der Multilingualität hat einen zweifachen Hintergrund: zum einen soll das GENESIS-System multilingual arbeiten, zum anderen bietet Multilingualität eine gewisse Gewährleistung für die Oberflächenferne und somit semantischen Charakter der Ausgangsstruktur.

Dieses Papier soll die aufgetretenen Probleme beleuchten und die Konsequenzen formulieren, die wir für unser eigenes Projekt daraus ziehen.

2. Das System MUMBLE

Das MUMBLE-System unterscheidet vier Ebenen, die ineinander überführt werden (siehe Abbildung 2.1). Die Knoten verschiedener hierarchischer Ränge der "message", d.h. der Eingabestruktur werden vermittels explizit deklarierter "realization-classes" (i.e. Satzbauplänen) in uninstantiierte Phrasenstrukturen überführt ("realization"), die dann zu einer baumartigen Struktur zusammengesetzt werden ("attachment"). Bei der "phrase-structure-execution" wird dieser Baum dann mit den weiteren Informationen der Eingabestruktur belegt. Die "morphology" setzt dann die bereits erfolgten Lexikalisierungen in morphologisch korrekte Formen um.

---

[1] Das MUMBLE-System wurde an der University of Massachusetts in Amherst als Generator für englische Texte entwickelt.

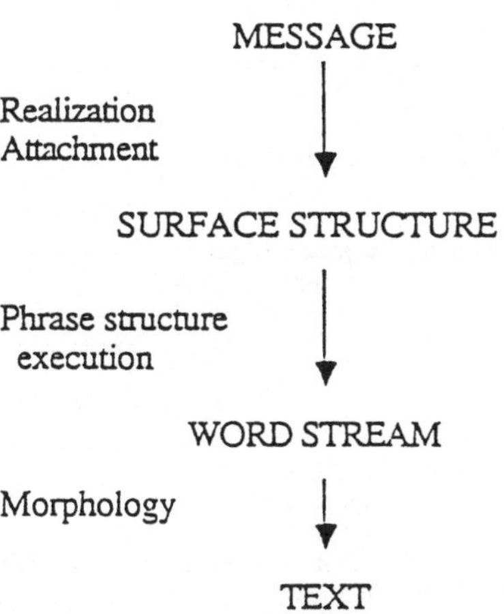

Abbildung 2.1: *Repräsentationsebenen und Überführungsschritte in MUMBLE*

Der Programmablauf bei der Generierung entspricht nicht dieser linearen Struktur; vielmehr werden die verschiedenen Schritte jeweils mit Einzelstrukturen durchlaufen, wobei immer soviel als möglich an Text realisiert wird.

Abbildung 2.2 gibt eine Eingabestruktur für MUMBLE wieder. Es wird ersichtlich, daß bereits der Generator-Input stark oberflächenbezogene Informationen enthält. Noch deutlicher wird dies bei der Behandlung von Anaphora: hier liegen in der Eingabestruktur keine Angaben über den betreffenden Referenten vor, sondern eine grammatische Beschreibung des zu wählenden Pronomens.

Neben normalen Deklarativsätzen beherrscht die für unsere Experimente benutzte MUMBLE-Version auch Passivkonstruktionen, Fragen (W- und Satzfragen), sowie die Einbettung von Relativ- und Objektsätzen.

```
(general-clause
  :head (CHASE/S-V-O_two-explicit-args

             (general-np
              :head ( np-proper-name
                             "Fluffy")

              :accessories (:number singular
                            :gender masculine
                            :person third
                            :determiner-policy  no-determiner ))

             (general-np
              :head (np-common-noun "mouse")
              :accessories (:number plural
                            :gender neuter
                            :person third
                            :determiner-policy initially-indefinite )
              :further-specifications
                 (((:attachment-function restrictive-modifier
                    :specification ( predication-to-be  *self*
                                        (adjective "little)))
                 )) )

  :accessories (:tense-modal present
                :progressive
                :unmarked )
  ))
```

Abbildung 2.2: *Eingabestruktur für den Satz "Fluffy chases little mice."*

3. Vorgehen bei der Modifikation von MUMBLE für das Deutsche

a) Einige Phänomene lassen sich auf dem Weg einer einfachen Stringsubstitution im Lexikon oder
den morphologischen Komponenten lösen. So sieht MUMBLE z.B. ein bequemes Handling für
unregelmässige Formen des Verbs oder des Plurals des Nomens vor. Dies funktioniert, solange im
Deutschen und im Englischen gleiche Kategorien vorliegen. Komplexer ist dagegen die Anpas-
sung der Morphologie naturgemäß da, wo das Englische keine dem Deutschen entsprechenden
Eigenschaften aufweist, wie z.B.:

a1) *Numerus- und Genuskongruenz des Determiners:*

Sie erfordert den Rückgriff auf die Konstituentenstruktur (in diesem Fall die NP), um vom
Bezugsnomen die entsprechenden Informationen zu holen. Insbesondere musste das Lexi-
konformat für Substantiveinträge so verändert werden, daß ein Genus als morphologische
Klasse spezifiziert werden kann.

Noch aufwendiger ist das Erreichen der Kasus-Kongruenz, weil MUMBLE zu dem Zeitpunkt, an dem die morphologische Oberflächenbearbeitung stattfindet, bereits nur noch auf
einem Phrasenstruktur-Baum arbeitet, in dem funktionale Informationen wie 'Subjekt',

'direktes Objekt' etc. bereits in Wortstellungsinformation umgesetzt sind. Da das Deutsche diese Information auf morphologischem Wege wiedergibt, müssen diese Informationen bei der morphologischen Behandlung noch zugänglich sein. In den bei MUMBLE verwendeten Morphologieklassen für Verben kann syntaktische Kasusinformation an die Nominalgruppen weitergegeben werden. Allerdings muß dann die Konstituentenstellung ebenfalls bereits festgelegt sein.

Für die Opposition definit - indefinit konnte dagegen auf die entsprechende für das Englische bereitgestellte Information zurückgegriffen werden, die darüberhinaus auch mit der Numerus-Information zusammen verwaltet wird, womit auch die Numerus-Kongruenz, obwohl im Englischen nur bei indefiniten Artikeln relevant, leicht herzustellen war.

a2)   Verbalmorphologie
Numeruskongruenz zwischen Subjekt und Prädikat und einfache Tempora wurden schon von der englischsprachigen MUMBLE-Version erzeugt, wobei auch eine weitgehende Übereinstimmung mit den Kategorien des Deutschen besteht. Problematisch ist dagegen die Wahl des Auxiliars bei den zusammengesetzten Zeiten (auch hier muss das Lexikonformat für Verben geändert werden) sowie die Personal-Kongruenz. Kein Problem ist die Behandlung unregelmässiger Verbformen, die im Lexikon eingetragen werden.

a3)   Nominalmorphologie:
MUMBLE generiert Pluralia, falls im Lexikon kein unregelmässiger Plural angegeben ist, durch Anhängen eines Plural-'s. Die Abhängigkeit der Pluralendung im Deutschen von der morphologischen Klasse erfordert ein wesentlich aufwendigeres Verfahren. Da die vorläufige Lösung, alle Pluralformen ins Lexikon einzutragen, nicht befriedigt, haben wir die SUTRA-S-Morphologiekomponente [Emele, Momma 85] des SEMSYN-Systems [Rösner 86] in MUMBLE integriert.

Festzuhalten ist, daß bereits für die hier genannten Phänomene an den verschiedensten Stellen des MUMBLE-Systems, insbesondere auch in den eher prozeduralen Teilen, in sehr inhomogener Weise und mit viel Kleinarbeit Änderungen vorgenommen werden mussten. Unseres Erachtens ist dies auf die einsprachige Konzeption des Systems zurückzuführen.

b)   Auf den ersten Blick paradox dazu erscheint, daß sich syntaktisch tiefergreifende Probleme eher leicht lösen lassen, und zwar in der erwünscht deklarativen Weise, nämlich vermittels der sogenannten "realization-classes". Sie bieten ein bequemes Mittel zur Deklaration von fertigen Satzbauplänen (im Sinne von Phrasen-Strukturregeln), zur Spezifikation von Auswahlrestriktionen für diese Patterns und zur Übergabe von Elementen der Eingabestruktur an diese Patterns als Parameter. Die bisher verwendeten Realisierungsklassen, die nur auf die lokale Expansion der einzelnen Konstituenten in Linie ausgerichtet sind, stossen an ihre Grenzen bei den bekannten Diskontinuitätsproblemen wie dem nachgestellten Verbalpräfix.

FAZIT:

MUMBLE ist als einsprachiges System konzipiert und hier liegt seine Leistungsfähigkeit. Für ein multilinguales System wäre auf jeden Fall eine stärkere Auslagerung einzelsprachspezifischer Gegebenheiten aus dem Programmcode in eher deklarative Komponenten wünschenswert, bis hin zu einer völlig modularen Abtrennung der Grammatik.

Ein solche Komponente zur deklarativen Spezifizierung einer einzelsprachlichen Grammatik sollte, nach der hier beschriebenen Erfahrung, mindestens die folgenden abstrakten Features und eine Möglichkeit zu deren Deklarierung und deren Handhabung bieten:

1. Möglichkeit zur Spezifikation von automatisch zu verwendenden Sonderformen im Lexikon.

2. Spezifikation von Kongruenzen zwischen beliebigen Paaren von abstrakten oder terminalen Elementen der Zwischenstruktur unter gleichzeitiger Angabe der grammatischen Kategorien, bezüglich derer die Kongruenz besteht.

3. Deklarative Aufführbarkeit von regelmässigen Paradigmen und Spezifikation von Flexionsklassen, denen die Lexikoneinträge zugeordnet werden können.

4. Eine prinzipiell freie Wortstellung, die erst durch die explizite Angabe von Stellungsregeln geordnet wird.

4. Literatur

[Emele, Momma 85] Martin Emele, Stefan Momma *SUTRA-S - Erweiterungen eines Generator-Front-End für das SEMSYN-Projekt.* Studienarbeit, Universität Stuttgart, 1985

[Meteer 87 (et al.)] Marie W. Meteer, David D. McDonald, Scott D. Anderson, David Forster, Linda S. Gay. Alison K. Huettner, Penelope Sibun. *MUMBLE-86: Design and Implementation.* COINS Technical Report 87-87, University of Massachusetts, 1987

[Rösner 86] Dietmar Rösner. *Ein System zur Generierung von deutschen Texten aus semantischen Repräsentationen.* Dissertation, Universität Stuttgart, 1986

Teaching a Second Language to a Computer:
A Programmer's View

Owen Rambow

Odyssey Research Associates
301A Harris B. Dates Drive
Ithaca NY 14850-1313*

This report gives a quick summary of some experiences made during the conversion of a text generation system from English to German language generation. The system is Dietmar Rösner's SEMTEX. Starting point for generation in SEMTEX is a text plan in the form of a list of semantic representations. The generator-kernel translates the semantic representations into syntactic structures. The sentence is linearized and the lexemes are inflected in the surface component SUTRA-S, developed form Stephan Busemann's SUTRA by Martin Emele and Stefan Momma[1].

During the conversion it became apparent that there are two different types of tasks. On the one hand, the language-specific knowledge for English had to be entered. This task required little actual programming and thus no conceptual work for the programmer. The language-specific knowledge includes the dictionaries, the morphological data and the word order rules. On the other hand, several new algorithms had to be added to make decisions that need not be made in German. This task if far more difficult for the programmer[2]. These algorithms are language-independent in the sense that if the same distinction is made in two languages, then the same algorithm can be used. For example, it would have been possible to simply use the German morphological algorithm; only the inflection morphemes would have had to be changed. The experiences can be summed up as follows:

1. The deeper the level, the less *language-specific knowledge* needs to be replaced. While the knowledge of the morphological component was almost completely replaced some rules from the linearization component could be retained, and the changes in the generator-kernel were rare and minor.

2. Those algorithms that deal with problems specific to German (and thus difficult for anglophone learners of German) could be simplified or eliminated. Problems that are specific to English (and thus difficult for German students of English) needed additional algorithmic coding.

---

*This work was supported by the Air Force Systems Command at Rome Air Development Center under Contract No. F30602-85-C-0098. The views and conclusions contained in this paper are those of the author and should not be interpreted as necessarily representing the official policies, either expressed or implied, of the Air Force or the U.S. Government.

[1]For a complete description of SEMTEX, see [Ros86]; for a complete description of SUTRA-S, see [EM85]. An overview of the system in English can be found, for example, in [Ros87] or [Ros88].

[2]Of course, the distinction between language-specific knowledge and algorithms does not mean that the knowledge cannot be coded procedurally.

3. The semantic representation itself turns out to be language-dependent in a particular sense.

A somewhat more detailed summary of some problems follows. Two sample texts are added as an appendix.

1 Morphology

English morphology is far simpler than German morphology. Since significantly less knowledge is needed, the algorithm that accesses this knowledge could also be significantly simplified[3]. For example, for every German noun the dictionary must indicate the class of inflection; the inflection morpheme is then determined as a function of number, case and inflection class by consulting "morphemic trees". In English, however, there is only one criterion for inflection: number. Only if the plural is irregular is there an entry in the dictionary. All morphemic trees can be replaced by one single pair of morphemes, $(\emptyset, -s)$. The algorithm that accesses the trees is thus superfluous. Similar analyses hold for the other word classes.

One point in which English morphology is more complicated is gender. Less knowledge is needed since most nouns can be covered by a default (neuter); the size of the dictionary can be greatly reduced. However, in addition to German's three genders there is a fourth gender, the dual. The correct pronominal form for a dual noun can be the masculine, the feminine or the inclusive (*he or she*) pronoun. The decision is based on semantic considerations. Accessing the dictionary is not sufficient, additional algorithms are necessary.

2 Word Order

Word order is similar in both languages. The algorithm can largely be retained. However, word order in dependent and topicalized clauses, which differs from standard word order in German, does not require special treatment in English. Both the relevant knowledge and the applicable part of the algorithm can be eliminated.

It is more difficult to determine the position of the adverb and of adverbial phrases in English. For instance, one class for temporal adverbs is sufficient for German (*Er wird* nie *gesehen werden* and *Er wird* zweimal *gesehen werden*), but not for English (*He will* never *be seen* but *He will be seen* twice). One possible solution is to further subdivide the class of temporal adverbs and to indicate in the linguistic dictionary to which class a particular adverb belongs. The position rules would have to be extended to reflect the different subclasses.

Furthermore, the position of the adverb in English is not always uniquely determined. This is true in particular for process adverbs. For example, *leidenschaftlich* and *passionately*, respectively, can be inserted into the following sentences at the marked positions. All four English variants correspond to the German sentence.

*Sie wird ihn * geküßt haben.*
*She * will * have * kissed him *.*

---

[3]As stated above, English morphology could have been dealt with in the context of the German algorithm. But reasons of efficiency exclude retaining the larger apparatus.

In English small shifts in meaning can be achieved by choosing a particular position for the adverb, or some positions can seem preferable for certain adverbs[4]. For a generator devoted to a particular task or a particular type of text a default position will most probably be sufficient. However, if highly nuanced and expressive English is to be generated, then an algorithm that deals with this problem will have to be devised. The decision will rely on semantic information. (The semantic information can come either from lexical semantics or from domain knowledge.)

3 Generator-Kernel

Changes in the generator-kernel were restricted to some prepositions that had to be changed or added in the government patterns of some verbs. For example, in German the agent in a nominalized "change"-concept simply requires the default realization with a genitive (*Zunahme der Zahl*). In English, a preposition is needed (*increase in the number*). The algorithm for introducing prepositions already existed, since some realizations of roles require prepositions in German as well. The object-oriented programming style of this component greatly facilitated the necessary additions and changes to the language-specific knowledge. For example, the rule given as an example above covers a range of (semantically related) cases such as *drop in*, *decrease in* etc.

Extensions to the Kernel would be needed in two areas which frequently pose special problems to German students of English: aspect and tense. German has no differentiation comparable to English's progressive and unmarked aspects (except for the regional construction *Es ist am regnen*). The decison between the aspects in English is based on a wide range of factors. Sometimes, purely linguistic considerations impose a particular choice (for example, *to be* as copula never takes the progressive). More frequently, however, the type of semantic representation will determine (or partly determine) aspect (for example, the first clause of a *while*-construction is likely to be a progressive). And in many cases the choice is based purely on domain knowledge. The algorithm has not yet been defined.

English has the same morphological tenses as German, but the usage of the present, present perfect and past tenses differs from that of the *Präsens*, *Perfekt* and *Präteritum* in German. In SEMTEX, tense is determined as a function of points of speech, event (interest) and reference. This is possible in English as well, as Reichenbach has shown (see [Rei47]). The conclusion might be that merely the language-specific rules need to be changed, not the algorithm that interprets them. But it turns out that this is not sufficient: the times of reference and interest are defined differently for English. Two English sentences that have the same tense (and the same Reichenbachian distribution of points of speech, event and reference) might be translated into German sentences with different tenses. Consider the following sentences:

(1) *Ich bin hier seit 1985.*
(2) *Ich bin hier seit 1985 dreimal gewesen.*
(3) *I have been here since 1985.*
(4) *I have been here three times since 1985.*

According to Reichenbach's analysis for English tenses, in sentences (3) and (4) the times of speech and reference coincide and follow the time of the event. SEMTEX, however, would, for (2), see the

---

[4]These shifts in meaning and preferred positions are fairly elusive. They are an effect of the fact that an adverb qualifies most stronlgy the immediately following word. Hence, for example, *He was brutally being tortured* seems awkward since the *being* is the auxiliary of the passive, and *brutally* can only be applied to an action, not to its suffering. *Incessantly* would be acceptable in that position.

times of event and reference as coincidental and preceding the time of speech, and for (1) consider all three times as being coincidental. Thus, the notions of points of speech, event and reference need to be redefined or refined, and the algorithms that use pre-linguistic (domain-) knowledge to determine them need to be adapted.

4   The Semantic Representation

The semantic representation is the link between domain knowledge and the linguistic component. SEMTEX transforms each of its units into exactly one sentence. Each unit expresses in a language-independent way the contents of the sentence. For languages as closely related as English and German, if a semantic representation can be realized in one language, then there is no problem in realizing it in the other one as well. However, in translating a list of representations that form a plan for connected text there is the possibility that unidiomatic or rough passages are generated. For example, sentences (2) correspond to sentences (1), but a sentence like (3) would be far more idiomatic and preferable:

(1) *Die Arbeitslosenquote betrug Ende April 9,4 Prozent. Sie hatte sich Ende Dezember des letzten Jahres auf 9,3 Prozent belaufen.*
(2) *At the end of April the unemployment rate had a value of 9.4 percent. At the end of the same month a year earlier it was at 9.3 percent.*
(3) *At the end of April the rate of unemployment was 9.4 percent, up from 9.3 percent a year ago.*

Sentence (3) cannot be derived from sentences (2) by linguistic, i.e. syntactic and/or lexical semantic means. Instead, sentence (3) requires a separate semantic representation (which, of course, may be derivable from those of sentences (2) using domain knowledge).

Of course, such phenomena occur only in broad context. But broad contexts are typical for any real use of language. Thus, a generator of the present kind might capture the problem of multi-sentence text by using a variety of language-dependent underlying text-plans.

5   Conclusion

The most striking experience during the conversion was the speed with which SEMTEX learned elementary English. Replacing large amounts of German language-specific knowledge with small amounts of English language-specific knowledge is an easy task. One might wish to conclude that English is an easier language, and to a certain extent this is true: it might be easier, for both man and machine, to quickly acquire a working knowledge of English than of German. However, the different points at which English will require algorithms different from those implemented for German, and in particular the fact that these algorithms will frequently need to interact with the pre-linguistic level, show that much delicate work still lies ahead before SEMTEX is truely bilingual.

Appendix: Sample Texts

The German text generated by SEMTEX:

Zunahme der Zahl der Arbeitslosen
NÜRNBERG/BONN (cpa) 5.12.1985
Die Zahl der Arbeitslosen ist im Dezember spürbar angestiegen. Sie hat von 2210700
auf 2347100 zugenommen. Die Arbeitslosenquote betrug Ende Dezember 9.4 Prozent.
Sie hatte sich Ende Dezember des lezten Jahres auf 9.3 Prozent belaufen. Der DGB hat
erklärt, er sehe in der Vergrößerung der Zahl der Arbeitslosen ein negatives Zeichen.

After two months of work on the conversion, SEMTEX produced the following paragraph from
a text plan similar to the one of the paragraph above. Except for a misplaced comma it is
gramatically correct. However, several of the more difficult problems outlined in the paper have
not yet been tackled, so that the language is unidiomatic and can easily be identified as produced
by a "foreigner".

Increase in the Number of Unemployed
NÜRNBERG/BONN (cpa) December 5, 1985
The number of unemployed in West Germany has increased slightly during November.
It has increased from 2,148,000 by 61,900 to 2,210,700. At the end of November the
unemployment rate had a value of 8.8 percent. At the end of the year-ago period it
had a value of 8.7 percent. Gerd Muhr, the speaker of the DGB, declares, it sees a bad
sign in the increase in the number of unemployed.

References

[EM85] Martin Emele and Stefan Momma. *SUTRA-S: Erweiterungen eines Generator-Front-End
für das SEMSYN-Projekt.* Technical Report, Universität Stuttgart, 1985.

[Rei47] H. Reichenbach. *Elements of Symbolic Logic.* Macmillan, New York, 1947.

[Ros86] Dietmar Rösner. *Ein System zur Generierung von deutschen Texten aus semantischen
Repräsentationen.* PhD thesis, Universität Stuttgart, 1986.

[Ros87] Dietmar Rösner. The automated news agency SEMTEX – a text generator for German. In
G. Kempen, editor, *Natural Language Generation: New Results in Artificial Intelligence,
Psychology and Linguistics*, pages 138–148, Kluwer Academic Publishers, Boston, 1987.

[Ros88] Dietmar Rösner. The SEMSYN generation system: ingredients, applications, prospects.
In *Proceedings of the Second Conference on Applied Natural Language Processing*, ACL,
Austin, 1988.

Tree Adjoining Grammars mit Unifikation

Karin Harbusch

FB 10 - Informatik IV
Universität des Saarlandes
Im Stadtwald 15
D - 6600 Saarbrücken 11
harbusch%sbsvax.uucp@germany.csnet

Abstract :

Auf dem Gebiet der Analyse natürlicher Sprache hat sich die *Unifikation* als ein Forschungsschwerpunkt herauskristallisiert.

Die Unifikation erfolgt dabei immer gebunden an eine kontextfreie Regel. Man kann sich nun fragen, ob es nicht größere sinnvolle Einheiten im Strukturbaum gibt, an die die Unifikation gebunden werden könnte. Mithilfe des Formalismus der *Tree Adjoining Grammars* (TAGs) werden gerade solche komplexeren Einheiten, nämlich Teilbäume des Strukturbaumes spezifiziert und ihre lokale Kombinierbarkeit definiert.

Ich werde im folgenden zunächst die beiden Formalismen TAG und PATR kurz beschreiben. Eine Definition zur Verknüpfung dieser beiden Formalismen, der *Tree Adjoining Grammars mit Unifikation*, stellt den Kernpunkt des Beitrages dar. Zum Abschluß werden einige Vorteile gegenüber den Formalismen in Reinform diskutiert und auf offene Probleme hingewiesen.

1. Tree Adjoining Grammars

Der Formalismus der Tree Adjoining Grammars wurde ursprünglich von A. K. Joshi, L. S. Levy und M. Takahashi 1975 vorgestellt (siehe [4]) und bildet seither die Grundlage für verschiedenste theoretische und praktische Betrachtungen. Einen gute Einführung versehen mit vielen Beispielen findet sich z. B. in [3].

Eine **Tree Adjoining Grammar**, kurz **TAG**, besteht aus der Menge der **Terminale** T, der Menge der **Nichtterminale** N, einem ausgezeichneten Nichtterminal S, dem **Startsymbol**, der Menge der **initialen Bäume** I und der Menge der **auxiliaren Bäume** A.

Ein **initialer Baum** ist ein Baum mit einer Wurzel, die mit dem Startsymbol beschriftet ist, inneren Knoten, die Nichtterminale als Beschriftung tragen und terminalen Blattwörtern.

Um neue nicht explizit in der Grammatik kodierte Bäume zu bilden, braucht man noch eine Menge spezieller Bäume, die in die initialen Bäume eingefügt werden können. Die Bäume aus dieser zweiten Baummenge, der Menge der **auxiliaren Bäume**, haben im Blattwort genau einen Nichtterminalknoten, den **Fußknoten**, der mit dem gleichen Nichtterminal wie der Wurzelknoten des Baumes beschriftet ist. Alle übrigen Blattknoten sind mit Terminalen beschriftet und alle inneren Knoten mit Nichtterminalen.

Das Kombinieren von Bäumen (**Adjoining** oder **Adjunktion**) ergibt sich einfach als das Löschen eines Nichtterminalknotens in einem, gegebenenfalls durch Adjunktionen bereits modifizierten, initialen Baum (im folgenden Beispiel das VP in Baum α) und das Einsetzen eines auxiliaren Baumes mit dem gleichen Nichtterminal an der Wurzel (Baum β) an Stelle des gelöschten Nichtterminals. Die in den ursprünglichen Knoten eingehende Kante geht in die Wurzel des auxiliaren Baumes ein und die aus dem Knoten ausgehenden Kanten gehen nun aus dem Fußknoten aus.

Aus einer endlichen Menge von Strukturbeschreibungen - der Menge der initialen und auxiliaren

Bäume - erreicht man so die Bildung beliebig großer Strukturen (**Ableitungen**), deren Blattwörter die **Sprache der Grammatik** definieren.

Am folgenden natürlichsprachlichen Beispiel sieht man bereits die generelle Philosophie der Beschreibung von linguistischen Phänomenen mit TAGs (viele natürlichsprachliche Beispiele finden sich in [6]). Mit Hilfe der initialen Bäume werden die einfachen Satz- bzw. Propositionsstrukturen beschrieben, die auxiliarer Bäume dienen zur Beschreibung lokal erweiternder Konstrukte.

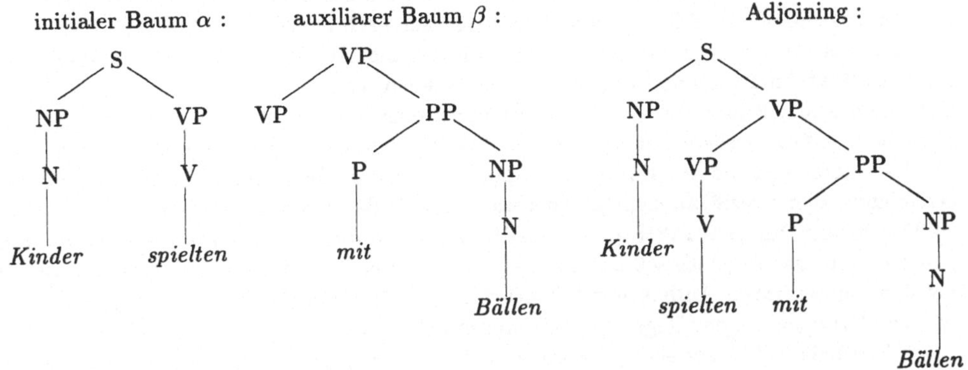

2. PATR-Unifikation

Eine gute Einführung in die Theorie der Unifikation findet sich z. B. in [7]. Ich möchte hier als eine Ausprägung den PATR-Formalismus (siehe [5]) vorstellen. Eine **Regel** in PATR besteht aus einer **Konstituentenliste** und einer **Spezifikationsliste**. In der Konstituentenliste wird eine kontextfreie Regel beschrieben, wobei das am weitesten links stehende Element der Liste die linke Seite der Regel darstellt. Alle weiteren Listenelemente von links nach rechts beschreiben die rechte Seite der kontextfreien Regel.

Diese Regeln bilden eine kontextfreie Grammatik, bestehend aus der Menge der **Terminale** T, der Menge der **Nichtterminale** N, einem ausgezeichneten Nichtterminal S, dem **Startsymbol** und der Menge der **Produktionen** $P \subseteq (N \times (N \cup T)^*)$.

Die Spezifikationsliste, die die Unifikationsregeln beschreibt, ist mit der Konstituentenliste dadurch verbunden, daß jede Konstituente als Nummer eine natürliche Zahl (die Numerierung beginnt bei Null) erhält, über die sie mittels der Spezifikation näher beschrieben wird. Eine Spezifikation in der Spezifikationsliste hat die Form (path {path | value}), wobei path aus einer Nummer, die auf eine Konstituente zeigt, und einer Liste von atomaren Attributnamen besteht und value ein Atom ist. Eine Spezifikation der Form (path path) beschreibt die Identifikation der Endpunkte der Pfade und eine der Form (path value) die Definition eines Values für einen Pfad. Verbindet man Nachfolger in solch einer Liste mit einer (gerichteten) Kante und repräsentiert man solche Pfade mit dem gleichen Präfix nur einmal, so daß ab der Unterscheidung eine Pfadverzweigung eingeführt wird, erhält man als graphische Darstellung der Spezifikationsliste einen **Directed Acyclic Graph**, kurz DAG genannt.

Unter **Unifikation**, dem Prozeß, der nun diese Regeln verarbeitet, versteht man die widerspruchsfreie Vereinigung der Spezifikationsteile einer kontextfreien Konstituentenregel. D. h., zwei Pfade, ausgehend vom gleichen Ursprung (die gleiche Nummer tragend), dürfen keine unterschiedlichen Values haben und nach Ausführung einer kontextfreien Ableitung eines Eingabewortes von S, dem Startsymbol, aus, müssen alle Pfade an ihrem Endpunkt einen Value tragen.

Beispielgrammatik, die zum initialen Baum α aus dem Beispiel zu TAGs korrespondierende kontextfreie Grammatik mit Unifikationsregeln versieht :

((S NP VP) (((0 subjekt) (1)) ((0 verbalkomplex) (2)) ((1 syntax) (2 syntax))))
((NP N) (((0 syntax) (1 syntax)) ((0 head) (1 stamm))))

((VP V) (((0 syntax) (1 syntax)) ((head) (1 stamm)))
((N *Kinder*) (((0 syntax num) pl) ((0 syntax gen) n) ((0 syntax pers) 3)) ((0 stamm) *kind*))
((V *spielten*) (((0 syntax num) pl) ((0 syntax pers) 3) ((0 tempus) prät) ((0 stamm) *spiel*))

3. TAGs mit Unifikation

Die Vorgehensweise bei der Verknüpfung der beiden Mechanismen wird schon intuitiv klar, wenn man jeden inneren Knoten in einem initialen oder auxiliaren Baum als linke Seite einer Konstituentenregel und seine Söhne in ihrer Reihenfolge von links nach rechts als rechte Seite dieser Regel interpretiert. Solch einer Regel ordnet man nun wie gewohnt die Spezifikationsliste zu und erhält so eine **Spezifikationsbeschreibung** für die Bäume einer TAG.

Wenn man jedem Knoten in allen diesen Bäumen eine eindeutige Nummer gibt und diese in die jeweilige Spezifikationsliste einfügt, statt der lokalen Nummer in der kontextfreien Regel, kann man die Spezifikationen von den Knoten entkoppeln und jedem Baum seine Spezifikationsliste, die die Vereinigung aller Spezifikationslisten an Knoten dieses Baumes ist, zuordnen.

Die **Definition der Adjunktion mit Unifikation** soll dieser Betrachtungsweise auch Rechnung tragen, d. h. das Ergebnis soll das gleiche sein wie im Fall der 'reinen' Unifikation angewandt entlang dem kontextfreien Aufbau des Strukturbaumes, der dem durch 'reine' Adjunktion (fest vorgegebene Gruppierung der Regeln) entstandenen entspricht.

Dieses Ergebnis soll *direkt* erzeugt werden, sich also bei jeder Adjunktion aktuell berechnen lassen. Als Problem tritt dabei auf, daß Informationen über den Knoten, in dem adjungiert wird, fließen können, die durch den Einbau eines neuen Teilbaumes gegebenenfalls verändert werden.

Dieser **'Filterwirkung'** trägt die folgende Definition Rechnung.
Im Knoten X, in dem adjungiert wird, werden die folgenden drei Mengen berechnet :
1. ↑X besteht aus allen Spezifikationen, in denen X rechte Seite einer kontextfreien Regel ist,
2. ↓X besteht aus solchen, in denen X linke Seite einer Regel (außer Valuedefinition) ist und
3. oX besteht aus allen Valuedefinitionen, die in diesem Knoten gemacht werden.
Bei der Adjunktion wird nun dieser Knoten X mit allen Spezifikationen, in denen die Nummer des Knotens vorkommt, aus dem Baum entfernt, der auxiliare Baum, wie bei der Definition von 'reinen' TAGs, eingesetzt (d. h. es wird eine Kante vom Vater von X zum Wurzelknoten und Kanten von Fußknoten zu allen Söhnen von X gezogen) und die neue Spezifikationsliste an Wurzel- und Fußknoten des eingesetzten Baumes folgendermaßen berechnet :

- Unifiziere die Spezifikationsliste der Wurzel des auxiliaren Baumes (d. h. alle Spezifikationen des Baumes, in denen die Nummer der Wurzel vorkommt) mit ↑X. Da der Wurzelknoten des auxiliaren Baumes nur linke Seite einer kontextfreien Regel sein kann, entstehen durch die Unifikation so gerade alle Verbindungen, die ursprünglich X zu seinem Vaterknoten hatte, zu allen von der Wurzel aus zugänglichen Informationen.

- Unifiziere die Spezifikationsliste des Fußknotens des auxiliaren Baumes mit ↓X. So entsteht aus den Verbindungen von X zu seinen Söhnen die Anbindung der Information aus dem Fußknoten an die Söhne von X.

- Die Value-Definition oX wandert im auxiliaren Baum nach einer **Vererbungsuntersuchung** hinter den längsten explizierten Pfad, unter dem der Value benutzt werden kann. So wird die widerspruchsfreie Definition aller Values von X im auxiliaren Baum gewährleistet.

Diese Vererbungsuntersuchung betrachtet den Weg aus Kanten auf dem Strukturbaum von der Wurzel zum Fußknoten eines auxiliaren Baumes. Die Spezifikationen entlang dieses Weges werden daraufhin untersucht, ob sie den Pfad aus Attributen, unter dem der Value definiert wurde, verlängern. Generell können als Beziehungen unter benachbarten (bzgl. dieses Weges) Spezifikationslisten die Präfix- (P), Gleichheits- (G) oder Unzusammenhangsrelation (U) bestehen. Diese generelle lokale Information wird von oben und unten (bzgl. der Wegenden) nach Kürzungsregeln (P P = P, P G = P, G P = P, G G = G) zusammengefaßt, bis man auf ein U oder das andere Ende des Weges stößt. An diesen erreichten Endpunkten wird der Value definiert (das kann also auch zweifach sein, z. B. wenn Unterbrechungen auftreten).

Im folgenden Beispiel werden die Bäume aus der Beispiel-TAG in Abschnitt 1 mit Spezifikationslisten versehen. Dazu wurden die beiden Bäume α und β mit eindeutigen Nummern versehen. Zu jedem Baum korrespondiert eine Spezifikationsliste.

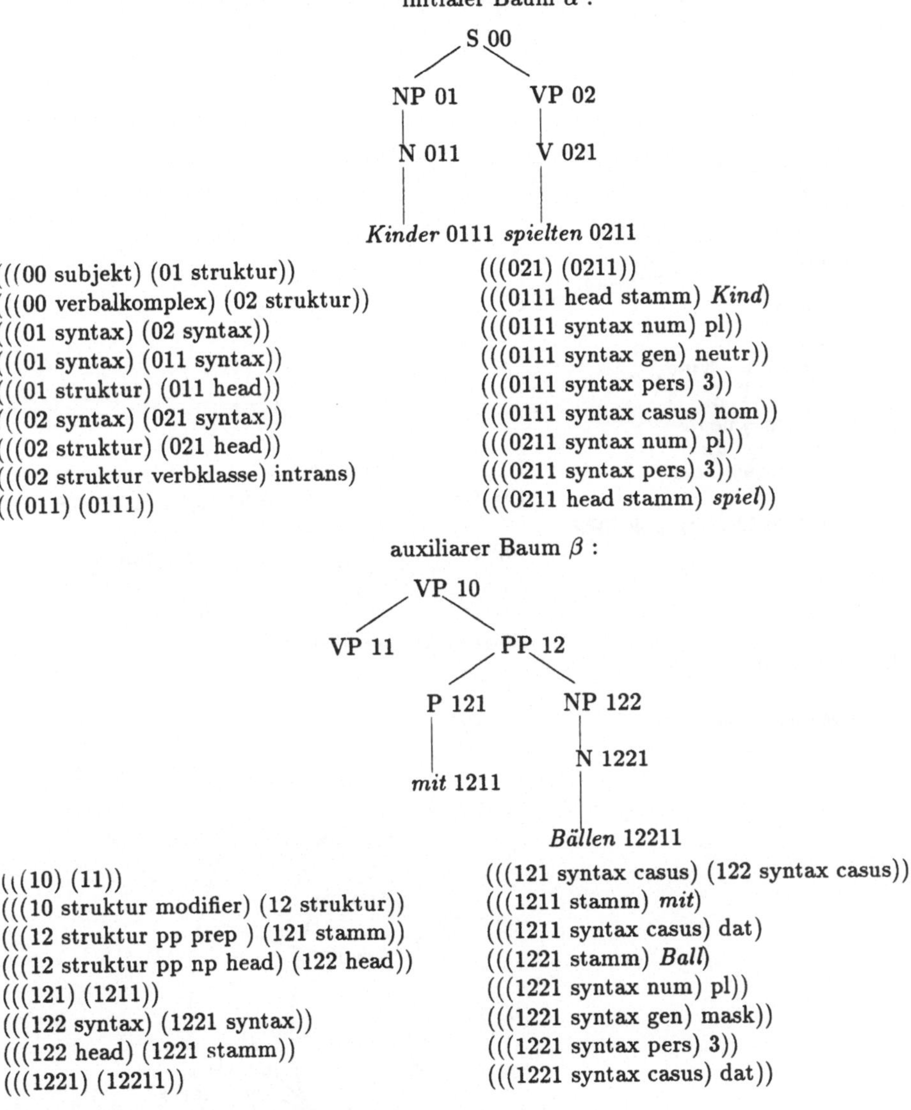

(((00 subjekt) (01 struktur))
(((00 verbalkomplex) (02 struktur))
(((01 syntax) (02 syntax))
(((01 syntax) (011 syntax))
(((01 struktur) (011 head))
(((02 syntax) (021 syntax))
(((02 struktur) (021 head))
(((02 struktur verbklasse) intrans)
(((011) (0111))

(((021) (0211))
(((0111 head stamm) *Kind*)
(((0111 syntax num) pl))
(((0111 syntax gen) neutr))
(((0111 syntax pers) 3))
(((0111 syntax casus) nom))
(((0211 syntax num) pl))
(((0211 syntax pers) 3))
(((0211 head stamm) *spiel*))

((10) (11))
(((10 struktur modifier) (12 struktur))
(((12 struktur pp prep) (121 stamm))
(((12 struktur pp np head) (122 head))
(((121) (1211))
(((122 syntax) (1221 syntax))
(((122 head) (1221 stamm))
(((1221) (12211))

(((121 syntax casus) (122 syntax casus))
(((1211 stamm) *mit*)
(((1211 syntax casus) dat)
(((1221 stamm) *Ball*)
(((1221 syntax num) pl))
(((1221 syntax gen) mask))
(((1221 syntax pers) 3))
(((1221 syntax casus) dat))

Die Mengen $\uparrow$, $\downarrow$ und o in VP in α sehen wie folgt aus :

$\uparrow$VP = {((00 verbalkomplex) (02 struktur)), ((01 syntax) (02 syntax))}

$\downarrow$VP = {((02 struktur) (021 head)), ((02 syntax) (021 syntax))}

oVP = {(02 struktur verbklasse) intrans)}

In folgender Abbildung sieht man im direkten Vergleich die DAGs zu jedem Knoten vor und nach der Adjunktion von Baum β in Knoten VP in Baum α. Die eindeutigen Knotennummern werden nach der Adjunktion dadurch erzeugt, daß die Nummer des Knotens, in dem adjungiert wurde, als geklammerter Präfix vor jeder Nummer im auxiliaren Baum erscheint. Die Zusammenhänge vor der Adjunktion sind durch durchgezogene und gestrichelte Linien gekennzeichnet, die nach der Adjunktion durch durchgezogene und strichpunktierte Linien.

Die ursprünglich über den Knoten VP mit der Nummer 02 laufenden Informationen werden nun während des Weges von der Wurzel zum Fußknoten des adjungierten Baumes modifiziert. Die Value-Definition wurde an Wurzel- und Fußknoten hinzugefügt, was aber durch die Identifikation der gesamten DAGs verdeckt wird.

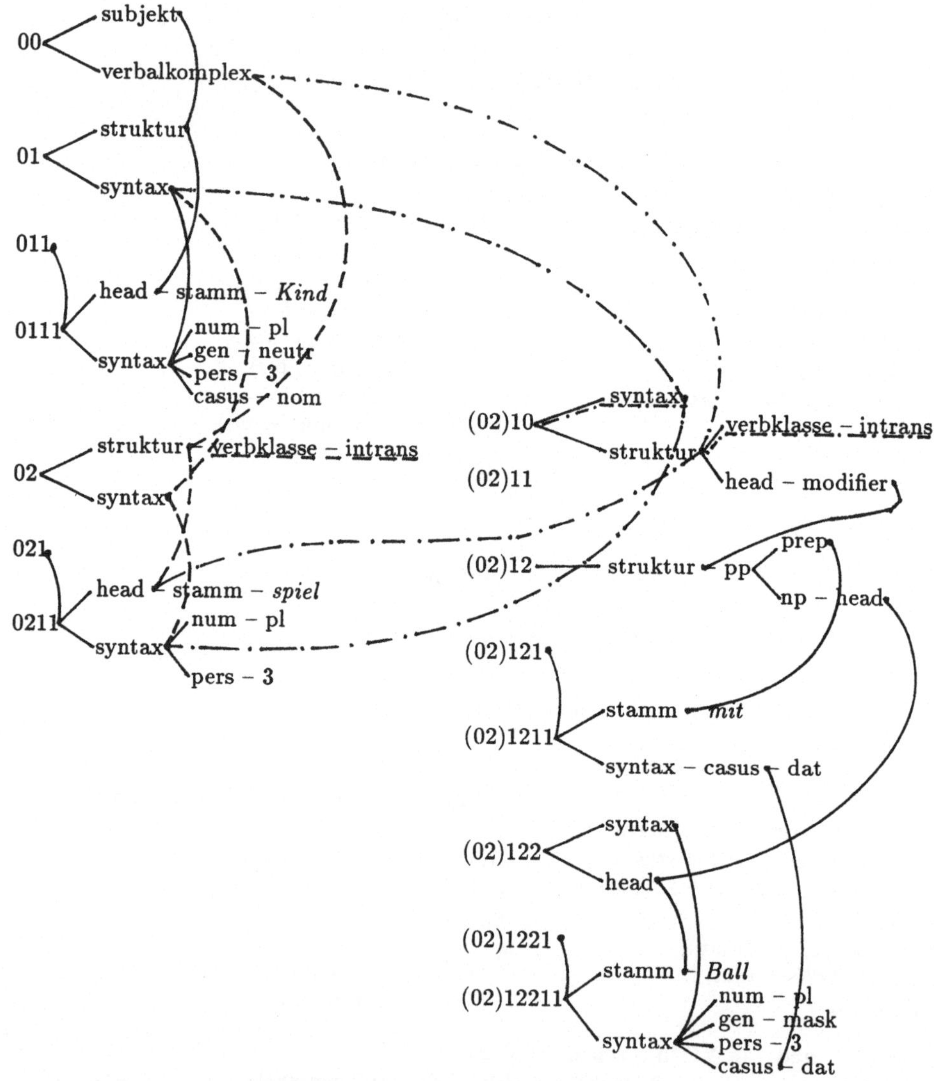

4. Vergleich mit den Formalismen in Reinform

Mit den TAGs hat man einem Formalismus, der theoretisch gut erforscht ist. Für die linguistische Anwendung ist hier der Sprachumfang wichtig, der einige kontextsensitive Sprachen beinhaltet, in denen man seine linguistischen Probleme als Einheit in jeweils einem Baum kodieren kann und das beschränkte Längenwachstum bei Adjunktionen, das dem der natürlichen Sprache entspricht (siehe [6]). Außerdem lassen sich TAGs auch im schlechtesten Fall in $O(n^4)$ Zeiteinheiten parsen (siehe [2]).

Man erkennt aber auch schnell den Hauptnachteil der TAGs. Die leichte Kodierbarkeit von Subkategorien und die Formulierung von Bedingungen mit Variablen darauf stellt an die TAGs die gleiche unüberwindliche Anforderung wie an eine kontextfreie Grammatik. Hier zeigt sich die enge Verwandtschaft der beiden Formalismen. Aus dieser Verwandtschaft heraus kann man die Definition von TAGs mit Unifikation ebenfalls motivieren. Man überträgt den gleichen Schritt, den man bei der Erweiterung von kontextfreien Grammatiken hin zu Unifikationsgrammatiken gemacht hat, auf TAGs.

Bei der Unifikation sind als wichtige Eigenschaften herauszustreichen, daß sie den oben angesprochenen Wunsch der Formulierung von Bedingungen mit Variablenbenutzung bei kontextfreien Grammatiken erfüllt, wobei sie eine simple Beschreibungsmethode dieser Bedingungen anbietet. Diese Einfachheit ist eng mit dem weiteren Argument gekoppelt, daß man sich nicht um die explizite Sequentialisierung der Bedingungen kümmern muß (Reihenfolge- und Richtungsunabhängigkeit der Unifikationsdefinition). Daher sehen alle Bedingungen, egal ob sie eine Definition, eine Überprüfung oder eine Propagierung von Information bedeuten, syntaktisch gleich aus. Das erleichtert das Grammatikschreiben, da man sich nicht festlegen muß, welcher Art eine Bedingung sein soll. Sie wird aus der gegebenen Situation heraus korrekt interpretiert.

All diese Eigenschaften können bei der Vereinigung der beiden Formalismen nicht erhalten bleiben, da sie zum Teil widersprüchlich sind. Wichtig ist aber, daß auf der Seite der TAGs die Einheiten, in denen die zusammenhängende Kodierung von linguistischen Problemen vorgenommen wird, erhalten bleiben. Wir haben weiterhin initiale und auxiliare Bäume, die immer noch den gleichen Sprachumfang abdecken.

Man kann nun aber Spezifikationslisten zu Bäumen hinzufügen. So erweitert sich der Sprachumfang auf alle Konstrukte, die eine reine Unifikationsgrammatik bewältigen kann (jeden kontextfreien Teil einer Unifikationsgrammatik kann man als TAG schreiben).

Auf der Seite der Unifikation ist die einfache Kodierbarkeit von Bedingungen und die Definition der Unifikation vollständig erhalten geblieben.

Die Eigenschaft der Monotonie bei Unifikationsgrammatiken geht aber verloren, da bereits propagiertes Wissen zurückgenommen werden kann (keine Vererbung des Features zwischen Wurzel und Fußknoten im adjungierten Baum) oder modifiziert werden kann (z. B. Verlängerung von Attribut-Pfaden). Diese zuletzt angesprochene Eigenschaft sehe ich als Vorteil an, da man so Hypothesen aufstellen oder Defaults definieren kann, die bei einer Adjunktion überschrieben werden. Die größere Mächtigkeit ist, da TAGs bereits über eine ausreichende verfügen, nicht beabsichtigtes Ziel bei der Erweiterung gewesen. So bleibt eine sinnvolle Einschränkung der Unifikation bei dieser Definition dem Benutzer selbst überlassen. Hier kann man sich den Angriffspunkt für weitere Überlegungen vorstellen, die zu einschränkenden Definitionen von TAGs mit Unifikation führen.

Eine weitere wichtige Frage, an der aktuell gearbeitet wird, ist es, ein effizientes Parsingverfahren für diesen neuen Formalismus zu entwickeln. Man ersetzt den Chart-Parser für die kontextfreien Regeln durch einen TAG-Parser, der lokal die Unifikationsbedingungen überprüft (siehe [1]). Jenachdem, wieviel Anteil der TAG-Teil der Definition bei der aktuellen Grammatik hat, kann man sich vorstellen, daß man weiterhin polynomiell parsen kann. Die Frage ist, ob man hier generelle Komplexitätsaussagen machen kann.

5. Zusammenfassung

Mit der Definition von TAGs mit Unifikation erhält man einen Formalismus, mit dem man linguistische Zusammenhänge besser darstellen kann, da man Einheiten sinnvoll zusammenfassen kann und nicht algorithmisch mit der Anwendung von Regeln argumentieren muß (aber kann, falls man will). Diese Aussage sollen im nächsten Arbeitsschritt größere Beispielgrammatiken belegen.

References

[1] **B. Buschauer, P. Poller, A. Schauder, K. Harbusch** : *Parsing von TAGs mit Unifikation,* erscheint als Memo in der Reihe KI-Labor, Fachbereich Informatik, Universität des Saarlandes, Saarbrücken, 1988.

[2] **K. Harbusch** : *Effiziente Analyse natürlicher Sprache mit TAGs,* erscheint in : Proceedings des Symposiums über 'Computerlinguistik und ihre theoretischen Grundlagen', Saarbrücken, im Springer-Verlag, in der Reihe 'Informatik-Fachberichte', Berlin, 1988.

[3] **A. K. Joshi** : *An Introduction to Tree Adjoining Grammars,* Technical Report MS-CIS-86-64, LINC-LAB 31, Department of Computer and Information Science, Moore School, University of Pennylvania, Philadelphia, 1985.

[4] **A. K. Joshi, S. Levy, M. Takahashi** : *Tree Adjoining Grammars,* in : Journal of Computer Systems and Science, Vol. 10, Seite 136-163, 1975.

[5] **L. Karttunen** : *D-PATR : A Development Environment for Unification Grammars,* CSLI - Report CLSI-86-61, Center For The Study Of Language And Information, Stanford, 1986.

[6] **T. Kroch, A. K. Joshi** : *Linguistic Relevance of Tree Adjoining Grammars,* Technical Report MS-CIS-85-16, Department of Computer and Information Science, Moore School, University of Pennylvania, Philadelphia, 1985.

[7] **S. M. Shieber** : *An Introduction to Unification-Based Approaches to Grammar,* CSLI - Lecture Notes Number 4, Center For The Study Of Language And Information,Stanford, 1987.

Einige Erweiterungen
disjunktiver Merkmalsbeschreibungen

Roland Seiffert
IBM Deutschland
WT LILOG
Postfach 80 08 80
7000 Stuttgart 80

Abstract

In der vorliegenden Arbeit werden einige Erweiterungen disjunktiver Merkmalsbeschreibungen diskutiert, die im Rahmen von **STUF** (**S**tuttgart **T**ype **U**nification **F**ormalism) im Projekt LILOG entwickelt wurden. Gegenüber den bisherigen Ansätzen sind dies insbesondere Konzepte zur Behandlung von **Termen mit fester und variabler Stelligkeit** in einem Formalismus und zur Strukturierung von Wissensbasen durch die Verwendung von **Wissensdomänen**.

1. Überblick

In dieser Arbeit möchte ich einen kurzen Überblick geben über einige Erweiterungen, die der in LILOG verwendete Unifikationsformalismus **STUF** (**S**tuttgart **T**ype **U**nification **F**ormalism) gegenüber anderen Formalismen wie z.B. Kasper (87) enthält.

Die wichtigsten dieser Erweiterungen sind

- closed types
- Wissensdomänen

Durch Einführen von *closed types* gibt STUF die Möglichkeit, innerhalb desselben Formalismus sowohl mit Termen fester als auch variabler Stelligkeit zu arbeiten. Dies bedeutet, daß je nach Anwendung die geeignete Wahl getroffen werden kann.

Das Konzept der *Wissensdomänen* oder *domains* dient zur Strukturierung des Wissens in einer STUF-Wissensbasis. Die Idee dabei ist, immer nur die Struktur der Typen zu zeigen, die zur aktuellen Domäne gehören und alle anderen Typen als unstrukturiert aufzufassen. Dadurch können die sichtbaren Strukturen kleiner gehalten werden und es kann verhindert werden, daß zusammenhanglose Informationen aus verschiedenen Domänen bei der Unifikation vermischt werden.

Zunächst wird kurz die Syntax zur Definition von Typen in STUF eingeführt. Ich habe hier eine gegenüber der tatsächlichen Implementierung etwas eingeschränkte Syntax verwendet, um die Darstellung zu vereinfachen. Insbesondere habe ich auf alternative Möglichkeiten zur Deklaration von Multidominanz verzichtet. Im Gegensatz zu FML von Kasper (87) orientiert sich die STUF-Syntax nicht an der Syntax für logische Formeln, sondern ist angelehnt an Konzepte aus PATR-II (siehe Shieber et al. 1983) und FUG (siehe Kay 1985). Insbesondere werden Unifikation und Generalisierung durch Klammerung von Formeln mit [] bzw. {} dargestellt und Multidominanz wird durch Pfadgleichungen ausgedrückt.

Eine **Typdeklaration** besteht aus einem Namen für den zu definierenden Typ und einer Typdefinition, also einer STUF-Formel:

    Name := Definition .

Eine **Typdefinition** in STUF hat die Form:

N	wobei N ein Typname der augenblicklichen Domäne ist
N!D	wobei N ein Typname der Domäne D ist
[t1 ... tn]	wobei alle ti Typdefinitionen sind
{ t1 ... tn }	wobei alle ti Typdefinitionen sind
a : t	wobei a ein Attribut und t eine Typdefinition ist
< p1 > = ... = < pn >	wobei alle pi Pfade, also Ketten von Attributen, sind

Die Definition von closed types erfolgt durch

closed(t)

wobei t allerdings gewissen Einschränkungen genügen muß. Dabei ist closed(t) ein Metaausdruck, der aussagt, daß es sich bei t um einen Typ mit fester Stelligkeit handeln soll. Details hierzu sind im Abschnitt über Typen mit fester Stelligkeit zu finden.

Eine **STUF-Wissensbasis** besteht aus einer Menge von Domänen, wobei für jede Domäne eine Menge von Typdeklarationen vorhanden ist. Dabei müssen nicht alle Domänen notwendigerweise auch durch STUF-Formeln beschrieben werden. Es genügt, wenn jede Domäne Prozeduren zur Unifikation, Generalisierung und zum Subsumptionstest für ihre Elemente bereitstellt.

Als Beispiel hier ein kleiner Ausschnitt aus einer fiktiven STUF-Wissensbasis:

DOMAIN stuf.

```
NP        := [ np_syn
                np_sem
              ] .
np_syn    := [ syn :    [ cat :     np!atom
                          bar:       2!atom
                        ]
             ] .
np_sem    := [ sem :    ............
             ] .
Hund      := [ NP
                sem:    [ sort:    Hund!sort
                        ]
                lex:    "Hund"!string
             ] .
```

DOMAIN sort.

```
Hund      := [ Säugetier
                Haustier
              ] .
Säugetier := ........
```

....

Im Gegensatz zu Aït-Kaci (1984) sind in STUF keine rekursiven Typdefinitionen erlaubt. Deshalb können Typen in STUF immer in eine **voll expandierte Form** gebracht werden, indem rekursiv alle Definitionen von verwendeten Typen eingesetzt werden. Im folgenden gehe ich immer davon aus, daß eine STUF-Formel in voll expandierter Form gegeben ist.

2. Typen mit fester Stelligkeit

In der Computerlinguistik gibt es im Bereich der Unifikationsgrammatiken zwei unabhängig voneinander gewachsene Klassen von Grammatikmodellen. Auf der einen Seite sind dies Ansätzen, die zur Beschreibung linguistischer Objekte komplexe Merkmalsstrukturen einsetzen. Auf der anderen Seite gibt es sehr stark logikorientierte Modelle, die PROLOG direkt zur Codierung linguistischer Information und deren Verarbeitung einsetzen. Unifikation ist in diesem Modell dann immer die Termunifikation.

Obwohl es klar ist, daß die Strategien auf beiden Seiten sehr ähnlich sind, gibt es immer wieder heftige Diskussionen, welcher Ansatz nun welche Vor- oder Nachteile besitzt.

Ich möchte die Argumente dieser Auseinandersetzung hier nicht weiter erläutern, sondern in diesem Abschnitt eine Erweiterung im STUF Typensystem vorstellen, die die Vorteile der beiden Repräsentationen, Merkmalsstrukturen mit variabler Stelligkeit und Terme mit fester Stelligkeit, in einem System vereinigt.

Zur Behandlung von Termen mit fester und variabler Stelligkeit in einem Formalismus benötigt man die Möglichkeit, auszudrücken, daß der Wert eines bestimmten Attributs undefiniert sein muß. Daher wird die STUF zugrunde liegende Subsumptionshierarchie durch Einführung der Typen S und U erweitert. Dabei soll S für alle definierten Typen stehen und U für undefinierte.

Die Menge, die T denotiert, wird in zwei disjunkte Teilmengen für die Denotate für S und U zerlegt. Es gelten also die Äquivalenzen

    [S U] < = > F
    { S U } < = > T

Die Subsumptionshierarchie für STUF gegenüber der für FML kann man graphisch so darstellen:

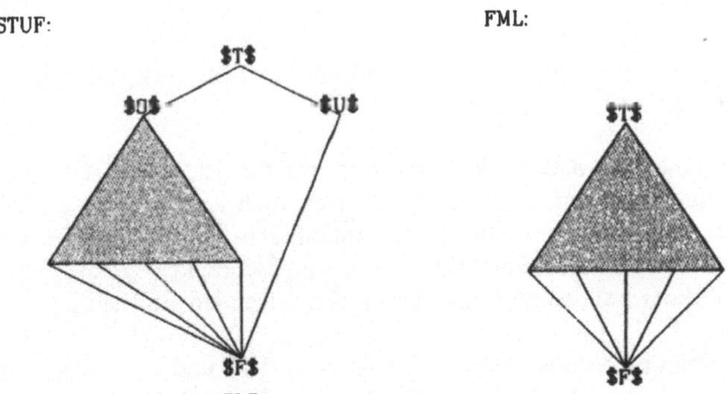

Zunächst sollen nur konjunktive STUF-Formeln betrachtet werden. Jede dieser Formeln kann in die Form

    [a1 : t1 ... an : tn]

gebracht werden. Bei freier Stelligkeit (open types) können zu dieser Formel noch beliebig weitere Attribut-Wert-Paare hinzugefügt werden. Bei fester Stelligkeit (closed types) ist dies nicht möglich, es kann nur noch zusätzliche Information über die Werte bereits vorhandener Attribute hinzugefügt werden.

Sei CF eine rein konjunktive Formel in STUF, dann ist der Definitionsbereich dom(CF) definiert als die Menge der Attribute, die in CF erwähnt werden und einen von T verschiedenen Wert t haben.

Geht man von einer festen, endlichen Menge ATTRIBUTE von Attributen aus, so kann man jede konjunktive Formel **totalisieren**. Dazu fügt man bei freier Stelligkeit für alle Attribute, die nicht in dom(CF) sind, ein Attribut-Wert-Paar a : T ein, bei fester Stelligkeit a : U.

Sei z.B. ATTRIBUTE = { a, b, c, d, e }, dann ergibt die Totalisierung:

    open   [a : t1 b : t2 d : t3] [a : t1 b : t2 c : T d : t3 e : T]
    closed [a : t1 b : t2 d : t3] [a : t1 b : t2 c : U d : t3 e : U]

Durch Einführung von Attribut-Wert-Paaren a : U für alle nicht vorhandenen Attribute bei closed types wird erreicht, daß jede konjunktive Verknüpfung mit einer Formel, die für a einen Wert ungleich T oder U enthält, zu F führt.

Syntaktisch wird in STUF eine konjunktive Formel CF dadurch als closed type definiert, daß man closed(CF) schreibt. Semantisch bedeutet dies genau die oben beschriebene Totalisierung mit Einführung von Attribut-Wert-Paaren a : U.

Natürlich wird in der Implementierung die Totalisierung nicht tatsächlich ausgeführt, sondern lediglich markiert, daß es sich bei einer konjunktiven Teilformel um einen closed type handelt. Die Unifikationsroutine muß dann bei der Bearbeitung von closed types garantieren, daß die Einschränkungen der Attributmengen eingehalten werden.

Durch diese Definition ist es in STUF möglich, Typen mit freier und fester Stelligkeit innerhalb eines Formalismus miteinander zu unifizieren. Das Ergebnis der Unifikation eines open types mit einem closed type kann dabei nur wieder ein closed type sein, da jedes Attribut, das im open type mit T versehen ist, bei der Unifikation mit dem entsprechenden Attribut des closed types den Wert U erhält.

Beispiel:

    closed([a:t1 b:t2 c:t3]) & [a:t4 c:t5]   =   closed([a:[t1 t4] b:t2 c:[t3 t5]])
    [a:t1 b:t2 c:t3] & closed([a:t4 c:t5])   = F

Die bisher gemachte Einschränkung, daß closed(CF) nur erlaubt ist, wenn CF eine rein konjunktive Formel ist, ist sehr gravierend. Allerdings macht es auch keinen Sinn, closed(t) für jede beliebige Formel t zuzulassen, da man dann keinen eindeutigen Definitionsbereich dom(t) angeben kann. Daher müssen die zulässigen Formeln für t so eingeschränkt werden, daß dom(t) eindeutig festliegt. Dies ist dann der Fall, wenn t eine der beiden folgenden Formen hat:

(1)   [a1 : t1 ... an : tn]   dann ist dom(t) = { ai | ti < = / = > T und ti < = / = > U }
(2)   { CF1 , ... , CFn }   wenn alle CFi die Form (1) haben und dom(CF1) = ... = dom(CFn)

Zu beachten ist, daß die eingebetteten Formeln jetzt beliebige Disjunktionen enthalten dürfen. Dies ist deshalb unkritisch, da eingebettete Disjunktionen die Attribut-Menge in der Toplevel-Formel nicht beeinflussen können.

Eine einfache Erweiterung besteht darin bei closed(t) für t auch Formeln zuzulassen, die Pfadgleichungen enthalten, also z.B.

    closed([a : x b : y <c> = <d e>])

Dies ist in STUF deshalb unproblematisch, da durch die Definition einer Pfadgleichheit immer auch die Existenz der genannten Pfade eingeführt wird, d.h. ein solcher Pfad erhält als Wert S und kann daher nie wieder durch Unifikation mit U als undefiniert markiert werden.

Um die Schwierigkeiten zu zeigen, in die man gerät, wenn man den Pfaden stattdessen als Wert T gibt, hier ein Beispiel:

$$t1 := closed([a:x <b> = <c>]) .$$
$$t2 := closed([a:x <b> = <d>]) .$$

Unifiziert man nun t1 und t2 so erhält man:

$$t := [t1\ t2] = closed([a:x])$$

Bei dieser Unifikation "verschwinden" also plötzlich Pfade aus der Struktur, was zum einen der Intuition beim Aufschreiben der Pfadgleichung entgegen läuft und zum anderen zu technischen Problemen in der Unifikationroutine führt.

Daher haben wir uns dazu entschlossen, die Pfade implizit mit S zu versehen. Im obigen Beispiel sind dann t1 und t2 nicht mehr unifizierbar.

3. Wissensdomänen

In Systemen wie PATR-II oder FUG spielen *Atome* eine wichtige Rolle. Mit ihnen werden die Blätter der gerichteten Graphen markiert, und nur durch Konflikte zwischen verschiedenen Atomen oder einem Atom und einer komplexen Struktur kann schließlich eine Unifikation fehlschlagen.

Bei Aït-Kaci (1984) werden anstelle von Atomen *Sorten* eingeführt. Dabei finden sich Sorten dann nicht mehr nur an den Blättern einer Struktur, sondern jeder Psi-Term wird mit einem Sortensymbol, dem *Head*, versehen. Dadurch erhalten Aït-Kacis Psi-Terme das Aussehen eines üblichen Terms in der Prädikatenlogik, nämlich ein Funktor und Argumente. Allerdings unifizieren nicht nur gleiche Heads, sondern die Unifikation der Sortensymbole wird gemäß einer separaten Verbandsstruktur durchgeführt.

In STUF wird keiner dieser beiden Ansätze verfolgt. Stattdessen haben wir das Konzept der **(Wissens-) Domänen** (*knowledge domains*) eingeführt. Die Grundidee dabei ist es, alle Typen in STUF als in irgendeiner Weise strukturiert aufzufassen. Dabei soll diese Struktur aber nur in der Domäne sichtbar sein, der die Typen angehören. Ein Beispiel für eine in Domänen strukturierte Wissensbasis habe ich bereits im Abschnitt 1. gegeben. Dort wurden z.B. die Sortendefinitionen in einer gesonderten Domäne behandelt, die wiederum aus STUF-Formeln bestand. Dies muß aber nicht in jeder Domäne so sein. Im allgemeinen geben wir keine Einschränkungen an, wie die verschiedenen Domänen intern strukturiert sind. Die einzige Forderung ist, daß jede Domäne Prozeduren zur Unifikation, Generalisierung und zum Subsumptionstest bereitstellen müssen und daß die Ergebnisse dieser Prozeduren den Gesetzen eines distributiven Verbandes genügen.

Atome im Sinne von PATR-II kann man z.B. folgendermaßen modellieren:

Sei ATOM die Menge der Atome. Dann sind die Objekte der Domäne D_{ATOM} Teilmengen der Menge ATOM. Dabei entspricht die leere Menge {} dem Typ F. Für die Operationen Unifikation, Generalisierung und Subsumption verwenden wir die üblichen Mengenoperationen:

$$\text{unify}_{ATOM}(X,Y) = Z \qquad \text{gdw.} \qquad Z = X \cap Y$$
$$\text{generalize}_{ATOM}(X,Y) = Z \qquad \text{gdw.} \qquad Z = X \cup Y$$
$$\text{subsumes}_{ATOM}(X,Y) \qquad \text{gdw.} \qquad Y \subseteq X$$

Da die Potenzmenge einer gegebenen Menge unter den üblichen Mengenoperationen einen distributiven Verband bildet, genügt diese Modellierung den angegebenen Bedingungen.

Benutzt man die Domänen sehr intensiv, um die Wissensbasen eines Systems zu strukturieren, kann man u.U. durch geschickte Implementierung domänenspezifischer Operationen einen erheblichen Effizienzgewinn gegenüber der Behandlung in einer komplexen STUF-Domäne erzielen. Außerdem wird durch die Strukturierung der Wissenbasen die Übersichtlichkeit und Verständlichkeit des Gesamtsystem wesentlich verbessert.

Integriert man Domänen in STUF, muß man auch die Frage beantworten, welche Semantik Operationen wie z.B. die Unifikation haben, wenn Objekte aus **verschiedenen** Domänen als Argumente gegeben sind. In der hier beschriebenen Version von STUF haben wir den Ansatz gewählt, daß Typen aus verschiedenen Domänen **grundsätzlich inkompatibel** sind. Dies gilt sowohl für verschiedene externe Domänen als auch für komplexe Formeln die mit einem Typ einer externen Domäne verknüpft werden sollen.

Damit gelten insbesondere die folgenden Äquivalenzen:

$$[\, a_{D1}\ b_{D2}\,] \ <\, =\, > \ \$F\$ \qquad \text{falls } D1\ =/=\ D2$$
$$[\, a_{D}\ t\,] \ <\, =\, > \ \$F\$ \qquad \text{falls } t\ \text{''komplex''} \text{ ist}$$
$$[\, a_{D}\ b{:}\$U\$\,] \ <\, =\, > \ a_{D}$$

Die Entscheidung für diese Semantik ist in gewisser Weise willkürlich. Man könnte sich ebenso dafür entscheiden, daß Typen aus verschiedenen Domänen grundsätzlich kompatibel sind, aber das Ergebnis einer Unifikation eben nicht anders angegeben werden kann als durch eine Konjunktion dieser beiden Typen. Mit dieser Variante erhielte man in STUF Formeln, die eine Verallgemeinerung der Psi-Terme von Aït-Kaci in dem Sinne bilden, daß beliebig viele ''Heads'' für jeden Term möglich sind. Ein Beispiel für eine solche Formel wäre dann:

$$[\, a_{D1}\ b_{D2}\ c{:}t1\ d{:}t2\,]$$

Dabei kann man die Typen a und b aus den Domänen D1 bzw. D2 als die ''Heads'' der komplexen Formel auffassen. Eine Unifikation mit einer anderen Formel ähnlicher Struktur führt dann dazu, daß immer Typen aus gleichen Domänen tatsächlich miteinander unifiziert werden, wogegen die Angabe einer weiteren Domäne nur zu ihrer Hinzunahme zur Formel führt.

Eine dritte Möglichkeit ist es, zu definieren, daß verschiedene externe Domänen grundsätzlich inkompatibel sind, dagegen jede externe Domäne mit komplexen Formeln kompatibel ist. Damit erhält man genau den Ansatz von Aït-Kaci, da nun für jede komplexe Formel nur noch (höchstens) ein Head angegeben werden kann.

4. Zusammenfassung

In der vorliegenden Arbeit wurden einige Erweiterungen disjunktiver Merkmalsbeschreibungen vorgestellt, die **STUF** gegenüber den bisherigen Ansätzen aufweist. Es wurde gezeigt, wie sich **Terme mit fester und variabler Stelligkeit** in einem Formalismus integrieren lassen. Außerdem wurde das Konzept der **Wissensdomänen** zur Strukturierung von großen Wissensbasen entwickelt.

STUF wurde im Rahmen des ersten Prototyps eines textverstehenden Systems, der im Projekt LILOG entwickelt wurde, zur Codierung sämtlicher linguistischer und nicht-linguistischer Wissensbasen eingesetzt.

Literatur

Aït-Kaci (1984) H. Aït-Kaci: *A Lattice Theoretic Approach to Computation Based on a Calculus of Partially Ordered Type Structures*. Ph.D. Thesis, University of Pennsylvania.

Beierle (1988b) C. Beierle, U. Pletat, H. Uszkoreit: *An Algebraic Characterization of STUF*. To appear in: Tagungsband des Symposiums "Computerlinguistik und ihre theoretischen Grundlagen", Saarbrücken 1988. Informatik-Fachberichte, Springer.

Bouma (1988) G. Bouma, E. König, H. Uszkoreit: *The Application of the Stuttgart Type Unification Formalism to Syntactic and Semantic Processing*. In: IBM Journal of Research and Development, March 1988.

Johnson (1987) M.E. Johnson: *Attribute-Value Logic and the Theory of Grammar*. Ph.D. Thesis, Stanford University.

Karttunen (1984) L. Karttunen: *Features and Values*. In: Proceedings of the 12th International Conference on Computational Linguistics. Stanford, CA.

Kasper (1987) R.T. Kasper: *Feature Structures: A Logical Theory with Application to Language Analysis*. Ph.D. Thesis, University of Michigan.

Kay (1985) M. Kay: *Parsing in Functional Unification Grammar*. In: Natural Language Parsing: Psychological, Computational, and Theoretical Perspectives. Cambridge University Press. Cambridge, GB. pp251-278

Seiffert (1988) R. Seiffert: *Operationen in erweiterten Typenunifikationsformalismen*. Diplomarbeit. Institut für Informatik, Universität Stuttgart.

Shieber (1983) S.M. Shieber, H. Uszkoreit, F.C.N. Pereira, J.J. Robinson, M. Tyson: *The Formalism and Implementation of PATR-II*. In: Research on Interactive Acquisition and Use of Knowledge. Artificial Intelligence Center, SRI International. Menlo Park, CA.

Smolka (1988) G. Smolka: *A Feature Logic with Subsorts*. LILOG Report 33. IBM Deutschland, Stuttgart.

Uszkoreit (1986) H. Uszkoreit: *Categorial Unification Grammar*. In: Proceedings of the 11th International Conference on Computational Linguistics. Bonn, Germany.

Uszkoreit (1988) H. Uszkoreit: *From Feature Bundles to Abstract Data Types: New Directions in the Representation and Processing of Linguistic Knowledge*. In: A. Blaser (ed.): Natural Language at the Computer - Contributions to Syntax and Semantics for Text Processing and Man-Machine-Communication. Proceedings of the Scientific Symposium Held on the Occasion of the 20th Anniversary of the Science Center Heidelberg of IBM Germany. TR 88.02.002. IBM Deutschland.

<u>Non-Constituent-Coordination</u>
<u>ohne Funktionale Komposition und Typenanhebung</u>

Birgit Wesche
IBM Deutschland - WT LILOG
Postfach 80 08 80
7000 Stuttgart 80

Eines der vordringlichsten Anliegen bei der Entwicklung eines natürlich-sprachlichen Systems ist es, die Komplexität des Verarbeitungsprozesses so gering wie möglich zu halten. Grammatikregeln müssen so restriktiv formuliert sein, daß sie bei spezifischen sprachlichen Strukturen - und nur bei diesen - greifen, um somit unerwünschte Mehrfachanalysen aufgrund von reinen Strukturambiguitäten zu vermeiden. Dieses war der motivierende Gedanke für die Entwicklung des folgenden Ansatzes im Rahmen einer kategorialen Unifikationsgrammatik. Der Ansatz ist somit aus computerlinguistischen Überlegungen begründet. Da jedoch eine bestimmte Art grammatischer Regeln in einer Kategorial-Grammatik in Frage gestellt wird, hat dieser Ansatz auf der anderen Seite auch theoretisch-linguistische Tragweite. Die grundlegende grammatische Regel, auf die man in einer Kategorialgrammatik trifft, ist die der Funktionalen Applikation. Ein Beispiel für Rechtsapplikation:

```
Funktor     Argument     ->     Wert
NP/N        N            ->     NP
das         Haus         ->     das Haus
```

Es gibt zwei Arten von Kategorien: Basiskategorien (meistens N und S) und hieraus abgeleitete Kategorien (e.g. N/N = Adj., NP/N = Determiner, etc.). Die Regel der Funktionalen Applikation (unterteilt in Rechts- und Linksapplikation) besagt, daß ein Funktor, welcher eine abgeleitete Kategorie sein muß, mit einem Argument, welches entweder eine Basiskategorie oder wiederum eine abgeleitete Kategorie sein kann, nach links oder rechts - angegeben durch die Richtung des "Slashes" in der Funktorkategorie - kombiniert, um eine neue Kategorie zu bilden.

Die Operation der Unifikation unterstützt die Sprachverarbeitung in folgender Hinsicht. Da die Spezifizierung von Kategorien in einer Kategorialgrammatik lediglich auf die Charakterisierung von syntaktischen Eigenschaften abzielt, bestünde unter rein kategorialgrammatischen Annahmen kein Unterschied zwischen der Struktur A):

```
A)     Johan   läuft    ->   S
       NP      S\NP     ->   S
```

und der Struktur B):

```
B)   * Johan   laufen   ->   S
       NP      S\NP     ->   S
```

Die Anreicherung der syntaktischen Kategorien mit morphologischen Merkmalen in Form von Attribut-Wert-Paaren ergibt folgendes Bild. Mit der Operation der Unifikation - der rekursiven Vereinigung von Merkmalsstrukturen, vorausgesetzt die Merkmale sind miteinander kompatibel - kann die Ableitung der Struktur B) - * Johan laufen - verhindert werden, da die jeweiligen morphologischen Merkmale bezüglich der Numerus-Werte (Singular versus Plural) nicht miteinander kompatibel sind und somit nicht zu einer akzeptablen Struktur unifizieren.

Mit den beiden Regeln der funktionalen Applikation lassen sich in einer kategorialen

Unifikationsgrammatik ein Großteil sprachlicher Strukturen handhaben. Ein Gefüge, welches sich jedoch nicht mehr ohne weiteres über Rechts- oder Linksapplikation verarbeiten läßt, ist die Struktur einer Koordination. Dies hat viele Kategorialgrammatiker dazu bewegt, zwei weitere Grammatikregeltypen einzuführen: die der Funktionalen Komposition und die der Typenanhebung. Funktionale Komposition bestimmt eine spezielle Kombinierbarkeit zweier Funktoren, während Typenanhebung eine unäre Regel ist, welche eine Kategorie kontextabhängig in eine andere anhebt.
Ein Kontext, der die mögliche Anwendung von Funktionaler Komposition auslösen könnte, ist im folgenden Beispiel gegeben:

```
auf      dem      und      unter    dem      Tisch
PP/NP    NP/N     Conj.    PP/NP    NP/N     N
```

Über Funktionale Applikation ließe sich zwar das zweite Konjunkt zu einer Präpositionalphrase ableiten. Mit der Spezifizierung der Funktor-Kategorie "und" als (X\X)/X wird aber gefordert, daß die syntaktische Kategorie des ersten Konjunkts gleich der des zweiten sein soll. Zu koordinieren wäre in obigem Fall also: "auf dem und unter dem". Die beiden Funktor-Kategorien einer Präposition und eines Determiner lassen sich jedoch nicht über Funktionale Applikation kombinieren. Hier greift jetzt die Regel der Funktionalen Komposition, die, am obigen Beispiel demonstriert, wie folgt operiert:[1]

```
Funktor    Funktor    ->    Wert
PP/NP      NP/N       ->    PP/N
```

allgemein: A/B   B/C   ->   A/C

Präposition und Determiner können so also miteinander kombinieren zu der neuen Funktorkategorie PP/N, welche jeweils sowohl als erstes wie auch als zweites Konjunkt als Argument der Funktorkategorie "und" fungieren kann. Für die Ableitung der Koordination selbst genügt wiederum die Regel der Funktionalen Applikation. Lediglich die Argumente der Funktorkategorie "und" werden über Funktionale Komposition hergeleitet.

Einen Kontext für die Notwendigkeit der Regelanwendung der Typenanhebung sieht z.B. Steedman (1987:12) bei folgendem Konstrukt:

```
I       will         cook       and Betty may eat the mushrooms.
NP      (S\NP)/VP    VP/NP      ....
```

Die Funktorkategorien "will" und "cook" können noch über Funktionale Komposition zu (S\NP)/NP kombiniert werden. Diese Kategorie kann nun aber weder über Applikation noch über Komposition mit der NP zu ihrer Linken zusammengefaßt werden. Nimmt man jedoch eine Typenanhebung auf der Subjekt-NP vor - welches bedeutet, eine Abbildung der jeweiligen Argumentkategorie auf eine Funktion über eine Funktion vorzunehmen, welche gerade wiederum die ursprüngliche Kategorie als Argument nimmt - so wird diese NP zu der Kategorie S/(S\NP) und über Funktionale Komposition ist wieder die Kombinierbarkeit der beiden so entstandenen Funktorkategorien möglich:[2]

---

[1]   Dies ist nur eine von vier möglichen Kompositionsregeln. Die übrigen drei lauten wie folgt:
```
A/B     B\C     ->    A\C
B/C     A\B     ->    A/C
B\C     A\B     ->    A\C
```

[2]   Im folgenden bedeuten die Anmerkungen "TR", "FA", "FC" in den Beispielableitungen entsprechend "Type Raising", "Functional Application", "Functional Composition".

```
I           will    cook    ...

NP          (S\NP)/NP

⇓  TR


S/(S\NP)
____________________

        S/NP
```

Die resultiernde Kategorie (S/NP) ist dann die Kategorie, die als Argument der Funktorkategorie "und" fungiert. Es stellt sich nun jedoch das Problem, daß die Regeln der Funktionalen Komposition und der Typenanhebung nicht nur im speziellen Fall einer Non-Constituent-Coordination angestoßen werden, sondern auch in beliebigen anderen Kontexten, in denen zwei Funktoren der spezifizierten Form nebeneinanderstehen, oder eine Kategorie, wenn angehoben, mit nachstehendem Funktor kombinierbar gemacht werden kann. Allein der in der Computerlinguistik sich so großer Beliebtheit erfreuender Satz: "Johan liebt eine Frau" kann auf vier Arten abgeleitet werden, welche allerdings lediglich reine Strukturambiguitäten darstellen.

```
        Johan       liebt       eine    Frau
        NP          (S\NP)/NP   NP/N    N

1.                              ______________  FA
                                         NP
                        ________________________  FA
                                 S\NP
                ________________________________  FA
                         S


2.                              ______________  FC
                              (S\NP)/N
                        ________________________  FA
                                 S\NP
                ________________________________  FA
                         S


      ( Johan     liebt       eine    Frau  )
        NP        (S\NP)/NP   NP/N    N

3.      ______                              TR
        S/(S\NP)
        ________________________            FC
              S/NP
        ________________________________    FC
                     S/N
        ________________________________________  FA
                         S
```

Dies kann schlimmstenfalls "in certain cases to an exponential growth of derivations" führen (Wittenburg 1987:75). Der Ansatz zur Behandlung von koordinativen Strukturen jedoch, der hier verfolgt wird, kann im schlimmsten Fall lediglich zu einer Verdopplung der Analysen führen.

Die Idee für diesen Ansatz ist der Methode entlehnt, mit der sich in einer kategorialen Unifikationsgrammatik Long-Distance Phänomene behandeln lassen. Im Falle einer topikalisierten Phrase beispielsweise läßt sich wie folgt verfahren. Tritt für die Funktorkategorie Verb an einer spezifizierten Position nicht das geforderte subkategorisierte Argument auf, operiert auf diesem Verb-Funktor die unäre Regel der GAP-INTRODUCTION. Diese verwandelt die Verb-Kategorie in die in ihr angegebene nächsthöhere Struktur, welche ihrerseits die Informationen über die aufgetretene Lücke - die topikalisierte Phrase - in Merkmalsstrukturen mit sich trägt. Nun kann der Satz weiter mit den bekannten Regeln abgearbeitet werden, wobei die GAP-Informationen dem jeweiligen neuen Ableitungsergebnis weitergereicht werden. Als letztes operiert dann die Regel GAP-ELIMINATION, die besagt, daß die Merkmalsspezifikationen bezüglich der Lücke in der vorerst abgeleiteten Satz-Kategorie mit denen der topikalisierten Phrase übereinstimmen müssen. Ist dies der Fall, kann zu der Kategorie S kombiniert werden. Dies sei, leicht vereinfacht, an folgendem Beispiel verdeutlicht (der Verb-Funktor wird hierbei in Verb-Erst-Stellung kodiert angenommen):

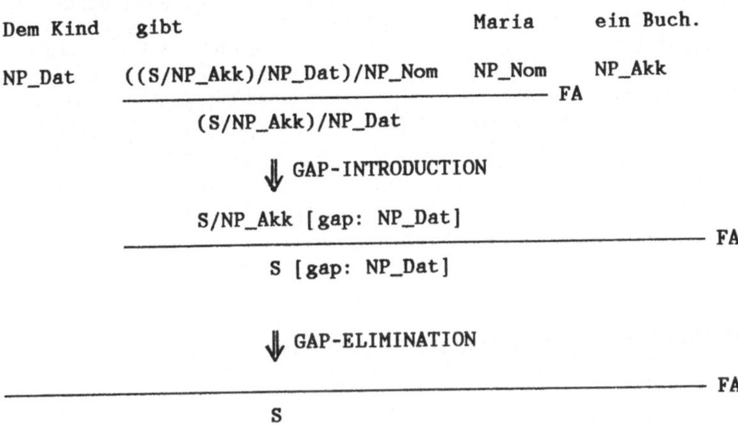

Gleichermaßen wie für Sätze mit topikalisierten Phrasen oder WH-Elementen im Vorfeld die Regel der Funktionalen Applikation, gekoppelt mit denen der GAP-INTRODUCTION und -ELIMINATION, für die Ableitung genügt, wäre ein ähnliches Verfahren nun für koordinative Strukturen der folgenden Art denkbar:

Für diesen Fall von Non-Constituent-Coordination wäre somit nicht die Einführung der Funktionalen Kompositionsregel notwendig, welche ihrerseits auch in vielen anderen Kontexten applizieren würde. Die Regeln der GAP-INTRODUCTION und -ELIMINATION ihrerseits können lediglich dazu führen, daß jede Funktor-Argument Kombination außer direkt über Funktionale Applikation zusätzlich noch über erstere Regeln abgeleitet wird, also schlimmstenfalls eine Verdopplung der Analysen. Durch adäquate Merkmalsspezifizierungen sowohl in diesen GAP-Regeln als auch in der Funktionalen Applikationsregel läßt sich diese Übergeneralisierung jedoch merklich einschränken. Weiterhin kann durch entsprechende Attribut-Wert-Wahl für Funktor und Argument über die Regel der Funktionalen Applikation gesteuert werden, daß die Koordinationslücke in den koordinativen Strukturen, die mit dieser Art der Analyse erfaßt werden können (jegliche Art von Gapping ist bisher außer acht gelassen), jeweils in der rechtsperiphären Position der Konjunkte auftritt.

Es ist wichtig anzumerken, daß hier nicht angenommen wird, daß es sich bei den Lücken aufgrund von Bewegung (WH-Movement, Topikalisierung) und den Lücken aufgrund von Tilgung in Koordinationen um ein und dasselbe sprachliche Phänomen handelt. Es gibt jeweils ein Regelpaar GAP-INTRODUCTION und -ELIMINATION für Bewegungsinstanzen und eines für Koordinations-Umgebungen, die sich beide durch wohldefinierte Merkmalsspezifizierungen klar voneinander unterscheiden. Lediglich der Mechanismus der Lückeneinführung und -eliminierung an sich ist beiden gemein. Die Interaktion der verschiedenen GAP-Regeln sei an folgendem Beispiel verdeutlicht, in dem ein Fall von Right-Node-Raising über einem Satz mit Verb-Zweit-Stellung vorliegt:

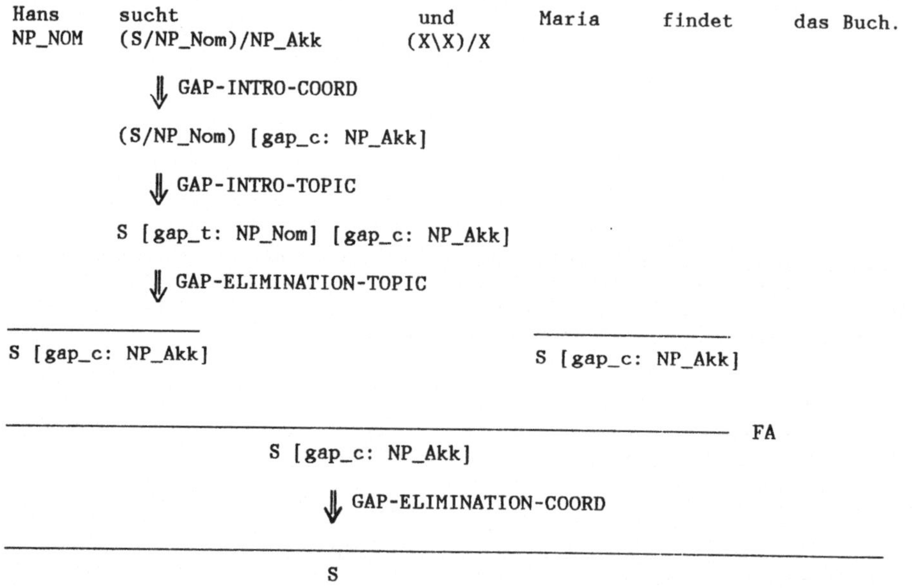

Die Möglichkeit, die GAP-Regeln auf diese Weise miteinander interagieren zu lassen, eliminiert gleichzeitig die Notwendigkeit, aufgrund dieser Art von Kontexten die unäre Regel des Type Raising einzuführen, wie es z.B. Steedman (1987) vorschlägt.

```
Hans      sucht                    und     Maria   findet   das Buch.
NP_Nom    (S\NP_Nom)/NP_Akk        (X\X)/X
```

⇓ TR

```
S/(S\NP_Nom)
──────────────────────────── FC        ──────────────── FC
     S/NP_Akk                               S/NP_Akk

        ────────────────────────────────────────── FA
                     S/NP_Akk
        ──────────────────────────────────────────────────────── FA
                            S
```

Der vorliegende Ansatz kommt somit für die Behandlung von Non-Constituent-Coordination mit den speziellen Regeln der GAP-INTRODUCTION bzw. -ELIMINATION und der grundlegenden Regel der Funktionalen Applikation aus. Zudem ist der Koordinationslücke aus Tilgung über die GAP-Regel besser Rechnung getragen als über eine Funktionale Kompositionsregel, in der nur allgemein die Möglichkeit der Kombination zweier adjunkter Funktoren spezifischer syntaktischer Kategorien festgelegt ist. Weiterhin können Koordinationscharakteristika lokal und somit direkt über die Koordinations-GAP-Regeln gesteuert werden, so daß man dem Anspruch einen erheblichen Schritt näher kommt, den Applikationsradius der grammatischen Regeln genau einzugrenzen. Abschließend sei nochmals hervorgehoben, daß der Vorteil in dieser Art von Regeln darin liegt, daß sie nicht so komplexe Auswirkungen auf die Analyse von nicht-koordinativen Strukturen haben wie vergleichsweise die vier verschiedenen Funktionalen Kompositionsregeln plus Type Raising, und die generative Kapazität der Grammatik sich somit in einem berechenbaren Rahmen bewegt. Eine entscheidende Bedeutung kommt hierbei der Möglichkeit der Merkmalsspezifizierungen und der über sie operierenden Operation der Unifikation zu, mithilfe derer sich Regeln in einer Kategorialgrammatik für die spezifischen Ableitungen präzise formulieren lassen.[3]

Literatur:

Bouma 1988 Bouma, G. (1988): Modifiers and Specifiers in Categorial Unification Grammar. In: Linguistics 26. Berlin: Mouton de Gruyter. pp.21-46.

Steedman 1987 Steedman, M. (1987): Gapping as Constituent Coordination. Unpublished manuscript. 60p.

Uszkoreit 1986 Uszkoreit, H. (1986): Categorial Unification Grammars. In: Proceedings of COLING '86. pp.187-194.

Wittenburg 1987 Wittenburg, K. (1987): Predictive Combinators: A Method for Efficient Processing of Combinatory Categorial Grammars. In: Proceedings of the ACL '87. pp.73-80.

---

[3] Die hier vorgestellten Regeln zur Behandlung von Non-Constituent-Coordination sind größtenteils integriert in die LILOG-Prototyp-Umgebung, implementiert in STUF (Stuttgart Type Unification Formalism). Die LILOG-Grammatik umfaßt keine weiteren Regeln außer den hier angesprochenen GAP-Regeln und den Regeln der Funktionalen Applikation.